Canadian Immigration and Refugee Law for Legal Professionals

Lynn Fournier-Ruggles

CONTRIBUTORS

Peter McKeracher
Ana Rasmusson
Ralph Gutkin
Lavinia Inbar

2009
Emond Montgomery Publications Limited
Toronto, Canada

Emond Montgomery Publications Limited
60 Shaftesbury Avenue
Toronto ON M4T 1A3
http://www.emp.ca/college

Printed in Canada.

We acknowledge the financial support of the Government of Canada through the Book Publishing Industry Development Program (BPIDP) for our publishing activities.

Acquisitions and developmental editor: Peggy Buchan
Marketing manager: Christine Davidson
Copy editor: David Handelsman, WordsWorth Communications
Production editor: Cindy Fujimoto, WordsWorth Communications
Proofreader: Debbie Gervais, WordsWorth Communications
Indexer: Paula Pike, WordsWorth Communications
Cover designer: John Vegter

Library and Archives Canada Cataloguing in Publication

Fournier-Ruggles, Lynn
    Canadian immigration and refugee law for legal professionals /
Lynn Fournier-Ruggles.

Includes index.
ISBN 978-1-55239-286-7

    1. Emigration and immigration law—Canada.   2. Refugees—Legal status, laws, etc.—Canada.   3. Canada. Immigration and Refugee Protection Act.   I. Title.
KE4454.F69 2008   342.7108'2   C2008-906927-7
KF4483.I5F69 2008

To the Three Ds

Table of Contents

Chapter 10   Enforcement Procedures ... 327

Chapter 11   Immigration Appeal Division 375

CHAPTER 1

Introduction

LEARNING OBJECTIVES

After reading this chapter you should be able to:

- List and describe the sources of immigration law.

- Find relevant immigration cases from the Immigration and Refugee Board, Federal Court, and Supreme Court of Canada.

- Find relevant sections from the *Immigration and Refugee Protection Act* and the IRP Regulations.

INTRODUCTION

Canada is a wealthy country with a highly developed social support system, a diverse population, and incredible natural resources. As a result, it is a highly attractive destination for people from around the world.

According to Citizenship and Immigration Canada (CIC), more than 15 million people immigrated to Canada since its confederation in 1867. In the last ten years, approximately 220,000 immigrants and refugees were admitted to Canada in each year. The Canadian government works to manage immigration by encouraging the influx of skilled workers and entrepreneurs, offering protection to people fleeing violence or human rights violations in their own countries, and reuniting families by allowing dependants of immigrants to come into our country. Canada has an annual immigration target of 1 percent of the total population.

Canada's **immigration** management scheme is created by the *Immigration and Refugee Protection Act* (IRPA), which was passed into law in 2001, replacing the *Immigration Act* of 1976. The government department that administers this statute and its regulations is Citizenship and Immigration Canada (CIC). CIC is a federal department responsible for the following general functions:

- admitting **immigrants**, foreign students, visitors, and temporary workers who enhance Canada's social and economic growth;

- resettling, protecting, and providing a safe haven for **refugees**;

- helping newcomers adapt to Canadian society and become Canadian **citizens**; and

- managing access to Canada to protect the security and health of Canadians and the integrity of Canadian laws.

Because there are so many applicants wanting to move to Canada, CIC applies formal criteria to determine which applicants will be permitted to come in. Generally, preference is given to applicants who are likely to make a positive contribution to the economy, or at the least not burden it. However, other factors, such as family reunification, may also be considered. Canada is also committed to providing a safe refuge for people fleeing persecution, by admitting refugees regardless of their financial circumstances.

In general, Canada supports the entry of foreign nationals who

- have valuable skills needed by Canadian employers;

- have the means, ability, and ambition to become entrepreneurs in Canada, or to extend the operation of existing, successful business enterprises to Canada;

- have come to Canada for protection when fleeing persecution in their own countries, particularly under conditions of war; or

- are the family members or dependants of immigrants (family reunification is a priority).

In general, Canada does not support the entry of foreign nationals who

- have a history of criminality or close connections to organized crime; or

- will likely pose a heavy burden on Canada's social support systems (for example, the health care system) without contributing to the Canadian economy.

The IRPA deals with two main categories of newcomers: immigrants and refugees. There are several classes of immigrants, and two categories of refugees, all of which will be explored in this text. The difference between an immigrant and a refugee is that an immigrant is a person from another country who wishes to live in Canada permanently, while a refugee is a person fleeing persecution who comes to Canada for safety. Many refugees later choose to stay, but making Canada their home is not their primary motivation for coming here. The term "immigration" may also be used generally to include both immigrants and refugees.

SOURCES OF IMMIGRATION LAW

Immigration in Canada is governed by both domestic law and international law. Domestic law governing immigration includes the Constitution, the *Canadian Charter of Rights and Freedoms*, federal and provincial statutes and regulations, and case law. The primary sources of immigration law are the federal *Immigration and Refugee Protection Act*, the regulations under that statute, and case law interpreting the statute and regulations. The *Citizenship Act* is another important federal statute. Federal–provincial agreements governing immigration to a particular province are also domestic law.

International law includes multinational treaties and conventions. Canada has signed a number of international agreements that affect our immigration rules—for example, the 1951 United Nations Convention Relating to the Status of Refugees. By signing these agreements, Canada has committed to structure our domestic law in a manner that is consistent with them.

Some of these treaties are multilateral involving many countries. Others relate to only a few specific countries—for example, the North American Free Trade Agreement (NAFTA), which contains specific provisions to facilitate temporary business entry among Canada, the United States, and Mexico.

Additionally, s. 7 of the IRPA grants the minister of Citizenship and Immigration the power to enter into agreements with other countries or with an international organization. These agreements must be approved by the federal Cabinet and must be consistent with the purposes of the IRPA.

To some degree, international principles have been **codified** in our domestic law—such as the refugee provisions of the IRPA. The IRPA is the focal point for the study of immigration law in Canada, and it is thoroughly explored in this text. However, before examining the details of this statute and its regulations, it is useful to take a step back and survey the wider landscape.

The Constitution

The **Constitution** is the supreme law of the land. It is the basic framework under which all other laws are created, and it establishes the basic principles to which all other laws must conform. Until 1982, Canada's Constitution was the *British North America Act* (later renamed the *Constitution Act, 1867*), a statute of England. It set up the framework for Canada's democracy, but only England had the power to make constitutional amendments. The *Canada Act 1982* finally changed this, and brought the power to amend the Constitution home to Canada's Parliament. A truly Canadian Constitution was created with the *Constitution Act, 1982*, which contains both the *Constitution Act, 1867* and the *Canadian Charter of Rights and Freedoms*.

DIVISION OF POWERS (SECTIONS 91 AND 92 OF THE CONSTITUTION ACT, 1867)

The *Constitution Act, 1867* created a **federal system of government**, which means that law-making powers are divided between the national government and the provincial governments according to subject matter. The national government (usually called the "federal government"), located in Ottawa, the nation's capital, has jurisdiction over matters of national interest that affect all Canadians from coast to coast. This government also has law-making jurisdiction with respect to the territories. The provincial governments have jurisdiction over local matters within each province.

Federal powers are set out in s. 91 of the *Constitution Act, 1867*, and include the authority to regulate immigration, national defence, and criminal law. The basic rule governing the division of powers is that matters that require a national standard fall within the jurisdiction of the federal government. For example, immigration and refugee laws that govern who is permitted to enter and live in Canada are issues that affect Canada's status in the international community, which makes it important that the same legal standards are applied across the country.

Provincial powers are set out in s. 92 of the *Constitution Act, 1867*, and generally include authority over all matters of a local or private nature in the province, such as property, hospitals, schools and child protection. In Canada, a large degree of legislative responsibility is delegated to the provinces. This means that there are many more provincial statutes, and accompanying regulations, than there are federal ones.

Examples of the Law-Making Powers of the Federal and Provincial Levels of Government

Federal Government Law-Making Powers by Subject Matter (Section 91)	Provincial Government Law-Making Powers by Subject Matter (Section 92)
Interprovincial/international trade	Property laws
National defence	Civil rights (contract, tort)
Currency	Hospitals
Criminal law	Matters of a local nature (local trade and public works)
Naturalization and aliens	Municipalities
Residual powers	Generally, all matters of a merely local or private nature in the province
Peace, order, and good government	

For example, s. 91(25) assigns jurisdiction over "naturalization and aliens," meaning immigration, to the federal government. For this reason, the *Immigration and Refugee Protection Act* and the *Citizenship Act* are both federal statutes. Section 92(13) assigns property and civil rights to the provincial governments. Accordingly, the Ontario *Residential Tenancies Act, 2006*, which deals with civil rights, is a provincial statute.

The federal government has a **residual power** to make laws for the peace, order, and good government of Canada in all matters that do not come within a provincial head of power. This means that any matters not specifically delegated to the provinces are matters over which the federal government has jurisdiction.

Occasionally, one level of government passes a law that appears to intrude on the jurisdiction of the other. Censorship is a good example of this. Controlling the sale of literature and images that may be offensive to some can be viewed as either a provincial concern (trade and commerce within a province), or a federal concern (obscenity as a criminal act).

Where someone alleges that a law is outside the jurisdiction of the government that passed it, courts are often called upon to settle the issue. If a law does not fit squarely into the camp of one or the other, the federal government takes jurisdiction, under the principle of **paramountcy**.

FEDERAL–PROVINCIAL AGREEMENTS: SHARING OF POWER (SECTION 95)

The *Constitution Act, 1867* makes a special provision for sharing power with respect to agriculture and immigration. With respect to immigration, s. 95 states that:

> In each Province the Legislature may make Laws in relation to ... Immigration into the Province; and it is hereby declared that the Parliament of Canada may from Time to Time make Laws in relation to ... Immigration into all or any of the Provinces; and any Law of the Legislature of a Province relative to ... Immigration shall have effect in and for the Province as long and as far only as it is not repugnant to any Act of the Parliament of Canada.

In other words, a province may make laws in relation to the immigration of people into the province, provided that those laws are not inconsistent or in conflict with any federal law. Therefore, in the area of immigration, there are concurrent powers of legislation between the two levels of government, but if there is a conflict between federal and provincial legislation, it is the federal legislation that prevails, according to the principle of paramountcy.

The IRPA provides that the minister of Citizenship and Immigration, with the approval of the Cabinet, may enter into agreements with the provinces. The following federal–provincial agreements were in force as of April 2008:

- Canada-Quebec Accord Relating to Immigration and Temporary Admission of Aliens;

- immigration agreements between Canada and each of: Alberta, Manitoba, Saskatchewan, Nova Scotia, and Ontario;

- agreements for cooperation on immigration between Canada and each of Yukon, Prince Edward Island, Alberta, and British Columbia; and

- agreements on provincial nominees between Canada and each of Nova Scotia, Alberta, Newfoundland and Labrador, and New Brunswick.

Canada-Quebec Accord

Canada and the province of Quebec have had immigration agreements since 1971, the most recent being the 1991 Canada-Quebec Accord. The Canada-Quebec Accord is the most significant and comprehensive immigration agreement between Canada and a province. Under it Quebec has the sole responsibility for selecting all independent immigrants and refugees outside of Canada who wish to settle in Quebec. The individuals selected by the province are then referred to CIC, which tests for inadmissibility on the grounds of medical risk or burden, security threat, and criminality. (The grounds of inadmissibility are discussed in Chapter 3 of this textbook.)

Canada remains responsible for setting minimum national standards for the admission of all immigrants and visitors, and for the administrative function of processing applications and physical admission to Canada at ports of entry. Quebec may impose additional selection criteria for immigrants to Quebec, and is responsible for integrating immigrants into the community.

Immigration Agreements and Cooperation Agreements

Immigration agreements and cooperation agreements facilitate cooperation and the exchange of information between the federal government and the provinces during the development of immigration programs and policies. For example, the Canada-Ontario Immigration Agreement, signed in 2005, provided that the federal government would transfer $920 million to the province over five years to assist with the integration of new immigrants, including language training.

Agreements on Provincial Nominees

Because of the shared responsibility for immigration, potential immigrants to Canada can apply to immigrate to Canada, or may apply specifically to a province through the Provincial Nominee Program. Agreements on provincial nominees allow a province or territory to nominate people as immigrants if the province believes that these people will contribute to the economic growth of the province.

The Provincial Nominee Program is based on agreements between the federal government and most of the provincial governments. These agreements allow each participating province to nominate immigrants to settle in that province. A potential immigrant to Canada who wishes to be a provincial nominee must first apply to one of the participating provinces and complete that province's nomination process. The specific criteria vary from province to province, and the province will consider the application based on its particular immigration needs.

After an applicant has been nominated by a province or territory, a separate application to Citizenship and Immigration Canada for permanent residence must also be made, and that application is assessed on the basis of Canadian immigration regulations. (This program is discussed further in Chapter 5.)

THE CANADIAN CHARTER OF RIGHTS AND FREEDOMS

The *Canadian Charter of Rights and Freedoms* is part of the Constitution of Canada. It was designed to help accomplish one of the most important constitutional functions—to express the fundamental values and principles of our society. Canada prides itself on being a free and democratic society that protects the welfare of its members. The Charter reflects that pride by providing a mechanism to balance individual freedoms against the need to protect society's more vulnerable members.

Rights and freedoms protected by the Charter include the following:

- freedom of expression (s. 2(b))

- freedom of religion (s. 2(a))

- right to life, liberty, and security of the person (s. 7)

- right to equality (s. 15).

The Charter provides that government legislation and actions cannot infringe on these rights and freedoms unless the infringement can be reasonably justified in a free and democratic society. Therefore, the Charter has two important effects:

1. If any law or government policy contravenes the terms of the Charter, that law or policy may be declared unconstitutional and of no force and effect by a court or administrative tribunal.

2. Any action of an agent or representative of any level of government that contravenes any right or freedom protected in the Charter can be challenged in the courts.

The precise scope of the Charter's application has been a matter of debate and litigation. Although it is clear that the Charter applies to the content and effects of government law and to the nature and effects of government action, it has sometimes been difficult to define what is meant by "government" action. Many organizations and regulated industries in Canada have some connection to government; and there have been many cases argued that turn on whether the actions of a quasi-governmental organization is government action.

Unregulated private activity is not intended to be subject to the Charter. The purpose of the Charter is to set limits on what the government can do—to protect minority rights in a democracy where the majority elects government. Because the Charter only applies with respect to government activity or decisions, the protection of equality rights has also been legislated in human rights legislation.

The purpose of human rights legislation is similar to the purpose of the Charter, but its scope stretches beyond government to regulate the actions of landlords, employers, and providers of goods and services—whether they be individuals, businesses, or private institutions. For example, if an apartment building owner refused to rent to people with children, this type of discrimination would be addressed by human rights legislation.

Reasonable Limits on Rights and Freedoms

Section 1 of the Charter is a very important provision that provides that all rights and freedoms are subject to "such reasonable limits prescribed by law as can be demonstrably justified in a free and democratic society." Each time a court considers whether a law is in violation of the Charter, it must consider whether the law imposes a reasonable limit as described in s. 1. A law will be struck down only when both of the following conditions exist:

1. the law violates a right or freedom; and

2. the law cannot be justified as a reasonable limit in the particular circumstances.

For example, freedom of expression may be curtailed by the duty of society to protect children from being exploited in pornography. In many instances the courts will conclude that although a right or freedom was violated, this violation was justifiable.

The reasons of the Supreme Court of Canada in the following four cases exemplify the power of the Charter to shape the law in Canada.

Andrews v. Law Society of British Columbia

The Supreme Court first ruled on the equality provisions set out in s. 15 in 1989, in *Andrews v. Law Society of British Columbia*, where it was held that the Law Society of British Columbia's requirement that lawyers be Canadian citizens violated s. 15 of the Charter. The wording of s. 15(1) is as follows:

> Every individual is equal before and under the law and has the right to the equal protection of the law without discrimination and, in particular, without discrimination based on race, national or ethnic origin, colour, religion, sex, age or mental or physical disability.

The Court held that the grounds of discrimination listed in s. 15 were not exhaustive, and analogous grounds, such as "citizenship," were also covered. The respondent Andrews was a British subject and permanent resident in Canada. He met all the requirements for admission to the British Columbia bar except that of Canadian citizenship. When he was refused admission, he successfully challenged the citizenship requirement on the ground that it violated his right to equality.

As the first s. 15 case, *Andrews* gave us the foundational analysis for Charter challenges involving equality. The Supreme Court held that s. 15 provides for every individual a guarantee of equality before and under the law, as well as the equal protection and equal benefit of the law without discrimination. The Court expanded the scope of the right to equality by rejecting an equality test—known as the "similarly situated should be similarly treated" test—which was used by the lower court for interpreting s. 15. This approach permitted distinctions, such as with respect to citizenship, provided that all non-citizens were treated the same, and all citizens were treated the same.

Instead, the Supreme Court held that discrimination is a distinction based on grounds relating to the personal characteristics of the individual or group, which has the effect of imposing disadvantages not imposed on others. Distinctions based on personal characteristics attributed to an individual solely on the basis of association with a group will rarely escape the charge of discrimination, while those based on an individual's merits and capacities will rarely be so classed. This guarantee is not a general guarantee of equality; its focus is on the application of the law. The effect of the impugned distinction or classification on the complainant must also be considered.

The Court noted that citizenship may be properly required for certain legitimate reasons; however, it concluded that barring an entire class of persons from certain forms of employment, solely on the ground of a lack of citizenship status and without consideration of educational and professional qualifications or the other attributes or merits of individuals in the group, infringes s. 15 equality rights.

Note that although *Andrews* held that s. 15 of the Charter prohibited discrimination against permanent residents, discrimination in some circumstances will be tolerated, either because it is justifiable under s. 1 of the Charter, or because the Charter itself makes a distinction between citizens and non-citizens—for example, only citizens may vote in elections. Also, the IRPA legitimately discriminates against non-citizens with respect to the right to live in Canada permanently and not be deported.

Singh v. Minister of Employment and Immigration

In *Singh* the Supreme Court of Canada considered whether s. 7 of the Charter applied to the adjudication of refugee claims, as set out in the former *Immigration Act* of 1976, and, if so, whether those procedures denied the s. 7 requirement of fundamental justice.

The wording of s. 7 is as follows:

Everyone has the right to life, liberty and security of the person and the right not to be deprived thereof except in accordance with the principles of fundamental justice.

Although Singh was not a Canadian citizen, the Court found that he was entitled to the protection of s. 7, which the Court held applied to "every human being who is physically present in Canada and by virtue of such presence amenable to Canadian law." Thus, the Supreme Court extended Charter protection to any persons in Canada, regardless of whether or not they have any legal right to be here.

The Court found that the denial of the right of a refugee claimant not to "be removed from Canada to a country where his life or freedom would be threatened" amounted to a deprivation of security of the person within the meaning of s. 7.

The Court determined that, at a minimum, the concept of fundamental justice in s. 7 includes the notion of procedural fairness. The procedural scheme under the former *Immigration Act* for refugee determinations was not in accordance with fundamental justice, because the hearings were based on written submissions only. The Court held that "where a serious issue of credibility is involved, fundamental justice requires that credibility be determined on the basis of an oral hearing." Only an oral hearing would be adequate in such circumstances to fairly assess a refugee claimant's credibility.

The Court further held that failure to provide an oral hearing was not reasonable or justifiable, and therefore could not be saved under s. 1. As a result of the *Singh* decision, the former refugee determination system was replaced by the Immigration and Refugee Board (IRB), which holds quasi-judicial oral hearings for refugee claimants who are in Canada.

Canada (Minister of Employment and Immigration) v. Chiarelli

Section 7 was raised again in *Canada (Minister of Employment and Immigration) v. Chiarelli* to challenge the former *Immigration Act* of 1976, but this time unsuccessfully. Sections 27(1)(d)(ii) and 32(2) of the *Immigration Act* required that deportation be ordered for persons convicted of an offence carrying a maximum punishment of five years or more, without regard to the circumstances of the offence or the offender. Chiarelli, a permanent resident, was declared inadmissible on the ground of criminality and ordered deported.

Chiarelli's criminal record classified him such that he was barred from admission to Canada, and the minister was authorized to issue a certificate dismissing Chiarelli's appeal. In other words, Chiarelli was not accorded the usual right to appeal, where all the circumstances of the case are considered regarding the deportation order. Chiarelli argued that these provisions were contrary to the s. 7 principles of fundamental justice. However, the Supreme Court of Canada held the following:

in determining the scope of the principles of fundamental justice as they apply to this case, the Court must look to the principles and policies underlying immigration law. The most fundamental principle of immigration law is that non-citizens do not have an unqualified right to enter or remain in the country.

The Court noted the distinction between citizens and non-citizens recognized in the Charter—only citizens are accorded the right "to enter, remain in and leave Canada" under s. 6(1). Additionally, the Court held the following:

there has never been a universally available right of appeal from a deportation order on "all the circumstances of the case." Such an appeal has historically been a purely discretionary matter. Although it has been added as a statutory ground of appeal, the executive has always retained the power to prevent an appeal from being allowed on that ground in cases involving serious security interests.

But, more to the point, with regard to the s. 7 requirement of fundamental justice, the Court held that

Parliament has the right to adopt an immigration policy and to enact legislation prescribing the conditions under which non-citizens will be permitted to enter and remain in Canada. It has done so in the *Immigration Act*. ... [N]o person other than a citizen, permanent resident, Convention refugee or Indian registered under the *Indian Act* has a right to come to or remain in Canada. ... One of the conditions Parliament has imposed on a permanent resident's right to remain in Canada is that he or she not be convicted of an offence for which a term of imprisonment of five years or more may be imposed. This condition represents a legitimate, non-arbitrary choice by Parliament of a situation in which it is not in the public interest to allow a non-citizen to remain in the country. ... [T]he personal circumstances of individuals who breach this condition may vary widely. The offences ... also vary in gravity, as may the factual circumstances surrounding the commission of a particular offence.

However there is one element common to all persons who fall within the class of permanent residents described in the s. 27(1)(d)(ii). They have all deliberately violated an essential condition under which they were permitted to remain in Canada. In such a situation, there is no breach of fundamental justice in giving practical effect to the termination of their right to remain in Canada. In the case of a permanent resident, deportation is the only way in which to accomplish this. There is nothing inherently unjust about a mandatory order. ... It is not necessary, in order to comply with fundamental justice, to look beyond this fact to other aggravating or mitigating circumstances.

Thus, in a nutshell, while s. 7 of the Charter does provide minimum procedural protections, it generally does not shield non-citizens from deportation.

Suresh v. Canada (Minister of Citizenship and Immigration)

In the case of *Suresh v. Canada (Minister of Citizenship and Immigration)*, the Court again addressed the issue of deportation, but with the additional element that the person was a Convention refugee who faced a risk of torture if deported. In this case, inadmissibility was due to membership in a terrorist organization.

Suresh was a Convention refugee from Sri Lanka who applied for landed immigrant status. He was ordered deported on security grounds, based on the opinion of the Canadian Security Intelligence Service that he was a member and fundraiser for the Liberation Tigers of Tamil Eelam, an organization engaged in terrorist activity in Sri Lanka, and whose members were subject to torture in Sri Lanka.

Section 53 of the *Immigration Act* of 1976 permitted deportation of persons who had been engaged in terrorism or were members of terrorist organizations, and who also posed a threat to the security of Canada, "to a country where the person's life or freedom would be threatened." The question was raised as to whether such deportation violated the procedural protection found under s. 7 of the Charter.

The Court held that while s. 53 did not infringe the Charter, deportation to face torture is generally unconstitutional, and some of the procedures followed in Suresh's case did not meet the required constitutional standards. Therefore, he was entitled to a new deportation hearing:

> [T]he procedural protections required by s. 7 in this case do not extend to the level of requiring the Minister to conduct a full oral hearing or a complete judicial process. However, they require more than the procedure required by the Act under s. 53(1)(*b*)—that is, none—and they require more than Suresh received.

In terms of the larger question of whether or not to deport a refugee when there is a risk that this would subject the refugee to torture, the Court held that it was a matter of balancing interests:

> Canadian jurisprudence does not suggest that Canada may never deport a person to face treatment elsewhere that would be unconstitutional if imposed by Canada directly, on Canadian soil. To repeat, the appropriate approach is essentially one of balancing. The outcome will depend not only on considerations inherent in the general context but also on considerations related to the circumstances and condition of the particular person whom the government seeks to expel. On the one hand stands the state's genuine interest in combatting terrorism, preventing Canada from becoming a safe haven for terrorists, and protecting public security. On the other hand stands Canada's constitutional commitment to liberty and fair process. This said, Canadian jurisprudence suggests that this balance will usually come down against expelling a person to face torture elsewhere.

So, while generally it would be a violation of the Charter to deport a refugee where there were grounds to believe there was a substantial risk of torture, the Court left open the possibility that in an exceptional case such deportation might be justified.

Case Law

Case law is judge-made law. The ability of courts to create law as well as interpret it is significant, as demonstrated in the Charter cases described above. Case law also includes the **common law**, which is a body of legal principles and rules that trace back to Britain. These rules are called "common" because they were applied so many times that they became widely known and considered well-settled rules of law. This is similar to the concept of **customary international law**, where customs and practice take on legal significance over time. Common-law principles still apply in Canada with respect to areas of law that are not fully codified by statute, such as contract law and tort law, but there are no common-law rules for immigration law.

Case law also includes tribunal and judicial decisions that interpret the Constitution, statutes, and regulations. To achieve predictability and consistency, by treating similar cases in a similar manner, our courts make decisions in accordance with **precedent**. "Rules" created by judges in legal decisions bind the decision makers in future decisions, at least where those decisions turn on the same or similar facts. The decisions of higher level courts (provincial courts of appeal, or the Supreme Court of Canada) must be respected and followed in lower courts unless the facts of the new case before the lower court differ substantially.

Statutes and Regulations

Statutes are written "codes" of law, also called legislation, which typically deal with a particular subject matter, such as the IRPA. Many statutes are accompanied by **regulations**, which fill in the details of how the law is to be implemented.

Statutes are created by a legislature: either the federal Parliament in Ottawa or the provincial or territorial legislatures in each of the provinces and territories. The legislature is the elected arm of government and is accountable to the voters. Provided that constitutional principles are not violated, such as those found in the *Charter of Rights and Freedoms*, a legislature can change the rules developed over time in case law, by using clear language in a statute. Also, courts may make decisions about the proper interpretation of statutory provisions, and this body of case law becomes part of the law under that statute.

Many statutes, including the IRPA and the *Citizenship Act*, authorize the creation of regulations, which provide the practical details of how the statute is to be implemented. Regulations are sometimes described as being "created under statutes." They are a subordinate form of legislation, drafted by the staff of the Cabinet of the governing party. Unlike statutes, regulations need not be approved and passed by the legislature.

Regulations tend to be very practical and can include lists, schedules, diagrams, forms, and charts. The information contained in regulations is just as important as that found in the primary legislation. If a statute has regulations made under it, the regulations will be found published in their own volumes separate from the statute, and will be revised according to the same schedule as the statute itself. However, regulations cannot exist independently without a parent statute. For a regulation to lawfully exist, it must have a parent statute that contains a provision designating regulation-making authority. If no such provision exists, no regulations may be enacted.

Policy

Policies explain the operation of legislation and regulation. Government **policy** is not law; however, it is a very important source of guidance and direction. How the law is actually applied in practice often evolves as a matter of government policy, especially where the law leaves room for discretion in administrative decision making. Policies can be formal or informal, and they can be written or unwritten. They can also have a wide range of objectives, such as promoting fairness and prioritizing the government's use of resources. For example, it is policy that CIC gives priority to processing and finalizing applications within six months in the family class for spouses, common-law and conjugal partners, and dependent children.[1]

The objectives and operation of government policy must be in compliance with legislation and regulations. If policies are found to operate in a way that is inconsistent with legislation or regulations, they must not be applied. Government policy documents are often made available to the public online on government websites.

ADMINISTRATIVE LAW

Much of immigration law is administrative law—the body of law that governs how government administrators and employees exercise the decision-making powers granted to them under statute. Depending on the requirements of the statute, administrative decisions may be made quickly and routinely, such as by a visa officer who issues a temporary resident visa to a foreign national, or they may be quasi-judicial—involving a hearing and an impartial decision maker. Often decisions start out as routine, but if an applicant is denied the right or benefit sought, she may challenge the decision, and it will be reheard, usually by an independent board or tribunal.

Administrative tribunals require a greater degree of procedural fairness than do routine administrative decisions made by staff, and they function in a similar manner to courts, with both sides making arguments and providing evidence to the decision maker. At the least, the person seeking a decision is entitled to be heard—to know the reasons for the decision and to be given an opportunity to respond. However, this does not necessarily extend to the right to a full oral hearing with the submission of evidence, examination and cross-examination of witnesses, and argument similar to a trial. The degree of procedural fairness required depends on the wording of the statute in question.

Whether a decision is administrative or quasi-judicial (with a hearing before a tribunal), the decision must be fair—based on the relevant criteria, and made by an unbiased decision maker. An advantage of administrative tribunals is that hearing procedures are generally much less formal than court procedures, and matters can be resolved more quickly.

Administrative decisions may also be judicially reviewed by a divisional court. On judicial review, the court considers whether the tribunal acted within its jurisdiction (according to the statute and regulations), whether it exercised its discretion in a reasonable manner, and whether its procedures were fair.

This is different from an appeal, which reconsiders the legal merits of the decision. On appeal, a court may overturn a decision if the decision was based on an erroneous interpretation or application of the law. In other words, the decision was "wrong."

Decisions of administrative tribunals may be appealed to a court only if expressly permitted by the statute that creates and governs that tribunal. The rationale for limiting appeals of tribunal decisions is that essentially an appeal involves replacing a tribunal's decision with a court's decision. This undermines one of the advantages of tribunals—their expertise in their particular subject area. It is a principle of administrative law that deference should be given to administrative decisions by government officials and tribunals, because they possess expertise in the particular regulatory regime—such as immigration and refugee law.

HISTORY OF IMMIGRATION LAW IN CANADA

Prior to Canada's first *Immigration Act*, Canada's immigration rules were taken from those of Great Britain.[2] For example, some provinces had enacted immigration laws primarily aimed at restricting the immigration of visible minorities. Historically, the ability for an alien to enter Britain was entirely dependent on the will of the King or Queen of England or officials appointed by the monarch. The power of the King or Queen to control immigration was gradually limited by statute law.

Patterns of Immigration

Immigration to what is now Canada predates the historical record. However, there are several scientific theories about the first migration to North America. Among them are the theory that Stone Age hunters followed game from Siberia into Alaska across a land bridge that once existed across what is now the Bering Strait, and the theory that Asian seafarers arrived by boats. Regardless of how or exactly when they arrived, these first migrants were probably the ancestors of Canada's First Nations peoples.

European immigration began in earnest in the early 17th century with French settlers and fur traders. In the 18th century came a wave of British Loyalists leaving the newly formed United States of America. In the 19th century a large number of immigrants came from Britain. In the 20th century large numbers of immigrants began pouring in from just about everywhere, beginning with the first huge wave from continental Europe right at the beginning of the century. This period of immigration in the 20th century has been described in the CIC's publication *Forging Our Legacy: Canadian Citizenship and Immigration, 1900-1977*, as follows:

> This huge influx of people represented a watershed in Canadian immigration history. From that time until today, Canada has never received the number of immigrants that it did in 1913, when over 400,000 newcomers arrived on Canadian soil. But throughout this century immigrants did continue to choose Canada as their new country, and a second great wave (the last one to date) occurred between 1947 and 1961. Although this wave, like the first, featured newcomers from continental Europe, southern Europe, especially Italy, and central Europe became much more important sources of immigrants. By contrast, immigration from Great Britain declined substantially from the earlier period (1900-1914).[3]

Although British immigration declined, British citizens still received preferential treatment over other immigrants. Various policies and laws restricted immigration from people considered to be not of the right colour or culture. Among the best-known examples of this institutionalized racism were the Chinese head tax and the *Chinese Immigration Act* of 1923, which replaced the head tax but effectively shut down Chinese immigration until its repeal in 1947.

When the Second World War erupted, anti-foreigner sentiment prevailed and many non-British people were interned, most famously the Japanese:

> In Canada itself, probably no group of people experienced as much hardship and upheaval as the Japanese Canadians. Their ordeal began on 8 December 1941, the day after the Japanese bombed Pearl Harbor. Within hours of that attack, Ottawa ordered that fishing boats operated by Japanese-Canadian fishermen be impound-

ed and that all Japanese aliens be registered with the Royal Canadian Mounted Police. The worst blow was delivered on 25 February 1942. On that day, Mackenzie King announced in the House of Commons that all Japanese Canadians would be forcibly removed from within a hundred-mile swath of the Pacific coast to "safeguard the defences of the Pacific Coast of Canada." Thus began the process that saw a visible minority uprooted from their homes, stripped of their property, and dispersed across Canada. Japanese Canadians, unlike their counterparts in the United States, were kept under detention until the end of the war. After the conclusion of hostilities, about 4,000 of them succumbed to pressure and left Canada for Japan under the federal government's "repatriation" scheme. Of these, more than half were Canadian-born and two-thirds were Canadian citizens.[4]

After the Second World War, unlike after the First World War, the Canadian economy boomed, paving the way for more liberal immigration policies, including policies for the acceptance of European displaced persons and refugees. Although these policies were more liberal, non-white immigrants were still explicitly considered undesirable and fully a third of the postwar wave of immigrants were British.

In the mid-1960s, Canada's immigration policies finally began to change. Instead of basing the selection of immigrants on race, Canada adopted new selection criteria: education and skills. For the first time, significant numbers of non-British, non-European, non-white immigrants were being welcomed from Africa, Asia, Latin America, and the Caribbean.

These more liberal immigration policies have continued to the present day. According to the Citizenship and Immigration Canada website, the top ten source countries for immigration to Canada in 2006 (the year for which the most recent statistics are available), are as follows:

Top Ten Countries of Birth for New Canadians in 2006

Country	Number of new citizens	Percentage
1. China	34,351	13.24
2. India	33,702	12.99
3. Pakistan	17,022	6.56
4. Philippines	15,475	5.96
5. Iran	8,060	3.10
6. South Korea	7,524	2.90
7. Romania	5,867	2.26
8. Sri Lanka	5,630	2.17
9. United States	5,076	1.95
10. Jamaica	4,812	1.85
Top 10 countries	**137,519**	**53.04**
Other	**121,748**	**46.95**
Total Canada	**259,267**	**100.00**

Source: Adapted from Citizenship and Immigration Canada, "Backgrounder: Citizenship Fast Facts," February 16, 2007, www.cic.gc.ca/english/department/media/backgrounders/2007/2007-02-16.asp.

Today, one out of every six Canadian residents was born outside of Canada. Canada accepts proportionately more immigrants than any other country in the world, including the United States.

In 2007, Canada admitted 236,758 new permanent residents. Currently, the government plans to admit between 240,000 and 265,000 new permanent residents in 2008.[5]

Although these numbers seem large, it should be noted that the immigration rate is approximately 0.7 percent of Canada's population, which numbers about 33,415,000.[6]

Legislative History

The history of modern Canadian immigration is inextricably linked to the legislative history of immigration in Canada. Currently, the two most important pieces of legislation with respect to Canadian immigration law are the *Immigration and Refugee Protection Act* and the *Citizenship Act*. These are the two Acts that guide decisions about who gets to come to Canada, and who gets to stay and enjoy all the rights of citizenship. The story of the predecessors of these statutes is as follows.

The *Immigration Act* of 1906 was a highly restrictive piece of legislation. It created a head tax for immigrants, barred many people and increased the government's power to deport:

> There had been laws since 1869 prohibiting certain kinds of immigration and since 1889 allowing designated classes of immigrants to be returned whence they came. The 1906 Act differed in degree, significantly increasing the number of categories of prohibited immigrants and officially sanctioning the deportation of undesirable newcomers.[7]

The 1906 Act was closely followed by the *Immigration Act* of 1910. This Act was even more exclusionary than the 1906 Act, allowing Cabinet the authority to exclude "immigrants belonging to any race deemed unsuited to the climate or requirements of Canada." The 1910 Act also strengthened the government's power to deport people, such as anarchists, on the grounds of political and moral instability.[8]

The policy considerations behind these two statutes and the various related laws and immigration policies were, for the most part, to encourage British and American immigration to Canada, and to discourage all other groups. An amendment to the 1906 Act, in effect in 1908, sharply curtailed Asian immigration in particular. This amendment, known as the "continuous-journey regulation," required immigrants to travel to Canada by continuous passage from their country of origin. This requirement was mostly designed to affect Indian and Japanese immigrants because of the difficulty in gaining continuous passage to Canada from those countries.

However, Canada needed cheap labour: people willing to work hard for low wages and under harsh conditions. The more desirable British and American immigrants were not willing to fill that need and although the Chinese who had worked on the building of the railway had proven themselves willing and hardworking, the existing laws severely restricted their entry into the country. "Canadian industrialists therefore turned increasingly towards central and southern Europe for the semi-skilled and unskilled labourers needed to supply the goods and services required by the new settlers."[9]

Immigration from eastern, southern, and central Europe continued to swell Canada's population up until just before the First World War. However, the decline of the Canadian economy and the subsequent war, which created increased suspicion and dislike of "foreigners," put the brakes on the boom in immigration. During the war, intolerance and harassment were suffered by those in Canada deemed "enemy aliens" because they originated from the now enemy countries. This was despite the fact that most of these so-called foreigners had settled in Canada and were contributing members of Canadian society.

Not only did many Canadians treat these "enemy aliens" badly, the government itself acted against them—for example, by interning many in camps at the start of the war. The government also passed legislation that penalized "enemy aliens," most strikingly the *Wartime Elections Act*:

> The *Wartime Elections Act*, invoked in the 1917 federal election, was perhaps the most extraordinary measure taken against enemy aliens. In addition to giving the federal vote to women in the armed forces and to the wives, sisters, and mothers of soldiers in active service (Canadian women as a whole had not yet won the right to vote in federal elections), the Act withdrew this right from Canadians who had been born in enemy countries and had become naturalized British subjects after 31 March 1902.[10]

These now disenfranchised, naturalized British subjects (Canadian citizenship did not yet exist) had fulfilled a three-year residency requirement so they were hardly newcomers. The *Naturalization Act*, passed in 1914, increased the residency requirement to five years. (British subjects did not have to be "naturalized" and obtained the full rights of Canadian nationals after only one year of residency.)

After the war, the economy suffered and the fear and dislike of foreigners escalated. One of the defining events of this period of Canadian immigration history was the Winnipeg General Strike of 1919:

> The spiralling cost of living, widespread unemployment, and disillusionment with "the system" gave rise to a wave of labour unrest that rolled across the country in 1918 and 1919, intensifying fears of an international Bolshevik conspiracy. Nothing did more to inflame anti-foreign sentiment and heighten fears of revolution than the Winnipeg General Strike of May 1919.[11]

The government's legislative reaction was again to target so-called foreigners:

> Ultimately, the decisive intervention of the federal government brought about an end to the conflict. Persuaded that enemy aliens had instigated the strike, the government succeeded in 1919 in amending the *Immigration Act*, to allow for their easy deportation. It then had ten strike leaders arrested and instituted deportation proceedings against the four who were foreign-born. When a protest parade on 21 June turned ugly, Royal North West Mounted Police charged the crowd, leaving one person dead and many others wounded. "Bloody Saturday," as it came to be called, led to the arrest and deportation of 34 foreigners and effectively broke the Winnipeg General Strike. But it would leave a long-lasting legacy of bitterness and unrest across Canada.[12]

The revised *Immigration Act* was further used to vigorously limit non-British immigration:

The revised *Immigration Act* and the Orders in Council issued under its authority signalled a dramatic shift in Canadian immigration policy. Prior to the First World War, immigration officials had chosen immigrants largely on the basis of the contribution that they could make to the Canadian economy, whereas now they attached more importance to a prospective immigrant's cultural and ideological complexion. As a result, newcomers from the white Commonwealth countries, the United States, and to a lesser extent the so-called preferred countries (that is, northwestern Europe) were welcomed, while the celebrated "stalwart peasants" of the Sifton era were not, unless, of course, their labour was in demand.[13]

Whereas in 1923 the *Chinese Immigration Act* was enacted to prevent virtually all Chinese immigration, in 1922 the regulations of the *Immigration Act* were relaxed by the government of Mackenzie King, who over the next few years repealed most of the legislation preventing European immigration. However, during the Great Depression of the 1930s, government policy and legislation again were used to close the doors to non-British immigrants as well as to refugees, including Jewish refugees attempting to flee Nazi Germany. Many immigrants were barred from entry and tens of thousands who were in Canada were deported in those years. With the outbreak of the Second World War, fear and suspicion of foreigners escalated. Many were interned in camps, most famously the Japanese, many of whom had been born in Canada.

Besides being racist, Canadian immigration laws were sexist, well into the mid-20th century:

> Married women, for example, did not have full authority over their national status. Classified with minors, lunatics and idiots "under a disability," they could not become naturalized or control their national status as independent persons, except in very special circumstances.[14]

The *Canadian Citizenship Act*, which came into force in 1947, addressed some of these issues of racism and sexism. This was Canada's first citizenship statute. Before that, there was no Canadian citizenship as we understand it today. Before 1947, "Canadians" were British subjects. It wasn't until the *Canadian Citizenship Act* came into being that Canadians became citizens of their own country. The new statute also gave married women autonomy with respect to their status—the nationality of a married woman was no longer dependent on that of her husband.

> With the enactment of this revolutionary piece of legislation Canada became the first Commonwealth country to create its own class of citizenship separate from that of Great Britain. ... In a moving and historic ceremony, staged on the evening of 3 January 1947 in the Supreme Court of Canada chamber, 26 individuals were presented with Canadian citizenship certificates. Among them were Prime Minister William Lyon Mackenzie King, who received certificate 0001, and Yousuf Karsh, the internationally acclaimed Armenian-born photographer.[15]

A new *Immigration Act*, the first new such Act since 1910, was enacted in 1952. Although this Act included provisions designed to exclude non-whites, it also provided the government with the discretion—a discretion that it exercised—to admit large numbers of refugees and others who would have otherwise been inadmissible.

But the turning point in Canada's legislative history was probably the *Immigration Act* of 1976:

> The *Immigration Act*, the cornerstone of present-day immigration policy, was enacted in 1976 and came into force in 1978. It broke new ground by spelling out the fundamental principles and objectives of Canadian immigration policy. Included among these are the promotion of Canada's demographic, economic, cultural, and social goals; family reunification; the fulfillment of Canada's international obligations in relation to the United Nations Convention (1951) and its 1967 Protocol relating to refugees, which Canada had signed in 1969; non-discrimination in immigration policy; and cooperation between all levels of government and the voluntary sector in the settlement of immigrants in Canadian society.[16]

Another important development was the creation of a second citizenship act—the *Citizenship Act*—which replaced the *Canadian Citizenship Act* and came into force in 1977. Amendments to the new Act have been made over the years, and it is still in force today. The new statute also addressed previous racist policies, particularly the different treatment received by "aliens" as opposed to those originating from Britain and the British Commonwealth (who would qualify for Canadian citizenship without being called before a judge for a hearing or taking the oath of allegiance in a formal ceremony):

> It was to rectify … anomalies and the unequal treatment accorded different groups of people that *An Act Respecting Citizenship* was first introduced in the House of Commons in May 1974. It received Royal Assent on 16 July 1976 and came into force, along with the Citizenship Regulations, on 15 February 1977. Henceforth, improved access and equal treatment of all applicants would be the guiding principles in the granting of Canadian citizenship.[17]

The new *Citizenship Act* provided equal rights and privileges, and equal obligations and duties, to Canadians, whether they were born in Canada or born elsewhere and acquired Canadian citizenship. It also permitted dual citizenship, allowing Canadians the benefits of citizenship of another country as well.

THE IMMIGRATION AND REFUGEE PROTECTION ACT AND ITS REGULATIONS

In contrast to many of Canada's earlier laws, the current legislative framework for immigration is based on non-discriminatory principles and is grounded in the values enshrined in the Charter. The current immigration act, the *Immigration and Refugee Protection Act*, came into force on June 28, 2002, replacing the *Immigration Act* of 1976. The IRPA introduced new provisions designed to increase national security and public safety measures, balanced by provisions intended to make it simpler for admissible persons to enter Canada.

The IRPA provides a framework for the operation of our immigration and refugee systems, setting out general rules and principles, the rights and obligations of permanent and temporary residents and protected persons, and key enforcement provisions. The regulations under it provide the specific details needed for its implementation and operation. The regulations change relatively frequently, and immigration consultants must monitor information sources such as the Citizenship and Immigration Canada website (www.cic.gc.ca).

The IRPA is divided into parts, and these parts are subdivided into divisions and then sections and subsections. A table of contents for the IRPA is produced in the box below.

IRPA Table of Contents

Sections 1 to 10: these sections set out the short title of the Act, provide definitions and objectives, and give the minister authority to appoint officers, make regulations, and set up international and provincial agreements

Part 1: Immigration to Canada

    Division 1: Requirements Before Entering Canada and Selection

    Division 2: Examination

    Division 3: Entering and Remaining in Canada

    Division 4: Inadmissibility

    Division 5: Loss of Status and Removal

    Division 6: Detention and Release

    Division 7: Right of Appeal

    Division 8: Judicial Review

    Division 9: Protection of Information

    Division 10: General Provisions

Part 2: Refugee Protection

    Division 1: Refugee Protection, Convention Refugees and Persons in Need of Protection

    Division 2: Convention Refugees and Persons in Need of Protection

    Division 3: Pre-removal Risk Assessment

Part 3: Enforcement

Part 4: Immigration and Refugee Board

Part 5: Transitional Provisions, Consequential and Related Amendments, Coordinating Amendments, Repeals and Coming into Force (Sections 187 to 275)

Schedule: Sections E and F of Article 1 of the United Nations Convention Relating to the Status of Refugees

IRPA Objectives and Interpretation Tools

The IRPA sets out separate objectives for the provisions regarding immigrants and the provisions regarding refugees. The objectives offer important guidance to immigration officers, the Immigration and Refugee Board, and the courts with respect to how the statute should be applied and interpreted.

With respect to immigration, the objectives of the IRPA, set out in s. 3(1), can be summarized as follows:

- maximize the social, cultural, and economic benefits of immigration;

- enrich and strengthen the social and cultural fabric of Canadian society, while respecting the federal, bilingual, and multicultural character of Canada;

- support and assist the development of minority official languages communities in Canada;

- support the development of a strong and prosperous Canadian economy, in which the benefits of immigration are shared across all regions of Canada;

- reunite families in Canada;

- integrate permanent residents into Canada, while recognizing mutual obligations for new immigrants and Canadian society;

- support consistent standards and prompt processing;

- facilitate the entry of visitors, students, and temporary workers for purposes such as trade, commerce, tourism, international understanding, and cultural, educational and scientific activities;

- protect the health and safety of Canadians and maintain the security of Canadian society;

- promote international justice and security by fostering respect for human rights and by denying access to Canadian territory to persons who are criminals or security risks; and

- cooperate with the provinces to better recognize the foreign credentials of permanent residents.

With respect to refugees, the objectives of the IRPA, set out in s. 3(2), can be summarized as follows:

- recognize that the priority of the IRPA is to save lives and protect displaced and persecuted persons;

- fulfill Canada's international legal obligations with respect to refugees and affirm commitment to international efforts to assist with resettlement;

- grant fair consideration to those who come to Canada claiming persecution;

- offer safe haven to persons with a well-founded fear of persecution based on race, religion, nationality, political opinion, or membership in a particular social group, as well as those at risk of torture or cruel and unusual treatment or punishment;

- establish fair and efficient procedures that will maintain the integrity of the Canadian refugee protection system, while upholding Canada's respect for the human rights and fundamental freedoms of all human beings;

- support the self-sufficiency and the social and economic well-being of refugees by facilitating reunification with their family members in Canada;

- protect the health and safety of Canadians and maintain the security of Canadian society; and

- promote international justice and security by denying access to Canadian territory to persons, including refugee claimants, who are security risks or serious criminals.

The IRPA also contains a section (s. 3(3)) that directs all decision makers to interpret and apply the IRPA in a manner that

- furthers the domestic and international interests of Canada;

- promotes accountability and transparency by enhancing public awareness of immigration and refugee programs;

- facilitates cooperation among the government of Canada, provincial governments, foreign states, international organizations, and non-governmental organizations;

- ensures that decisions taken under the IRPA are consistent with the Charter, including its principles of equality and freedom from discrimination and of the equality of English and French as the official languages of Canada;

- supports the government's commitment to enhancing the vitality of the English and French linguistic minority communities in Canada; and

- complies with international human rights instruments to which Canada is signatory.

Appeals under the IRPA are heard by the Immigration and Refugee Board of Canada—an administrative tribunal. The IRB has three divisions: the Immigration Division, the Immigration Appeal Division and the Refugee Protection Division. Within these divisions, members perform the following functions: hold admissibility hearings to determine whether individuals may enter or remain in Canada; hold detention reviews; hear and decide appeals on immigration matters (such as removal orders, sponsorship refusals, and residency requirements); and decide refugee claims made by individuals in Canada. IRB decisions may be subject to judicial review by the Federal Court of Canada.

IRPA Regulations and Rules

Regulations under the IRPA are made by the Cabinet and must be published in the *Canada Gazette* along with a regulatory impact analysis statement. These explanatory notes are helpful in determining how the regulations are to be applied, and cover the following points:

- description of the regulation, including its purpose and function

- alternatives to the regulation that were considered

- benefits and cost to the public of the regulation

- consultations that took place with interested parties and the public in the drafting of the regulation

- compliance and enforcement issues

- gender-based analysis of the impact of the regulation

- contact person.

There are numerous regulations under the IRPA, covering a variety of subject areas. The largest is the Immigration and Refugee Protection Regulations, which consist of 21 parts, and provide detailed guidance regarding the application of the IRPA, including, for example, Part 5: Permanent Residents, Part 10: Visitors, and Part 14: Detention and Release. Other regulations include the following:

- Alejandra Flores Velasquez Immigration Exemption Regulations (S.O.R./91-693)

- Order Designating the Minister of Citizenship and Immigration as the Minister Responsible for the Administration of That Act (S.I./2001-120)

- Order Setting Out the Respective Responsibilities of the Minister of Citizenship and Immigration and the Minister of Public Safety and Emergency Preparedness Under the Act (S.I./2005-120)

- Protection of Passenger Information Regulations (S.O.R./2005-346).

In the context of immigration and refugee matters, **rules** are regulations that establish practices and procedures for the presentation of cases. They are generally binding, like any other regulations, unless they specifically provide otherwise. The rules are authorized by s. 161(1) of the *Immigration and Refugee Protection Act*, and include the following examples:

- Adjudication Division Rules (S.O.R./93-47)

- Convention Refugee Determination Division Rules (S.O.R./93-45)

- Immigration Appeal Division Rules (S.O.R./2002-230)

- Immigration Division Rules (S.O.R./2002-229)

- Refugee Protection Division Rules (S.O.R./2002-228).

Policy

Policy fills in the gaps left by the IRPA and its regulations, and is intended to promote consistency, fairness, and transparency. Most policy develops and evolves over time on an informal basis, as certain procedures that work well become accepted policy. Policy may also be formalized through a variety of policy instruments that codify informal policy or create new policy. Both CIC and the IRB use a variety of policy instruments, as described below.

CIC POLICY INSTRUMENTS

Consider the following policy instruments of CIC:

1. *Policy notes.* Policy notes are memoranda used to address issues that are temporary in nature, or that are limited to a specific region.

2. *Program manuals.* The minister of Citizenship and Immigration Canada publishes operations manuals to guide the activities of immigration officers. Immigration officers consult these manuals when applying the IRPA and its regulations; likewise, immigration practitioners should consult these documents when advising clients. The existing manuals can be found online at www.cic.gc.ca/english/resources/publications/index.asp and are as follows:

   - *Citizenship Policy (CP)*
   - *Enforcement (ENF)*
   - *Temporary Foreign Workers Guidelines (FW)*
   - *Legislation (IL)*
   - *Information Sharing (IN)*
   - *Inland Processing (IP)*
   - *Reference (IR)*
   - *Overseas Processing (OP)*
   - *Protected Persons (PP).*

   Keep in mind that although the operations manuals are very important, they are merely policy and do not have the force of law. Therefore, if a provision of a manual is inconsistent with the provisions of the IRPA or its regulations, it will not be valid.

3. *Operational bulletins.* Occasionally, operational bulletins are issued to deliver urgent or one-time-only instructions to staff to be used on a temporary basis while the program and policy manuals are updated. A notice of current operational bulletins can be found under "Operational bulletins" on the CIC website at www.cic.gc.ca/english/resources/ manuals/bulletins/index.asp.

IRB POLICY INSTRUMENTS

Consider the following policy instruments of the IRB:

1. *Chairperson's guidelines.* The chairperson's guidelines are authorized by s. 159(1)(h) of the *Immigration and Refugee Protection Act*, to provide guiding principles for resolving cases and to further the government's strategic objectives. The chairperson of the Immigration and Refugee Board is permitted to make guidelines and identify decisions as

important precedents, to better enable members of the IRB to carry out their duties. The chairperson's guidelines are not mandatory, but decision makers are required to justify cases of non-compliance. The following eight guidelines existed as of October 2008:

- Guideline 1: Civilian Non-Combatants Fearing Persecution in Civil War Situations

- Guideline 2: Guidelines on Detention

- Guideline 3: Child Refugee Claimants: Procedural and Evidentiary Issues

- Guideline 4: Women Refugee Claimants Fearing Gender-Related Persecution

- Guideline 5: Providing the PIF and No PIF Abandonment in the Refugee Protection Division (the PIF is the Personal Information Form that is completed for a refugee applicant)

- Guideline 6: Scheduling and Changing the Date or Time of a Proceeding in the Refugee Protection Division

- Guideline 7: Concerning Preparation and Conduct of a Hearing in the Refugee Protection Division

- Guideline 8: Guideline on Procedures with Respect to Vulnerable Persons Appearing Before the Immigration and Refugee Board of Canada.

The guidelines can be found online at www.irb-cisr.gc.ca/en/references/policy/guidelines/index_e.htm.

2. *Jurisprudential guides.* The jurisprudential guides are authorized by s. 159(1)(h) of the *Immigration and Refugee Protection Act.* Their purpose is to facilitate consistency in decision making with regard to similar cases. A jurisprudential guide reiterates the reasoning of the IRB in a specific decision, so that it can be applied in other similar cases. The jurisprudential guides are not mandatory, but decision makers are required to justify non-compliance with the guides in cases with similar facts.

3. *Persuasive decisions.* Persuasive decisions are decisions identified by the head of the Division, such as the RPD, as being well reasoned. Decision makers are encouraged to follow the same reasoning in their own decisions. Unlike with the jurisprudential guides, decision makers are not required to justify the choice not to follow persuasive decisions.

4. *Policies.* Policies are formal statements explaining the details of new IRB initiatives, such as outlining roles and responsibilities. A few examples of policies are as follows:

- Policy on Oral Decisions and Oral Reasons (September 2003)—reaffirms that delivery of decisions and reasons orally, at the conclusion of a hearing, is normal practice for the IRB

- Policy on the Use of Jurisprudential Guides (March 2003)—governs the exercise of the chairperson's authority to identify a decision as a jurisprudential guide

- Fast Track Policy: Hearings Process (March 2005)—establishes a framework for identifying and processing simple claims more quickly than complex claims.

5. *Chairperson's instructions.* Chairperson's instructions provide formal direction to individual IRB staff. They are more narrow and specific than the policies described above.

Annual Report to Parliament on Immigration

Under s. 94 of the IRPA, the minister is required to table an annual report with Parliament on the operations of the *Immigration and Refugee Protection Act*. This plan must include:

- information on selection of foreign nationals including details on cooperation with the provinces;

- the number of foreign nationals who became permanent residents in the previous year, and projections for the future;

- the number of persons who entered Canada in the previous year under federal–provincial agreements;

- the number of persons who were given permanent resident status in the previous year for humanitarian and compassionate reasons, by the minister;

- the languages spoken by persons who became permanent residents;

- the number of times that immigration officers exercised the power to let in a person who would otherwise have been deemed inadmissible because the officers determined that the admission was justified; and

- a gender-based analysis of the impact of the IRPA.

For a copy of the most recent annual report to Parliament on immigration, visit the Citizenship and Immigration Canada website at www.cic.gc.ca/english/resources/publications/index.asp.

THE CITIZENSHIP ACT AND ITS REGULATIONS

The *Citizenship Act* does not discriminate between citizens by birth and immigrants who obtain citizenship, nor does it discriminate between men and women, or between people of different nationalities or race. All citizens share the same rights and privileges, such as the right to vote and hold office, and all share the same obligations and duties. Most notably, the *Citizenship Act* permits dual citizenship, allowing Canadians the benefits of citizenship of another country as well.

With a few exceptions, such as the children of diplomats, all persons born in Canada are Canadian citizens. Children born outside of Canada who have at least one Canadian parent are automatically citizens as well.

The *Citizenship Act* is divided into eight parts, as shown in the table of contents produced in the box below.

The *Citizenship Act* currently has two regulations: the Citizenship Regulations, 1993 and the Foreign Ownership of Land Regulations. The Act is explored in more detail in Chapter 6.

Citizenship Act Table of Contents

Sections 1 and 2: these sections set out the short title and definitions

Part I: The Right to Citizenship

Part II: Loss of Citizenship

Part III: Resumption of Citizenship

Part IV: Certificate of Citizenship

Part V: Procedure

Part VI: Administration

Part VII: Offences

Part VIII: Status of Persons in Canada

Schedule: Oath or Affirmation of Citizenship

NOTES

1. Citizenship and Immigration Canada, "OP 1: Procedures," in *Overseas Processing (OP)*, January 25, 2008, www.cic.gc.ca/english/resources/ manuals/op/index.asp.

2. For a description of the history of immigration law, see D. Galloway, *Immigration Law* (Concord, ON: Irwin Law, 1997), Chapter 1.

3. Citizenship and Immigration Canada, *Forging Our Legacy: Canadian Citizenship and Immigration, 1900-1977*, October 2000, www.cic.gc.ca/ english/resources/publications/index.asp.

4. Ibid.

5. Citizenship and Immigration Canada, *Backgrounder: 2007 Annual Report to Parliament on Immigration*, October 31, 2007, www.cic.gc.ca/english/ department/media/backgrounders/2007/index.asp.

6. Statistics Canada, "Canada's Population Clock," October 2008, www. statcan.ca/english/edu/clock/population.htm.

7. Supra note 3.

8. Ibid.

9. Ibid.

10. Ibid.

11. Ibid.

12. Ibid.

13. Ibid.

14. Ibid.

15. Ibid.

16. Ibid.

17. Ibid.

REFERENCES

Andrews v. Law Society of British Columbia. [1989] 1 S.C.R. 143.

Canada (Minister of Employment and Immigration) v. Chiarelli. [1992] 1 S.C.R. 711.

Canada-Québec Accord Relating to Immigration and Temporary Admission of Aliens. February 5, 1991. www.micc.gouv.qc.ca/publications/pdf/Accord_ canada_quebec_immigration_anglais.pdf.

Canadian Charter of Rights and Freedoms. Part I of the *Constitution Act, 1982.* R.S.C. 1985, app. II, no. 44.

Citizenship and Immigration Canada. *Facts and Figures 2006: Immigration Overview—Permanent and Temporary Residents*. 2007. www.cic.gc.ca/english/pdf/pub/facts2006.pdf.

Citizenship Act. R.S.C. 1985, c. C-29.

Constitution Act, 1867. 30 & 31 Vict., c. 3 (UK).

Constitution Act, 1982. R.S.C. 1985, app. II, no. 44.

Convention Relating to the Status of Refugees. 189 U.N.T.S. 150, entered into force April 22, 1954. www.unhchr.ch/html/menu3/b/o_c_ref.htm.

Immigration and Refugee Protection Act. S.C. 2001, c. 27.

Immigration and Refugee Protection Regulations. S.O.R./2002-227.

Singh v. Minister of Employment and Immigration. [1985] 1 S.C.R. 177.

Suresh v. Canada (Minister of Citizenship and Immigration). [2002] 1 S.C.R. 3.

RECOMMENDED READING

Knowles, Valerie. *Strangers at Our Gates: Canadian Immigration and Immigration Policy, 1540-1990*, rev. ed. (Toronto: Dundurn Press, 2007).

Malarek, Victor. *Haven's Gate: Canada's Immigration Fiasco* (Toronto: Macmillan of Canada, 1987).

REVIEW QUESTIONS

This chapter was divided into five main sections, each reflecting a key basis for understanding sources of immigration law. The headings below correspond to those in the chapter. You should now be able to answer the questions under each heading.

Sources of Immigration Law

1. What are the key federal statutes and regulations used in Canada for immigration, refugee, and citizenship matters?

2. Why is immigration a federal responsibility?

3. Give an example of how the federal government shares its federal powers related to immigration with the provinces and territories.

4. Are permanent residents, temporary residents, and refugees protected by s. 7 of the *Canadian Charter of Rights and Freedoms*? If yes, why? If no, why not?

5. Which Supreme Court decision holds that the concept of fundamental justice includes the notion that procedural fairness requires that where credibility is at issue, it must be determined on the basis of an oral hearing?

Administrative Law

1. What is administrative law?

2. What is a judicial review?

History of Immigration Law in Canada

1. List and provide one historical highlight from each of Canada's immigration statutes.

2. List and provide one historical highlight from each of Canada's citizenship statutes.

The Immigration and Refugee Protection Act and Its Regulations

This section of the chapter described the Act, its regulations, and other instruments that you will need as part of your professional toolkit.

1. Find and briefly summarize the following sections of the IRPA:

   - Section 2
   - Sections 8 and 10
   - Section 11
   - Section 12
   - Section 14
   - Section 15
   - Section 16
   - Section 18
   - Section 19

2. Find the section of the IRPA that requires the minister to table an annual report to Parliament.

The Citizenship Act and Its Regulations

1. Find the section of the *Citizenship Act* that defines who is a Canadian citizen.

2. Find the section of the *Citizenship Act* that details the requirements for citizenship.

3. Where in the *Citizenship Act* does the citizenship oath appear?

EXERCISE

Find the most recent *Annual Report to Parliament on Immigration* and determine the following:

- the government's plan to admit permanent residents by category,

- the government's plan to admit temporary residents, and

- the government's plan to admit protected persons as permanent residents.

CHAPTER 2

Decision Makers

LEARNING OBJECTIVES

After reading this chapter you should be able to:

- Identify key federal organizations involved in deciding immigration, citizenship, and refugee protection matters.

- Distinguish the role and function of Citizenship and Immigration Canada (CIC), the Canada Border Services Agency, the Immigration and Refugee Board (IRB), the Federal Court, and the Supreme Court.

- Identify the divisions of the Immigration and Refugee Board and distinguish the jurisdiction and function of each of those divisions.

- Distinguish the decision-making roles of the minister of CIC, the minister of Public Safety and Emergency Preparedness, minister's delegates, and decision makers in the IRB, including the chairperson and members.

- Understand the basis in law for decision making.

INTRODUCTION

Take a look in the government section of your phone book or try a web search to answer some of these questions:

- Who do you contact about how to have a client released from immigration detention?

- Who do you contact if your client's sponsorship of a family member has failed—Citizenship and Immigration Canada (CIC) or the Immigration and Refugee Board (IRB)?

- Who is responsible for removing people who should not be in Canada— CIC, the IRB, or the Canada Border Services Agency (CBSA)?

- If your application to sponsor a family member is refused, do you file an appeal with the board, the Federal Court, or the Supreme Court?

The answers to these questions are not straightforward. Canadian immigration and refugee laws and related processes are complex. A client may have "a file" with more than one organization, so determining which organization to contact depends on where the case stands in the process.

In Chapter 1 we learned about the various sources of law that are applied to manage the complexities of Canadian immigration. There is one more piece of the puzzle to add: the role of decision makers in immigration cases. Who makes decisions on cases? What decision-making powers do they have? Where do they get that authority? In this chapter, we look briefly at the following three levels of decision making and the related organizations involved in immigration and refugee protection matters:

1. the minister, including officers, for Citizenship and Immigration Canada, Public Safety and Emergency Preparedness Canada (PSEPC), and one of its agencies, the Canada Border Services Agency;

2. the Immigration and Refugee Board, and its four divisions; and

3. the courts.

We learn about who, within those organizations, has the statutory authority for making decisions, where they get their jurisdiction to make decisions, and what relationships exist among the three levels of decision making.

MINISTERS RESPONSIBLE FOR IMMIGRATION MATTERS

Section 4 of the *Immigration and Refugee Protection Act* divides responsibility for immigration and refugee functions between two ministers:

- the minister of Citizenship and Immigration, and
- the minister of Public Safety and Emergency Preparedness (PSEP).

Note that the Department of Public Safety and Emergency Preparedness is now called Public Safety Canada. We use the former title in this text because the relevant legislation does so.

The following descriptions of ministerial authority relate to either the minister of CIC or PSEP, unless otherwise specified.

Ministerial Authority and Decision-Making Powers

The minister of Citizenship and Immigration heads CIC, which is responsible for general areas of immigration and citizenship, including the following:

- immigration policy development, including guidance to staff in carrying out their functions and applying legislation;

- an annual immigration plan, which sets out the target numbers for immigration;

- immigration programs related to temporary and permanent immigration;

- the settlement and integration of newcomers to Canada;

- the resettlement of refugees;

- pre-removal risk assessments; and

- most policies related to admissibility.

The minister of Public Safety and Emergency Preparedness heads PSEP and has the policy lead for immigration enforcement functions, such as those carried out by the Canada Border Services Agency. Those functions include the management and operation of Canada's borders, including the following:

- arrests,

- detentions,

- removals, and

- port of entry functions.

The IRPA grants broad regulatory power to Cabinet through the **governor in council** to make rules and regulations in the form of **orders in council**. This enables the government to respond quickly to adapt the Act's broad provisions to changing circumstances. For example, the regulations stipulate the dollar amount for processing an application for a permanent resident visa. By an order in council, the regulations can easily be amended to change the amount payable for processing the application (s. 5).

The minister of CIC is required to table proposed regulations before each House of Parliament (the House of Commons and the Senate) so that they can be referred to the appropriate committee of that House when those proposals relate to the following provisions:

- examinations;

- rights and obligations of permanent and temporary residents;

- status documents;

- loss of status and removal, detention, and release;

- examination of eligibility to refer a refugee claim;

- the pre-removal risk assessment and principle of *non-refoulement*; and

- transportation companies (s. 5(2)).

The proposed regulation need only be tabled once, however, as it does not have to be presented to each House of Parliament again, even if it has been altered (s. 5(3)). As a result, amendments can be made without further examination by Parliament.

The IRPA empowers the minister to make decisions on a variety of matters. We will learn the basis in law for this authority, including the minister's power to delegate specific powers and decisions.

IMMIGRATION POLICY AND ADMINISTRATIVE FUNCTIONS

The minister of CIC is responsible for immigration policy development and immigration processes. Did you ever wonder who decides whether Canada should accept fewer or more immigrants? This is an area of responsibility of the minister of CIC, who in consultation with the provinces is responsible for setting the annual targets, including the number and types of foreign nationals who may come to Canada either as temporary or permanent residents.

The minister must table the annual immigration plan before Parliament by the first of November in each year. The minister also determines the requirements for foreign nationals such as the minimum standards they must meet in order to qualify as permanent residents. An example of this is the "pass mark" for skilled workers, investors, entrepreneurs, and self-employed persons, discussed in Chapter 5, "Permanent Entry."

The minister also has specific administrative authorities under the regulations to the IRPA. For example, the minister of PSEP can designate ports of entry and their dates and hours of operation.

ADMISSIBILITY AND ENFORCEMENT

Under Canadian immigration law, the minister decides whether a person is allowed to enter (is admissible) or is to be removed from Canada (see Chapter 3). The minister also has the discretionary power to grant temporary and permanent resident status to foreign nationals on the basis of humanitarian and compassionate grounds. This may apply both to those who wish to come to Canada and to those who wish to remain here but are inadmissible for technical, medical, or criminal reasons.

For example, you may have read or heard about cases in the news where a child is in need of life-saving surgery that is not available in the child's home country. How is it that the child may come to Canada for medical treatment, if she is not healthy enough to pass the required medical examination? This is an example of the minister of CIC exercising discretionary powers to allow entry. Although the child does not meet the statutory requirements for admission to Canada, the reasons for seeking entry to Canada are compelling enough for the minister to grant temporary authorization. The minister may issue a temporary resident visa—formerly known as a "minister's permit"—which is valid for a specific and limited period of time, and which can also be cancelled.

On the other hand, when an officer has reason to believe that a permanent resident or foreign national who is already in Canada has become inadmissible, the officer writes an "admissibility report" to be reviewed by the minister. The minister is authorized under s. 44(2) to take one of the following actions:

- allow the person to stay in Canada, if the minister concludes that the report is not well founded;

- issue a removal order, if the minister concludes that the report is well founded and that it falls within the jurisdiction of the officer who wrote the report; or

- refer the case to the Immigration Division of the Immigration and Refugee Board, if the minister concludes that the report is well founded, but that it does not fall within the jurisdiction of the officer who wrote it.

Consider the following scenario relating to the minister's authority to make decisions that could lead to a foreign national's removal from Canada. In this case scenario, the minister's authority has been delegated to officers, who carry out the immigration functions.

> *Jose Rodriguez came to Canada to visit his uncle Juan, who owns a small restaurant. One of Juan's employees quit suddenly so he asked Jose to come and work for him until he could find a replacement. Jose agreed and over a period of several weeks worked as a waiter and bus boy, and even helped out in the kitchen. His uncle paid him cash for his services. Jose was allowed entry to Canada as a temporary visitor but had no authorization to work. Jose is now considered to be in a state of non-compliance—namely, not in possession of a work authorization—and is now inadmissible. Jose came to the attention of immigration officials, and an officer "wrote a report" against Jose.*

In Jose's case, the minister (or, in practice, the minister's delegate) will review the officer's admissibility report and make a decision that ultimately could lead to Jose's removal from Canada. This process is explored in detail in Chapter 10, "Enforcement Procedures."

DELEGATION OF AUTHORITY

The minister's **delegation of authority** to others is necessary, given the sheer volume of immigration cases. The IRPA allows for certain ministerial powers, duties, requirements, and authorities to be delegated, to ensure that Canada's immigration, refugee protection, and citizenship programs can be delivered efficiently. Generally, the minister may **designate** persons wherever the word "officer" is used in the Act or its regulations with respect to a power, duty, requirement or authority. Each minister (of CIC or PSEP) may designate **officers** to carry out certain provisions of the Act and its regulations regarding their respective mandates, and may delegate their powers. An officer is a public servant who has been given specific powers and has been designated by the minister to carry out specific duties under the IRPA. There are several types of officers, including visa officers, examining officers, senior immigration officers, immigration officers, and CBSA officers. The minister's delegation of authority must be made in writing and must specify the powers and duties of officers (ss. 6 (1) and (2)).

SECURITY CERTIFICATES

A security certificate may be issued against a permanent resident or foreign national for removal purposes when there is reason to believe that the person poses a security threat and there is information that needs to be protected for security reasons. The purpose of the security certificate is to ensure that the government's classified information remains confidential: this has the effect of closing proceedings and ensuring the non-disclosure of certain information that could seriously harm the government's ability to protect its citizens.

A security certificate must be signed personally by both the minister of Public Safety and Emergency Preparedness and the minister of Citizenship and Immigration. Because of the lack of transparency and public accountability inherent in a closed process, this power must not be delegated under s. 77(1) of the IRPA.

The certificate is then referred to the Federal Court where a judge hears evidence in the absence of the person named to protect national security or the safety of any person. The judge will also hear evidence from the person named in the certificate. If the judge decides that the certificate is reasonable, then the certificate automatically becomes a removal order.

Officers

Officers are public servants who, for our purposes, work either for CIC or the CBSA. CIC officers are responsible for the delivery of the immigration program at Canadian missions abroad, and at national, regional, and local offices across Canada. Officers who work for CIC hold a number of positions and carry out a variety of duties, including the following:

- processing applications for temporary residence (such as authorizations for visitors, students, and temporary workers), permanent residence, refugee resettlement, and citizenship;

- providing settlement and integration services for newcomers;

- conducting research;

- reporting and analyzing international migration and refugee and social policy trends used for formulating government policy; and

- developing policy and programs.

Officers who work for the CBSA carry out a variety of duties related to immigration, including the following:

- examining people at ports of entry;

- detaining those people who may pose a threat to Canada; and

- removing people who are inadmissible to our country, including those involved in terrorism, organized crime, war crimes, or crimes against humanity.

Through the "Designation of Officers and Delegation of Authority" instrument signed by the minister of CIC on July 20, 2006, most of the powers vested in the minister by the IRPA in relation to the application of the law are delegated; the instrument includes a description of the duties and powers of officers granted to those persons working for CIC, the CBSA, and other agencies. The instrument also contains a section that sets out those authorities that have not been delegated. There is a separate designation and delegation-of-authority instrument signed by the president of the CBSA for those authorities that are under the specific mandate of the minister of Public Safety and Emergency Preparedness, such as those related to designating officers as peace officers.

Under the IRPA, officers have the power to examine people, perform search and seizure, and exercise the powers of a **peace officer**. Presented below is a general overview of officers' authorities. More on officers' authority to make decisions on applications is provided in later chapters.

EXAMINATION ON APPLICATION

When a person wishes to come to Canada, he must apply for temporary or permanent residence, usually before arriving. The application may be made abroad or at a port of entry, such as at the border or at an airport. It may be made orally or in writing depending on a number of factors described in later chapters.

Oral applications are made, for example, when a person landing at an airport asks to make a refugee claim, or someone at the Canada–US border, with a temporary or permanent resident visa, asks to enter Canada. Written applications may be made using forms provided by CIC, including applications for temporary or permanent residence. Applications are considered complete when all the instructions for completing the forms have been followed and all supporting documents have been submitted to the appropriate office.

Whether the person applies abroad or at a port of entry, the application must be assessed by an officer who is authorized to make a decision (IRPA s. 15(1)). The officer decides whether the person qualifies under an immigration program, such as the Family Class or Skilled Worker program, and whether the person has the right to enter Canada. Generally, the officers who work abroad and assess applications, at visa offices or consulates, are called **visa officers**; CBSA officers working at ports of entry, such as the Canada–US border, airports, or harbours, may have titles such as Border Services Officer or Enforcement Officer.

Visa officers typically review written applications, ensure their completeness, and evaluate the information. They may also interview applicants. CBSA officers, on the other hand, typically carry out their duties orally through examination procedures by questioning the person to elicit information—for example, about citizenship, residency, intention, employment, and length of stay at a port of entry. The details of the application procedures for specific immigration programs are explored in later chapters.

Section 28 of the Immigration and Refugee Protection Regulations provides that all persons who seek to enter Canada are deemed to be making an application and are therefore subject to an examination. Officers can compel an applicant to answer questions, to provide relevant documents, photographs, and fingerprints, and to submit to medical examinations. Officers act in an adjudicative capacity, which means they must be unbiased in their assessments and evaluations. They render binding decisions after reviewing and considering information received as evidence.

SEARCH AND SEIZURE

Some officers have been delegated authority for search and seizure powers; however, these powers may be exercised only when the officer has **reasonable grounds** to believe that a person who is trying to enter Canada has done any of the following:

- concealed his identity;

- hidden documents that are relevant to his admissibility; or

- concealed documents that may have been used for the purpose of smuggling or trafficking of persons.

The *Canadian Charter of Rights and Freedoms*, in ss. 8 to 10, provides that all persons in Canada, including foreign nationals, have the right to be secure against unreasonable search or seizure. Therefore, an officer may only exercise search and seizure powers if that officer has reasonable grounds to believe that one of the above criteria has been met. Reasonable grounds are a set of facts and circumstances that would satisfy an ordinarily cautious and prudent person, and that are more than mere suspicion.

Provided that there are reasonable grounds, an officer is authorized under the IRPA to conduct the following types of searches:

- search person, luggage, and personal effects (s. 139(1));

- board and inspect vessels to carry out a search (s. 15(3));

- seize vehicles and other items or assets used in relation to an immigration offence or to ensure compliance with the Act and its regulations; and

- seize documents that were fraudulently or improperly obtained or used, or likely to be fraudulently or improperly used, such as fraudulent passports (s. 139 and 140).

Consider the following:

A female traveller from the United States, Martina Vidi, is stopped at the Peace Arch border crossing from Washington into British Columbia. The CBSA officer has reasonable grounds to believe that Martina is concealing her identity. The officer instructs Martina to pull her car into a separate lane and advises her that she wishes to conduct a search. Martina complies. The search involves the examination of all of Martina's belongings: her purse, her briefcase, two suitcases, other personal effects, and her car. The officer's search is for the purpose of detecting documents or evidence that relate to Martina's identity, her admissibility, and any potential offences under the IRPA. Martina is asked to empty her pockets and to remove her jacket for examination. There is no physical contact between the officer and Martina, and no force or constraint is used in the search.

In the scenario above, Martina consented to the search, but if a person for some reason disagrees to a search, or behaves in any manner that puts the officer's safety at risk, the officer may detain the person, and compel compliance with the search. However, detaining the person triggers the right to be advised of the right to counsel. Section 10 of the Charter requires that all persons being arrested or detained, including anyone submitting to an involuntary personal search, must be advised of the reason for the detention and of the right to retain and instruct counsel without delay.

ARREST AND DETENTION

Certain CIC and CBSA officers—such as those bearing the titles Citizenship and Immigration Officer, Detentions; Citizenship and Immigration Officer, Enforcement; Citizenship and Immigration Officer, Port of Entry; Border Services Officer; and Case Presenting Officer[1]—have the authority and powers of a peace officer to arrest and detain permanent residents or foreign nationals pursuant to s. 138(1) of the IRPA. The authorization is generally given to the "title" relevant to the type of work performed.

Officers have the authority to **arrest** a permanent resident or foreign national who they believe has or may have breached the IRPA, and may **detain** him if the person poses a danger to the public, if his identity is in question, or if there is reason to believe that the person will not appear for an immigration proceeding. Officers may also detain a permanent resident or foreign national at a port of entry if

- it is necessary for the completion of an examination; and
- there are reasonable grounds to believe that the person is inadmissible for reasons of security or for violating human or international rights.[2]

Generally, an officer must have a warrant to arrest and detain a permanent resident, foreign national, or protected person (IRPA s. 55(1)). However, the IRPA makes an exception in s. 55(2) for the arrest and detention without a warrant of a foreign national:

(a) who the officer has reasonable grounds to believe is inadmissible and is a danger to the public or is unlikely to appear for examination, an admissibility hearing, removal from Canada, or at a proceeding that could lead to the making of a removal order by the Minister under subsection 44(2); or

(b) if the officer is not satisfied of the identity of the foreign national in the course of any procedure under this Act.

Recall our scenario involving Martina Vidi:

Suppose that Martina for some reason disagrees to the search or behaves in any manner that puts her or the officer's safety at risk. The officer has the authority to detain Martina without a warrant, and her detention compels her to comply with the search. Of course, this is predicated on the fact that the officer had reasonable grounds to believe that Martina was concealing her identify. At this point, Martina must be advised of her right to counsel.

Inadmissibility and enforcement matters are more thoroughly explored in Chapter 10, "Enforcement Procedures."

As peace officers, CIC and CBSA officers have the authority to apply for and obtain search warrants under ss. 487 to 492.2 of the *Criminal Code* and to execute warrants for arrest and detention. Generally, an officer applies for a search warrant to obtain information to establish a person's identity, locate a person wanted on an immigration arrest warrant, or obtain evidence related to an immigration investigation. An officer who wants to apply for a search warrant must make an application to a judge or justice of the peace, who issues the warrant.

MINISTER RESPONSIBLE FOR CITIZENSHIP MATTERS

In addition to immigration and refugee portfolios, the minister of Citizenship and Immigration also has authority over citizenship. In the same way that the IRPA confers immigration functions, s. 2(1) of the *Citizenship Act* allows for citizenship functions to be assigned to the appropriate member of Cabinet, which is currently the minister of CIC. These functions include the following:

- granting Canadian citizenship to new Canadians,

- providing documentation of citizenship to citizens, and

- promoting Canadian citizenship.

Under s. 23 of the *Citizenship Act* the minister may delegate those powers, in writing, to those responsible for applying the law. As a matter of policy, the power to determine citizenship status and to grant, retain, renounce, or resume citizenship is delegated only to Canadian citizens.[3]

IMMIGRATION AND REFUGEE BOARD

Established in 1989, the **Immigration and Refugee Board (IRB)** is a federal administrative tribunal that conducts admissibility hearings, detention reviews, immigration appeals, and refugee protection claims. It is sometimes called the "board" or by the name of one of its four divisions:

- the Immigration Division (ID),

- the Immigration Appeal Division (IAD),

- the Refugee Protection Division (RPD), and

- the Refugee Appeal Division (RAD).

Note that the RAD, although provided for in the IRPA, has not yet been created.

Each division performs specialized functions, such as adjudicating immigration matters and appeals or deciding claims for refugee protection. The IRB reports to Parliament through the minister of CIC and also works with the CBSA. However, it functions independently from government, and like all tribunals is expected to exercise its role in an impartial manner.

The board is composed of a chairperson, numerous members who preside over hearings and make decisions, and public servants who support the tribunal's operations. The board has a dual accountability structure in which the decision makers are responsible to the chairperson through their respective managers—namely, the deputy chairperson, assistant deputy chairperson, and coordinating members—and the public servants are responsible to separate managers—namely, the executive director, director general, regional director, and registrar.

Chairperson's Powers

The chairperson is the IRB's chief executive officer and has a range of statutory powers for the management of decision makers, including the authority to supervise and direct the work of the board, to designate coordinating members, to assign members to a division, and to delegate certain powers. The chairperson also has the authority to issue guidelines to decision makers and to identify any of the board's decisions as jurisprudential guides (IRPA s. 159(1)). As well, the chairperson has the exclusive authority to make the rules of practice and procedure for the tribunal; these powers may not be delegated (IRPA ss. 159(1) and 161).

The chairperson is assisted by two deputy chairpersons (appointed by the governor-in-council) and one director general (a public servant, appointed under the

Public Service Employment Act) to oversee the management of decision makers. With the exception of the power to make the rules of practice and procedure, the chairperson's authority may be delegated to a board member. In the case of the Immigration Division, the chairperson may only delegate Immigration Division powers to the director general, directors, or members of that division (IRPA s. 161).

Members' Powers

Decision makers at the IRB, in all divisions, are called **members**. Members are selected for their expertise and their experience in a variety of fields including but not limited to general law, immigration, refugee law, and human rights. Members of the IAD, RPD, and RAD are appointed for a term of service of no longer than seven years, while members of the ID are permanent members.

The governor in council appoints members to all divisions except the Immigration Division. Known as "adjudicators" under the 1978 *Immigration Act*, members of the Immigration Division are appointed under the *Public Service Employment Act*. In 2004, the process for appointing decision makers was reformed so that members are now selected through a merit-based process by an independent advisory panel and a selection board. From this selection process, the chairperson of the IRB then provides a list of candidates to the minister of CIC, who makes recommendations for appointment by the governor in council.

Members have the power and authority of a commissioner, and may do anything they consider necessary for a full and proper hearing. They may administer an oath, summon witnesses, and take evidence under oath. They may also choose to conduct hearings by telephone or by video conference, and may determine whether a hearing will be held in public or in private. Members have the authority to designate a representative in cases involving a minor or a person who is unable to appreciate the nature of the proceedings.

Should a person fail to appear for her hearing, the member assigned to hear the case has the statutory power to determine that the hearing has been abandoned. The member may also refuse a withdrawal by an applicant and make a finding of abuse of process. Members in all divisions of the IRB have the power to apply the Charter, and may declare a specific section of the IRPA inoperative if they find it to be in violation of a Charter right.

The Board's Four Divisions

Each of the board's four divisions has jurisdiction to hear and decide specific types of cases. What follows is a brief description of each division's decision makers and jurisdiction. Details of the procedures of each are described in later chapters.

IMMIGRATION DIVISION

Members of the ID are responsible for hearing and deciding matters regarding the following:

- admission or removal of permanent residents and foreign nationals, and

- review of immigration detentions.

Admissibility hearings involve a determination of whether a person should be allowed to enter or remain in Canada, or whether a person should be ordered removed from Canada. In our example of Jose, who was caught working without a work permit, the matter would likely be referred for a hearing before a member of the ID. At the hearing, the minister, represented by a hearings officer, would argue the case against Jose. The member would hear both sides of the case, and decide Jose's status in Canada.

Detention reviews under the IRPA determine whether there are sufficient reasons to continue the detention of a person who was detained on the grounds that he poses a danger to the public or is unlikely to appear at a hearing. Using our example, Jose could be detained "on immigration hold" if he was thought to be a danger to the public, or there was a risk he wouldn't appear for his admissibility hearing. At the detention review, Jose would appear before a member of the ID to argue his release while the hearings officer would argue against his release or ask for conditions to be imposed on a release order.

Members of the ID have the same powers as a commissioner appointed under Part I of the *Inquiries Act*. These powers include the power to summon witnesses and require them to give evidence, orally or in writing, and on oath, and produce documents. Members have the powers of a court of record in civil cases to issue summons and issue warrants for arrest when a person fails to appear for a hearing as summoned (Immigration Division Rules, rules 33, 34, and 35). Members of the ID are not bound by any legal or technical rules of evidence. They may receive and base their decision on any evidence they consider credible or trustworthy (IRPA s. 173).

Members of the ID are public servants. This is the only division of the IRB where decision makers are public servants rather than appointees of the governor in council. Recall that, unlike their counterparts in the board's other divisions, members of the ID have no time limit to their terms. These anomalous characteristics of the ID are essentially due to a government reorganization. Before 1993, public servants known as adjudicators conducted inquiries and detention reviews for the former Employment and Immigration Commission (EIC). In 1993 the adjudicators were transferred from the EIC to the IRB. When the IRPA was enacted in June 2002, the Adjudication Division was renamed the Immigration Division and its adjudicators were referred to as members of the ID. The ID is managed by the director general of the ID (nationally) and by directors in major cities such as Vancouver, Toronto, and Montreal.

IMMIGRATION APPEAL DIVISION

Members of the IAD have jurisdiction to hear and decide four types of appeals, as follows:

- sponsorship appeals from Canadian citizens and permanent residents whose applications to sponsor close family members to come to Canada have been refused;

- removal order appeals from permanent residents, foreign nationals with a permanent resident visa, and protected persons who have been ordered removed from Canada;

- loss-of-permanent-residence appeals from permanent residents by an immigration officer outside of Canada to have not fulfilled their residency obligation; and

- minister's appeals from the minister responsible for the CBSA, who may appeal a decision made by the ID at an admissibility hearing.

There are certain immigration matters where a person has a statutory right to appeal decisions to the IAD. Section 63 of the IRPA provides those appeal rights to sponsors, visa holders, permanent residents, protected persons, and the minister against a decision by the ID.

In hearing appeals, IAD members are not limited to reviewing findings of fact at the first hearing. Appeals are hearings **de novo**, which means starting afresh, and the IAD must receive any additional evidence, and base its decision on its own assessment of the evidence—including credibility of witnesses—even if the strict rules of evidence have not been met.[4] Members of the IAD are not bound by any legal or technical rules of evidence; they may receive and base their decision on any evidence they consider credible or trustworthy (IRPA s. 173). IAD hearing procedures are explored in greater detail in Chapter 10, "Enforcement Procedures."

Let's return to our scenario concerning Juan and his nephew Jose:

With all the problems that Juan, the restaurant owner, had in hiring his nephew Jose, he has encouraged his wife, Marie, to help out more at the restaurant. But this would require Marie to put their two children in daycare. As a Canadian citizen, she decides to sponsor her mother, Ana, with the plan that Ana will look after the children while Marie works at the restaurant. The sponsorship is refused. What recourse does Marie have now?

Permanent residents and Canadian citizens, like Marie in the example above, have the right to appeal the decision to refuse their sponsorship applications to the IAD. A member of the IAD will hear and decide the appeal. In this example, the appellant Marie will present her case, and a hearings officer will represent the minister at the appeal hearing as the respondent. The IAD is the only division that has "all the powers, rights and privileges vested in a superior court" pursuant to s. 174 of the IRPA. Members may swear in and examine witnesses, and may issue orders for the production and inspection of documents.

At the national level the IAD is managed by the deputy chairperson of the IAD. Locally, the assistant deputy chairpersons and coordinating members fulfill management roles in major cities such as Vancouver, Toronto, and Montreal.

REFUGEE PROTECTION DIVISION

With the coming into force of the IRPA in June 2002, the Convention Refugee Determination Division was renamed the Refugee Protection Division. Members of the RPD are responsible for hearing refugee claims made by persons in Canada and determining whether the claimants are refugees or not.

Refugee hearings are generally informal and non-adversarial. Members of the RPD are not bound by any legal or technical rules of evidence; they may receive and base their decision on any evidence they consider credible or trustworthy. They may inquire into any matter that they consider relevant to the establishment of a well-founded claim. Furthermore, members may take **judicial notice** of any facts, information, or opinion within the division's specialized knowledge (IRPA s. 170). Judicial notice is a rule in the law of evidence that allows a fact to be accepted as true without supporting evidence if the truth of that fact is so well known that it cannot be refuted. Refugee hearings are discussed in greater detail in Chapter 8, "In-Canada Refugee Determination Process."

Like the IAD, the RPD is managed at the national level by the deputy chairperson. Locally, the assistant deputy chairpersons and coordinating members fulfill management roles in major cities such as Vancouver, Toronto, and Montreal.

REFUGEE APPEAL DIVISION

Although the IRPA provides that an unsuccessful refugee claim may be appealed to the Refugee Appeal Division, this division has not yet been created. The relevant sections of the IRPA (ss. 110 and 111) have not yet been proclaimed into law. Until this changes, refugee claimants who are unsuccessful before the RPD have no right of appeal, and their only recourse is to apply for leave for a judicial review to the Federal Court, or to apply for a pre-removal risk assessment.

An organizational chart for the IRB and its four divisions is provided below.

Structure of the Immigration and Refugee Board

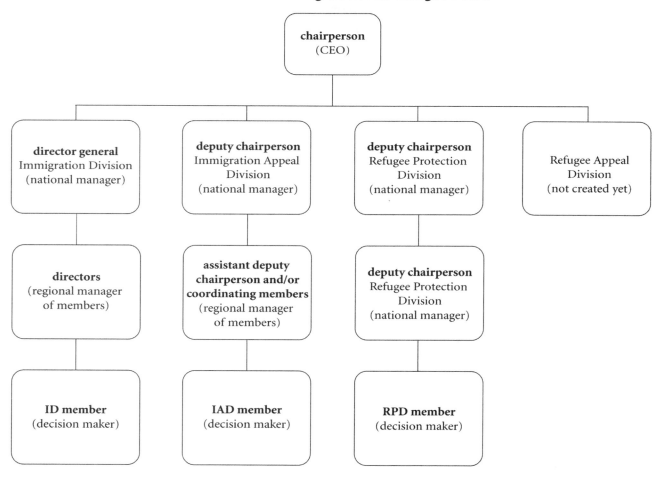

COURTS

Matters involving the IRPA may come before the courts by way of judicial review or appeal. Judicial review provides the means for the courts to oversee administrative decisions, such as those made by the divisions of the IRB. Although the courts defer to the expertise of administrative tribunals, and generally accept their findings of fact, on judicial review the court will determine whether the administrative decision-making process was fair and was based on the appropriate legal considerations.

Appeals from lower court decisions consider whether the decision maker erred in its interpretation of the law, or in its application of the law to the facts. Findings of fact, such as the credibility of a witness, are not generally reconsidered on appeal—only points of law are argued.

Because the IRPA is a federal law, the courts with jurisdiction over the interpretation and application of the IRPA are the federal courts. The trial court is the Federal Court, and the appeal court is the Federal Court of Appeal. If a significant legal issue is in question, decisions of the Federal Court of Appeal may be appealed to the final decision maker in Canada—the Supreme Court of Canada.

Federal Court and Federal Court of Appeal

The Federal Court has jurisdiction to review decisions, orders, and other administrative actions made by the IRB, CIC, and the CBSA. In this way the courts exercise a supervisory role. Judicial review may be sought by either party—the individual or the minister—provided that an application for leave to the Federal Court is made within the statutory time limit of 60 days after receiving the disputed decision. A Federal Court judge will either grant or deny leave for judicial review. The IRB may also refer any question of law, jurisdiction, or practice to the Federal Court at any stage of a proceeding.

The Federal Court derives its authority from s. 18.1(3) of the *Federal Courts Act*. Upon judicial review of an IRB decision, the Federal Court may do any of the following:

- send the matter back for redetermination by a different member or panel,

- quash the IRB decision and substitute its own decision, or

- uphold the IRB decision.

If a party is dissatisfied with a decision of the Federal Court, leave for appeal may be sought from the Federal Court of Appeal. However, s. 74(d) of the IRPA provides that an appeal may be made only if the court certifies that a serious question of general importance is involved, and states the question. The appeal then deals only with this particular question.

Non-lawyers, such as immigration consultants and paralegals, are not authorized to represent clients in Federal Court or the Federal Court of Appeal (see s. 11 of the *Federal Courts Act* and rule 119 of the Federal Courts Rules). In appropriate cases, non-lawyers who are representing immigration or refugee clients should explain the judicial review process and refer their clients to an immigration lawyer. For self-represented litigants, the Federal Court provides information on "Court Process and Procedures" online at http://cas-ncr-nter03.cas-satj.gc.ca/portal/page/portal/fc_cf_en/Process.

Supreme Court of Canada

The Supreme Court of Canada is the final court of appeal from all other Canadian courts, on all subject matters. Before a case can reach the Supreme Court of Canada, all other avenues of appeal must first be exhausted.

A party who is not satisfied with a Federal Court of Appeal decision has the right to seek leave to appeal to the Supreme Court of Canada, under s. 40(1) of the *Supreme Court Act*. The Supreme Court of Canada may grant leave to appeal only if the case involves a question of public importance, if it raises an important issue of law or mixed law and fact, or if the matter is, for any other reason, significant enough to be considered by the country's Supreme Court.

APPENDIX

A summary of the various decision makers discussed in this chapter, their functions, and their responsibilities and activities is provided in the table below.

Immigration and Refugee Decision Makers

Decision makers	Organization	Function	Responsibility or activity
Minister and designated or delegated officers	CIC	Immigration	◆ responsible for ◦ immigration policy development ◦ annual immigration plan ◦ temporary residents immigration processes ◦ permanent residents immigration processes ◦ settlement and integration of newcomers to Canada ◦ pre-removal risk assessments ◦ most policies related to admissibility
Minister and designated or delegated officers	PSEP/CBSA	Immigration/ Enforcement	◆ responsible for ◦ management and operation of Canada's borders and port of entry functions ◦ arrests ◦ detentions ◦ removals ◦ background checks of immigration applicants
Minister only	CIC PSEP/CBSA	Enforcement	◆ responsible for ◦ signing security certificates ◦ referring security certificates to the Federal Court
Member	IRB: Immigration Division	Immigration	◆ hears and decides ◦ admissibility hearings for persons who are inadmissible to or removable from Canada ◦ detention review hearings into the reasons for detention of persons under the IRPA ◆ issues removal orders in complex cases

(The table is continued on the next page.)

Immigration and Refugee Decision Makers (cont'd.)

Decision makers	Organization	Function	Responsibility or activity

Member	IRB: Immigration Appeal Division	Immigration	◆ hears and decides appeals against
			  ◇ the minister's decision to refuse a sponsorship application (sponsorship appeal)
			  ◇ a removal order decision by a member of the ID or the minister from a permanent resident, foreign national with a permanent resident visa, or protected person who has been ordered removed from Canada (removal order appeal)
			  ◇ an immigration officer's decision that a permanent resident has lost his permanent resident status (loss-of-permanent-residence appeal)
			  ◇ an appeal from the minister responsible for the CBSA, who may appeal a decision made by the ID at an admissibility hearing (minister's appeal)
			Note: The IAD does not hear appeals against a removal order for a person who is a security threat or war criminal, has committed crimes against humanity, is involved in organized crime, or is a serious criminal, as that person has no right of appeal.

Judge	Federal Court		◆ decides reasonableness of a security certificate ◆ conducts judicial review
Judges	Federal Court of Appeal		◆ hear appeals from the Federal Court

Judges	Supreme Court of Canada		◆ hear and decide an appeal only if
			  ◇ the case involves a question of public importance,
			  ◇ the case raises an important issue of law or mixed law and fact, or
			  ◇ the matter is, for any other reason, significant enough to be considered by the country's Supreme Court

Minister and designated or delegated officers	CIC	Refugee Protection	◆ responsible for
			  ◇ the resettlement of refugees
			  ◇ admissibility of refugee claimants in Canada
			  ◇ determinations of eligibility

Minister and designated or delegated officers	PSEP/CBSA		◆ responsible for
			  ◇ background checks of refugee claimants
			  ◇ removal of refugee claimants where a "danger opinion" exists

Member	IRB: Immigration Refugee Protection Division		◆ hears claims made by persons in Canada and determines whether the claimants are refugees or not
Minister and designated or delegated officers	CIC	Citizenship	◆ grant Canadian citizenship to new Canadians ◆ provide proof of citizenship ◆ handle citizenship promotion

NOTES

1. For a complete list of officers by title, refer to "Letter of Designation" signed by the vice-president, Enforcement Branch, CBSA, on April 21, 2006, available online at www.cbsa-asfc.gc.ca.

2. Canada Border Services Agency, "Fact Sheet: Arrests and Detentions," March 2004, http://cbsa-asfc.gc.ca/media/facts-faits/menu-eng.html.

3. Citizenship and Immigration Canada, "CP 2: Decision-Making," in *Citizenship Policy (CP)*, March 21, 2007, s. 1.5, www.cic.gc.ca/english/ resources/manuals/cp/index.asp.

4. *Kahlon v. Canada (Minister of Employment and Immigration)* (1989), 7 Imm. L.R. (2d) 91, 97 N.R. 349 (F.C.A.).

REFERENCES

Canada Border Services Agency. "About the CBSA." December 9, 2005. www.cbsa-asfc.gc.ca/menu-eng.html.

Canada Border Services Agency. "Fact Sheet: Arrests and Detentions." March 2004. www.cbsa-asfc.gc.ca/media/facts-faits/007-eng.html.

Citizenship Act. R.S.C. 1985, c. C-29.

Citizenship and Immigration Canada. *Annual Report to Parliament on Immigration 2005*. October 31, 2005. www.cic.gc.ca/english/resources/ publications/annual-report2005/index.asp.

Citizenship and Immigration Canada. "Citizenship and Immigration Canada: Serving Canada and the World." Catalogue no. Ci51-99/2003. 2003.

Citizenship and Immigration Canada. "ENF 9: Judicial Review." In *Enforcement (ENF)*. January 30, 2006. www.cic.gc.ca/english/resources/publications/ index.asp.

Citizenship and Immigration Canada. *Instrument of Designation and Delegation: Immigration and Refugee Protection Act and Regulations*. July 20, 2006. www. cic.gc.ca/english/resources/manuals/il/il3_e.pdf.

Citizenship and Immigration Canada. "IP 1: Temporary Resident Permits." In *Inland Processing (IP)*. April 29, 2005. www.cic.gc.ca/english/resources/ manuals/ip/index.asp.

Citizenship and Immigration Canada. "IR 6: Immigration Service Delivery Network Abroad." In *Reference (IR)*. September 2002. www.cic.gc.ca/english/ resources/publications/index.asp.

Criminal Code. R.S.C. 1985, c. C-46.

Deschênes, Claudette. "Letter of Designation: Authorization to Have the Authority and Powers of a Peace Officer," Canada Border Services Agency. April 21, 2006. www.cbsa-asfc.gc.ca/agency-agence/delegation/desig/po-ag-eng.html.

Federal Courts Act. R.S.C. 1985, c. F-7.

Federal Courts Immigration and Refugee Protection Rules. S.O.R./93-22.

Federal Courts Rules. S.O.R./98-106.

Immigration and Refugee Board. "Memorandum." In *Guide to Proceedings Before the Immigration Division*. August 26, 2005. www.irb-cisr.gc.ca/en/references/legal/id/idguide/idguide_memo_e.htm.

Immigration and Refugee Protection Act. S.C. 2001, c. 27.

Immigration and Refugee Protection Regulations. S.O.R./2002-227.

Immigration Division Rules. S.O.R./2000-229.

Inquiries Act. R.S.C. 1985, c. I-11.

Public Safety Canada. "Security Certificates." March 10, 2008. www.publicsafety.gc.ca.

Public Service Employment Act. S.C. 2003, c. 22.

Supreme Court Act. R.S.C. 1985, c. S-26.

Treasury Board of Canada Secretariat. "Section 3: Supplementary Information." In DPR 2004-2005: Immigration and Refugee Board. October 26, 2005. www.tbs-sct.gc.ca/rma/dpr1/04-05/IRB-CISR/IRB-CISRd45_e.asp#.

REVIEW QUESTIONS

This chapter was divided into four main sections that set out the responsibility for making decisions about immigration, refugee, and citizenship matters. The headings below correspond to those in the chapter. You should now be able to answer the questions under each heading.

Ministers Responsible for Immigration Matters

1. Which ministers are authorized by the IRPA to carry out immigration and refugee functions? Can you name them?

2. Provide an example of a minister's authority that cannot be delegated.

3. Provide examples of an officer's duties related to the examination of an application.

4. Under what circumstances can an officer exercise her search and seizure powers?

5. Can an officer arrest and detain an individual under the IRPA without a warrant?

Minister Responsible for Citizenship Matters

1. Which minister is responsible for citizenship functions?

2. Which statute provides this authorization?

Immigration and Refugee Board

1. What are decision makers at the IRB called?

2. Members of which divisions are appointed by the governor in council?

3. Which members are public servants?

4. Name the three active divisions of the Immigration and Refugee Board.

Courts

1. In which court is a judicial review conducted?

2. If a party is not satisfied with the decision of the Federal Court, can that party appeal to the Supreme Court of Canada?

CHAPTER 3
Inadmissibility

LEARNING OBJECTIVES

After reading this chapter you should be able to:

- Identify the eight grounds of inadmissibility to Canada under the *Immigration and Refugee Protection Act*.

- Understand when exemptions to these grounds of inadmissibility apply.

- Describe the three types of decisions that may be used by officers to identify persons who are inadmissible on the ground of membership in a group that engages in espionage, subversion, or terrorism.

- Describe the four types of decisions that may be used by officers to identify persons who are inadmissible on the ground of violating human or international rights.

- Distinguish among the three types of domestic crime that may make a person inadmissible to Canada: serious criminality, criminality, and organized criminality.

- Understand that different government agencies may be involved in assessing inadmissibility.

INTRODUCTION

The purpose of this chapter is to outline and discuss the grounds for refusing a person's application for permanent or temporary residence in Canada. These are known as the grounds of **inadmissibility**.

Section 19(1) of the *Immigration and Refugee Protection Act* (IRPA) states that Canadian citizens and persons under the *Indian Act* have an automatic right to enter and remain in Canada. Anyone else who wishes to do so must

- obtain permission to enter Canada, as either a temporary or permanent resident; and

- satisfy an officer that he is not inadmissible.

The first hurdle that a foreign national faces when applying to come to Canada is obtaining permission as either a temporary or permanent resident. This involves meeting the eligibility requirements for one of the numerous classes or subclasses under which a foreign national may apply, such as visitor, member of the family class, or refugee, to name just a few. Note that an applicant for entry must first establish eligibility under the relevant class or subclass before an officer will consider inadmissibility. This is because the background checks required to establish that an applicant is not inadmissible, such as police record checks, medical examinations, and other investigations, may be costly and time consuming. Because so many applicants will fail to meet the eligibility requirements, it is more efficient to consider inadmissibility only after eligibility is confirmed.

The various classes and subclasses are described in detail in Chapter 4, "Temporary Entry," Chapter 5, "Permanent Entry," Chapter 8, "Refugee and Humanitarian Resettlement Program," and Chapter 9, "In-Canada Refugee Determination Process."

Once eligibility is established, the foreign national may nevertheless be barred from entering or staying in Canada because of inadmissibility. A person who is found to be inadmissible may be denied a temporary or permanent resident visa, refused admission, or removed from Canada. The IRPA sets out eight grounds of inadmissibility, as follows:

1. security risk (s. 34),

2. human or international rights violations (s. 35),

3. serious criminality (s. 36(1)), criminality (s. 36(2)), and organized criminality (s. 37),

4. health reasons (s. 38),

5. financial reasons—that is, inability to provide for oneself or dependants (s. 39),

6. misrepresentation (s. 40),

7. failure to comply with the IRPA (s. 41), and

8. inadmissible family member (s. 42).

Generally, inadmissibility applies to all applicants in the same manner, regardless of the class or subclass under which they are requesting entry to Canada. For this reason, the chapter on inadmissibility precedes those dealing with eligibility requirements.

GROUNDS OF INADMISSIBILITY

Each of the eight grounds of inadmissibility is considered in detail below.

1. Security Risk (Section 34)

A permanent resident or foreign national may be found inadmissible on security grounds for several reasons, according to s. 34(1) of the IRPA, as follows:

- espionage or subversion against a democratic government, institution, or process;

- subversion by force of any government;

- terrorism;

- being a danger to the security of Canada; or

- violence that would or might endanger the lives or safety of persons in Canada.

The terms "espionage," "subversion," "democratic," and "terrorism" are not defined in the IRPA or its regulations. However, Citizenship and Immigrations Canada's *Enforcement (ENF)* operations manual provides the following definitions:[1]

- **Espionage** is the practice of spying. It is the gathering of information in a surreptitious manner and involves secretly seeking out information usually from a hostile country, to benefit one's own country.

- **Subversion** is the practice of overturning or overthrowing; it seeks to accomplish change by illicit means or for improper purposes related to an organization. Subversion need not be by force.

- **Democratic** describes government by the people, especially where the people hold the supreme political power.

- **Terrorism** is defined as "activities directed toward or in support of the threat or use of acts of violence against persons or property for the purposes of achieving a political objective; an act intended to cause death or serious bodily injury to a civilian, or to any other person not taking an active part in hostilities in a situation of armed conflict, when the purpose of such act, by its nature or context, is to intimidate a population or to compel a government or an international organization to do or to abstain from doing any act."

MEMBERSHIP IN A GROUP THAT ENGAGES IN ESPIONAGE, SUBVERSION, OR TERRORISM

A person may be found inadmissible for her own activities, or for belonging to an organization that engages in espionage, subversion, or terrorism. There are three types of decisions that may be used by officers as evidence of "a conclusive finding of fact" that a person is a member of such an organization. These decisions are listed in s. 14 of the Immigration and Refugee Protection Regulations (IRP Regulations), as follows:

- an Immigration and Refugee Board (IRB) determination that a foreign national or permanent resident has engaged in terrorism;

- an IRB determination that a person is a person referred to in section F of article 1 of the Convention Relating to the Status of Refugees (Refugee Convention)—that is, a person excluded from refugee protection for committing crimes against peace, war crimes, or a crime against humanity; or

- a court decision under the *Criminal Code* concerning the commission of a terrorism offence.

In deciding whether a terrorism offence has been committed, the courts look to the *Criminal Code*'s definition of **terrorist group** in s. 83.01, which reads in part:

> (a) an entity that has as one of its purposes or activities facilitating or carrying out any terrorist activity …
> and includes an association of such entities.

Reliance on the decisions of the IRB and the courts saves the time and expense of rehearing the issue of membership.

IDENTIFYING SECURITY THREATS

Officers rely on security screening checks as important tools for identifying known security threats. The many documents that an applicant must provide when applying for permanent or temporary residence offer important information about the applicant's identity, relationships, financial history, work and school activities, and background.

Officers may also consult police and intelligence reports and records of criminal convictions and previous dealings with Canadian immigration if these resources are available. When the identity of a person cannot be confirmed in Canada, fingerprints and photographs are taken and are used not only to identify the person but also to conduct background checks with international authorities. In cases where a security certificate has been issued against a person, this fact, in itself, is considered conclusive proof that a person is inadmissible.

EXEMPTIONS

In rare cases, a person who is found to have engaged in one or more of the activities listed in s. 34(1) may nevertheless be able to satisfy the minister of Public Safety and Emergency Preparedness (PSEP) that being in Canada would not be detrimental to the national interest. This decision is at the discretion of the minister, and may not be delegated.

2. Human or International Rights Violations (Section 35)

Permanent residents and foreign nationals who have committed violations of human or international rights outside of Canada are inadmissible. Specifically, s. 35 of the IRPA lists the following prohibited activities and conditions:

- committing an offence referred to in ss. 4 to 7 of the *Crimes Against Humanity and War Crimes Act*, while outside Canada;

- being a **prescribed senior official** in the service of a government that, in the opinion of the minister, engages in or has engaged in terrorism, systematic or gross human rights violations, genocide, a war crime, or a crime against humanity within the meaning of ss. 6(3) to (5) of the *Crimes Against Humanity and War Crimes Act*; or

Inadmissible on Security Grounds: The Case of Ernst Zundel

The infamous case of Ernst Zundel, a Holocaust denier, is a real-life Canadian case about a person who was found inadmissible on security grounds and removed from Canada. A German national, Zundel first came to Canada in 1958 when he was 19 years old. He lived here until 2000 never having obtained Canadian citizenship as his application was refused. During the 1980s, Zundel became well known as a Holocaust denier and disseminator of Nazi material. His company, Samisdat Publishers, produced the pamphlet "Did Six Million Really Die?" and the book *The Hitler We Loved and Why*, which led to criminal charges.

In the late 1990s, Zundel faced a complaint before the Canadian Human Rights Commission for spreading hatred against Jews on his website, but left Canada for the United States in 2000 before the hearing was completed. Zundel returned to Canada in 2003 when he was deported from the United States for overstaying. Around the same time, Germany issued a warrant for his arrest on hate charges.

On May 1, 2003, the solicitor general of Canada and the minister of Citizenship and Immigration signed a security certificate stating that Mr. Zundel was a danger to the security of Canada. Zundel was alleged to be inadmissible on the security grounds of "engaging in acts of terrorism, being a danger to the security of Canada, engaging in acts of violence that would or might endanger the lives or safety of persons in Canada or being a member of a group that there are reasonable grounds to believe has or will engage in acts of espionage, subversion or terrorism."[2]

Zundel was detained. As is required when a security certificate is issued, the matter went before the Federal Court for approval. On February 24, 2005, Justice Blais of the Federal Court of Canada found the security certificate to be reasonable and stated in his decision:

> Mr. Zundel has associated, supported and directed members of the Movement who in one fashion or another have sought to propagate violent messages of hate and have advocated the destruction of governments and multicultural societies. Mr. Zundel's activities are not only a threat to Canada's national security but also a threat to the international community of nations. Mr. Zundel can channel the energy of members of the White Supremacist Movement from around the world, providing funding to them, bringing them together and providing them advice and direction."[3]

The security certificate issued against Zundel was conclusive proof that Zundel was inadmissible and the removal order against him could be enforced. He had no appeal rights because of the serious grounds of inadmissibility. Zundel was deported to Germany, where upon his arrival he was arrested and charged with 14 counts of inciting racial hatred. In February 2007, Zundel was sentenced to a five-year term in prison.

■ being a person, other than a permanent resident, whose entry or stay in Canada is restricted pursuant to a decision, resolution, or measure of an international organization of states, of which Canada is a member, that imposes sanctions on a country against which Canada has imposed or has agreed to impose sanctions in concert with that organization or association.

The terms "crimes against humanity," "genocide," and "war crime" are defined in the *Crimes Against Humanity and War Crimes Act* at s. 4(3):

■ **Crimes against humanity** include murder, extermination, enslavement, deportation, imprisonment, torture, sexual violence, persecution, or any other inhumane act or omission that is committed against any civilian population or any identifiable group and that, at the time and in the place of its commission, constitutes a crime against humanity according to customary international law or conventional international law or by virtue of its being criminal according to the general principles of law recognized by the community of nations, whether or not it constitutes a contravention of the law in force at the time and in the place of its commission.

■ **Genocide** means an act or omission committed with intent to destroy, in whole or in part, an identifiable group of persons, as such, that, at the time and in the place of its commission, constitutes genocide according to customary international law or conventional international law or by virtue of its being criminal according to the general principles of law recognized by the community of nations, whether or not it constitutes a contravention of the law in force at the time and in the place of its commission.

■ **War crime** means an act or omission committed during an armed conflict that, at the time and in the place of its commission, constitutes a war crime according to customary international law or conventional international law applicable to armed conflicts, whether or not it constitutes a contravention of the law in force at the time and in the place of its commission.

Prescribed senior officials are referenced in s. 35(1)(b) as members of governments that the minister of PSEP has authority to designate as perpetrators of terrorism, systematic or gross human rights violations, genocide, war crimes, or crimes against humanity. The minister may add and remove countries from the list, so it changes from time to time.[4] Consider the following examples of designated governments:

■ the Bosnian Serb regime between March 27, 1992 and October 10, 1996;

■ the Siad Barre regime in Somalia between 1969 and 1991;

■ the former military governments in Haiti between 1971 and 1986, and between 1991 and 1994 except the period from August to December 1993;

■ the former Marxist regimes of Afghanistan between 1978 and 1992;

■ the governments of Ahmed Hassan al-Bakr and Saddam Hussein in power from 1968 to 2003;

- the government of Rwanda under President Habyarimana between October 1990 and April 1994, as well as the interim government in power between April 1994 and July 1994;

- the governments of the Federal Republic of Yugoslavia and the Republic of Serbia (Milosevic) between February 28, 1998 and October 7, 2000; and

- the Taliban regime in Afghanistan from September 27, 1996 to 2001.

IDENTIFYING RIGHTS VIOLATORS

There are four types of decisions that may be used by officers as evidence of "a conclusive finding of fact" that a person has committed human or international rights violations. These decisions are listed in s. 15 of the IRP Regulations, as follows:

- a UN-established international tribunal decision;

- an IRB determination that a foreign national or permanent resident has committed a war crime or a crime against humanity;

- an IRB determination that a foreign national or permanent resident is a person referred to in s. F of article 1 of the Refugee Convention—that is, a person excluded from refugee protection for committing crimes against peace, war crimes, or a crime against humanity; or

- a court decision under the *Criminal Code* or the *Crimes Against Humanity and War Crimes Act*.

As with the determination of security risks, reliance on the decisions of these bodies saves the time and expense of rehearing the issue. A security certificate issued against a person can be also be used as conclusive proof that a person is inadmissible for violating human or international rights.

EXEMPTIONS

As with security threats, in rare cases a person who is found to have engaged in one or more of the activities listed in s. 35 may nevertheless be able to satisfy the minister of PSEP that being in Canada would not be detrimental to the national interest. This decision is at the discretion of the minister, and may not be delegated.

3. Serious Criminality (Section 36(1)), Criminality (Section 36(2)), and Organized Criminality (Section 37)

Sections 36(1), (2), and (3), and 37 all deal with criminality. **Criminality** refers to domestic crime, as opposed to crimes against humanity or war crimes as proscribed by international law.

When a person is convicted of an offence outside Canada, it is necessary to compare the elements of Canadian law with those of the foreign jurisdiction to determine whether the person is inadmissible. The particular law under which the person was convicted in the foreign country is not relevant. Rather, what matters is the Canadian offence that matches the criminal act committed. The officer must establish that the foreign offence contains the essential elements of the offence in Canada to show that it is equivalent to the foreign offence. The officer can compare foreign law and foreign court documents and examine the person at the admissibility hearing.

CIC's *Enforcement (ENF)* operations manual[5] explains that the policy intent is "first and foremost to deny entry into Canada and thereby prevent Canadian territory being used as a safe haven by persons who are subject to a criminal proceeding in a foreign jurisdiction; or are fleeing from such proceedings."

Criminal charges that are dropped, or result in a not-guilty verdict, will not cause inadmissibility. However, if a person has been charged with a crime and the trial is still under way, the person may be inadmissible pending the results of the trial.

There are three categories of criminality: serious criminality (s. 36(1)), criminality (s. 36(2)), and organized criminality (s. 37). These are described below.

SERIOUS CRIMINALITY (SECTION 36(1))

Serious criminality is a ground of inadmissibility for both foreign nationals and permanent residents. Generally, the offence must be punishable by a maximum of ten years' imprisonment to qualify. However, this depends on whether the offence was committed in or outside Canada, and, if outside Canada, whether or not the person was convicted. These three subcategories of serious criminality are described below:

- *Convicted in Canada:* The person was convicted in Canada of an offence punishable by a maximum term of imprisonment of at least ten years, or of an offence for which a term of imprisonment of more than six months was imposed.

- *Convicted outside Canada:* The person was convicted of an offence that, if committed in Canada, would constitute an offence punishable by a maximum term of imprisonment of at least ten years.

- *Committed an act outside Canada:* The person committed an act that is an offence in the place where it was committed and that, if committed in Canada, would constitute an offence punishable by a maximum term of imprisonment of at least ten years.

If a permanent resident or foreign national is convicted of a serious crime while living in or visiting Canada, the minister alleges inadmissibility. Ordinarily, an officer receives information of the conviction from the court.

Exemptions

A person found inadmissible by reason of serious criminality may be exempted and permitted to enter or remain in Canada if pardoned or acquitted for the offence committed. With respect to such offences committed outside Canada, the person is exempt if rehabilitated.

These exemptions apply in the same way for the grounds of criminality and organized criminality. These exemptions are outlined in detail in the sections below.

CRIMINALITY (SECTION 36(2))

Whereas grounds of serious criminality apply to both foreign nationals and permanent residents, grounds of criminality apply only to foreign nationals. Permanent residents cannot be found inadmissible on the basis of this lesser threshold of criminality.

There are four subcategories of criminality under s. 36(2), but before describing these subcategories, it is necessary to understand the terminology of Canada's *Criminal Code*. The Code distinguishes between three kinds of offences, as follows:

- **summary conviction offences:** Less serious offences with a maximum sentence of six months and prosecuted using streamlined procedures;

- **indictable offences:** More serious offences such as murder, with longer periods of imprisonment and more complex prosecution procedures; and

- **hybrid or dual procedure offences:** Offences for which the Crown prosecutor chooses to proceed either by summary conviction or by indictment, in light of the circumstances of the alleged offence. An example is impaired driving.

For immigration purposes, a hybrid or dual procedure offence is "deemed to be an indictable offence, even if it has been prosecuted summarily," according to s. 36(3)(a) of the IRPA.

The four subcategories of criminality are as follows:

- *Convicted in Canada:* The person was convicted in Canada of an offence punishable by way of indictment, or of two summary conviction offences not arising out of a single occurrence.

- *Convicted outside Canada:* The person was convicted outside Canada of an offence that, if committed in Canada, would constitute an indictable offence, or of two summary conviction offences not arising out of a single occurrence that, if committed in Canada, would constitute offences.

- *Committed an act outside Canada:* The person committed an act outside Canada that is an offence in the place where it was committed and that, if committed in Canada, would constitute an indictable offence.

- *Committed an act on entering Canada:* The person committed, on entering Canada, a summary conviction offence prescribed by regulations.

Exemptions

The IRPA provides a few exemptions to inadmissibility on the ground of criminality, and Canada will admit persons who have been pardoned or acquitted, or, if otherwise inadmissible because of offences committed outside Canada, are either deemed to be rehabilitated or have satisfied the minister that they are rehabilitated. Each of these exemptions is considered below:

1. **Pardon:** A pardon may be granted under the *Criminal Code*, resulting in the offence being deemed to not have occurred. A person who is

pardoned from the offence at issue is exempt from inadmissibility. A foreign pardon must be equivalent to a pardon in Canada. This applies regardless of whether the offences occurred in or outside Canada.

2. **Acquittal:** An acquittal, or finding of not guilty, also exempts a person from inadmissibility. This applies regardless of whether the offences occurred in or outside Canada.

3. **Deemed rehabilitated:** A person whose conviction occurred outside Canada may be deemed rehabilitated, thereby removing the ground of criminal inadmissibility, if the following criteria under s. 18(2) of the IRP Regulations are met:

   a. at least ten years have elapsed since the completion of the sentence imposed (such as probation, prison term, fines, or restitution);

   b. the conviction is not considered serious in Canada;

   c. the conviction did not involve any serious property damage, physical harm to any person, or any type of weapon; and

   d. the offence committed would be punishable in Canada by a maximum term of imprisonment of less than ten years.

   Even if ten years have passed, the person seeking entry to Canada must disclose the conviction and should provide evidence that no further offence has occurred.

4. **Individual rehabilitation:** Unlike the deeming provision described above, to be considered for individual rehabilitation, one must apply. To be eligible, a person must show that at least five years have passed since the completion of the sentence imposed (such as prison term, suspended sentence, fines, or probation), and that the conviction equates to a hybrid or indictable offence in Canada. Applications must be submitted to a Canadian visa office, where the visa officer considers all relevant factors to approve or refuse the application.

Consider the following case scenarios regarding exemptions to inadmissibility on the ground of criminality under s. 36(2).

Sovann, a Cambodian national, is interested in applying for a student permit to complete a two-year culinary program offered at the University of British Columbia. Sovann is concerned that he may be inadmissible on the ground of criminality. In 1989, Sovann was convicted in the United States of "driving while impaired." Sovann did not serve any time in prison and he has no other convictions. In the United States, this may be prosecuted as a misdemeanour offence, often under a state motor vehicle law or municipal law. However, in Canada, impaired driving is a criminal offence under the Criminal Code and is listed as a hybrid offence.

Sovann may be deemed rehabilitated when more than ten years have elapsed since the payment of his fine in 1989. He must, because his offence is equivalent to a hybrid offence under Canadian law, apply at the Canadian visa office for individual rehabilitation at the time he submits his visa application. If his application is accepted, Sovann will be allowed to enter Canada, provided that he complies with the eligibility criteria for a student permit.

> *Juanita, a Colombian national, would like to apply for a temporary resident visa to attend her sister's wedding in Canada. Juanita is concerned that she may be criminally inadmissible to Canada. Juanita was convicted of shoplifting in April 2001 and was sentenced to one year's probation and required to attend counselling. She has no other convictions. The elements of Juanita's offence in her home country are equivalent to an offence (informally known as "theft under") in the Criminal Code. It is a hybrid offence that could be prosecuted either summarily or by indictment.*

Unfortunately for Juanita, she is inadmissible to Canada because hybrid offences are deemed indictable for immigration purposes. However, under s. 36(3)(c), Juanita is eligible to apply for rehabilitation after April 2007, which is five years after the completion of the imposed sentence to apply for rehabilitation. Because probation is considered part of a sentence or a conviction, Juanita must count five years from the end of the probation period, which is April 2002.

> *Kelly and Alicia are friends from Trinidad and Tobago. They both want to apply for temporary resident visas to Canada. Each of them is concerned that she may be criminally inadmissible to Canada. Kelly was convicted of a crime on June 18, 2003, and received a jail sentence of three months. Alicia was convicted of driving under the influence on April 3, 2003 and had her driver's licence taken away from her for three years.*

Kelly may apply for rehabilitation five years after the end of the sentence imposed. If Kelly's three-month jail sentence ended September 18, 2003, Kelly is eligible to apply for rehabilitation on September 18, 2008, as long as no other terms were imposed on her sentence.

Alicia's sentence ends on April 3, 2006. Because five years must elapse from the end date of the suspension or the date her driver's licence is reinstated, Alicia will be eligible to apply for rehabilitation on April 3, 2011.

Those not eligible for deemed rehabilitation or individual rehabilitation, because neither five nor ten years have elapsed since the completion of the sentence, may apply at a visa office for a **temporary resident permit (TRP)**. A TRP will be issued only in compelling circumstances, as described later in this chapter.

An applicant may request that an officer review the details of his case and assess inadmissibility on the ground of criminality. The applicant must fill out an application for rehabilitation and check off the box "for information only." There is no fee for this type of application, although the processing usually takes several months.

ORGANIZED CRIMINALITY (SECTION 37)

Both permanent residents and foreign nationals may be found inadmissible for being members of an organized crime group under s. 37 of the IRPA.

Specifically, this section applies when the permanent resident or foreign national

- is a member of an organization that is believed on reasonable grounds to be or to have been engaged in activity that is part of a pattern of criminal activity planned and organized by a number of persons acting in concert in furtherance of the commission of an indictable offence or in furtherance of the commission of an offence outside Canada that, if committed in Canada, would constitute an indictable offence, or engaging in activity that is part of such a pattern; or

- is, in the context of transnational crime, engaged in activities such as people smuggling, trafficking in persons, or money laundering.

There must be proof of membership, and of a pattern of criminal activity that is planned and organized by persons acting in concert to find a person inadmissible under this ground.

The *Enforcement (ENF)* operations manual proposes that officers typically wait for the courts to decide the organized criminality charges, before considering inadmissibility.[6] However, in cases where local authorities are not pursuing formal charges, officers may investigate and report the person as inadmissible if organized criminal activity is uncovered.

Exemptions

A refugee claimant whose only involvement with a criminal organization was to facilitate travel to Canada to make the refugee claim is exempt from inadmissibility. It would be unfair to return a person at risk whose only involvement with crime was necessary for survival, and such a person would not pose a risk of further criminality in Canada.

Any person found inadmissible on the ground of organized criminality may also be exempt from inadmissibility if the minister is satisfied that the person's presence in Canada would not be detrimental to the national interest.

4. Health Reasons (Section 38)

Only foreign nationals may be inadmissible for reasons of health. Permanent residents already accepted and living in Canada cannot later be found inadmissible if they develop a medical condition. Once permanent resident status is granted, health concerns arising later will not result in inadmissibility.

A foreign national who applies for temporary or permanent residence and who suffers from a health condition may be inadmissible according to s. 38(1) of the IRPA if the health condition

- is likely to be a danger to public health, such as a communicable disease;

- is likely to be a danger to public safety, such as a mental condition that causes unpredictable or violent behaviour; or

- might reasonably be expected to cause excessive demand on health or social services, such as a condition that requires ongoing expensive medical treatment.

The first two conditions are not limited to a person's physical condition, but also extend to a psychological incapacity that may create a danger to the health or safety of persons living in Canada.

Sexually transmitted viruses and diseases, such as human immunodeficiency virus (HIV) and syphilis, pose a danger to public health or safety only if there is evidence that the person engages in high-risk behaviour, such as sharing contaminated needles or engaging in unprotected sex, and the person is refusing to cooperate with public health authorities. This is in contrast to a disease such as tuberculosis: if it is active (and contagious), it is generally grounds for inadmissibility, mainly because it can be transmitted easily through coughing or sneezing. A person with inactive tuberculosis cannot transmit the disease, and may be admitted into Canada, provided that regular medical followups are undertaken to ensure that the disease continues to be inactive.

Persons who are HIV positive may pass the first two grounds only to be refused on the third ground of excessive demand on health or social services. The current guidelines for assessing HIV cases state that any applicant receiving antiretroviral therapy (ARV) is inadmissible because of excessive demand.

MEDICAL EXAMINATION

As part of the application process, permanent residence applicants and their dependants must undergo a medical examination at their own expense. Temporary residence applicants may also be required to do this, depending on factors such as country of origin, length of stay, and type of activity in Canada.

Additionally, a temporary residence applicant who normally would be exempt from the medical examination may be required to submit to one if an officer suspects illness or a medical condition that could render the applicant medically inadmissible. A suspicion may be raised if the applicant appears to be sick, or if questioning by the officer reveals that the applicant was recently discharged from the hospital, or is taking medication for a serious illness. The medical examination may be conducted as part of a port of entry examination, for example, when a temporary resident is seeking admission.

The medical examination must include the following:

- a physical and mental examination;

- a review of past medical history, laboratory tests, and diagnostic tests; and

- a medical assessment of records.

Those applicants who pass their medical examinations are issued a medical certificate that is usually valid for 12 months.

Only a **designated medical officer (DMO)**, a physician designated by CIC, is authorized to carry out a medical assessment. The DMO considers the following factors:

- the nature, severity, and probable duration of any health impairment from which the person is suffering;

- the danger of contagion;

- any unpredictable or unusual behaviour that may create a danger to public safety; and

- the supply of social or health services that the person may require in Canada and whether the use of such services will deprive Canadian nationals of these services (for example, the risk of a sudden incapacity).

A person may overcome inadmissibility and be admissible as a temporary resident if she is seeking medical treatment, provided that the medical treatment will not create excessive demand on health services.

The DMO prepares a medical profile based on the test results and gives an opinion about whether the person is admissible, inadmissible, or requires **medical surveillance**. A designation of medical surveillance does not bar a person from admission; rather, it provides for monitoring. For example, an applicant's inactive tuberculosis must be checked periodically to ensure that it does not become active and contagious.

The DMO's report is provided to the visa officer, who, in accordance with s. 20 of the IRP Regulations, must follow the medical opinion. The visa officer notifies the applicant if there is a finding of inadmissibility to give the applicant the opportunity to reply and provide further documentation, within a reasonable period of time, before rendering a final decision.

EXEMPTIONS

In some circumstances, foreign nationals who intend to stay in Canada for six months or longer are exempt from the requirement to submit to a medical examination if they are one of the following:

- a person entering Canada with the purpose of carrying out official duties, unless they seek to engage or continue in secondary employment in Canada;

- a family member of an accredited foreign representative under s. 186(b) of the IRP Regulations, unless that family member seeks to engage or continue in employment in Canada;

- a member of the armed forces of a country that is a designated state for the purposes of the *Visiting Forces Act* who is entering or is in Canada to carry out official duties, other than a person who has been designated as a civilian component of those armed forces, unless that member seeks to engage or continue in secondary employment in Canada;

- a family member of a protected person, if the family member is not included in the protected person's application to remain in Canada as a permanent resident; or

- a non-accompanying family member of a foreign national who has applied for refugee protection outside Canada.

Although family class spouses, common-law partners, or children of sponsors, Convention refugees, and protected persons must undergo medical examinations for health and public safety reasons, they cannot be found inadmissible on the basis of excessive demand on health or social services. Also, persons who are likely to be refused on the basis of excessive demand may avoid inadmissibility by having a satisfactory financial arrangement to cover the cost of the treatment and related expenses. For example, a person seeking to enter Canada for medical treatment would normally be inadmissible unless the visa officer was satisfied that the person could pay all associated costs for the medical treatment, including travel and accommodation.

5. Financial Reasons (Section 39)

A foreign national who applies for temporary or permanent residence must satisfy the visa officer of his ability to both be self-sufficient and support any dependants in Canada, physically and legally, pursuant to s. 39 of the IRPA.

At the time of processing an application abroad, the visa officer assesses the person's financial resources as well as any arrangements in place, such as job offers, and the person's potential employability. Upon the applicant's arrival in Canada, an officer verifies that the person has sufficient funds to cover the temporary stay or, in the case of an applicant seeking to establish permanent residence, that the person has employment or that his funds are sufficient for six months.

Certain classes of permanent residents, such as entrepreneurs under the business class, are admitted with additional financial conditions to be fulfilled within a predetermined amount of time.

EXEMPTION

Convention refugees and protected persons who apply for permanent residence in Canada are exempted by the IRPA from inadmissibility due to financial grounds.

6. Misrepresentation (Section 40)

Applicants are required to answer truthfully all questions and produce all relevant documents at the examination, according to s. 16 of the IRPA. Failure to do so could result in inadmissibility.

There are four situations of misrepresentation described in s. 40, but before we examine them it is worthwhile to consider the definitions of the following terms as stated in the *Enforcement (ENF)* operations manual:

- **Misrepresentation** (also referred to as false pretences): "Misstating facts to obtain money, goods, benefits or some other thing desired by a person who might otherwise not be entitled to it."

- **Withholding:** "to hold back from doing or taking an action; to keep (within); to refrain from granting, giving, allowing or 'letting it be known.' A person can misrepresent themselves by being silent just as easily as a person who actively states a 'mistruth.' A person who refuses or declines to answer a question, preferring instead to allow outdated or false information to be accepted as current or true information, is engaging in the activity of misrepresentation."

up to here
(for ILP only)

Keeping those definitions in mind, consider the four situations of misrepresentation, as follows:

1. A permanent resident or foreign national is inadmissible on the ground of misrepresentation for directly or indirectly misrepresenting or withholding material facts relating to a relevant matter that induces or could induce an error in the administration of the IRPA.

   For example, a person who provides false identity documents to conceal identity or to falsify a relationship would be found inadmissible on this ground. Persons found inadmissible while outside Canada may be banned for two years. Persons found inadmissible while in Canada may be banned from the date that the removal order is enforced, in accordance with s. 40(2)(a) of the IRPA.

   Under s. 22 of the IRP Regulations, refugee claimants are exempted from inadmissibility on this ground if the disposition of the claim is pending, as are protected persons.

2. A permanent resident or foreign national is inadmissible on the ground of misrepresentation for being or having been sponsored by a person who is found to be inadmissible for misrepresentation.

   The consequence is a two-year ban. Also, according to s. 64(3) of the IRPA, the sponsor loses the right to appeal unless the sponsored person is the sponsor's spouse, common-law partner, or child.

3. A permanent resident or foreign national is inadmissible on the ground of misrepresentation on a final determination to **vacate** a decision to allow the claim for refugee protection by the permanent resident or the foreign national.

   This refers to a refugee claimant who commits a misrepresentation in order to acquire Canada's protection. The Refugee Protection Division (RPD) has the authority to vacate a refugee determination under s. 109(1) of the IRPA, if it finds that the decision was obtained as a result of directly or indirectly misrepresenting or withholding material facts relating to a relevant matter. The consequence of such a finding is that the refugee claim is deemed rejected and the decision conferring refugee protection is vacated, or nullified, according to s. 109(3).

   Currently, the **notice of decision** by the RPD to vacate the claim is sufficient evidence of such a determination. However, if the sections of the IRPA that provide for an appeal before the Refugee Appeal Division are enacted, the person's appeal rights would have to be exhausted before a finding of inadmissibility could be made.

4. A permanent resident or foreign national is inadmissible on the grounds of misrepresentation on ceasing to be a citizen under para. 10(1)(a) of the *Citizenship Act*, in the circumstances set out in s. 10(2) of that Act.

   If a person loses Canadian citizenship because of misrepresentation, the officer obtains a letter confirming that the person has ceased to be a citizen from CIC, which has the responsibility for processing citizenship applications and maintaining citizenship records.

As with all other grounds of inadmissibility, a finding of misrepresentation may be made by visa officers to deny visas to applicants abroad, by port of entry officers to deny entry into Canada, as well as by officers in Canada to remove a person already admitted.

Consider the following case scenarios.

A vehicle with four individuals arrives at a Canadian port of entry and the driver is asked whether all the occupants in the car are Canadian citizens. The driver replies, "yes." One of the passengers is a foreign national and remains silent.

In this scenario the driver misrepresented the foreign national, and the foreign national withheld material facts by remaining silent. Both are grounds for inadmissibility.

An individual appears at a Canadian port of entry to claim refugee status. The individual is using someone else's passport, but advises the officer that he used this passport for the purposes of leaving his country because his life was in danger.

Normally, an individual who is using a false identity would be inadmissible to Canada on the basis of misrepresentation. However, the IRPA exempts persons who have claimed refugee protection if a determination of their claim is pending. This is an important exemption because without some degree of subterfuge refugees may not be able to escape from the countries they are fleeing.

A representative for a temporary residence applicant provides false information regarding the applicant's educational credentials. The applicant is truly unaware that the representative submitted false documentation until the officer brings this anomaly to the applicant's attention.

Misrepresentation is extended to those who may not be aware of a misrepresentation or whose actions or lack of actions were unintentional but resulted in misrepresentation. In the present case, the applicant is responsible for ensuring that the application is truthful and the supporting documents are genuine. The applicant could therefore be inadmissible for misrepresentation for submitting false documents even though he was not the one who fabricated the evidence.

EXEMPTIONS

Under s. 22 of the IRP Regulations, the misrepresentation provisions do not apply to protected persons and persons who have claimed refugee protection, provided that a disposition regarding their claim is pending. Additionally, under s. 176 of the IRP Regulations and s. 21 of the IRPA, misrepresentation provisions do not apply to those abroad who are family members of protected persons.

7. Failure to Comply with the IRPA (Section 41)

The ground of "non-compliance with the IRPA" is a catch-all covering contraventions of immigration law and regulations that are not captured by other grounds of inadmissibility. It is especially useful for enforcement of conditions that may be imposed on temporary and permanent residents.

Other examples of failure to comply include the failure to do the following:[8]

- appear for an examination;

- appear for an admissibility hearing;

- obtain the written authorization of an officer to return to Canada (required by s. 52(1) of the IRPA for a person who has been excluded);

- hold the relevant temporary or permanent visa under s. 20 of the IRPA (for example, a visitor or student who engages in employment without a work visa);

- leave Canada by the end of the period authorized for their stay as required by s. 29(2) of the IRPA (for example, a person who overstays her authorized visit); or

- abide by s. 29(2) of the IRPA to comply with any condition set out in s. 184 of the IRP Regulations (for example, members of a crew such as those on a ship who must leave Canada within 72 hours after they cease to be a member of the crew).

The most common reason for inadmissibility is arriving at a port of entry without a valid visa as required by s. 11 of the IRPA and ss. 6 and 7 of the IRP Regulations.

8. Inadmissible Family Member (Section 42)

A person may be inadmissible as a result of the inadmissibility of family members. Under s. 42, a foreign national, other than a protected person, is inadmissible on the ground of an inadmissible family member if

- the accompanying family member or, in prescribed circumstances, the non-accompanying family member, is inadmissible; or

- the foreign national is an accompanying family member of an inadmissible person.

A visa officer assesses the foreign national's application including information provided about dependants, such as background and medical records to determine whether they are inadmissible. A foreign national thus may be inadmissible because of the inadmissibility of a dependant, even if the dependant is not accompanying the foreign national to Canada, according to s. 23 of the IRP Regulations. The policy reason for this provision is forward looking: a non-accompanying dependant today could be tomorrow's sponsored applicant.

ASSESSING INADMISSIBILITY

The minister of Citizenship and Immigration Canada is responsible for most policies related to admissibility. However, the minister of Public Safety and Emergency Preparedness is responsible for policy regarding inadmissibility on the grounds of security, organized criminality, and violation of human or international rights.

Several immigration agencies may be involved in identifying inadmissible foreign nationals, depending on the place and circumstances. Consider the four different processes for determining inadmissibility:

1. A CIC visa officer may refuse to issue a visa to a person who makes an application for permanent or temporary entry while outside Canada, barring the person from coming to Canada.

2. At a port of entry, a Canada Border Services Agency (CBSA) officer may refuse entry and issue a removal order to any of the following:

   - a person who is a returning permanent resident with a Permanent Resident Card;

   - a new permanent resident with a permanent resident visa;

   - a foreign national with or without a temporary resident visa; or

   - a refugee claimant.

   (Recall that the CBSA is an agency of Public Safety Canada, formerly the Department of Public Safety and Emergency Preparedness.)

3. A CBSA officer may find that a permanent or temporary resident became inadmissible after admission to Canada, and issue a removal order.

4. The Immigration Division of the Immigration and Refugee Board may hold an **inadmissibility hearing** for cases referred to it by the minister (usually PSEP), at which a permanent or temporary resident may be found inadmissible, and a removal order issued. Additionally, the Immigration Appeal Division hears immigration appeals, including those against certain decisions on admissibility.

These processes are discussed fully in Chapter 10.

NOTES

1. Citizenship and Immigration Canada, "ENF 1: Inadmissibility," in *Enforcement (ENF)*, August 8, 2008, s. 3, at 7-8, www.cic.gc.ca/english/ resources/manuals/enf/index.asp.

2. *Zundel v. Canada (F.C.A.)*, 2004 FCA 145, [2004] 3 F.C.R. 638.

3. *Zûndel, Re*, 2005 FC 295, at para. 112.

4. Citizenship and Immigration Canada, "ENF 2: Evaluating Inadmissibility," in *Enforcement (ENF)*, s. 6.4, May 24, 2006, www.cic .gc.ca/english/resources/manuals/enf/index.asp.

5. Ibid., at s. 3.5.

6. Ibid., at s. 4.2.

7. Ibid., at s. 9.2.

8. These examples are taken from CIC's *Enforcement (ENF)* operations manual, supra note 1, at 28.

REFERENCES

Citizenship Act. R.S.C. 1985, c. C-29.

Criminal Code. R.S.C. 1985, c. C-46.

Immigration and Refugee Protection Regulations. S.O.R./2002-227.

Indian Act. R.S.C. 1985, c. I-5.

Visiting Forces Act. R.S.C. 1985, c. V-2.

REVIEW QUESTIONS

1. List and briefly describe the eight grounds of inadmissibility under the IRPA.

2. Provide an example of an action or condition that would render a person inadmissible under s. 34(1) of the IRPA.

3. What are the differences between s. 34(1) and s. 35(1) of the IRPA? Give examples.

4. Is failing to comply with the IRPA a ground for inadmissibility? Where is this section found in the Act?

5. In what situation is a person an inadmissible family member under the IRPA? Which section of the Act deals with this issue?

CHAPTER 4

Temporary Entry

LEARNING OBJECTIVES

After reading this chapter you should be able to:

- Differentiate among the four classes of temporary residents: visitors, students, workers, and temporary resident permit holders.

- Describe the general provisions for applying for a temporary resident visa, and understand the difference between a temporary resident visa and a temporary resident permit.

- Understand the general obligations of temporary residents.

- Describe how temporary residents can lose their status.

- Describe the requirements and application process for the visitor class, student class, and worker class.

- Explain the rights and obligations of Canadian employers in relation to temporary resident employees.

- Understand the international agreements that apply to the temporary entry of business workers.

- Describe the Live-In Caregiver Program, including the responsibilities of Canadian employers under the program.

- Explain the criteria for obtaining a temporary resident permit.

INTRODUCTION

We usually think about immigration to Canada as a permanent change that a person makes to seek opportunities and a better standard of living, escape poverty or violence, or reunite with family. However, another important type of immigration exists: temporary immigration. Canada's temporary immigration program allows thousands of people each year to visit, study, or work in Canada while providing benefits to our economy.

Temporary residents are foreign nationals who are permitted to remain in Canada for a specified period of time. Temporary residents must leave Canada by the end of the period authorized for their stay. They may re-enter Canada only if their authorization provides for re-entry.

There are four classes of temporary residents according to the *Immigration and Refugee Protection Act* (IRPA) and its regulations:

- visitors;

- students;

- workers; and

- temporary resident permit holders.

A clear distinction is made between each class on the basis of the activity that the foreign national intends to undertake while in Canada temporarily, such as visiting, studying, or working.

According to the minister of Citizenship and Immigration in the *Annual Report to Parliament on Immigration 2007*, temporary immigration is permitted to meet Canada's "labour-market needs, support Canadian businesses and influence our culturally diverse communities."[1] In 2006, Canada processed 987,378 applications from foreign nationals who required a visa to enter Canada temporarily as visitors; admitted 112,658 foreign workers who filled skill gaps in the domestic labour market; and permitted entry to 61,703 foreign students.[2]

What would happen if people stopped coming to Canada? Consider the economic impact of the 2003 outbreak of SARS (Severe Acute Respiratory Syndrome), which not only kept tourists away but also kept international students and business workers at home. Temporary resident programs are vital to Canada's prosperity. At the same time, Canada's immigration policy recognizes that it is important to balance the need to attract foreign nationals and process applications efficiently with the need to protect Canadians by denying access to those who pose a criminal or security threat and those who abuse our system by not leaving at the end of their permitted stay. These goals are reflected in the following immigration objectives in s. 3(1) of the IRPA:

> (g) to facilitate the entry of visitors, students and temporary workers for purposes such as trade, commerce, tourism, international understanding and cultural, educational and scientific activities;
>
> (h) to protect the health and safety of Canadians and to maintain the security of Canadian society; [and]
>
> (i) to promote international justice and security by fostering respect for human rights and by denying access to Canadian territory to persons who are criminals or security risks.

This chapter considers both the general requirements for all temporary residents and the specific requirements for each of the different temporary resident programs. It discusses the overriding restrictions that deny temporary access to Canada such as eligibility criteria. Also discussed are the obligations and conditions that must be fulfilled by foreign nationals after admission to Canada.

Generally, a foreign national who wishes to reside temporarily in Canada must submit to an application and approval process and obtain a temporary resident visa before coming to Canada. However, foreign nationals from "visa-exempt" countries are excluded from this requirement, as are those with special status.

TEMPORARY RESIDENT VISA

Generally, foreign nationals may not enter Canada to remain on a temporary basis without first obtaining a temporary resident visa (TRV), unless they are exempt from visa requirements, according to s. 7 of the Immigration and Refugee Protection Regulations (IRP Regulations). A temporary resident visa is an official document issued, or a stamped impression made on a document, by an officer from a Canadian visa office or a Regional Processing Centre (RPC). A visa office or Regional Processing Centre refers to a Canadian consulate, embassy, or high commission outside of Canada that processes immigration applications. Not all consulates or embassies process immigration applications. Different regions have different procedures. The visa is placed in the applicant's passport to identify the holder as a person who may become a temporary resident upon admission to Canada.

A temporary resident visa is not to be confused with a temporary resident permit (TRP), which is issued by an officer only in special cases, and is discussed at the end of this chapter.

For most foreign nationals, obtaining a temporary resident visa involves a formal, written application procedure. For those who are exempt, an oral application at the port of entry is sufficient. A temporary resident visa is issued when the officer is satisfied that the applicant meets the requirements of the IRPA and its regulations, specifically s. 22 of the IRPA and s. 179 of the IRP Regulations, which require that the applicant has

- fulfilled certain obligations;

- met the criteria for the particular class of temporary resident that he has applied under; and

- shown that he is not inadmissible.

Applications for a temporary resident visa may be refused for any of the following reasons:

- the applicant does not meet the eligibility criteria for the particular class of temporary resident;

- the applicant (or any family member) is inadmissible on the grounds of security risk, human or international rights violations, criminality, organized criminality, health risk, financial reasons, misrepresentation, or non-compliance with the IRPA, or because of an inadmissible family member (see Chapter 3, "Inadmissibility"); or

- the officer is not satisfied that the applicant will leave by the end of his stay.

There is no right to appeal to the Immigration and Refugee Board; however, the applicant may seek leave for a judicial review at the Federal Court. Also, if an applicant who was refused admission believes that the refusal was discriminatory and without bona fide justification, the applicant may file a complaint under the *Canadian Human Rights Act*.

Even when a temporary resident visa is obtained, it is not a guarantee of admission to Canada. All people seeking to come to Canada, including temporary residents, must be examined by an officer according to s. 18 of the IRPA. Therefore, when the applicant arrives at a Canadian port of entry seeking admission, an officer from the Canada Border Services Agency (CBSA) makes the decision whether or not to allow it. A change of circumstances between the time of acquiring a temporary resident visa and the time of arrival in Canada, or additional information available, could result in the applicant being refused entry. In other words, a temporary resident visa allows a person to travel to a Canadian port of entry in order to visit, work, or study in Canada, but does not in itself grant admission to Canada.

Temporary Resident Visa Exemptions

Although the general rule is that all foreign nationals who are seeking temporary residence require a temporary resident visa before arriving at a port of entry, the regulations grant exceptions to this rule. Some persons may be exempt on the basis of nationality, possession of certain documents, or purpose of the entry:

- *Nationality.* Citizens of numerous countries, including Australia, France, and Mexico, do not require a temporary resident visa to enter Canada. Nor do British citizens or citizens of a British overseas territory. Nor do nationals of the United States or permanent residents of the United States. Section 190(1) of the IRP Regulations provides a full list of nationality exemptions. The list of countries may change at any time, so it is important to consult the most current version of the IRP Regulations or the Citizenship and Immigration Canada (CIC) website at www.cic.gc.ca/ english/visit/visas.asp. For quick reference, the CIC website provides a list of countries and territories whose citizens require visas in order to enter Canada as visitors. This detail in the regulations allows the minister of CIC to quickly add or remove countries (by way of an order in council) in response to changing trends. For example, in 1997, the Canadian government imposed visa requirements on the Czech Republic in response to a trend of a rising number of Romany people from that country who travelled to Canada as visitors, then overstayed to make refugee claims, the majority of which were refused. To stem the flow of citizens from the Czech Republic, visa requirements were imposed. Ten years later, however, in October 2007 Canada lifted the visa imposition for Czech nationals wishing to visit Canada for fewer than 90 days. This was in response to pressure from the European Commission to lift requirements on eight then new European Union member nations, including the Czech Republic.

- *Documents.* Foreign nationals do not require a temporary resident visa to enter Canada if they hold particular documents, which include a diplomat's passport, a passport or travel document issued by the Holy See, a national Israeli passport, or certain Hong Kong passports. Section 190(2) of the IRP Regulations provides a full list of exemptions based on the applicant's documents.

- *Purpose of entry.* Foreign nationals may be exempted from the temporary resident visa requirement if they are members of a transportation crew, are airplane passengers landing in Canada for refuelling, or have come to Canada for an interview with a United States consular officer regarding re-admission to the United States. Section 190(3) of the IRP Regulations provides a full list of exemptions based on the applicant's purpose of entry.

Temporary Resident Visa Conditions

Temporary residents must comply with any conditions imposed under the IRP Regulations at s. 183. There are general conditions that are automatically imposed on all temporary resident visas that are issued, such as the requirement to leave by the end of the authorized period of stay. Other conditions vary depending on the class of temporary resident.

The officer at the port of entry authorizes the foreign national's entry as a temporary resident and will remind her of the conditions. If the officer has any doubts about the temporary resident's intention to live up to the general terms and conditions of admission, a security deposit may be imposed.

A **security deposit** is a sum of money in proportion to the obligations of the conditions and the costs associated with enforcement activities such as investigations, arrests, detentions, immigration hearings, and removals. The examining officer may still grant entry but will require the foreign national (or someone acting on her behalf) to post a bond or sign a performance bond, as authorized under s. 45 of the IRP Regulations. This section is used as a control measure to guarantee compliance.

Once entry has been granted, a temporary resident usually may not change status without permission. Doing so would be a violation of the IRPA, causing inadmissibility, and could result in removal. For example, under ss. 186 and 187 of the IRP Regulations, a temporary resident holding a **visitor visa**—that is, a temporary resident visa issued under the visitor class—is not allowed to work in Canada without a work permit; and under ss. 188 and 189, a temporary resident generally may not study without a study permit. Similarly, a temporary worker may not change jobs, and some international students may not change their approved type of educational institution without first applying to have the conditions amended.

A foreign national who wishes to change the type of visa or to change a condition must first apply to the Case Processing Centre (CPC-V) in Vegreville, Alberta. The following documents must be submitted:

- a completed Application to Change Conditions, Extend My Stay or Remain in Canada form (IMM 1249) for applicants in Canada who wish to change their type of visa or to change the conditions imposed upon entry;

- a Statutory Declaration of Common-Law Union form (IMM 5409), if applicable;

- a Use of a Representative form (IMM 5476), if applicable;

- a Document Checklist form (IMM 5558); and

- a cost-recovery processing fee receipt form (IMM 5401), which indicates that the cost recovery processing fee of $75 has been paid to an approved financial institution.

Processing may take 30 days, or more in some cases.

Temporary Resident Visa Requirements

There are basic criteria that must be met for all temporary resident visas, according to s. 179 of the IRP Regulations. These requirements must generally be met by all visitors, workers, and students seeking a temporary resident visa. A temporary resident visa may be issued only if an examination establishes that the foreign national

- has used the application documents that the IRPA requires for the particular temporary resident class;

- has applied to the appropriate visa office if he is outside Canada or to the Case Processing Centre in Vegreville if he is in Canada, in accordance with the requirements of the IRPA;

- will leave Canada by the end of the period authorized for staying in Canada;

- has paid the required processing fees;

- holds a passport or similar document that may be used to enter the country that issued it, or another country;

- meets the medical examination requirements contained in s. 30 of the IRP Regulations;

- meets the requirements applicable to the temporary resident class; and

- is not inadmissible.

Each of these criteria is considered in more detail below.

APPLICATION DOCUMENTS

A foreign national is deemed to have applied for a temporary resident visa as a member of the visitor, worker, or student class by submitting the following documents:

- a complete application form (IMM 5257B for visitors, IMM 1295 for workers, or IMM 1294 for students);

- a Statutory Declaration of Common-Law Union form (IMM 5409), if applicable;

- a cost-recovery processing fee receipt (form 5401), which indicates that the cost-recovery processing fee has been paid to an approved financial institution;

- a valid passport or travel/identity document, unless the foreign national is exempt from passport and travel document requirements under s. 52(1) of the IRP Regulations;

- recent passport-size photos for each family member (the name of the person should be written on the back of each photo);

- proof of custody and/or a letter of consent from the custodial parent where a child under 16 years of age is either travelling alone, without proper identification, or with adults other than a sole custodial parent or guardian (also, if a CBSA officer at a port of entry is concerned for the safety of a child, the child may be examined alone to determine whether the child was abducted or is a runaway); and

■ proof of current immigration status if the foreign national is not a citizen of the country in which she is applying (more information in this area is provided in the following section).

Applicants may also be required to provide other documents to convince the officer that they intend to return to their country of residence at the end of the period authorized for their temporary stay, such as a letter from an employer indicating that the applicant is expected to return.

Finally, there are also specific documents required for each type of temporary resident visa, as discussed later in this chapter.

PLACE OF APPLICATION

Since April 1, 2005, applicants *outside* Canada seeking a temporary resident visa as a student or worker are required to submit their application to the visa office that is responsible for serving one of the following jurisdictions:

■ a country in which the applicant was lawfully admitted; or

■ the applicant's country of nationality (or if the applicant is stateless, her country of habitual residence).

However, applicants already *in* Canada who are seeking a temporary resident visa as a student or worker, or a renewal, are required to submit their application to the Case Processing Centre in Vegreville. Applicants are also required to obtain a study permit or work permit, both of which are described later in this chapter.

The following list provides further clarification of the persons who are eligible to apply to CPC-V for a temporary resident visa or to vary or cancel the conditions imposed upon entry to Canada:

■ foreign nationals and their family members holding valid work or study permits;

■ foreign nationals and their family members holding temporary resident permits valid for a minimum of six months;

■ refugee claimants subject to an unenforceable removal order;

■ protected persons who are the subject of humanitarian and compassionate considerations, spouses or common-law partners in Canada, and live-in caregivers who have been determined eligible for permanent resident status;

■ persons whose study permits were authorized by a visa office abroad, where the permit was not issued at a port of entry; or

■ family members of athletes on a Canadian-based team, media representatives, members of the clergy, or military personnel assigned to Canada (s. 215 of the IRP Regulations).

Consider the following case scenario:

Rose, a Colombian national, is currently working in Arizona as a live-in caregiver for the British ambassador to the United States. Rose is 32 years old, speaks fluent English, and obtained a university degree in Colombia. After completing her education in Colombia, Rose moved to Arizona in order to care for the ambassador's three children. She has now worked for the ambassador for five years.

The ambassador is soon moving back to London, but has told Rose that the new Canadian ambassador would like to employ Rose in Ottawa. Rose has worked problem-free for the ambassador in Arizona although she was never authorized to work in the United States and she did not enter the United States legally. Rose would like to apply for a work permit in Buffalo under the Live-In Caregiver Program.

Unfortunately for Rose, she may not apply in Buffalo because s. 11(2) of the IRP Regulations prohibits her from doing so. Rose was not lawfully admitted to the United States at any time; therefore, she has no right to apply in Buffalo. Rose must submit her application in her country of nationality, Colombia.

On the other hand, a business person from India spending a day or two in France may apply for a Canadian temporary resident visa in Paris, as long as he was lawfully admitted to France; or a Pakistani student studying in Singapore may apply for a temporary resident visa and a study permit at the visa office there.

Section 11(2) is only applicable to persons who are physically present in the country in which they were lawfully admitted. For example, s. 11(2) will not permit a Peruvian national who is physically in Peru to make a temporary resident visa application by mail to the Canadian visa office in New York City.

Consider another case scenario:

Maria is a dual citizen of Mexico and Argentina. Maria is currently living in the United Kingdom; she entered the United Kingdom legally but then lost her immigration status because she failed to extend her work permit. Maria would like to apply for a temporary resident visa to Canada, but she is unsure where she can submit her application.

Maria is entitled to submit her application to the Canadian visa office in either Mexico or Argentina, where she will be required to attend an interview, because Maria is a citizen of both countries. Alternatively, Maria may submit her application to the Canadian visa office in London, because she was lawfully admitted to the United Kingdom. The fact that she lost her immigration status afterward does not exclude her from submitting her application to the visa office in London.

INTENTION TO LEAVE CANADA

A foreign national must satisfy an officer that he will leave Canada at the end of the period authorized for the temporary stay, according to s. 20(1)(b) of the IRPA. An officer relies on certain factors to determine whether an applicant intends to remain in Canada illegally, claim refugee status, or otherwise seek to remain in Canada, and thus not abide by the requirement to leave Canada at the end of the period authorized for his temporary stay:

1. whether the applicant has family or economic ties to the country of residence;

2. whether the applicant has the financial capability to be self-sufficient while in Canada;

3. the applicant's immigration status in the country of residence;

4. the economic and political situation of the applicant's country of residence; and

5. any other obligations or responsibilities that the applicant may have in the country of residence.

These factors are considered in more detail below; however, it is important to keep in mind that a foreign national who has a **dual intent** of becoming a permanent resident is not necessarily precluded from becoming a temporary resident. Provided that the visa officer is satisfied that the foreign national has the capacity and willingness to leave Canada by the end of the period authorized for his stay, a temporary resident visa may not be denied simply because the foreign national intends to apply for permanent status, according to s. 22 of the IRPA. For example, a person who has already submitted an application for permanent residence as a provincial nominee[3] may wish to visit Canada for the purpose of an "exploratory visit" while awaiting the processing of that application.

The foreign national must satisfy both the officer abroad and the officer at the port of entry that he has the ability and willingness to leave Canada at the end of the temporary period authorized. Therefore, the fact that a foreign national has been issued a visa does not in itself grant admission to Canada. Under s. 180 of the IRP Regulations, the foreign national must not only meet the requirements for issuance of the visa at the time it is issued but also continue to meet these requirements at the time of the examination on entry into Canada.

1. Family and Economic Ties

The officer examines whether the applicant has any family living in the country of residence, and whether the family will be accompanying the applicant to Canada. If the applicant does not have family in the country of residence or if the family lives outside the country of residence, the applicant will be deemed to not have family ties in the country of residence. This may lead the officer to believe that the applicant is less likely to be motivated to return there.

The officer also examines the applicant's employment status and financial stability in his country of residence. The officer determines whether the applicant is employed, and, if so, the amount of the salary. Has the applicant's employer approved a request for leave, and is the employer expecting the applicant to return to the job? This would suggest a genuine intention to return. The officer also considers whether the applicant owns any property in the country of residence, and, if so, the value of the property. Significant holdings, particularly a family home, suggest an intention to return to the country of residence.

2. Financial Self-Sufficiency

The applicant must prove that there are sufficient funds to cover living expenses for the applicant and any dependants while they are in Canada, and that there will be funds remaining to pay for the return trip home at the end of the temporary stay. The amount of money that an applicant needs varies according to the circumstances of the visit, such as how long the applicant will stay and whether the applicant will stay in a hotel or with friends or relatives. The following is a list of supporting documents that could be included as evidence of an applicant's financial resources:

- bank statements or deposit books that show accumulated savings, for both applicant and spouse;

- letters of employment, providing the name of the employer, the applicant's position/occupation, the date that the employment commenced, and annual earnings, for both applicant and spouse; and

- evidence of assets in the country of residence, such as deeds and car ownership, for both applicant and spouse.

In the event that the applicant lacks the means of self-support, but a host or family member in Canada is willing to provide adequate support for the applicant while in Canada, the officer examines the ability of the host or family member to do so. In such cases the following documents and evidence may be enclosed in support of the application:

- a letter of invitation from the host or family member in Canada, including a description of the financial assistance offered, such as accommodation, transportation costs, and medical costs;

- to prove the host or family member's income, either her last two Canada Revenue Agency Notice of Assessments, or a letter from her employer indicating her position, date employment commenced, and annual earnings; and

- evidence of the size of the host's or family member's family in Canada to ensure that sufficient income, known as the minimum necessary income, is available to support all dependants. The minimum necessary income is determined by reference to an annual Statistics Canada measure called the low income cut-off (LICO). See the figures in the table below, which are effective until December 31, 2008.

Size of family unit	Minimum necessary income
1 person (the sponsor)	$21,202
2 persons	$26,396
3 persons	$32,450
4 persons	$39,399
5 persons	$44,686
6 persons	$50,397
7 persons	$56,110
More than 7 persons, for each additional person, add	$5,713

Visa officers tend to be flexible in issuing temporary resident visas to parents and grandparents who have applications for permanent residence in process, and whose purpose of entering Canada is to visit—even if it is for a long period.

3. *Immigration Status*

The officer examines the applicant's immigration status in the country of residence. Section 11(2) of the IRP Regulations gives temporary resident visa applicants great flexibility to apply to come to Canada from any country as long as they were lawfully admitted and they remain physically present in that country during the processing of their applications.

Note, however, that there are situations where applicants are able to rely successfully on s. 11(2), but their applications are less likely to succeed because they lack credibility on the basis that the applicants will leave Canada at the end of the period authorized for their stay. Consider a Mexican citizen who enters the United States legally but then overstays the period authorized for his temporary stay. Section 11(2) permits this Mexican applicant to apply for a Canadian temporary resident visa at a visa office in Buffalo, because he was lawfully admitted to the United States—even though he is no longer entitled to be there. However, the fact that he overstayed his visa in the United States may undermine his efforts to convince the officer that he will not do the same if he is granted a Canadian temporary resident visa.

4. *Economic and Political Conditions*

The officer examines the economic and political situation in the applicant's country of residence. This is necessary because even if ties to the home country are strong, unstable economic or political conditions may cause a change of mind about returning home.

5. *Other Obligations and Responsibilities*

The officer may consider any other obligations or responsibilities that the applicant has in the country of residence if they are clearly disclosed during the examination. This may include personal responsibilities, such as caring for an aged parent, or business obligations to partners or employees. It is important to remember that the onus to provide sufficient evidence to support the applicant's case rests on the applicant. Failure to provide supporting documentation may result in the application for a temporary resident visa being refused.

PROCESSING FEES

Applicants for temporary resident visas and permits are required to pay processing fees. Processing fees vary for a single-entry temporary resident visa, multiple-entry temporary resident visa, transit visa, study permit, and work permit. There is no fee for a temporary resident visa if a work or study permit is issued at the same time.

The following table lists the processing fees for each type of temporary resident visa and permit, as of August 2008:

Type of temporary resident visa	Processing fee
Visitor visa—single entry to Canada	$75.00
Visitor visa—multiple entry	$150.00
Maximum family rate—this refers to the maximum processing fee per family for either single- or multiple-entry visa applications when all family members apply at the same time	$400.00
Work permit	$150.00
Work permit—group of three or more performing artists and staff	$450.00
Study permit	$125.00
Transit visa	No fee

Processing fees are non-refundable even if the application is refused; the fee is to cover the costs of processing the application, not for the decision. However, in certain circumstances, applicants for a temporary resident visa may be exempt from paying the processing fee.

The following visitor class applicants are exempt from paying the processing fee:

- foreign nationals applying for transit visas;

- persons who are issued courtesy visas as long as the person is listed in s. 296(2) of the IPR Regulations; persons listed in s. 296(2) include diplomats, who are always fee-exempt, whether the purpose of the visit is official or not;

- members of the armed forces who comply with the *Visiting Forces Act*;

- members of the clergy and religious groups; and

- competitors such as coaches, judges, team officials, medical staff, or members of a national or international sports organizing body participating in the Pan-American Games, or as a performer participating in a festival associated with any of those Games.[4]

The following student class applicants are exempt from paying the processing fee:

- foreign nationals who have been determined to be Convention refugees or members of a designated class prior to their arrival in Canada, and their family members;

- foreign nationals in Canada whose claim to be Convention refugees has been deemed admissible but has not yet been decided by the Refugee Protection Division, and their family members;

- diplomats accredited to Canada or another country, consular officers, representatives or officials of a foreign country, and their family members (for example, a dependent son of an accredited diplomat posted in Morocco who intends to study in Canada);

- students seeking renewal of their study permits who have become temporarily destitute through circumstances totally beyond their control or the control of any person on whom they are dependent for financial resources; and

- foreign nationals who are in Canada or who are coming into Canada under an agreement between Canada and a foreign country or an arrangement entered into with a foreign country by the government of Canada that provides for reciprocal educational opportunities (for example, participants in the Canada–US Fulbright Program).[5]

PASSPORT AND TRAVEL DOCUMENTS

The details of what documents are acceptable and what documents are unacceptable are set out in s. 52 of the IRP Regulations. Foreign nationals seeking to become temporary residents must hold a passport or travel document that is valid for the period authorized for their stay. Such documents, including certain passports, travel documents, identity documents, and *laissez-passers* (travel permits from the United Nations), are listed in s. 52(1) of the IRP Regulations.

There is also a list of individuals exempt from this requirement, provided in s. 52(2):

   (a) citizens of the United States; ...

   (c) residents of Greenland seeking to enter Canada from Greenland;

   (d) persons seeking to enter Canada from St. Pierre and Miquelon who are citizens of France and residents of St. Pierre and Miquelon;

   (e) members of the armed forces of a country that is a designated state for the purposes of the *Visiting Forces Act* who are seeking entry in order to carry out official duties, other than persons who have been designated as a civilian component of those armed forces;

   (f) persons who are seeking to enter Canada as, or in order to become, members of a crew of a means of air transportation and who hold an airline flight crew licence or crew member certificate issued in accordance with International Civil Aviation Organization specifications.

Furthermore, s. 52(3) provides a list of unacceptable documents that are not considered passports or identity or travel documents, such as documents purporting to have been issued by Somalia, the All Palestine Government, Bophuthatswana, Ciskei, Transkei, or Venda.

The validity of a temporary resident visa does not outlast the validity of a passport. Therefore, if the applicant's passport will soon expire, it should be renewed before the applicant applies for a temporary resident visa.

MEDICAL EXAMINATIONS

Medical examinations are required for applicants who will work in occupations where the protection of public health is essential. Regardless of the intended period of stay in Canada, a foreign national who is seeking to work in Canada in an occupation that is related to health services, or that requires close contact with other persons, must undergo a medical examination.

Such persons include schoolteachers, domestic workers, day nursery employees, clinical laboratory workers, medical students admitted to Canada to attend university, and physicians on short-term locums, because they may involve close contact with people for more than three hours per day and/or a risk of exchange of body fluids. Additionally, agricultural workers from designated countries and territories[6] are required to undergo a medical examination.

A medical examination is also generally required in the following situations, regardless of any public health concerns:

- the foreign national is seeking entry into Canada, or applying for a renewal of a work or study permit or authorization to remain in Canada, as a temporary resident for a period in excess of six consecutive months, including an actual or proposed period of absence from Canada of less than 14 days; or

- the foreign national resided or sojourned for six or more consecutive months in a designated country or territory during the one year immediately preceding the date of seeking entry to Canada.

Medical examinations must be performed by designated medical practitioners.[7] Furthermore, medical exams should be done at least two months before the expiry of the temporary resident's work or study permit, to avoid processing delays.

In certain circumstances, a foreign national seeking to stay in Canada for six months or longer may be exempt from the medical examination requirement. Section 30(2) of the IRP Regulations lists the following exempt persons:

- a person entering Canada with the purpose of carrying out official duties, unless that person seeks to engage or continue in secondary employment in Canada;

- a family member of an accredited foreign representative, as listed in s. 186(b) of the IRP Regulations, unless that family member seeks to engage or continue employment in Canada;

- a member of the armed forces of a country that is a designated state for the purposes of the *Visiting Forces Act* who is entering or is in Canada to carry out official duties, other than a person who has been designated as a civilian component of those armed forces, unless that member seeks to engage or continue in secondary employment in Canada;

- a family member of a protected person, if the family member is not included in the protected person's application to remain in Canada as a permanent resident; or

- a non-accompanying family member of a foreign national who has applied for refugee protection outside Canada.

Extension of a Temporary Resident Visa

A visitor who wishes to stay longer than the period of authorized stay must seek an extension before the expiry of the visa, by applying to the Case Processing Centre in Vegreville, Alberta. It is advisable to do so at least 30 days before expiration of the visa, to allow time for processing. An application for an extension of the temporary resident visa requires submission of the same documents required to change the type of visa or change a condition. These documents are as follows:

- a completed Application to Change Conditions, Extend My Stay, or Remain in Canada form (IMM 1249) for applicants in Canada seeking to extend their stay in Canada, to change the type of visa, or to change the conditions imposed upon entry;

- a Statutory Declaration of Common-Law Union form (IMM 5409), if applicable;

- a Use of a Representative form (IMM 5476), if applicable;

- a Document Checklist form (IMM 5558); and

- a cost-recovery processing fee receipt form (IMM 5401), which indicates that the cost-recovery processing fee of $75 has been paid to an approved financial institution.

Additionally, the temporary resident should provide the following:

- an explanation of why he wishes to stay in Canada longer;

- proof of identity;

- proof of current status in Canada (a valid and current visa);

- evidence of how he will support himself and any dependants in Canada; and

- a purchased ticket or funds set aside to prove an intention to leave Canada, and any other details including date and type of transportation.

Under s. 183(5) of the IRP Regulations, as long as the temporary resident applies to renew his status before it expires, status is retained until a decision is rendered on the application. If the applicant has a study or work visa and applies to extend the visa before it expires, he has the right to continue to study or work under the same conditions while in Canada.

Loss and Restoration of Temporary Resident Status

A temporary resident may lose temporary resident status under s. 47 of the IRPA. This can happen where a temporary resident becomes inadmissible, such as by overstaying the authorized period of stay. If found to be inadmissible, the temporary resident loses status and may be removed from Canada. The enforcement process is discussed in Chapter 10, "Enforcement Procedures."

When a visitor, worker, or student loses status as a temporary resident, an application may be made to have it reinstated or restored. According to s. 182 of the IRP Regulations, a temporary resident is allowed to seek restoration of status, for a fee, within 90 days after temporary resident status is lost. If the 90 days have passed, the person must leave Canada.

A restoration of status may be granted only in cases where the temporary resident continues to comply with the initial requirements for the stay in Canada after failing to comply with one or more of the subsequent requirements by

- remaining in Canada longer than the period authorized for her stay, but no longer than 90 days;

- changing the type of studies, educational institution, location of studies, or times and periods of studies, without applying to change these conditions on her study permit, if they were specified on her study permit as conditions; or

- changing employers, type of work, or location of work, without applying to change the conditions, if they were specified on her work permit.

Therefore, a temporary resident whose temporary resident status has expired is not eligible to apply for an extension but may apply for restoration of status, provided that the 90-day period has not passed. There is no guarantee that the application for restoration of status will be approved, because every application is assessed on its own merits. Therefore, the submissions should include an explanation for the failure to comply with the requirements of the temporary resident visa, and as much supporting evidence as possible.

Additionally, a foreign national may not apply for restoration of status if the loss of status resulted from non-compliance with conditions for which a six-month ban may be imposed. Section 200(3)(e)(i) of the IRP Regulations provides that

(3) [a]n officer shall not issue a work permit to a foreign worker if …

(e) the foreign national has engaged in unauthorized study or work in Canada or has failed to comply with a condition of a previous permit or authorization unless

(i) a period of six months has elapsed since the cessation of the unauthorized work or study or failure to comply with a condition.

Consider the following scenario:

Robert is working in Canada with a work permit and he is seeking an extension. Robert's work permit expired three weeks ago but he has continued to work in Canada. Robert did not intend to violate any conditions imposed on his work permit, but he thought that he would be receiving a reminder from CIC regarding the renewal.

What will Robert's status be if the CPC in Vegreville contacts Robert's employer and discovers that he was working after the work permit expired?

Robert may not be issued a new work permit unless a period of six months has elapsed from the date of the violation, according to the Act.

Furthermore, under s. 306 of the IRP Regulations, a completed application form IMM 1249 and a $200 restoration fee must be submitted to the Case Processing Centre in Vegreville. The restoration fee is in addition to the temporary resident visa fee, which must be paid again. The documents that must be submitted are the same as those listed above under the heading "Extension of a Temporary Resident Visa."

VISITOR CLASS

The visitor class is the simplest of the temporary resident classes. It includes tourists, vacationers, and family members and friends of Canadians who wish to come here for short periods of time. Tourists and vacationers contribute significantly to the Canadian economy, and it is important to welcome them with a minimum of red tape, while ensuring security and safety.

There are three types of visitor visas, as follows:

1. **Single-entry visa.** A single-entry visa allows a foreign national to enter Canada only once, usually only for six months. An exception exists for repeated entries into Canada from the United States or St. Pierre and Miquelon, provided that the foreign national does not enter another country.

2. **Multiple-entry visa.** A multiple entry visa allows a foreign national to enter Canada from another country multiple times during the validity of the visa. It may have a validity of up to five years.

3. **Transit visa.** A transit visa is required for travel through Canada to another country by anyone who would need a temporary resident visa to enter Canada and whose flight will stop here for less than 48 hours. The foreign national is required to show travel tickets.

The foreign national must satisfy the officer that he will comply with all the restrictions imposed on the visitor visa, such as not engaging in illegal work, according to s. 180 of the IRP Regulations. Generally, visitors are not allowed to work or study in Canada unless they are authorized to do so under the IRP Regulations. In many cases, a work or study permit is required.

However, there are categories of workers who do not require work permits to work in Canada. Similarly, in certain circumstances visitors are allowed to study in Canada without first obtaining a study permit. For example, a visitor may take a program of study up to six months in duration, without having to obtain a study permit.

Processing time guidelines suggest that foreign nationals should apply for a visitor visa at least one month before the intended departure date.

STUDENT CLASS

Consider the value of international students who bring with them new ideas and a global perspective. In 2007, 74,008 foreign students were admitted to Canada. One reason why studying in Canada may be an attractive option for the foreign student is the possibility of future permanent residence. For example, under the skilled worker class, an applicant receives credit for Canadian postsecondary education under the point system. To attract and retain foreign students, the minister of CIC unveiled a new program called the Canadian Experience Class, in September 2008. The program allows certain foreign students who are graduates of a Canadian postsecondary institution and possess professional, managerial, and skilled Canadian work experience to apply for permanent residence. The following sections consider the criteria and application process for foreign students.

WEBLINK

To learn how long it took to process Canadian visitor visas at visa offices around the world in 2007 (the year for which the most recent figures are available), go to the CIC website at www.cic.gc.ca/english/information/times/international/13-temp-visitors.asp.

Criteria for Entry

A foreign national who wishes to study in Canada must obtain a study permit unless she qualifies for an exemption (discussed below under the heading "Study Permit Exemptions"). A foreign national may be issued a study permit according to s. 216(1) of the IRP Regulations if an examination establishes that the foreign national meets the basic criteria applicable to all temporary resident applicants, as well as the criteria specific to students.

Visa officers look at many factors before deciding whether an applicant qualifies for a study permit. In addition to presenting the application form and basic documents that must be provided in support of all temporary resident visa applications, such as passport and travel documents (unless exempt), proof of immigration status, passport-size photos, and cost-recovery processing fee, applicants must also

- present a letter of acceptance from the educational institution where they intend to study;

- be able to pay the tuition fees for the course or program that they intend to pursue;

- be able to financially support themselves and any family members who are with them during their period of study;

- be able to cover the transportation cost for themselves and any family members to and from Canada;

- pass the CIC medical examination, if required;[8] and

- receive a Certificat d'acceptation du Québec (Quebec Certificate of Acceptance, or CAQ) if they intend to study in Quebec.

The **letter of acceptance** is a key document that must be included in the application. The following list of items, although not mandatory, should be included in the letter of acceptance to increase the chances of approval of the application:

- the full name, date of birth, and mailing address of the student;

- the course of study for which the student was accepted;

- the estimated duration or date of completion of the course;

- the date on which the selected course of study begins;

- the last date on which a student may register for a selected course;

- the academic year of study that the student will be entering;

- whether the course of study is full-time or part-time;

- the tuition fee;

- any conditions related to the acceptance or registration, such as academic prerequisites, completion of a previous degree, and proof of language competence;

- clear identification of the educational institution, usually confirmed through its letterhead; and

- where applicable, licensing information for private institutions, usually confirmed through letterhead.[9]

Not everybody is required to submit a letter of acceptance from an educational institution. For example, under s. 219(2)(a) of the IRP Regulations, accompanying family members of a student or a worker are exempt from the acceptance-letter requirement. Additionally, under ss. 219(2)(b) and 219(3), students whose study permits will expire in less than 90 days are not required to submit a letter of acceptance from an educational institution when applying for an extension. The extension may only be issued for a validity period of 90 days starting the day that the students receive written notification from their educational institutions of successful completion of their studies.

All applicants for study permits destined to a Quebec educational institution at the primary, secondary, college, or university level must obtain a Certificat d'acceptation du Québec issued by the Ministère des Relations avec les citoyens et de l'Immigration du Québec (MRCIQ) before being eligible for a study permit, even for part-time courses or for courses delivered by private institutions.

Because education is within the jurisdiction of each province, CIC makes it clear in its information guides to international students that it is up to the student to inquire about the quality of the schools in which they intend to enroll.

A study permit will not be issued for preschool, kindergarten, courses of general interest or self-improvement, distance learning courses, or audited courses attended without credit.

Application Documents

The following application documents are available online at www.cic.gc.ca/english/information/applications/student.asp:

- *Studying in Canada: Applying for a Study Permit Outside Canada* guide (IMM 5269)

- Application for a Study Permit Made Outside of Canada form (IMM 1294)

- Statutory Declaration of Common-Law Union form (IMM 5409), if applicable

- Use of a Representative form (IMM 5476), if applicable

- Document Checklist for a Study Permit form (IMM 5483).

Processing time guidelines suggest that foreign nationals should apply for a study permit at least one month before the intended departure date. In 2007 CIC was able to process 71 percent of applications within 28 days.

CIC announced a policy on April 18, 2005 that allows postsecondary international students to transfer between programs of study and institutions without applying for a change to the conditions of their study permit.

Consider the following case scenario:

Claudia from Costa Rica wishes to attend the University of Toronto to obtain a B.Sc. degree in mathematics. Claudia wishes to submit the minimum number of documents required in order to be issued her study permit.

The documents that must accompany Claudia's application for a study permit are proof of acceptance into the B.Sc. program at the University of Toronto, which is an accredited educational institution, a passport, because Costa Rica is no longer on the list of visa-exempt countries, and proof of funds to pay for the program and to support herself while in Canada.

Claudia changes her mind after beginning her studies at the University of Toronto. She now wants to conclude her degree in mathematics at the University of British Columbia but doesn't know whether she needs to apply for a change to the conditions of her study permit.

Claudia is permitted to continue studying because she will take the same degree at another accredited university.

Health Insurance

Although the issuance of the study permit does not require proof of private health insurance, student applicants must obtain private health insurance prior to arrival in Canada because provincial health insurance coverage varies depending on the province of destination. For example, Saskatchewan and the Northwest Territories extend immediate coverage to foreign students while British Columbia, Alberta, and Nova Scotia extend health coverage only after various waiting periods. For Quebec-destined students, health insurance may be a precondition to the issuance of the CAQ.

Place of Application

Some foreign nationals are permitted to apply for a student visa at a Canadian port of entry, such as United States nationals or persons who have been lawfully admitted to the United States for permanent residence, and residents of Greenland, St. Pierre, and Miquelon. Nevertheless, these foreign nationals must comply with the requirements applicable to the student class, pursuant to s. 216(1) of the IRP Regulations.

Temporary residents in Canada with a valid study permit must submit their applications for renewal or to change conditions on their study permit to CPC-V.

Study Permit Extensions

A foreign national may apply to CPC-V for the renewal of her study permit if the following conditions are met:

- the renewal application was made before the expiry of the current study permit (processing time guidelines suggest that the application for renewal should be made at least 30 days before the expiry date of the current study permit);

- all conditions imposed on entry into Canada have been complied with;

- the foreign national is in good standing at the educational institution, in accordance with s. 217(1) of the IRP Regulations; and

- the foreign national is in compliance with the eligibility criteria for a study permit pursuant to s. 216.

Because it may take some time to process a renewal, a foreign national is allowed to continue studying in Canada with an expired study permit if the following conditions are met:

- the renewal application was made before the expiry of the current study permit;

- the foreign national has remained in Canada since the expiry of the study permit; and

- the foreign national continues to comply with the conditions, other than the expiry date, set out on the expired study permit, in accordance with s. 189 of the IRP Regulations.

Consider the following case scenario:

Lara is an international student attending Seneca College in Toronto. Lara applied for the renewal of her study permit two weeks before it expired. Unfortunately, Lara has not yet received a decision regarding her application for renewal and her student visa has expired.

What would you advise Lara? Under ss. 186(u) and 189, Lara has implied status and has the right to continue studying under the same conditions as long as she remains in Canada. Consequently, the original study permit continues to be valid until a decision is made and Lara is notified (s. 183(5)).

Study Permit Exemptions

Not everyone is required to obtain a study permit in order to study in Canada. Foreign nationals are exempt from the requirement of a study permit if they fall under one of the following categories:

- family members and members of the private staff of diplomats or foreign accredited representatives (s. 188(1)(a) of the IRP Regulations);

- persons seeking to study a short-term program of study of six months or less (s. 188(1)(c)) unless they are seeking to work on campus;

- members of the armed forces of a country designated for the purposes of the *Visiting Forces Act*, even if they want to study for more than six months (s. 188(1)(b) of the IRP Regulations); or

- minor children in Canada, other than children of a temporary resident not authorized to work or study, who intend to study at the preschool, primary, or secondary level (s. 30(2) of the IRPA). However, it is important to clarify that minor children applying outside Canada do require a study permit.

Consider the following case scenario:

Carlos, a Mexican priest, has been granted temporary resident status for a period of one year for the purpose of assisting a congregation. During this time, Carlos would like to enroll in a four-month language-training course, and once completed, Carlos would like to engage in a four-month religious studies course.

Does Carlos require a study permit? Carlos may complete the two courses without a study permit, because each course of study is less than six months in duration and can be completed within the original period of stay authorized upon entry—namely, one year.

However, if Carlos wants to enroll in another short-term course of an additional four months, this would exceed the period of temporary resident status authorized upon entry. In that case, Carlos must apply for an extension of his temporary resident status. However, the reason for his request for an extension must be to continue assisting the congregation, and not for the purpose of completing the course. Carlos would likely be granted an extension of his temporary resident status and could then enroll in the short-term course without a study permit.

Study Permit Restrictions

A study permit is a written authorization issued to foreign students that authorizes them to engage in studies in Canada,[10] subject to certain restrictions. An officer may impose, vary, or cancel conditions on the study permit. These conditions may include one or more of the following:

- type of studies or course that the foreign national may take;

- educational institution that the foreign national may attend;

- location of studies;

- time and period of studies;

- time and place at which the foreign national shall report for medical examination or observation;

- time and place at which the foreign national shall report for the presentation of evidence in compliance with applicable conditions;

- duration of stay in Canada; or

- prohibition of engaging in employment, except for students attending an accredited educational institution on a full-time basis, who are in possession of a valid and subsisting study permit and who are allowed to work on campus without a work permit (s. 186(f) of the IRP Regulations).

Work for Foreign Students

Although CIC requires foreign students to arrive in Canada with sufficient funding for the duration of their study period, many students find the need to earn extra income. This need is recognized in the IRPA and IRP Regulations, which provide that foreign students may work while pursuing postsecondary education in Canada in certain circumstances. In some cases, a work permit is not required, as in the case of a student who works on campus. In others, a permit is required, as in the case of a student who works off campus or one who is enrolled in postgraduate studies or a co-op program. Each of these situations is discussed below.

WORK NOT REQUIRING A PERMIT (ON CAMPUS)

A foreign national in Canada on a valid study permit is authorized to work on campus without a work permit, provided that the student is enrolled full-time at a public or other authorized postsecondary institution, and that the student maintains full-time status at the institution (s. 186(f) of the IRP Regulations).

"On campus" is defined as the employment facilities within the boundaries of the campus. The student may only work on the campus of the educational institution at which she is registered. In the event that the school has more than one campus, the student may work at a different location, provided that it is within the same municipality. The student may not work at campuses outside of the municipality (s. 186(f) of the IRP Regulations).

Students working as graduate assistants, teaching assistants, or research assistants are considered to be within the scope of "on campus" employment, provided that the students have been recommended by officials of their department; the work to be performed is directed by a department head or a faculty member; and the work takes place in a research institute or program in an affiliated hospital or research unit.

Consider the following case scenario:

Sara has obtained a temporary resident visa and will visit Canada in September. Upon arriving, Sara wants to enroll in a five-month, full-time, postgraduate linguistics certificate program offered by Humber College. Sara also intends to work on campus to further assimilate the Canadian culture.

Recall that s. 188(1)(c) of the IRP Regulations states that a foreign national may study in Canada without a study permit if the duration of the program is six months or less. However, this exemption does not apply to a foreign national who wishes to work on campus. In the present case, Sara should be advised that although she does not need a study permit to study in the five-month course at Humber College, she does need a study permit to work on campus.

WORK REQUIRING A PERMIT (OFF CAMPUS)

There are two situations in which a foreign student may be eligible to work off campus, as follows:

1. *They have become destitute through circumstances beyond their control.* Students may apply for a work permit if, by reason of circumstances beyond their control, they become temporarily destitute

according to s. 208 of the IRP Regulations. Such circumstances may include war, upheaval, or collapse of the banking system in the home country.

2. These students may be granted an **open work permit**, which allows the student to work for any employer for a specific period of time. Usually, the time period coincides with the duration of the current term of study, rather than with the duration of the entire program or with the duration of the study permit.

3. *They are enrolled as full-time students at a postsecondary educational institution that participates in the Off-Campus Work Permit Program.* A student may apply for an off-campus work permit if the student is attending a publicly funded postsecondary institution that has signed an arrangement to participate in the program with its provincial or territorial government. The list of participating institutions can be found on the CIC website at www.cic.gc.ca/english/study/institutions/participants.asp.

These students are required to comply with the following criteria to qualify for an off-campus work permit. They must

- hold a valid study permit;

- be enrolled in a participating institution;

- have full-time student status for at least 6 months of the 12 months preceding the application for a work permit;

- have maintained satisfactory academic standing; and

- have signed a form authorizing the institution, the province, and CIC to share the student's personal information in order to confirm that the above criteria are met.[11]

Furthermore, students are not eligible to apply for a work permit under this program if they

- have a partial or full scholarship or award from the Canadian Commonwealth Scholarship Program, from the Government of Canada Awards Program funded by the Department of Foreign Affairs and International Trade (DFAIT), or from an award or internship program funded by the Canadian International Development Agency (CIDA);

- are registered in programs that consist either exclusively or primarily of an English-as-a-second-language or French-as-a-second-language (ESL/FSL) program;

- have completed their studies and are no longer considered as full time; or

- have previously held an off-campus work permit and failed to maintain their eligibility under the program or failed to comply with the terms and conditions of their work or study permit.[12]

Consider the following case scenarios:

Melissa is a student in the science and technology program at Capilano University in British Columbia. Melissa is interested in obtaining an off-campus work permit but is unsure when she will be eligible to submit her application. Melissa began full-time studies in September and continued through the end of February (with the exception of the Christmas break). During this time, she has maintained good grades.

Melissa will be eligible for a work permit in March because she has been enrolled in full-time studies from September to February, which equals six months, she continues to be enrolled in full-time studies, and she has maintained satisfactory academic standing at the time of her application.

Melissa's friend George, a fellow student at the university, is also interested in applying for an off-campus work permit, and he would like to know when he will be eligible to apply for a work permit. George was enrolled in full-time studies from January until the end of April. He took four months off for summer break, and resumed full-time studies in September.

George will not be eligible to apply for a work permit until he has completed a full six months of studies. George studied full time from January until the end of April, and then resumed full-time studies in September after taking a four-month break. George will be eligible to apply in November, because January to April equals four months, and September to October equals two months, which totals six months.

Students who have obtained a work permit may only work part time a maximum of 20 hours per week off campus while school is in session. Students are allowed to extend that to full-time work only when the school is in a scheduled break, such as winter or spring break.

However, the legislation does not prohibit students from working both 20 hours per week off campus and 20 hours per week on campus. This legislative oversight may threaten a student's ability to continue full-time studies and to maintain satisfactory academic standing as required to remain eligible for the program.[13]

WORK REQUIRING A PERMIT (POSTGRADUATE WORK PERMITS)

Foreign nationals currently in possession of a valid study permit and about to graduate from a postsecondary institution may apply for a postgraduate open work permit.[14] An open work permit enables the foreign national to seek and accept employment, and to work for any employer for a specified period of time. An open work permit also exempts the foreign national from the requirement of obtaining a confirmation from Human Resources and Social Development Canada (HRSDC), which is generally required to obtain a work permit. More information about open work permits and HRSDC is provided below under the heading "Worker Class."

A foreign national seeking to obtain a postgraduate work permit/open work permit must meet the following criteria:

- the student must have graduated from a postsecondary institution from a program of at least eight months' duration;

- the student must still be in possession of a valid study permit upon submission of a postgraduate work permit; and

- the application for a postgraduate work permit must be submitted within 90 days of receiving a written confirmation from the institution indicating that the academic program was successfully completed, such as a transcript or notice of graduation.

Careful consideration must be given to the transition from off-campus work permit to postgraduate work permit. If the study permit is set to expire within the 90-day period, the student must apply for a "bridging extension" to her valid study permit prior to applying for a postgraduate work permit. Once granted, the postgraduate work permit may be valid for a period not longer than that in which the graduating student studied at a Canadian postsecondary institution, and may not exceed three years.

Additionally, when a graduating student is in possession of a valid off-campus work permit, the student may continue to use this work permit in the 90 days following the date of graduation. This off-campus work permit may also be used to commence postgraduate work until the postgraduate work permit is issued.[15]

Once the one-year postgraduate work permit expires the student must apply for a Labour Market Opinion (also referred to as an LMO or HRSDC confirmation) to maintain work permit status. The LMO is discussed below under the heading "Worker Class."

WORK REQUIRING A PERMIT (CO-OP WORK PROGRAM)

Students whose work experience is an essential and integral component of their program of study may be eligible for a work permit under a co-op or internship program. To be eligible, the following conditions must be met:

- the student must be in possession of a valid study permit;

- the student's intended employment must be an essential part of the program of study in Canada;

- the employment must be certified as part of the academic program by a responsible academic official of the institution;

- the student's co-op or internship employment may not form more than 50 percent of the total program of study; and

- the student must not be a medical intern or extern, nor a resident physician (except in veterinary medicine).[16]

Note that international students, scholars, and scientists may also be eligible to obtain work permits for work related to a research, educational, or training program. These work permits are issued under specific programs funded by the Canadian International Development Agency, the International Development Research Centre of Canada (IDRC), Atomic Energy of Canada Ltd., the National Research Council of Canada (NRC), and the Natural Sciences and Engineering Research Council of Canada (NSERC).[17]

WORKER CLASS

Foreign workers contribute to Canada's economy by filling labour market shortages and boosting trade. We will focus on the normal eligibility requirements for a foreign national who wishes to work temporarily in Canada, including the process for vetting the job offer, and the responsibilities of Canadian employers. Finally, we describe the various foreign worker programs in Canada.

Under ss. 194 to 196 of the IRP Regulations, foreign nationals who wish to work temporarily in Canada are part of the worker class of temporary residents and are generally required to have a job offer and a work permit, unless exempt under s. 186. "Work" is defined under s. 2 of the IRP Regulations as "an activity for which wages are paid or commission is earned, or that is in direct competition with the activities of Canadian citizens or permanent residents in the Canadian labour market."

The temporary worker program relies on the cooperation of three departments, as follows:

- CIC (to, for example, process applications abroad);

- Human Resources and Social Development Canada (HRSDC), also known as Service Canada (to provide letters of confirmation to employers required by the foreign worker); and

- the Canada Border Services Agency (to conduct port of entry examinations).

Generally, a foreign national seeking to work in Canada is required to comply with a three-tier process involving each of these departments, as follows, in this order:

1. obtain an HRSDC confirmation from HRSDC;

2. obtain a work permit from CIC; and

3. enter Canada after an examination by a CBSA officer at the port of entry.

HRSDC Confirmation

The HRSDC's main responsibility is to provide an **HRSDC confirmation**, also known as a **Labour Market Opinion (LMO)**, regarding whether the issuance of a work permit to a foreign worker will have either a neutral or positive effect on Canada's economy. Several factors are considered, such as wages, working conditions, the availability of Canadians or permanent residents to do the work, and the skills and knowledge transfer and job creation that may result from employing a foreign worker. These factors are considered in more detail below under the heading "Factors."

Generally, Canadian employers who wish to employ a foreign worker must obtain an HRSDC confirmation from HRSDC before the foreign worker may apply for a work permit from CIC. There are, however, a number of important exemptions and special programs, explained later in this chapter, which may apply in particular industries or circumstances to permit circumvention of the requirement of obtaining an HRSDC confirmation.

FACTORS

Unless an exemption applies, the HRSDC considers several factors when assessing an employment offer, including the following:

1. *Verification of the employment offer.* Verification that the employment offer is genuine must be provided.

2. *Recruitment efforts.* The employer must demonstrate reasonable efforts to hire Canadians or permanent residents for the position, before offering it to a foreign worker. The onus is on the employer to prove that there were no Canadians available for the position, or that Canadian applicants could not be trained for the position in a reasonable amount of time.

3. *Union consultation.* All relevant unions and professional associations must be consulted with respect to the potential employment of a foreign worker, and letters of consent from them must be attached to the application for the LMO. Additionally, the employment of the foreign worker must not adversely affect the settlement of any labour dispute in progress or the employment of any person involved in that dispute.

4. *Job creation.* A position that is likely to help job creation or job retention for Canadian citizens or permanent residents has a greater chance of being approved.

5. *Transfer of skills.* Workers who are likely to transfer skills and knowledge for the benefit of Canadians or permanent residents are favoured.

6. *Labour shortages.* Consideration will be given to whether the worker is likely to fill a labour shortage in the Canadian market because of a skills shortage.

7. *Wages and working conditions.* The wages and working conditions offered must be sufficient to attract Canadian citizens or permanent residents, and retain them in that work. Jobs offering less than adequate remuneration will not be approved.

It is crucial that the submissions include information regarding the above factors, such as details about recruitment efforts and their results, and a detailed explanation of how the company would benefit from the foreign worker's employment—with respect to profitability, employee's skills, and positive spillover effects on Canadians.

OCCUPATIONS UNDER PRESSURE

In response to the need of Canadian employers to fill critical job shortages, the HRSDC has developed a regional list of **occupations under pressure** that makes it easier for employers to hire foreign workers for certain jobs. This list has been extended to seven regions of Canada: Alberta, British Columbia, Manitoba, Nova Scotia, Ontario, Prince Edward Island, and Quebec.

Employers seeking to hire workers for listed occupations are only required to conduct minimum advertising efforts rather than the more comprehensive recruitment efforts (two to three weeks) usually required. Employers are only required to advertise on the government of Canada's national Job Bank (or the equivalent in Saskatchewan, Quebec, or the Northwest Territories) for seven calendar days or demonstrate that they have ongoing recruitment mechanisms in place, by using recognized job Internet sites, unions, professional associations, corporate websites, professional journals, newspapers, or newsletters.

EXPEDITED PROCESSES

The application for an LMO can take anywhere from 2 to 25 weeks, depending on the jurisdiction. Therefore, it is incumbent on the immigration practitioner to be aware of the options for expediting the application process. In this section, we discuss the benefits of using three programs to expedite the process: the Expedited Labour Market Opinion Pilot Project for employers in British Columbia and Alberta, the pre-approval blanket LMO program for employers wishing to hire several foreign workers, and the concurrent processing initiative.

Expedited Labour Market Opinion Pilot Project

In British Columbia and Alberta, the processing of an HRSDC confirmation can take anywhere from 18 to 25 weeks. To address the long processing time, HRSDC created an **Expedited Labour Market Opinion Pilot Project** in 2007 to accelerate the application process for hiring temporary foreign workers in certain occupations in these provinces. The pilot project has since been expanded to include 33 occupations, as listed in the table below.[18]

carpenters (journeyman/woman)	manufacturing and processing labourers
civil engineers	mechanical engineers
commercial janitors, caretakers	mechanical engineering technologists
construction labourers	petroleum engineers
crane operators (journeyman/woman)	pharmacists
delivery drivers	registered nurses
dental technicians	residential cleaning and support workers
electrical and electronics engineers	retail salespersons and sales clerks
food and beverage servers	roofers
food counter attendants	ski and snowboard instructors
food service supervisors	specialized cleaners
heavy-duty equipment mechanics	steamfitters, pipefitters
hotel front desk clerks	surveyor helpers
hotel and hospitality room attendants	tour and travel guides
industrial electricians	welders
industrial meat cutters	machinists
ironworkers	

Employers in British Columbia and Alberta seeking to participate in this pilot project must have been in operation for a minimum of 12 consecutive months, and during the 12 months the employer must have employed at least one worker. Proof of the 12-month operation requirement may include the business's remittance forms from the Canada Revenue Agency for the past 12 months.

Employers who qualify to participate in the pilot project will receive an **Expedited Labour Market Opinion (E-LMO)** for any of the 33 occupations, provided that the chosen occupations are in line with the business activity. The employer must then submit an application form, including the employer's identification and access code that were provided in the E-LMO letter. This confirms for the HRSDC that the employer is eligible for the pilot project and expeditious processing.

Under this pilot project, employers are required to comply with the usual requirements pertaining to advertising, employment conditions, and wages.

Pre-approval Blanket LMO Program

HRSDC has instituted a **pre-approval blanket LMO program**, allowing employers who wish to ultimately hire several foreign workers for the same type of position to obtain a **blanket LMO**. A blanket LMO is an "approval in principle" that HRSDC issues to an employer so that the employer can recruit foreign workers, knowing that once suitable workers are found, a positive LMO will be issued. This program is an obvious benefit to large companies with multiple hiring needs.

To acquire a blanket approval, the employer must submit an ordinary application form, but clearly indicate that it is making a request for pre-approval. Information about the foreign workers is left out, as they have not yet been recruited. Once approved, the employer recruits foreign workers and provides their information to HRSDC. A positive LMO is issued to each successfully recruited worker. The foreign worker must then submit an application for a work permit to CIC.

Concurrent Processing Initiative

The **concurrent processing initiative** became available in August 2006. It permits Canadian visa officers in offices outside Canada to start the processing of a foreign worker's work permit application while the LMO is pending. The foreign worker must satisfy the concurrent processing eligibility criteria, including the requirements that

- the foreign worker's job is listed in the HRSDC's National Occupational Classification (NOC) system at the O, A, or B level; and

- the foreign worker is applying for a work permit at a Canadian visa office outside Canada.

A foreign worker who wishes to be considered under this initiative must

1. apply for a temporary work permit with all the supporting documentation, save for the LMO;

2. indicate awareness of the need to obtain a positive LMO, and provide proof that an application for an LMO has been submitted to HRSDC by the employer;

3. submit a copy of the offer of employment or employment contract, indicating the proposed duration and conditions of employment;

4. appear to be credible, and satisfy the requirements of the offer of employment, and meet other requirements as applicable; and

5. pay the application processing fee.[19]

The CPC in Vegreville employs a similar, though informal, policy to not refuse an application for a work permit where the LMO is pending if there is evidence that the employer acted in a diligent manner when applying for the LMO within a reasonable time prior to the expiry of the foreign employee's current work permit.

Before employers consider the concurrent processing alternative, they should be aware that if CIC has not received the LMO within 90 days of the date of the letter accompanying the instructions for medical examinations, the visa officer will refuse the foreign worker's application. Therefore, if a significant period of time has elapsed (60 days) since the application for a work permit was submitted to CIC and the LMO is still pending, it may be wise to follow up with HRSDC to inquire about how much longer it will likely take to obtain a determination. In light of this restriction, concurrent processing may not be feasible in jurisdictions where the processing for an LMO is lengthy.

Furthermore, the concurrent processing initiative is not available for the Live-In Caregiver Program, the Seasonal Agricultural Worker Program, or the Low Skill Pilot Project, each of which is discussed in the next section.

Exemptions and Special Programs

Under ss. 204 to 208 of the IRP Regulations, certain jobs and work categories do not require an HRSDC confirmation, and others are included in special programs that make acquiring the HRSDC confirmation much quicker. Whenever possible, the Canadian employer should seek an exemption from HRSDC approval, or an appropriate special program, as the HRSDC process may be lengthy and there is no assurance of success.

Some of the strategies available to foreign workers to circumvent the time-consuming need for an LMO are discussed below.

ACADEMICS PROGRAM

HRSDC and CIC, in cooperation with universities, degree-granting colleges, and unions representing Canadian academics, set out the criteria for the academics program. It was created with the purpose of assisting degree-granting, postsecondary educational institutions in Canada to meet their staffing and teaching needs by seeking internationally the best-qualified and most suitable candidates for full-time academic staff positions.

Prior to the hiring of a foreign academic for a position in Canada, the institution must meet the following criteria:

- advertise vacant positions in Canada;

- advertise the position for a month to allow broad exposure of the vacancy to Canadians and permanent residents;

- ensure that any vacant position advertised abroad is also advertised simultaneously in Canada;

- demonstrate that the advertising medium used—Internet, print, or electronic—is effective in attracting appropriate candidates for the position;

- include in the advertisement the following: "All qualified candidates are encouraged to apply; however, Canadians and permanent residents will be given priority";

- meet all conditions of applicable collective agreements;

- complete the Foreign Academic Recruitment Summary outlining the educational institution's hiring decision and providing summaries of Canadian applicants verified by the vice-president or other senior academic official of the educational institution; and

- complete a yearly summary report on recruitment practices for Canadian academics and results.[20]

The academics program does not extend to community colleges unless they are affiliated with a university and their students are able to obtain degrees, nor does it apply to the Collèges d'enseignement général et professionnel (Cégep) in Quebec.

The IRPA includes a variety of foreign academics who, while required to obtain a work permit, are exempt from obtaining an LMO, as follows:

- post-doctoral fellows and research award recipients;

- leaders in various fields;

- guest lecturers and visiting professors;

- citizens of the United States and Mexico appointed as professors under the university, college, and seminary levels of the North American Free Trade Agreement (NAFTA); and

- citizens of Chile appointed as professors under the Canada–Chile Free Trade Agreement.[21]

Additionally, the following foreign academics are exempt from obtaining both an LMO and a work permit:

- academic consultants and examiners, provided that they are eminent individuals seeking entry to evaluate academic programs or research proposals;

- graduate assistants, provided that they are considered to be within the scope of on-campus employment; and

- self-funded researchers, provided that they comply with the business visitor's criteria.

SEASONAL AGRICULTURAL WORKER PROGRAM

The **Seasonal Agricultural Worker Program (SAWP)** permits the entry of foreign nationals to work in the agricultural sector in Canada. SAWP was developed by HRSDC and CIC in cooperation with agricultural producers and a number of foreign countries including Mexico and several Commonwealth Caribbean countries.[22]

SAWP currently operates in British Columbia, Alberta, Saskatchewan, Manitoba, Ontario, Quebec, New Brunswick, Nova Scotia, and Prince Edward Island, and meets the needs of specific agricultural commodity sectors.

Prior to hiring a foreign worker under SAWP, a Canadian employer must meet the following criteria:

- demonstrate efforts to hire Canadian agricultural workers or unemployed Canadians through HRSDC and provincial employment programs;

- prepare a human resources plan explaining the efforts to find Canadian workers, eight weeks before the start of the work;

- offer the foreign worker the same wages paid to Canadian agricultural workers doing the same work;

- pay for the foreign worker's airfare to and from Canada (a portion of this cost can be recovered through payroll deductions);

- provide free seasonal housing to the foreign worker that has been approved by the appropriate provincial/municipal body;

- pay the immigration visa cost-recovery fee for the worker (this fee or a portion of this fee can be recovered through payroll deductions);

- ensure that the foreign worker is covered by workers' compensation;

- ensure that the foreign worker is covered under private or provincial health insurance during his stay in Canada; and

- sign an employment contract outlining wages, duties, and conditions related to the transportation, accommodation, health, and occupational safety of the foreign worker.[23]

CIC will issue a work permit of no more than eight months, provided that the foreign worker meets the work permit's eligibility criteria pursuant to s. 200 of the IRP Regulations.

INFORMATION TECHNOLOGY WORKERS PILOT PROJECT

In response to the pressing need of Canadian employers to fill significant shortages in the software industry, CIC collaborated with HRSDC, Industry Canada, and the Software Human Resource Council on the development of a pilot project to simplify the entry of foreign workers in the software industry.

Under this pilot project, no confirmation letter from HRSDC is required and the applicant's work permit application may be processed more quickly, provided that the applicant's entry into the Canadian labour market would have no negative impact on Canadian job seekers and the applicant is offered a job in one of the following seven occupations:

- Senior Animation Effects Editor (NOC 9990.1)

- Embedded Systems Software Designer (NOC 9990.2)

- MIS Software Designer (NOC 9990.3)

- Multimedia Software Developer (NOC 9990.4)

- Software Developer—Services (NOC 9990.5)

- Software Products Developer (NOC 9990.6)

- Telecommunications Software Designer (NOC 9990.7).[24]

Applicants who hold a bachelor's degree need not have taken a program in information technology—a bachelor's degree in any field is acceptable. In the event that the applicant holds a college diploma or certificate, the course of study must contain a computing element. Applicants are also required to have a minimum of two years of relevant work experience and must have a sufficient level of English or French proficiency to carry out their work duties.

To be accepted into the pilot project, employers must offer acceptable wages. Information on wages and salaries is available on the Service Canada Labour Market Information website at www.labourmarketinformation.ca, and information on job description requirements is available on the National Occupational Classification website at www5.hrsdc.gc.ca/noc-cnp/app/index.aspx.

Consider the following scenario:

ABC Company, a provider of information technology consulting services, wishes to hire Yousef, an Egyptian national, as an "information technology solutions consultant." Yousef speaks and writes English well. He has a bachelor's degree that is equivalent to a similar degree from a recognized university in Canada. Additionally, Yousef has more than six years of experience working with a wide variety of computer operating systems, computer languages, and computer database programs.

Should Yousef apply for a work permit under the Information Technology Workers pilot project? Yes. Yousef meets all of the requirements to qualify as a Software Products Developer under the pilot project, which exempts him from obtaining an HRSDC confirmation. Yousef may be granted a work permit from CIC, provided that he meets the work permit's eligibility criteria pursuant to s. 200 of the IRP Regulations.

Consider another scenario:

Kevin, a British national, is a specialized programmer of tool and die machines. He received a job offer from a Canadian company that is looking to fill a labour shortage in its workforce. The company has submitted an application to HRSDC. In its application, the company has documented the labour shortage in Canada and described its employment offer, which is consistent with Canadian standards and wage rates. Additionally, the company has argued that Kevin's recruitment will result in the transfer of new skills and knowledge to the Canadian market and labour force that will enable it to hire and train additional Canadian workers.

Unfortunately, Kevin is criminally inadmissible to Canada, because he was convicted of a crime two days after the employer submitted the application to HRSDC.

In the above scenario, would HRSDC refuse the employer's application? The employer's application to HRSDC will most likely be approved, provided that the hiring of Kevin will not adversely affect the settlement of any labour dispute in progress.

However, the inadmissibility of Kevin, as a foreign worker, to Canada on criminal grounds may result in a refusal of his work permit. It is important to understand that HRSDC's role is to review the proposed wages and working conditions, the availability of Canadians or permanent residents to do the work in question, the skills and knowledge transfer, and the job creation for the benefit of Canadians or permanent residents that may result from confirming the employment of a foreign worker. Assessing an applicant's inadmissibility is outside the scope of the HRSDC's official duties.

LOW SKILL PILOT PROJECT

In July 2002, HRSDC introduced the Pilot Project for Occupations Requiring Lower Levels of Formal Training (NOC C and D), also known as the **Low Skill Pilot Project**. The main objective of the Low Skill Pilot Project is to meet the labour market demand for temporary foreign workers in jobs that are listed in parts C and D of the National Occupational Classification, which includes labourers, cleaners, cashiers, and drivers.

Foreign workers must have at least a high school diploma or two years of job-specific training to qualify under the Low Skill Pilot Project, while employers must agree to do the following in order to qualify:

- pay the full transportation costs for the foreign worker to and from the country of origin;

- cover all recruitment costs related to hiring the foreign worker;

- ensure that affordable and suitable accommodation is available for the foreign worker;

- provide temporary medical insurance coverage for the duration of the employment;

- register the foreign worker with the provincial workers' compensation/ workplace safety insurance plan;

- sign an employment contract; and

- demonstrate continued efforts to recruit and train Canadian workers.[25]

Under the Low Skill Pilot Project, the maximum duration of the LMO is restricted to 24 months, and the work permit is issued for the same period as the LMO. Additionally, the pilot project specifies that at the end of the authorized period of stay, the foreign worker is required to return to the country of origin for at least four months before applying for another work permit under the pilot project. In other words, the worker may stay and work in Canada for two years, then must return home for four months, then may work in Canada again for a further two years, and so on.

There is no prohibition against spouses and dependent children accompanying a foreign worker to Canada for the 24 months of work; however, questions may be raised about the applicant's bona fides and ability to support dependants while in Canada. Furthermore, spouses of workers admitted under the pilot project are not eligible for an open work permit and children may be required to pay international student rates to attend school.

SIGNIFICANT BENEFIT

Consistent with ss. 204 to 208 of the IRP Regulations, senior managers, executives, and individuals with specialized knowledge may apply for a work permit without having first obtained an HRSDC confirmation, provided that their presence in Canada will result or is likely to result in a **significant benefit** to Canada. The meaning of significant equates to important or notable.

When assessing requests for work permits based on significant social or cultural benefits, immigration officers are required to consider the impact that the foreign worker would have on Canada's labour market and economy. If an individual's work in Canada is likely to produce a significant social or cultural benefit, then "the balance of practical considerations argues for the issuance of a work permit in a time frame shorter than would be necessary to obtain an HRSDC opinion."[26]

Officers rely on the following objective measures when assessing whether a foreign worker's presence in Canada will result in a significant social or cultural benefit:

- the foreign worker's degree;

- whether the foreign worker has significant full-time experience in the occupation sought (ten or more years of experience);

- awards and accolades conferred upon the foreign worker;

- membership in organizations requiring excellence of its members;

- whether the foreign worker has judged or critiqued others' work in the field of specialty;

- scientific or scholarly contributions in the field; and

- publications authored by the foreign national in academic or industry publications.

INTRA-COMPANY TRANSFERS

The **intra-company transfer** category was designed to assist multinational businesses to move executives temporarily, when required for business purposes. It applies to executives who would not necessarily provide a significant benefit to the social, cultural, or economic threads of Canadian life, and therefore would not qualify under the significant benefit category.

The intra-company transfer category permits "international companies to temporarily transfer qualified employees to Canada for the purpose of improving management effectiveness, expanding Canadian exports, and enhancing the competitiveness of Canadian entities in overseas markets."[27] In other words, the admission of an intra-company transferee to Canada is subject to the relationship between the Canadian and foreign company. The intra-company transferee will be admitted with the purpose of assisting in the operations of a foreign company's Canadian parent, subsidiary, branch, or affiliate company.

To qualify as an intra-company transferee exempt from obtaining an LMO, a foreign worker must

- seek entry to undertake employment in Canada for a multi-national business that is or will be doing business in both Canada and in the foreign country;[28]

- assume a position in an executive, senior managerial, or specialized knowledge capacity;

- have been employed in a similar full-time position for a minimum of one year in the three years prior to coming to Canada; and

- comply with all immigration requirements for temporary entry.

Additionally, the foreign worker must submit the following documentation:

- confirmation of her continuous employment (full time, not accumulated part time) with the enterprise outside Canada for one year within the three-year period immediately preceding the date of application;

- an outline of her position in an executive or managerial capacity or one involving specialized knowledge, including title, place in the organization, and job description;

- an outline of her position in Canada, including title, place in the organization, and job description;

- in the case of a foreign national possessing "specialized knowledge," evidence that the person has such knowledge and that the position in Canada requires it;

- an indication of her intended duration of stay; and

- a description of the relationship between the enterprise in Canada and the enterprise in the foreign country, and, upon request, evidence of this, such as annual reports, articles of incorporation, financial statements, partnership agreements, and business tax returns.

There are no restrictions on which country the foreign executive is from. Consider the following scenario:

Ernesto, an Italian executive with San Pelligrani, a renowned bottled-beverage company, is being transferred to run San Pelligrani's Canadian subsidiary. The company relationship qualifies San Pelligrani under the affiliate definition in the intra-company transfer category. The Canadian office employs 350 people.

Ernesto has worked as an executive with San Pelligrani in Italy for the last 15 years. He is in good health and has no criminal record. Ernesto would like to submit the bare minimum in documentation for the intra-company transfer work permit application.

Ernesto's application requires only a company support letter and the fees for the work permit. The letter from the foreign company is crucial as it will support the fact that Ernesto has come from an executive position; that he will be moving into a similar role in the Canadian office; and that the corporate relationship between the foreign entity and the Canadian entity exists and complies with the IRP Regulations.

As was discussed earlier, HRSDC confirmation is not needed because intra-company transferees in the executive category do not require HRSDC approval. Rather, they are confirmation-exempt per s. 205 of the IRP Regulations. A copy of the applicant's university degree is also unnecessary because the educational background of the applicant in the executive transfer category is not required. Indeed, the executive need not have graduated from high school. Rather, he must hold an executive position in the company abroad, be coming to occupy an executive position in the Canadian affiliate, and have worked for the company for at least one year in the past three years in an executive or senior managerial role.

Executives and senior managers are permitted to renew their initial intra-company transfer work permits up to a maximum of seven years. Specialized knowledge workers may renew their work permits up to a maximum of five years. After the maximum period is reached, the foreign worker must leave Canada and the Canadian labour market for at least one year. When the year is over, the foreign worker may reapply and begin the cycle again.

Mergers and Acquisitions

If the multinational company that employs the foreign worker is subject to a corporate merger or acquisition,[29] the corporate relationship between the foreign business and the Canadian business may be affected. Because this is a critical component of the foreign worker's eligibility under this category, a merger or acquisition may have consequences for a foreign worker who currently possesses a work permit under the intra-company transfer category.

If it can be established that a qualifying relationship between the foreign and Canadian businesses[30] continues to exist, even though there have been changes in ownership internally, the foreign worker may still qualify as an intra-company transferee. The Canadian company need only document the corporate restructuring with CIC. This would be the case if the foreign and Canadian companies remained related through a common parent company, which held the shares of both subsidiaries.

However, if the entities no longer meet the requirements for this relationship, then any foreign intra-company transferee currently working for the Canadian entity would not qualify to continue working for the new entity. The foreign worker will be required to either obtain a new work permit under another HRSDC-exempt category (if possible) or obtain an HRSDC confirmation in order to obtain a work permit. Foreign workers must address the issue as soon as possible with CIC to avoid any risk of misrepresentation and, in a worst-case scenario, risk of the foreign worker being barred from entry to Canada.

Where the employee's position has changed only in name, but all other duties remain the same, eligibility for a work permit is not affected. An amendment of the work permit may be all that is needed. However, where the responsibilities have changed, eligibility may require reassessment. The foreign worker must be in an executive, senior managerial, or specialized knowledge position to continue qualifying for the intra-company transfer work permit. If the foreign worker's job description has changed such that she is no longer eligible, an application must be made for a new work permit.

Consider the following scenario:

> *Robert holds a work permit as an intra-company transferee. Because of a merger transaction, Robert's position changed, but the description of his duties remains the same. The merger transaction did not affect the corporate relationship between the Canadian entity and the foreign entity.*

Robert's eligibility is not affected; however, he should seek an amendment to the work permit to reflect the change.

Finally, in all cases it is important to assess whether the corporate relationship between the Canadian entity and foreign entity continues to be valid. Is the Canadian employer still doing business, either directly or through a parent, branch, affiliate, or subsidiary, in another country to which the employee can reasonably be expected to be transferred at the end of their assignment in Canada?

INTERNATIONAL AGREEMENT

A foreign national may be issued a work permit without an LMO to perform work in Canada pursuant to an international agreement between Canada and one or more countries, according to s. 204 of the IRP Regulations. Among the international agreements to which Canada is signatory are the North American Free Trade Agreement and the General Agreement on Trade in Services (GATS).

NAFTA

The North American Free Trade Agreement, arguably the most important agreement for those practising US and Canadian immigration law, was created to facilitate trade among its three signatory countries: Canada, the United States, and Mexico. NAFTA facilitates trade as well as the movement of persons involved in the trade of goods or services. Business people covered by NAFTA are not required to obtain an LMO and can gain quicker, easier temporary entry into Canada.

NAFTA covers three categories of foreign workers: business visitors, professionals, and intra-company transferees. It is important not to confuse "intra-company transfer," a category discussed earlier, with the intra-company transferee category under NAFTA, which applies only to citizens of Mexico and the United States.

From a Canadian immigration perspective, a **business visitor** under NAFTA refers to citizens of the United States or Mexico who seek to engage in international business activities related to research and design; growth, manufacturing, and production; marketing; sales; distribution; after-sales service; and general service.[31] Because business visitors are restricted from entering the Canadian labour market and their primary source of remuneration must remain outside Canada, they are not required to obtain an LMO or a work permit. However, business visitors must apply at the port of entry for a visitor's record and must comply with the usual admissibility requirements for temporary entry.

A **professional** under NAFTA refers to a citizen of the United States or Mexico who has pre-arranged employment[32] with a Canadian employer and whose occupation is listed in the 60-plus occupations/professions covered by NAFTA, such as accountants, computer systems analysts, engineers, management consultants, and technical writers. Professionals must be qualified to work, as evidenced by degrees, diplomas, professional licences, accreditation or registration, and must comply with existing immigration requirements for temporary entry.

The professional must be qualified to provide professional services in Canada; therefore, both the qualifications of the individual and the position in Canada must be considered. For example, a lawyer must be seeking to enter Canada as a lawyer and not as a paralegal. Alternatively, a paralegal cannot be admitted to work as a lawyer unless the applicant is also qualified as a lawyer as indicated in the Minimum Education Requirements and Alternative Credentials list in appendix 1603.D.1 of NAFTA.

Additionally, an individual must be seeking to enter Canada to work in a position for which he possesses the required qualifications. For example, a physiotherapist cannot be admitted to Canada to be a corporate executive, because physiotherapy is not his field of qualification.

The list of Minimum Education Requirements and Alternative Credentials provides more than 60 professions and their equivalent minimum educational requirements and alternative credentials to assess the qualifications of foreign professionals.[33]

On initial entry, the professional is given work permit status for a maximum duration of one year. Extensions are also issued for up to one year, provided that the individual continues to comply with the requirements for professionals.

The professional category does not allow self-employment in Canada. However, responding to unsolicited inquiries about services that the professional may be able to perform, or establishing an office from which to deliver pre-arranged services to clients, does not constitute self-employment.

The **intra-company transferee** is the third category under NAFTA. As mentioned previously, it is different from the intra-company transfer category under the IRPA because it applies only to citizens of Mexico and the United States (whereas that category under the IRPA applies to foreign nationals from any country). However, because of the harmonization of IRPA and NAFTA provisions, there are now no differences in entry requirements and work permit durations.

Citizens of the United States or Mexico whose employment pertains to an executive or managerial capacity or one involving specialized knowledge for an enterprise in the United States or Mexico that has a parent, branch, subsidiary, or affiliate relationship with a Canadian company may qualify. The executive is required to have been continuously employed in a similar position outside Canada for one year in the previous three-year period. Like all other visitors, intra-company transferees must also comply with existing immigration requirements for temporary entry.

Consider the following scenario:

Ricardo, a Mexican citizen, arrives at a Canadian port of entry to apply for a work permit. On arrival he advises the CBSA officer that he has been offered employment by the Canadian subsidiary of a Mexican company where he worked as a senior marketing manager from May 2007 until he left approximately two months ago.

Ricardo may be granted a work permit because he qualifies as a NAFTA intra-company transferee pursuant to LMO exemption CEC T24 under s. 204(a)(i) of the IRP Regulations. Ricardo is a Mexican citizen who has worked for the Mexican parent company in a managerial capacity for more than one year in the three-year period preceding the presentation of his application for adjudication.

Both professionals and intra-company transferees may alternatively be admitted under the general service provision of the business visitor category, if they are not seeking to enter the Canadian labour market and their primary source of remuneration remains outside Canada—in other words, if they meet the business visitor criteria.

GATS

The General Agreement on Trade in Services is similar to NAFTA in several respects, including the categories under which a foreign worker may apply and the fact that such categories are HRSDC-exempt.

Under GATS, each of the 153 member nations has made individual commitments concerning trade in services. Additionally, GATS has set out unique rules for the entry of professionals.

A **GATS professional** refers to a person who seeks to engage in an activity at a professional level in a designated profession, and meets the following criteria. A GATS professional must

WEBLINK

As of July 23, 2008 the World Trade Organization website listed 153 member nations. The current list of member nations is available at www.wto.org/english/ thewto_e/whatis _e/tif_e/org6_e.htm.

- possess citizenship of a member nation, or the right of permanent residence in Australia or New Zealand;

- have an occupation that falls within the definition of an eligible GATS profession;

- work as part of a short-term services contract obtained by a company in another member nation; and

- have the necessary academic credentials and professional qualifications, which have been duly recognized, where appropriate, by the professional association in Canada.[34]

The list of GATS professional occupations and their equivalent requirements can be found in appendix D of "FW 1: Foreign Worker Manual" in the CIC operations manual *Temporary Foreign Workers Guidelines (FW)*.[35]

GATS professionals are not permitted to work in service sectors that relate to education, health services, culture, and sports services. Visas are restricted to a maximum duration of 90 days; thus, extensions beyond the 90 days are not permitted under the GATS professional category.[36]

THE LIVE-IN CAREGIVER PROGRAM

The Live-In Caregiver Program (LCP) applies to the care of children aged 18 or under, an elderly person aged 65 or older, or a person with a disability.

The LCP was introduced to address the shortage of live-in care workers in Canada. It is important to distinguish the LCP from other categories of persons who may perform a domestic or caregiving function, such as the following:

- *Participants in an international youth exchange program.* This is a reciprocal exchange program that enables youth to engage in short-term work or study activities in Canada. Participants may find work as a nanny or mother's helper.

- *Diplomatic staff.* Employees of diplomatic staff, such as domestic workers, may enter Canada as accredited members of a diplomat's suite.

These categories are not part of the LCP; therefore, the persons who apply under them are not eligible to apply for permanent residence in Canada.

The HRSDC requirements for the LCP, which must be met by the employer, and the CIC and CBSA requirements, which must be met by the foreign worker, are outlined below.

HRSDC Requirements

The LCP applies only to caregivers who live in the home of the person cared for. This is so even if the home is not the employer's residence. For example, an employer may hire a live-in caregiver to look after an elderly parent who lives at a separate address. It is also possible for a live-in caregiver to reside in two different locations in circumstances where the caregiver will care for a child whose parents share custody. In this instance, both locations should be disclosed to HRSDC. It is also acceptable under the LCP for one parent to act as the employer even though the children live with the other parent.

To obtain an HRSDC confirmation, an employer must satisfy the following requirements:

- submit a Foreign Live-In Caregiver Application form (EMP 5093 for Ontario and EMP 5198 for British Columbia);

- submit the employment contract, signed by the employer and live-in caregiver;

- offer prevailing wage rates and acceptable working conditions (see the table below);

- show proof of adequate recruiting efforts in Canada before making a job offer, unless exempted (see the table below);

- provide the live-in caregiver with suitable accommodation in a private home at the same location as the person being cared for, including a private and furnished room; and

- employ the live-in caregiver on a full-time basis.

Quebec employers must apply for a Certificat d'acceptation du Québec (Quebec Certificate of Acceptance, or CAQ) from the Ministère de l'Immigration et des Communautés culturelles in addition to applying for a labour market opinion. British Columbia employers must register with the provincial government in addition to applying for a labour market opinion.

The following table sets out the minimum standards for wages and working conditions, and describes the advertising requirements in each province.

Regional Wages, Working Conditions, and Advertisement Requirements for the Live-In Caregiver Program (LCP)

Region	Prevailing wage	Maximum hours	Room and board	Advertising requirements
Alberta	$9.17 per hour $9.62 per hour as of October 1, 2008	44 hours per week Must pay for 44 hours per week	$73.85 per week $320 per month $336 per month as of October 2008	None
British Columbia	$8 per hour	40 hours week	$75 per week $325 per month	None
Manitoba	$8.75 per hour $9.30 per hour as of September 1, 2008	8 hours per day or 40 hours per week Hours worked beyond standard hours are considered overtime and compensated at 150 percent of the regular wage rate	Maximum combined deductions: $50 per week or $200 per month Meals not taken cannot be deducted Deductions cannot lower minimum wage by more than $1.00 for each meal and $7.00 per week for room	Major local newspaper for one weekend (*Winnipeg Free Press* or *Winnipeg Sun*) and one week in the Job Bank
New Brunswick	$7.75 per hour	44 hours per week	Allowed but wages cannot be below provincial minimum wages	Local newspaper or Job Bank
Newfoundland and Labrador	$8.00 per hour	40 hours per week	"Reasonable" rental charges for room	At least one advertisement in a province-wide newspaper (i.e., the *Evening Telegram*, Saturday edition) and two weeks' advertisement in the Job Bank
Nova Scotia	$8.10 per hour	No provisions Overtime to be paid after 48 hours of work	$65 per week	One week in the Job Bank Advertisement must include wages, working conditions, and room and board if they are to be charged to the worker
Ontario	$9.25 per hour	48 hours per week	$369.42 per month	None
Prince Edward Island	$7.75 per hour $8.00 per hour as of October 1, 2008	48 hours per week	$45 per week Meals not taken cannot be deducted	Two weeks in the Job Bank
Quebec	$8.50 per hour	40 hours per week	No deduction allowed for room and board	None
Saskatchewan	$9.50 per hour	40 hours per week	$250 per month	None
Northwest Territories	$9.68 per hour $10.16 per hour as of October 1, 2008	44 hours per week	$400 per month $420 per month as of October 1, 2008	None

Region	Prevailing wage	Maximum hours	Room and board	Advertising requirements
Nunavut	$9.68 per hour $10.16 as of October 1, 2008	44 hours per week	$400 per month $420 as of October 1, 2008	None
Yukon	$8.37 per hour	44 hours per week	$152 per month	None

Source: Adapted from Human Resources and Social Development Canada, "Regional Wages, Working Conditions and Advertisement Requirements for the Live-In Caregiver Program (LCP), July 29, 2008, www.hrsdc.gc.ca/en/workplaceskills/ foreign_workers/advertreq/wageadreq.shtml#tphp.

In most provinces an employer is required to advertise the live-in caregiver position to find qualified Canadians or permanent residents. Advertisement in newspapers is not the only type of acceptable recruitment available—also valid are flyers, networking, recruitment agencies, friends, and local and ethnic newspapers. If an employer has published an ad in a language other than English or French, a translation should be enclosed with the LMO application.

An employer is permitted to seek candidates who possess desired skills, such as the ability to speak in a language other than English or French, or to cook. However, such preferences are not weighted by the officer when assessing an application under the live-in caregiver program.

Live-in caregivers must obey the restrictions imposed by the LCP. For example, a live-in caregiver may not work for more than one employer at a time. Additionally, a live-in caregiver may not work for a health agency or labour contractor, or in day-care or foster care.

It is acceptable for an employer to make an offer of employment to a live-in caregiver for less than 12 months. However, if this is the case, the employer will most likely be contacted by HRSDC to find out why, because CIC generally issues a minimum duration of one year for the work permit.

In the event that the live-in caregiver changes employers, the new employer must obtain a new HRSDC confirmation, the new employer and live-in caregiver must sign an employment contract, and the live-in caregiver must apply for a new work permit.

CIC Requirements

The CIC criteria, including educational, training, and language requirements, must be met by foreign live-in caregivers seeking to qualify for the Live-In Caregiver Program. Specifically, the requirements for applicants who wish to work outside of Quebec are as follows:

1. *Educational requirement.* Successful completion of the equivalent of Canadian secondary school.

2. *Training/work experience requirement.* Either the training requirement or the work experience requirement below:

   - Training requirement—successful completion of six months of full-time classroom training in the field or occupation related to the job in question. (Full time is considered at least 25 to 30 hours per week of educational instruction.) Additionally, the training must be in a classroom setting; therefore, correspondence courses are not acceptable.

- ■ Work experience requirement—completion of at least 12 months of full-time paid employment, including at least six months of continuous employment with one employer, in the related field or occupation (for example, in a daycare, hospital, or senior citizen home), within three years immediately prior to the day on which the person submits an application for a work permit to a visa office.

3. *Language proficiency requirement.* The ability to read, listen, and speak English or French at a level sufficient to communicate effectively in an unsupervised setting, such as to respond to emergency situations by contacting a doctor, an ambulance, the police, or the fire department, answer the door and the telephone, and administer medication. In the event that the officer is not convinced that the applicant has sufficient language proficiency, the officer may request an interview.

4. *Mandatory employment contract.* The employer must forward the original employment contract to the live-in caregiver. The contract must be signed by the employer (not by the employer's representative or another employee on behalf of the employer) and by the live-in caregiver. Furthermore, the employment contract must be consistent with provincial employment standards.

Live-in caregivers seeking to work in Quebec need only 6 months of work experience in the related occupation, as opposed to the 12 months of experience outlined above. However, the live-in caregiver is required to obtain a Quebec Certificate of Acceptance before applying for the work permit, and the employer is required to facilitate access to French courses outside regular working hours.

Consider the following case scenario:

Maria, a Filipino national, is seeking to apply for a work permit under the LCP. Maria has obtained a job in Canada as a live-in caregiver to care for a Canadian employer's two minor children. The employer has obtained the required HRSDC confirmation.

Maria would like to know whether she is eligible to obtain a work permit under the LCP. Maria has 17 years of work experience as a caregiver taking care of her own three children at home. She has a high level of English proficiency and has completed a high school program.

Would Maria qualify for a work permit? Unfortunately for Maria, her work experience does not comply with the requirements set out by the LCP, because her work experience is not paid work experience. Although there may be situations where the applicant is employed as a live-in caregiver by a relative, applicants must satisfy the officer that they were actually paid for work performed.

Application Documents

The following documents must be submitted in support of a live-in caregiver application:

- an application for a Work Permit Made Outside of Canada form (IMM 1295B);

- a copy of the HRSDC confirmation;

- the original mandatory employment contract;

- proof of the equivalent of Canadian secondary school graduation;

- proof of training (diploma and transcripts) or proof of work experience (letters of reference from previous employers);

- identity documents, such as a valid subsisting passport, original birth certificate, marriage certificate, or divorce certificate if applicable;

- the processing fee;

- proof of medical examinations;

- police clearances for all the areas where the applicant resided more than six months; and

- evidence of the intention to leave Canada at the end of the period authorized for the temporary stay per s. 20(1)(b) of the IRPA.

Consider the following case scenario:

Boupha, a Cambodian national, submitted her application for a work permit under the LCP to the Canadian embassy in Bangkok. Boupha completed a college diploma in physiotherapy and then completed seven months of full-time training for live-in caregivers in a classroom setting, within the past year.

Boupha has included in her work permit application all of the requisite documents that establish her experience in accordance with the requirements of the IRPA and the IRP Regulations. In addition, Boupha is including the documents that the Canadian employer forwarded to her, these being the HRSDC confirmation and the employment contract signed by the Canadian employer's legal representative. Boupha signed the employment contract prior to submitting her application to the Canadian embassy. Finally, Boupha also included the identity documents and police clearances for her and all members of her family. Boupha would like to know whether her application is complete.

Section 8.2 of "OP 14: Processing Applicants for the Live-In Caregiver Program" in the CIC operations manual *Overseas Processing (OP)* sets out the documents required for LCP applications. It specifically provides that the employment contract must be signed by both the employer and by the applicant. It is not sufficient that the contract was signed by the legal representative of her employer.

In the event that the live-in caregiver continues to work for the same employer and is seeking to renew the work permit, the live-in caregiver must submit the following documents:

- a letter from the employer stating that the live-in caregiver will continue to be employed full time for another year; and

- a new employment contract extending the original employment contract for another year.

There is no need for a new HRSDC confirmation.

In the event that a live-in caregiver is between jobs and has not yet found a new employer, the live-in caregiver may apply for a bridge extension. A bridge extension is an interim work permit valid for a period of two months, which gives the live-in caregiver the opportunity to find a new employer within that period.

Place of Application

Applicants seeking an initial work permit under the LCP must submit their applications to a visa office abroad. This may be a little confusing, as applicants already in Canada with a temporary resident visa are entitled to submit an application to the CPC-V.[37] In fact, CPC-V is responsible for processing applications in Canada for work permits and renewals, study permits, and live-in caregiver's applications for permanent residence in Canada.[38] However, applicants seeking an initial work permit under the LCP must apply outside Canada, regardless of whether they are in Canada with a temporary resident visa.

Consider the following case scenario:

July is a student completing a six-month live-in caregiver program at Humber College. July will graduate from this program in May 2009 and would like to submit her application for a work permit under the LCP soon after completing the program. She would also like to eventually become a permanent resident. July is unsure where to submit her application for a work permit.

July must submit her application for a work permit to the visa office that corresponds to her country of nationality. Applicants seeking an initial work permit under the LCP must submit their applications outside Canada to qualify under the LCP and therefore be eligible for permanent residence in Canada. Consequently, if July submits her application to the CPC-V, she will not qualify under the LCP and will not be eligible for permanent residence in Canada after the two-year mark. July, however, may apply to CPC-V for extensions of her work permit and, once she is eligible for permanent residence, she may submit her application to CPC-V as well.

Applying for Permanent Residence

Family members may not accompany live-in caregivers to Canada. Even when an employer agrees that a family member may reside with the caregiver in the employer's residence, there are no guarantees that any subsequent employer would agree to the same terms.[39] To mitigate the harsh consequences of this to many caregivers who leave their own children behind, the LCP allows caregivers and their family members to apply for permanent residence after the live-in caregiver has worked for two years in Canada, within the three years of arrival to Canada.

Live-in caregivers applying for permanent residence may request **parallel processing** for some or all of their family members residing in or outside Canada.[40] Alternatively, live-in caregivers may sponsor family members at a later date after becoming permanent residents themselves.

Additionally, a live-in caregiver who has received first-stage approval (approval in principle) of the permanent resident application is entitled to apply for an open work permit. This allows the live-in caregiver to accept employment and to work for any employer for the time period specified on the work permit.

Because a live-in caregiver's work permit is valid for only one year at a time, it must be renewed every year to maintain eligibility under the LCP. The work permit may be extended up to a maximum of three years, during which the two years of full-time employment to qualify for permanent residence must be completed. The three-year mark was established to give the live-in caregiver flexibility to compensate for periods of unemployment, illness, vacation, or maternity leave.

Work Permit from CIC

CRITERIA FOR ENTRY

The CIC criteria used to determine eligibility for a work permit are mainly based on the factors discussed earlier, which are applicable to all temporary residents— namely, intention to leave Canada at the end of the authorized temporary stay; possession of a passport; compliance with the medical examination requirements (s. 30 of the IRP Regulations); and admissibility. In addition, under s. 200 of the IRP Regulations, the foreign worker must satisfy the requirements related to the worker class, which include the following:

- a genuine offer to work in Canada from a Canadian employer (s. 203 of the IRP Regulations);

- approval of the employment offer by HRSDC (unless exempted); and

- compliance with the requirements of the job in Canada, such as education, training, and experience.

Generally, a foreign worker must prove access to sufficient funds for living expenses, to be eligible for a work permit. Exceptions include refugee claimants subject to an unenforceable removal order, students who have become temporarily destitute, and temporary resident permit holders as long as their permit is valid for at least six months (s. 200 of the IRP Regulations).

It is important to note that a work permit does not guarantee admission to Canada. The foreign worker must meet the requirements for issuance of the work permit at the time the visa is issued, and must continue to meet these requirements at the time of the examination by a CBSA officer on entry into Canada, according to s. 180 of the IRP Regulations. Therefore, a foreign worker may be refused at the port of entry if she does not comply with the requirements for issuance of the work permit (for example, if she is inadmissible on the ground of criminality), regardless of whether she has obtained an employment confirmation.

APPLICATION DOCUMENTS

In addition to the documents required to support any temporary resident application—namely, an application form (IMM 1295B), cost-recovery processing fee, passport and travel documents (unless exempted by s. 52(1) of the IRP Regulations), proof of immigration status, and passport-size photos—an applicant must provide documents relevant to the worker class, including

- an "approved job offer," letter, or contract from the foreign worker's prospective employer;

- a copy of the HRSDC confirmation, unless the occupation or category is HRSDC-exempt; and

- background documents showing qualifications and experience as evidence that she meets the requirements for the job (s. 200(3)(a) of the IRP Regulations).

If the application is for Quebec, the foreign worker must also provide a copy of the Quebec Certificate of Acceptance.

PLACE OF APPLICATION

The general rule is that a foreign worker must apply outside Canada for a work permit; however, there are situations where a work permit may be obtained at the port of entry or within Canada (ss. 198 and 199 of the IRP Regulations).

The following persons must apply outside Canada:

- all persons who require a temporary resident visa;

- seasonal agricultural workers;

- live-in caregivers;

- all persons who require a medical examination, unless valid medical examination results are available at the time of entry; and

- international youth exchange program participants other than US citizens or permanent residents, unless approved by the responsible visa office (that administers the DFAIT-granted quota) abroad (Canadian experience class exemption code C21).[41]

Unless they are identified in the above list of persons who must apply outside of Canada, the following persons may apply at a port of entry:

- all nationals or permanent residents of the United States, and residents of Greenland and St. Pierre and Miquelon (contiguous territories);

- persons whose work does not require HRSDC confirmation; and

- persons whose work requires HRSDC confirmation, as long as the confirmation has been issued before the worker seeks to enter.[42]

Additionally, the following persons are eligible to apply for a work permit within Canada:

- holders of valid work or study permits and their family members;

- members of a crew;

- religious members, provided that they have a positive LMO;

- students applying for postgraduate work permits;

- holders of temporary resident permits that are valid for a minimum of six months, and their family members;

- refugee claimants and persons subject to an unenforceable removal order;

- in-Canada applicants and their family members who are deemed eligible for permanent resident status, which include live-in caregivers, spouses or common-law partners, protected persons, and persons who qualify on humanitarian and compassionate grounds;

- persons whose work permits were authorized by a visa office abroad, where the permit was not issued at a port of entry;

- Mexican citizens admitted to Canada as temporary residents, who may apply for a work permit under any NAFTA category; and

- US citizens admitted as visitors, who may apply in Canada under the professional or intra-company transferee NAFTA categories only (s. 199 of the IRP Regulations).

A foreign worker may be accompanied by a spouse or common-law partner and dependent children. The family members do not need to complete separate applications, but they must be named and included either as accompanying or non-accompanying family members in the foreign worker's application.

In the event that accompanying family members want to work in Canada, they must apply for separate work permits and must meet the same standards, including the HRSDC confirmation if applicable. They may, however, benefit from applying for their work permit from within Canada.

WORK PERMIT RESTRICTIONS

A work permit is a written authorization to work in Canada issued by an officer. Generally, it is based on a specific position with a specific employer, and is subject to one or more of the following restrictions:

- type of employment in which the foreign worker may work;

- employer for whom the foreign worker may work;

- location where the foreign worker may work; and

- length of time the foreign worker may work.

In the event that the foreign worker seeks to engage in work with a different employer, a new HRSDC confirmation will be required, unless the occupation is HRSDC-exempt (s. 52(1) of the IRP Regulations). This is in addition to the requirement to obtain a new work permit.

An open work permit may also be available in some cases. It has the advantage of not being job-specific. Therefore, a foreigner with an open work permit may work for any Canadian employer, without first having a confirmed offer of employment. An open work permit may carry some restrictions, such as the length of time that the foreign worker may work in Canada or the location of where the foreign worker may work.

The following persons are eligible to apply for an open work permit:

- live-in caregivers who have met the requirements for permanent residence (s. 113 of the IRP Regulations);

- members of the spouse or common-law in Canada class (s. 124 of the IRP Regulations);

- spouses or common-law partners of foreign representatives and family members of military personnel;

- spouses or common-law partners of foreign workers whose work is at a level that falls within NOC skill levels O, A, or B;

- spouses or common-law partners of work permit holders who have been nominated for permanent residence by a province, irrespective of the skill level of the principal applicant's occupation;

- destitute students;

- persons who are deemed to be convention refugees or persons in need of protection (s. 95(2) of the IRPA);

- persons for whom eligibility or admissibility requirements have been waived under humanitarian and compassionate grounds and who, as such, are eligible to become permanent residents (s. 25(1) of the IRPA);

- family members of the above who are in Canada; and

- international students who have graduated from a Canadian postsecondary institution.

In addition to a work permit, some foreign workers require a temporary resident visa to enter Canada. If a temporary resident visa is required, the foreign worker need not make a separate application—it will be issued at the same time as the documentation necessary for the foreign worker to enter Canada as a temporary worker.

WORK PERMIT EXTENSIONS

A foreign worker may apply to CPC-V for the renewal of a work permit as long as the foreign worker complies with the following conditions:

- the renewal application was made before the expiry of the current work permit (processing time guidelines suggest that the foreign worker should apply for a renewal at least 30 days before the expiry date); and

- the foreign worker has complied with all conditions imposed on entry into Canada.

It is important to note that a foreign worker is allowed to continue working in Canada under the conditions of an expired work permit if the following conditions are met:

- the renewal application was made before the original work permit expired;

- the foreign worker has remained in Canada since the expiry of the work permit; and

- the foreign worker continues to comply with the conditions, other than the expiry date, set out on the expired work permit (s. 186(u) of the IRP Regulations).

A work permit becomes invalid when it expires or when a removal order that is made against the permit holder becomes enforceable (s. 209 of the IRP Regulations).

WORK PERMIT EXEMPTIONS

Not everyone is required to obtain a work permit in order to work in Canada (s. 186 of the IRP Regulations). Some categories of workers who are exempt from needing a temporary work permit include the following:

- business visitors;

- diplomats;

- foreign athletes;

- military personnel;

- crew members;

- clergy;

- performing artists;

- public speakers;

- news reporters;

- expert witnesses, examiners, and evaluators; and

- students engaging in part-time work on campus.

Business visitors should not be confused with business persons. A business visitor is a separate category that carries separate requirements from those of a business person. A business visitor is a foreign worker who seeks to engage in international business activities in Canada without directly entering the Canadian labour market (s. 187(1) of the IRP Regulations). Thus, the business visitor's primary source of remuneration is outside Canada, and the principal place of business and actual place of accrual of profits remains predominantly outside Canada. For example, a foreigner who wants to enter Canada for the purpose of purchasing Canadian goods for a foreign business is a business visitor, as is a foreigner who wants to enter Canada for the purpose of receiving training by a Canadian parent of the corporation that employs the foreign worker outside Canada.

In contrast, a **business person** is someone who seeks entry through some sort of pre-arrangement—for example, as a salaried employee under a personal contract with a Canadian employer or through a contract with the professional's employer in the home country. The business person class includes foreign workers who are seeking to enter Canada under an international agreement such as NAFTA or GATS.

Intra-company transferees are also included in the business person classification because they are covered under international agreements. A business person does not require an LMO but must apply for a work permit.

Consider the following case scenario:

Maps & Software Inc. is a US company that manufactures marine maps and computer software. Maps & Software Inc. does not have any subsidiaries or affiliates in Canada. The company is interested in sending three of its employees to Toronto to conduct research for a new mapping software device that will assist mariners in navigating Lake Ontario. Once research is finalized, the three employees are to return to the United States with their findings; and once the product is manufactured, it will be available to anyone who wants to purchase it.

In this case, the three employees of the US company are not required to obtain work permits, for the following reasons: there is no Canadian employer contracting for their services; the US company will be the direct beneficiary of the foreign workers' efforts; and the employees' source of remuneration for the work performed remains outside Canada. Consequently, the three workers satisfy the business visitor's criteria, which exempts them from having to obtain a work permit. Additionally, because they are US nationals, they can apply for the business visitor's visa at the port of entry.

Members of the clergy are not required to obtain a work permit to work in Canada; however, they are required to ask for a **visitor's record** at the port of entry.

Consider the following case scenario:

Larry, a US national who lives in Utah, has recently been hired by a Canadian church to serve as its minister for the upcoming year. Larry has been given contradictory information regarding whether he needs a work permit. Some have said that everyone who works in Canada needs a work permit, and others have told him that members of the clergy may work without a work permit in Canada.

Larry needs to request a visitor's record from the port of entry reflecting the one-year duration of his clergy work in Canada. However, he will not need a work permit because work done during the course of a legitimate business visit is a type of exempt work. Furthermore, members of the clergy are exempt from the need for a work permit under s. 186(l) of IRP Regulations, which states:

A foreign worker may work in Canada without a work permit ... as a person who is responsible for assisting a congregation or group in the achievement of its spiritual goals and whose main duties are to preach doctrine, perform functions related to gatherings of the congregation or group or provide spiritual counselling.

Performing artists are also exempt from obtaining a work permit, provided that they are not in an employment relationship with a Canadian organization or business that has contracted them for their services in Canada. For example, singers performing at a private event are exempt from obtaining a work permit, whereas exotic dancers performing at bars or clubs or actors performing in a Canadian-based production, are not exempt from obtaining a work permit.[43]

TEMPORARY RESIDENT PERMIT

A foreigner may be barred from entering Canada as a temporary resident either because of inadmissibility or failure to meet the requirements of the IRPA. Sometimes it is still possible to enter Canada with a **temporary resident permit (TRP)**, formerly known as a "minister's permit."

It is important to ensure that all other options for temporary entry are thoroughly explored before applying for a TRP. For example, in a case of inadmissibility due to criminality, has the person since been deemed rehabilitated or pardoned and therefore become admissible?

Consider the following situations where granting of a TRP may be appropriate:

1. *Medical treatment.* A foreigner wishes to come to Canada for pre-arranged medical treatment, but is inadmissible on health grounds. In this instance an officer may consider whether the treatment is unavailable in the home country, the cost of the treatment, and how the medical costs will be covered. Unless the foreigner is suffering from a communicable or contagious disease, and precautions cannot guarantee that there will be no threat to anyone en route or in Canada, a TRP may be issued.

2. *Minor crimes.* A foreigner wishes to come to Canada as a visitor, but is inadmissible on the ground of criminality. A TRP may still be issued if the following are true: the offence was minor (did not involve drugs, physical violence, or damage to property); there are no more than two convictions; there is no pattern of criminal behaviour; the individual has completed all sentences; and there is a high probability that the individual will successfully settle in Canada without committing further offences. However, it will be necessary to demonstrate a compelling need for admission to Canada, even if the offence was minor and all other conditions were met. For example, the foreigner may be seeking entry to Canada in order to visit a dying parent.

In contrast, cases that may not warrant favourable consideration include cases of an inadmissible sponsored parent needing medical treatment who has other children or family members in the home country to provide care, or a criminally inadmissible spouse with a risk of violence or repeat offence. Additionally, TRPs are not granted to those who want to restore their temporary resident status as a visitor, student, or worker when their status has expired.

Criteria

A foreign national who is inadmissible, or does not meet the requirements of the IRPA, may be eligible for a TRP and become a temporary resident if an officer is of the opinion that admission is justified in the circumstances, according to s. 24(1). Whether or not to grant the TRP is at the discretion of the officer, who measures the risk posed by the foreign national to Canadians and Canadian society against the foreign national's need for admission. The foreign national's circumstances must be compelling and sufficient to overcome inadmissibility.

The TRP may be cancelled at any time. However, it is important to note that it remains valid until any one of the following events occurs:

- the permit is cancelled under s. 24(1) of the IRPA;

- the permit holder leaves Canada without obtaining prior authorization to re-enter Canada;

- the period of validity specified on the permit expires; or

- a period of three years elapses from the permit's date of validity (s. 63 of the IRP Regulations).

A TRP carries privileges greater than those accorded to visitors, students, and workers. For example, foreign workers holding a TRP are allowed to submit applications inland for a work or study permit, and may have access to health or other social services.

Additionally, TRP holders may be eligible for permanent residence as long as they remain continuously in Canada on a permit for at least three years and do not become inadmissible on other grounds. Therefore, permit holders must be cautious about a break in continuity, which may affect their eligibility for permanent residence. A break in continuity occurs when permit holders, without authorization for re-entry, leave Canada, or when they neglect their responsibility to seek an extension of their status prior to the expiry of their permit. It is therefore recommended that permit holders do not leave Canada unless their TRP specifically authorizes re-entry, and that they apply for an extension of their status at least 30 days before the permit expires.

Place of Application

TRPs are issued at both Canadian ports of entry and CIC inland offices, whereas temporary resident extensions are only issued inland.

A foreign national outside Canada wishing to apply for a TRP must do so at the visa office. The visa office will assess the application and refuse it or approve it. If approved, the TRP will be issued at the port of entry, when the approved person arrives in Canada. The visa office does not issue the TRP itself.

Therefore, a foreign national outside Canada may apply at the port of entry or visa office for a TRP. Depending on the circumstances, an officer at a port of entry may agree to consider this type of application. However, it is generally not advisable to apply at the port of entry, given that an officer always reserves the right to refuse entry and may require the person to leave immediately. Although processing times at a visa office can take several months, this route may be safer than taking the risk of appearing at a port of entry.

If the officer approves the TRP, the duration of the permit will be determined on the basis of the facts and circumstances presented by the applicant. For example, a person seeking to enter Canada for a short business trip will be issued a TRP that is valid for the duration of that trip and no longer.

Consider the following case scenario:

Cecilia is seeking an extension of her work permit. She continues to work, even though her work permit expired a week ago. Unfortunately, Cecilia forgot to send her application for renewing her work permit to CPC-V before it expired. An inadmissibility finding is made against Cecilia on the basis of her violating Canadian immigration laws by working without a valid work permit.

What does Cecilia have to do to obtain a new work permit? When there has been an inadmissibility finding, a TRP is required to enter or stay in Canada, no matter what type of inadmissibility (s. 24(1) of the IRPA). It should be noted that Cecilia should not apply for an extension because her work permit has already expired. Additionally, Cecilia is not eligible to apply for restoration of status because she has been found inadmissible. Thus, the fact that 90 days have not passed since the expiration of her work permit is irrelevant (s. 182 of the IRP Regulations).

APPENDIX

The following box provides a reference list of important definitions and topics that relate to temporary entry to Canada.

Reference for Temporary Entry to Canada	
Provision	**IRPA and IRP Regulations**
Definition, application	IRPA s. 22
Obligations—general	IRPA ss. 20 and 29
Obligations—work, study	IRPA s. 30
Loss of status	IRPA s. 47
Temporary resident authorization (visa)	IRPA s. 22 and IRP Regulations ss. 179 to 185
Definitions: "study permit," "work"	IRP Regulations ss. 1, 2
General entry requirements	IRP Regulations s. 7
Place of application	IRP Regulations s. 11(2)
Medical examinations	IRP Regulations s. 30
Security deposit	IRP Regulations s. 45
Passport requirement	IRP Regulations s. 50
Passport exemptions	IRP Regulations ss. 52, 190
Employer requirements, offences	IRP Regulations ss. 124, 125, 126
Workers—no permit	IRP Regulations ss. 186 and 187
Students—no permit	IRP Regulations ss. 188 and 189
TRV exemptions	IRP Regulations s. 190
Visitors	IRP Regulations ss. 191 to 193
Workers: applications, permits, renewals	IRP Regulations ss. 194 to 209
Students: applications, permits, restrictions	IRP Regulations ss. 210 to 222

NOTES

1. Citizenship and Immigration Canada, *Annual Report to Parliament on Immigration 2007*, 2007, www.cic.gc.ca/english/resources/publications/annual-report2007/message.asp.

2. Ibid.

3. Provincial nominees are persons who are nominated by a Canadian province or territory. They are selected because they possess the skills, education, and work experience necessary to make an immediate economic contribution to the province or territory that nominates them and are ready to establish themselves successfully as permanent residents in Canada.

4. Citizenship and Immigration Canada, "OP 11: Temporary Residents," in *Overseas Processing (OP)*, s. 5.9, February 24, 2006, www.cic.gc.ca/english/resources/manuals/op/index.asp.

5. Citizenship and Immigration Canada, "OP 12: Students," in *Overseas Processing (OP)*, s. 5.13, April 11, 2005, www.cic.gc.ca/english/resources/manuals/op/index.asp.

6. Designated countries or territories are those that have been determined to have a higher incidence of serious communicable disease than Canada. The list of designated countries/territories includes most countries with the exception of countries in Western Europe, the United States, Australia, New Zealand, and Japan. The list of designated countries/territories is available on the CIC website at www.cic.gc.ca/english/information/medical/dcl.asp.

7. The list of designated medical practitioners is available on the CIC website at www.cic.gc.ca/dmp-md/medical/aspx.

8. Foreign students must meet the same medical requirements as those that apply to all temporary residents to Canada.

9. Supra note 5, s. 5.6.

10. Ibid., s. 5.1.

11. Citizenship and Immigration Canada, "FW 1: Foreign Worker Manual," in *Temporary Foreign Workers Guidelines (FW)*, s. 5.38E, June 11, 2008, www.cic.gc.ca/english/resources/manuals/fw/index.asp.

12. Ibid., s. 5.38.

13. Citizenship and Immigration Canada, *Off-Campus Work Permit Program for International Students: Guide for Designated Institutional Representatives*, August 2008, www.cic.gc.ca/english/study/institutions/guide-dir.asp.

14. As of April 21, 2008, and for the first time, international students can apply to obtain an open work permit under the Post-Graduation Work

Permit Program, with no restrictions on the type of employment and no requirement for a job offer.

15. Supra note 11, s. 5.39E.

16. Citizenship and Immigration Canada, *Applying for a Work Permit— Student Guide* (IMM 5580), July 2008, www.cic.gc.ca/english/ information/applications/guides/5580e.asp#coop.

17. Ibid.

18. Human Resources and Social Development Canada, "Expedited Labour Market Opinion Pilot Project," February 26, 2008, www.hrsdc.gc.ca/en/ workplaceskills/foreign_workers/elmopp/elmoppone.shtml.

19. Citizenship and Immigration Canada, "Concurrent Processing: NOC, Levels O, A and B," July 16, 2008, www.cic.gc.ca/english/work/processing .asp.

20. Human Resources and Social Development Canada, "Hiring Foreign Academics in Canada," February 26, 2008, www.hrsdc.gc.ca/en/ workplaceskills/foreign_workers/academic.shtml.

21. Ibid., www.hrsdc.gc.ca/en/workplaceskills/foreign_workers/acadexemp .shtml.

22. Human Resources and Social Development Canada, "Hiring Foreign Agricultural Workers in Canada," June 27, 2008, www.hrsdc.gc.ca/en/ workplaceskills/foreign_workers/sawp.shtml.

23. Ibid.

24. Citizenship and Immigration Canada, "Working Temporarily in Canada: Special Categories—Information Technology Workers," July 31, 2007, www.cic.gc.ca/english/work/special-tech.asp.

25. Human Resources and Social Development Canada, "Pilot Project for Occupations Requiring Lower Levels of Formal Training," June 5, 2008, www.hrsdc.gc.ca/en/workplaceskills/foreign_workers/lowskill.shtml.

26. Supra note 11, s. 5.29.

27. Ibid., s. 5.31B.

28. There must be a qualifying business relationship between the Canadian and foreign company. Furthermore, the companies must be "doing business," which means "regularly, systematically, and continuously providing goods and/or services by a parent, branch, subsidiary, or affiliate in Canada and the foreign country, as the case may be" (ibid.).

29. Mergers refer to "the joining together of two entities into a single entity called a surviving entity; the surviving entity assumes all of the assets and liabilities of the merged entities, i.e. it purchases the stock, assets and liabilities of the other entities, absorbing them into one corporate structure." Acquisitions refer to "the takeover of the controlling interest of

one entity by another and both entities retain their legal existence after the transaction" (supra note 11, appendix 1).

30. The terms and conditions of the intra-company transferee's work permit will continue to be valid if the Canadian employer is still doing business either directly or through a parent, branch, affiliate, or subsidiary in another country to which the employee can reasonably be expected to be transferred at the end of their assignment in Canada (supra note 11, appendix 1).

31. Supra note 11, appendix G, s. 1.8.

32. Evidence of pre-arranged employment includes a signed contract with a Canadian enterprise, or evidence of an offer of employment from a Canadian employer, or a letter from the American or Mexican employer on whose behalf the service will be provided to the Canadian enterprise. Professionals seeking self-employment in Canada are excluded (supra note 11, s. 3.4).

33. Supra note 11, appendix G, s. 3.8.

34. Supra note 11, appendix D.

35. Supra note 11.

36. Ibid.

37. Citizenship and Immigration Canada, "IP 4: Processing Live-In Caregivers in Canada," in *Inland Processing (IP)*, s. 5.2, April 24, 2008, www.cic.gc.ca/english/resources/manuals/ip/index.asp.

38. Ibid.

39. Citizenship and Immigration Canada, "OP 14: Processing Applicants for the Live-in Caregiver Program," in *Overseas Processing (OP)*, s. 5.10, March 2003, www.cic.gc.ca/english/resources/manuals/op/index.asp.

40. Ibid., s. 5.11.

41. Supra note 11, s. 5.23.

42. Ibid.

43. Supra note 11, s. 5.8.

REFERENCES

Canadian Human Rights Act. R.S.C. 1985, c. H-6.

Citizenship and Immigration Canada. "IP 6: Processing Temporary Resident Extensions." In *Inland Processing (IP)*. March 29, 2006. www.cic.gc.ca/english/resources/manuals/ip/index.asp.

Citizenship and Immigration Canada. "OP 14: Processing Applicants for the Live-In Caregiver Program." In *Overseas Processing (OP)*. March 2003. www.cic.gc.ca/english/resources/manuals/op/index.asp.

Citizenship and Immigration Canada. "Sponsorship of Parents, Grandparents, Adopted Children and Other Relatives—The Sponsor's Guide (IMM 5196)." 2008. www.cic.gc.ca/english/information/applications/guides/5196E10.asp.

Citizenship and Immigration Canada, RDM. *Facts and Figures 2007.* July 11, 2008. www.cic.gc.ca/english/resources/statistics/facts2007/03.asp.

Immigration and Refugee Protection Act. S.C. 2001, c. 27.

Immigration and Refugee Protection Regulations. S.O.R./2002-227.

Visiting Forces Act. R.S.C. 1985, c. V-2.

REVIEW QUESTIONS

1. What kind of documents can an applicant who wants to visit Canada provide to prove that she will leave at the end of the authorized stay?

2. What is a TRV?

3. Name the different types of Canadian temporary resident visas and describe briefly their use.

4. What does the visa officer consider when processing an application for a TRV?

5. Under which conditions can temporary residents lose their status and privilege?

6. To change the terms and conditions of their authorization or extend their stay, what must temporary residents do?

7. Describe the main document that a person must submit in order to obtain a student visa.

8. List the specific terms and conditions listed on a work visa.

9. Some business visitors may enter Canada more easily under the provisions of trade agreements with Canada. Name two such agreements and describe them briefly.

CHAPTER 5

Permanent Entry

LEARNING OBJECTIVES

After reading this chapter you should be able to:

- Describe the general provisions for applying for permanent residence.
- Differentiate among the three classes of permanent residents.
- Understand the general rights and obligations of permanent residents.
- Understand the purpose of the Family Class program and skilled worker class.
- List the requirements for applying for permanent residence as a member of the family class and the application process.
- Explain the rights and obligations of sponsorship.
- Describe sponsorship appeals before the Immigration Appeal Division.
- Describe the federal skilled worker requirements and application process, and explain the National Occupational Classification.
- Understand the point system, how to calculate points, and the pass mark.
- Differentiate among the three categories of business class immigrants.
- Describe the business class requirements and application process.
- Generally describe the procedure for humanitarian and compassionate applications.

INTRODUCTION

Immigration to Canada is beneficial to both Canada and newcomers to our country: in the *Annual Report to Parliament on Immigration 2007*,[1] the minister of Citizenship and Immigration reminds us that newcomers traditionally select Canada for work or because of our humanitarian tradition of protecting the vulnerable. The government recognizes the need for maintaining a strong and skilled labour force and for strengthening Canada's social fabric and cultural diversity. However, our aging population and low birth rate mean that Canada must look to immigration to fill our labour shortages. Moreover, as other countries are experiencing similar challenges, Canada must remain competitive in the global market in order to attract workers with the right skill sets to contribute significantly to our economy.

The management of immigration programs includes balancing the need to attract newcomers with the need to protect Canadians by denying access to people who pose a health, criminal, or security threat, and those who would abuse our immigrant or refugee systems. In studying the various immigration programs, you will find examples of this balancing act. On the one hand are programs designed to attract newcomers who can contribute to Canada, and on the other hand are overriding restrictions that deny access.

A foreign national who wishes to reside in Canada must go through a lengthy application process and a complex approval process. Nevertheless, the time and associated financial costs of applying have not discouraged the thousands of people who apply and are accepted as permanent residents each year.

In 2006, Canada admitted over 251,000 permanent residents in the following classes, or categories:[2]

- family class: family members of Canadian citizens and permanent residents made up 28 percent (70,506);

- economic class: members of this class, including skilled workers, business people, provincial or territorial nominees, and live-in caregivers, made up 54.9 percent (138,257);

- refugees and protected persons: members of this group made up 12.9 percent (32,492); and

- persons admitted on humanitarian and compassionate grounds: members of this group made up 4 percent (10,223).

Under s. 70(2) of the Immigration and Refugee Protection Regulations (IRP Regulations), to become a permanent resident, a foreign national must submit an application under a specific immigration program in one of these four basic classes of permanent residence, as is appropriate to the situation. The application is assessed by an **immigration visa officer** (a public servant working in a Canadian consulate or visa office abroad), who may issue the permanent resident visa.

This chapter explores the requirements and rules of eligibility that apply to all permanent resident applicants. It also explores those requirements particular to the family class, economic class, and subclasses, and, finally, permanent residency based on humanitarian and compassionate considerations, which may apply in rare circumstances.

Permanent resident status under the Refugee and Humanitarian Resettlement program is described in Chapter 8.

GENERAL PROVISIONS

Under s. 6 of the IRP Regulations, all foreign nationals who wish to make Canada their permanent home must first apply and obtain a **permanent resident visa**. The permanent resident visa allows the foreign national to travel to Canada and, after a successful examination at a port of entry, to enter Canada as a permanent resident.[3]

With the enactment of the *Immigration and Refugee Protection Act* (IRPA), the term permanent resident came into use, replacing the former term, "landed immigrant." Both terms carry the same meaning. The IRPA distinguishes between permanent residents and temporary residents. A permanent resident has more rights than a temporary resident, such as a visitor, business traveller, or student, but fewer rights than a Canadian citizen.

Before applying for Canadian citizenship, a foreign national must obtain **permanent resident status**. A person with permanent resident status enjoys most of the same rights and responsibilities as Canadians guaranteed under the *Canadian Charter of Rights and Freedoms*, such as the right to live, work, and study in Canada and the legal obligation to pay taxes and respect Canadian laws. However, a permanent resident may not run for political office and may not vote—these privileges are reserved for citizens. Furthermore, although s. 27 of the IRPA gives permanent residents the absolute right to enter and remain in Canada, they must comply with statutory requirements or risk having their status revoked.

The IRP Regulations require all applications for permanent residence to be made in writing using the forms provided by Citizenship and Immigration Canada (CIC), which are available on the CIC website at www.cic.gc.ca. Applicants must also pay related processing fees (s. 10(1)). These fees are listed on the CIC website at www.cic.gc.ca/english/information/fees/fees.asp. The IRP Regulations also stipulate that counsel (anyone assisting with the application and charging a fee for services) must be an *authorized representative* and must provide contact information in the application (s. 10(2)).

After a foreign national meets all immigration criteria, she is permitted to travel to Canada with a permanent resident visa in hand; however, she is not yet considered to have permanent resident status until admitted as such to Canada. Permanent resident status is acquired on the date of the foreign national's admission to Canada, formerly known as the landing date. Upon arrival at the port of entry, the foreign national is examined by an officer who decides whether to admit the person as a permanent resident. Generally, the officer examines the person to confirm her intention to establish permanent residence in Canada, and to confirm that there is nothing new, such as an invalid medical examination or expired permanent resident visa, that would make the foreign national or her family members inadmissible (s. 70(1) of the IRP Regulations).

Permanent Resident Card

Once in Canada, a permanent resident uses the **Permanent Resident Card (PR card)**[4] to show proof of immigration status. The PR card is a wallet-sized plastic card that is mailed to the person after arrival in Canada, provided that CIC is informed of the person's correct address within 180 days of her arrival. The PR card is valid for only five years and must be renewed thereafter.

The CIC website provides instructions and a guide on how to apply for a renewal or replacement card. The application must be sent to the Case Processing Centre in Sydney, Nova Scotia together with a processing fee of $50 per person.

According to the IRP Regulations, the PR card is considered to be property of the Crown (s. 53(2)) and can be revoked if any of the following events occur:

- a new card is issued;

- the permanent resident becomes a Canadian citizen or loses permanent resident status;

- the PR card is lost, stolen, or destroyed; or

- the permanent resident dies (ss. 59(2) and 60).

Generally, a permanent resident may apply for citizenship after accumulating three years of residence in Canada. This process is fully explored in Chapter 6, "Citizenship."

Loss of Permanent Resident Status

Unlike citizenship, permanent residence is technically not "permanent," because a person can lose this status. Section 2(1) of the IRPA defines a permanent resident as a person who has acquired permanent resident status and has not subsequently lost it under s. 46.

Section 46 sets out four ways in which persons may lose permanent residence status:

1. if they become Canadian citizens;

2. if they fail to comply with the residency obligations under s. 28 of the IRPA;

3. if a removal order made against them comes into force; or

4. if a final determination is made that they are not refugees or not entitled to protection.

1. BECOMING A CANADIAN CITIZEN

A person who becomes a Canadian citizen is no longer a permanent resident. Citizenship includes all the rights of permanent residence, plus additional rights. Chapter 6 explains in detail the process for becoming a Canadian citizen; generally, a permanent resident must be a resident of Canada for at least three years (1,095 days) in the last four years (1,460 days). Days spent in Canada as a temporary resident may be counted toward the residency requirements.

2. RESIDENCY OBLIGATIONS

A person can lose permanent resident status by failing to fulfill residency obligations. Although a permanent resident is not required to spend all of his time in Canada, generally he must physically reside here for 730 days out of every five years, according to s. 28 of the IRPA. There are some exceptions to the residency obligation. In certain circumstances, time outside Canada may be counted as equivalent to days in Canada, according to s. 28(2)(a). These circumstances exist where permanent residents reside as follows:

- outside Canada while accompanying a Canadian citizen who is their spouse or common-law partner or, in the case of a child, their parent;

- outside Canada while employed on a full-time basis by a Canadian business or in the federal public administration or the public service of a province; or

- outside Canada while accompanying a permanent resident who is their spouse or common-law partner or, in the case of a child, their parent and who is employed on a full-time basis by a Canadian business or in the federal public administration or the public service of a province.

A person who loses permanent resident status because of failure to meet residency obligations (s. 46(1)(b) of the IRPA) may appeal to the Immigration Appeal Division of the Immigration and Refugee Board (IRB) under s. 63(4) of the IRPA.[5]

3. REMOVAL ORDER

A person who is subject to a removal order as a result of inadmissibility can lose permanent resident status. The grounds of inadmissibility, such as security and criminality issues, are discussed in detail in Chapter 3, "Inadmissibility."

Each case is reviewed on its merits by an immigration official delegated by the minister of Public Safety and Emergency Preparedness, who decides whether to allow the person to remain in Canada or to refer the case to the Immigration Division of the Immigration and Refugee Board for a decision, according to s. 44(2) of the IRPA.

4. FINAL DETERMINATION THAT A PERSON IS NOT A REFUGEE OR IS NOT ENTITLED TO PROTECTION

A person who becomes a permanent resident following a determination that she is a Convention refugee or a person in need of protection may lose permanent resident status and be removed from Canada if fraud or misrepresentation was involved in her refugee claim. Misrepresentation may involve false statements and documents, as well as omissions, such as failing to disclose a relevant fact. In such situations, the minister makes an application to the Refugee Protection Division under s. 109 of the IRPA to vacate the original decision because of fraud or misrepresentation. An application to vacate a decision is a request to the Division to "do away with" the original decision to grant protection. The Division, on a final determination, may decide to vacate the original decision for refugee protection, which consequently also leads to the loss of the person's permanent residency.

FAMILY CLASS

As discussed in Chapter 1, one of the stated objectives of Canadian immigration policy is to facilitate family reunification (s. 3(1)(d) of the IRPA). Accordingly, several changes were made to the Family Class program when the IRPA came into force, to support the reunification of Canadians and permanent residents with their close family members, as follows:

- The definition of "family" was modernized to include common-law and same-sex partners.

- The age to sponsor a relative was reduced from 19 years of age to 18.

- The definition of "dependent child" was expanded to increase the age from under 19 to under 22.

- Adoption provisions were introduced, in keeping with the principle of the "best interests of the child."

- An "in-Canada" class for sponsored spouses and partners was created.

- The length of the sponsorship requirement was reduced from ten years to three years, for spouses and common-law partners.

- Medical grounds, such as a medical condition placing excessive demand on health and social services, were eliminated as a basis for inadmissibility, for spouses and dependants under 22.

The IRPA also eliminated the sponsor's right of appeal to the Immigration Appeal Division in cases where the family member was found inadmissible for reasons of security, human or international rights violations, serious criminality, or organized criminality.

The Family Class program includes two separate processes, as follows:

1. **Sponsorship application process:** A *sponsor* or *sponsorship applicant* is a person in Canada who wants to reunite with a family member. There is a separate application and approval process for becoming a sponsor. A sponsor must be a Canadian citizen or permanent resident, according to s. 13(1) of the IRPA, and must meet other criteria such as financial requirements.

2. **Permanent residence application process:** The *permanent residence applicant* is the foreign national who wishes to live in Canada as a permanent resident, according to s. 12(1) of the IRPA. The applicant must meet the regulatory definition of a "member of the family class" and meet specific criteria[6] to qualify for permanent residence. The application and approval are separate but related processes from the sponsor.

Both these processes must be successfully completed before an applicant may become a permanent resident as a member of the family class. Consider the following case scenario:

Gary is a 48-year-old Canadian citizen. He has been divorced for several years, and lives in Toronto, Ontario where he shares custody of his two children: Thomas, 9, and Samantha, 7. Ellie is a 45-year-old American citizen with two daughters: 17-year-old Amanda and 12-year-old Martha. Ellie's husband, Paul, died when Martha was a baby.

Gary met Ellie through Paul years ago when they were all undergraduates at Cornell University in New York. Ellie and Paul were married in 1988 and remained close friends with Gary, who moved back to Canada after graduation. Gary's job required him to travel frequently to the United States, so it was easy to maintain his friendship with Ellie throughout the years, even after Paul died. After Gary divorced, his relationship with Ellie became intimate, leading to a marriage proposal and a legal marriage. Even though Gary could seek a job transfer to the United States through his company, he doesn't want to relocate there because he would lose joint custody of his two school-aged children. Ellie, however, is more flexible about where she can live and is even welcoming a change to start a new life with Gary. Together, they decided that Gary should sponsor Ellie and the girls as permanent residents so they can all live as a family in Canada.

Does Gary meet the legal requirements to sponsor Ellie and her children? Do Ellie and her children, Amanda and Martha, qualify for sponsorship? To answer these questions, we will examine the various elements of the Family Class program including a review of provisions of the IRPA and its regulations. We will learn about the two separate but interrelated processes for sponsoring a person to Canada and for applying as a permanent resident under the family class.

Throughout the text, we refer to "immigration officers" and "visa officers." The sponsor's application is processed in Canada by an immigration officer, who is a public servant working at a Case Processing Centre. The sponsored person's application for permanent residence is processed abroad by a visa officer. Visa officers are Canadian public servants who work at Canadian missions abroad and perform multiple duties, including assessing applications from foreign nationals who wish to become permanent residents.

For the sake of simplicity, we will focus on the sponsorship of a spouse and dependent children, as in our case scenario. However, where the requirements are different for sponsoring other members of the family class, they are explained.

Sponsors Under the Family Class

Family class immigration involves sponsorship by a qualifying individual—the sponsor. The sponsor undertakes responsibility for the basic living expenses of the family member being sponsored, for a prescribed period. The list of persons who may be sponsored include the following:

- spouses, common-law partners, and conjugal partners;

- dependent children;

- children intended for adoption;

- parents, grandparents, and their dependent children;

- brothers, sisters, nephews, nieces, or grandchildren if they are either orphaned, not a spouse or common-law partner, and under 18; and

- any relative if the sponsor is alone in Canada and has none of the above family members to sponsor.

REQUIREMENTS OF THE SPONSOR

The process of sponsoring a person for permanent residence begins with the sponsor—in our case scenario, Gary. The framework is found in s. 13(1) of the IRPA, and further details are provided in the regulations. The sponsor must be either a Canadian citizen or permanent resident who is at least 18 years old, resides in Canada, and has filed an application to sponsor a member of the family class (see below under the heading "Sponsorship Kits and Applications for Permanent Residence"), according to s. 130(1) of the IRP Regulations.

Generally, the sponsor must reside in Canada. An exception is made where a Canadian citizen residing outside of Canada satisfies immigration officials that he will resume residence in Canada once the sponsored person becomes a permanent resident. This allows a Canadian citizen whose work may require him to live outside of Canada for a period of time to begin the sponsorship process. However, permanent residents, while living abroad, may not sponsor.

Gary meets the age, status and residence requirements of the definition of a sponsor. He must, however, meet other conditions to satisfy immigration officials that he will be able to carry out his obligations as a sponsor.

Bars to Sponsorship

Just as a bank will conduct a credit check to ensure you have the ability to repay a loan, the government wants to limit the risk of a sponsor defaulting on his obligations. Sponsorship requires Gary to provide the basic living expenses for Ellie and her children; therefore, he must prove there is nothing that would prevent him from fulfilling this commitment. The immigration officer who processes Gary's application must be satisfied that there is nothing in Gary's history, such as criminality, that would make him a risk for sponsorship.

Certain activities, as set out in s. 133 of the IRP Regulations, would bar Gary from sponsorship. A person may not sponsor or be a co-signer[7] if any of the following bars to sponsorship exist:

- *The person is subject to a removal order.* The IRPA requires permanent resident sponsors to reside in Canada. A person subject to a removal order is at risk of not being able to fulfill this obligation.

- *The person has been detained in any penitentiary, jail, reformatory, or prison.* Such a person has no ability to provide financial support.

- *The person has been previously convicted of a specified offence.* These offences include a sexual offence (or an attempt or threat to commit such an offence), either in Canada or abroad, against anyone, or an offence resulting in bodily harm (including threats to or attempts at doing so) against a relative. This bar addresses concerns that a sponsored family member could be at risk of sexual abuse or family violence.[8] A history of such offences within five years of the sponsorship application is barred unless the sponsor was pardoned or acquitted. For convictions outside Canada, the sponsor must show rehabilitation or acquittal.

- *The person is in default of spousal or child support payments ordered by a court in or outside of Canada.* A sponsor who is in default of a court-ordered or court-registered support obligation must first resolve this matter with the local provincial or territorial authorities to remove this bar.

- *The person is in default of a debt[9] owed under the IRPA.* Sponsorship includes signing a legally binding contract with the minister of CIC. As long as there is an unpaid debt, the minister will not enter into another legal contract with a person who is in default of payment.

- *The person is not an undischarged bankrupt under the Bankruptcy and Insolvency Act.* A bankrupt person is considered a poor financial risk.

- *The person is in receipt of social assistance other than for reasons of disability.* A sponsor who receives social assistance cannot provide for his own basic necessities, let alone those of others. Only under exceptional circumstances may this bar be waived under humanitarian and compassionate grounds.

- *The person is in default of a previous sponsorship undertaking.* Such a person is considered to be a poor risk because he has not previously honoured a legal, financial obligation with the minister of CIC.

Gary read about all the conditions he must meet to be a sponsor, and has determined that there is nothing that would bar him from sponsoring Ellie. To complete his application, Gary will also be required to sign two documents that set out his obligations: an undertaking with the minister of CIC and a sponsorship agreement with Ellie.

Undertaking

A sponsor must make a formal commitment to financial responsibility for the family members for three to ten years, depending on the sponsorship relationship and the age of the family members being sponsored, according to the IRP Regulations. This commitment is called an *undertaking* and is included with the sponsor's application—Application to Sponsor and Undertaking form (IMM 1344A). The undertaking is a legal contract with the minister of Citizenship and Immigration, signed by the sponsor.

The basis for this requirement is to ensure that relatives receive the support they need to establish themselves in Canada so that they will not become a financial burden on the community and require social assistance. By signing the undertaking, the sponsor agrees to repay the Canadian government for any social assistance payments made to the sponsored family members.

When Gary signs the undertaking, he is entering into a binding contract with the minister of Citizenship and Immigration. As the sponsor, he remains obligated to provide basic requirements regardless of any change in circumstances, such as a marital breakdown, unemployment, or even the death of Ellie. Gary agrees to provide Ellie, the sponsored person, and Amanda and Martha, Ellie's family members, with basic necessities, including food, clothing, shelter, dental care, eye care, and other health needs not covered by public health services, from the day they enter Canada until the end of the specified period of the undertaking.

The undertaking takes effect the day that Ellie is admitted to Canada as a permanent resident. Generally, the duration of the undertaking is for ten years but there are exceptions depending on the relationship of the person being sponsored and can vary with the age of a dependent child, as follows:

- a three-year commitment for a spouse, common-law partner, or conjugal partner of the sponsor;

- the earlier of ten years or until the child turns 25, for a dependent child who is less than 22 years of age and is the child of the sponsor, or the sponsor's spouse, or common-law or conjugal partner;

- three years for a dependent child who is 22 years of age or older and is the child of the sponsor or the sponsor's spouse, or common-law or conjugal partner; and

- for anyone else, ten years.

Consider our example of Gary:

Ellie is Gary's spouse; therefore, the duration of the undertaking for Ellie is for three years from the date that she arrives in Canada as a permanent resident.

Gary's obligations toward Amanda and Martha (the dependent children of his spouse, Ellie) are tied to their economic dependency and their ages, and therefore are longer in duration. The girls will both be under 22 years of age on the date of becoming permanent residents, so Gary would calculate his undertaking to be 10 years or when the girls reach the age of 25, whichever comes first, as follows:

Amanda is 17 years old. If she is 17 when she becomes a permanent resident, the duration of Gary's undertaking with the minister of CIC will be for 8 years: 17 years old + 8 years undertaking = 25 years old. Martha is 12 years old. If she is 12 when she becomes a permanent resident, the duration of Gary's undertaking with the minister of CIC will be for the full 10 years: 12 years old + 10 years undertaking = 22 years old.

Sponsorship Agreement

In addition to signing the undertaking with the minister of CIC, Gary must also sign an agreement with Ellie. This sponsorship agreement is separate and different from the undertaking as its purpose is to set out the mutual obligations and rights of the sponsor and the sponsored person.

The Sponsorship Agreement form (IMM 1344B) is included in the sponsor's application package. After Gary signs it, he sends it to Ellie so that she has the opportunity to read it and understand her rights and responsibilities. The document makes it clear that the undertaking remains in effect notwithstanding events such as the granting of citizenship or a change in circumstances, such as marital breakdown.

Unfortunately, not all sponsored persons are aware of their rights. Some women, for reasons such as poor language skills, poor education, and cultural norms, are vulnerable to a range of domestic abuse including physical and financial control, isolation, and violence. A woman may stay in a relationship under threat of deportation because she is unaware of her rights and believes that she must remain in an abusive relationship or face deportation. This is false.

To address this issue, the Sponsorship Agreement form provides the following:

> Sponsored persons and/or their family members who are being abused or assaulted by their sponsors should seek safety away from their sponsors even if this means they will have to apply for social assistance benefits. A sponsor cannot force Citizenship and Immigration Canada to remove you from Canada.

Let's suppose that Gary and Ellie separate or divorce: Gary would continue to be financially responsible for Ellie (if this happens within the three years of his undertaking) and for the girls (also for the duration of his undertaking). Ellie and her children would not be forced to leave Canada as some sponsored persons are led to believe: they have the right to remain in Canada because they are permanent residents.

Sponsors of all ages, and sponsored persons of at least 22 years of age, must sign the Sponsorship Agreement. If the sponsored person is a spouse, common-law partner, or conjugal partner, then that person, regardless of age, must sign the agreement.

Gary the sponsor and Ellie the spouse will both sign the Sponsorship Agreement. Amanda and Martha are both under the age of 22 and therefore will not sign the document. The sponsorship agreement provides details of Gary's obligations to support Ellie and her girls during the period of the undertaking by providing basic requirements such as food, shelter, clothing, and medical care. The agreement also provides that Ellie is obligated to make reasonable efforts to provide necessities for herself and her children.

Financial Requirements

Generally, sponsors must show that they have the financial means to provide for all their family members, including those already residing in Canada and those they intend to sponsor. The minimum necessary income requirement is published annually by Statistics Canada in **low income cut-off (LICO)** levels.

Low Income Cut-Off Test

The applicable LICO level is based on urban areas of 500,000 inhabitants or more, regardless of where the sponsor lives. The sponsor's income must generally come from Canadian sources—with two exceptions:

- sponsors who commute from Canada to work in the United States may use their US employment income, provided that it is declared as income on their Canadian income tax return; and

- sponsors living in Canada, who declare income from foreign sources on their Canadian income tax returns, may use this foreign income to meet the financial requirements for sponsorship.

Sponsors must provide their latest Notice of Assessment from the Canada Revenue Agency to report total income, as referenced in s. 133(1)(j)(i) of the IRP Regulations and shown on line 150 of the Notice of Assessment.

If, at some time in the future, Ellie wishes to sponsor her widowed mother, she will be required to pass the LICO test.

How to Calculate LICO

The LICO level is determined on the basis of the total number of family members. In sponsorship situations, the number of family members includes all members of a sponsor's own family and all sponsored persons and their family members, including family members listed as non-accompanying. See the 2008 LICO table below:

Low Income Cut-Off (LICO) Table for 2008

Size of family unit	Minimum necessary income
1 person (the sponsor)	$21,202
2 persons	$26,396
3 persons	$32,450
4 persons	$39,399
5 persons	$44,686
6 persons	$50,397
7 persons	$56,110
More than 7 persons, for each additional person, add	$5,713

Source: Citizenship and Immigration Canada, *Sponsorship of Parents, Grandparents, Adopted Children and Other Relatives: The Sponsor's Guide* (IMM 5196 E) June 2008, www.cic.gc.ca/english/pdf/kits/guides/5196E.pdf.

Generally, the LICO table is updated each year, so look for effective dates. The LICO table above is effective until December 31, 2008. Annual LICO tables can be found in *Sponsorship of Parents, Grandparents, Adopted Children and Other Relatives: The Sponsor's Guide* (IMM 5196 E) on the CIC website at www.cic.gc.ca/english/information/applications/family.asp. Click on the Instruction Guide link to access the current table.

Consider this example, in which Ellie decides to sponsor her mother:

The size of Ellie's family unit is equal to 7 as follows: Ellie must count herself, her 2 children, and her spouse, Gary, and his 2 children, which totals a family unit equal to 6, assuming that all 4 children are dependent. She must also count the number of people being sponsored, which is equal to 1, in this case, her mother.

If we use the table provided as an example, Ellie must show that she has an annual income of at least $56,110. Any income Ellie earns in Canada is reported in her Notice of Assessment from her income tax return for the last 12 months: this is how she proves she meets this minimum to qualify on financial grounds to sponsor her mother. If Ellie has not earned enough money, she can ask Gary to act as a co-signer to make up the financial gap, provided that their pooled resources meet the minimum income requirement of $56,110.

Co-signer

A sponsor who does not have the necessary financial means to be a sponsor may take on a **co-signer** to make up the difference financially. Consequently, the co-signer must also sign the undertaking. A co-signer must meet the following criteria:

- be either the spouse or common-law partner of the sponsor;

- meet the same eligibility requirements as the sponsor; and

- assume the same obligations as the sponsor.

Together the sponsor and co-signer become **jointly and severally liable** if there is a default. This means that either of them may be required to pay the full amount, should the other lack funds to contribute—the obligation is not divided in half.

Assume that when Ellie sponsors her mother, she asks her spouse, Gary, to act as a co-signer because she does not have sufficient funds to pass the LICO test. In this situation, both Ellie and Gary become jointly responsible for the sponsorship of Ellie's mother.

Exceptions

The LICO financial obligations do not apply to all relatives. Excepted persons are set out in s. 133(4) of the IRP Regulations, and include the following:

- a spouse, common-law partner, or conjugal partner;

- a dependent biological child, where the child has no dependent children of her own;

- a child under the age of 18 whom the sponsor intends to adopt in Canada; or

- a child under the age of 18 where the sponsor is a guardian of the child.

Although the sponsor is not required to meet the LICO test for these cases, she must still complete a financial evaluation using CIC's Financial Evaluation form (IMM 1283).

In our case scenario, Gary is exempted from the LICO test because he is sponsoring his spouse and her dependants.

Members of the Family Class

This is the second part of the process, which focuses on the applicants for permanent residence. In our first case scenario, Ellie is seeking to come to Canada as a permanent resident along with her dependent children, Amanda and Martha. In order to do so, she and her daughters must meet the definition of "members of the family class" as set out in the IRP Regulations.

People who wish to come to Canada permanently may choose to apply under the Family Class program because they have family members in Canada with whom they wish to be reunited, such as in Ellie's case. Members of the family class may include the following, according to s. 117(1):

- spouses and common-law or conjugal partners 16 years of age or older;

- fathers or mothers;

- grandfathers or grandmothers;

- dependent children, including children adopted overseas;

- orphan children under 18 to be adopted in Canada, if they are the sibling, niece or nephew, or grandchild of the sponsor; and

- children under 18 to be adopted in Canada.

Sponsors who do not have a closely related family member who is either a Canadian citizen or a permanent resident, or who could be sponsored as a member of the family class, may sponsor one distant relative regardless of age or relationship. Unlisted relatives include independent children, aunts, uncles, nieces, nephews, and cousins.

The IRP Regulations also create a class for sponsored spouses or common-law partners in Canada (s. 123) and their dependent children, if the spouse or common-law partner has legal temporary status in Canada, such as a visitor, student, or business worker.

A person who applies for permanent residence under the Family Class program must not only meet the regulatory definition of a member of the family class but fulfill other requirements, as follows:

- have an eligible sponsor;

- be able to prove identity, age, and relationship to the sponsor and other family members, whether those family members are accompanying or not;

- be admissible to Canada, including family members, whether they are accompanying or not; and

- have a valid and subsisting passport or travel document.

RELATIONSHIP TO THE SPONSOR

Applicants for permanent residence must provide proof of their age and identity by providing birth certificates and identity documents. Canadian immigration policy also places the onus on the applicant to establish the nature of the relationship to the sponsor, as defined in the IRP Regulations.

For relationships such as marriages, common-law partnerships, conjugal partnerships, and adoptions, a person must show that the relationship to the sponsor is genuine. Immigration visa officers are trained to look for relationships of convenience or bad-faith relationships and can refuse an application if they have evidence that an applicant entered into a relationship for the purpose of immigrating to Canada, according to ss. 4 and 4.1 of the IRP Regulations.

It is important to know the kind and variety of documentation one must provide to establish the *bona fides* of a relationship. In the case of biological relatives, such as parents, grandparents, siblings, and children, if no documentary evidence exists to support the relationship, applicants may be required to produce DNA evidence.

SPOUSAL RELATIONSHIPS

The definition of a spouse under the IRPA includes a married spouse, common-law partner, conjugal partner, and same-sex partner. Under previous immigration law, a person could sponsor another person to which he or she was engaged to be married. However, it was difficult to assess whether the engagement would actually result in a marriage, and, consequently, when the current IRPA came into force, this ground for sponsorship was eliminated. If the applicant for permanent residence is engaged to be married, he or she must wait until after the marriage to apply as a spouse, or may apply as a common-law partner if the couple lived together continuously for at least 12 months.

Excluded Relationships

An applicant for permanent residence applying as the sponsor's spouse, common-law partner, or conjugal partner is excluded as a member of the family class, according to ss. 5 and 117(9) of the IRP Regulations, if any of the following circumstances exist:

1. the applicant is under 16 years of age; or

2. the sponsor is already sponsoring a spouse, common-law partner, or conjugal partner, and the undertaking has not ended; or

3. the sponsor is the spouse of another person; or

4. the sponsor is a spouse who has lived separate and apart from the applicant for at least one year and either

   a. the sponsor is the common-law partner of another person or the conjugal partner of another foreign national, or

   b. the applicant is the common-law partner of another person or the conjugal partner of another sponsor; or

5. the applicant was a non-accompanying family member of the sponsor and was not examined when the sponsor previously applied to Canada as a permanent resident.

Relationships of Convenience

The sponsorship of a spouse, common-law partner, or conjugal partner is barred where the relationship between the sponsor and the applicant exists only for immigration purposes.

A "relationship of convenience" is a relationship that is entered into for the sole purpose of gaining permanent residence, as described in s. 4 of the IRP Regulations. A *new relationship* is a relationship of convenience formed after a previous relationship was dissolved for the purpose of entering into the relationship of convenience, as described in s. 4.1 of the IRP Regulations.

With respect to new relationships, case law has held that there are two elements, both of which have to be present to bar sponsorship. In other words, the applicant only needs to negate one. The two elements are as follows:

- the applicant must have gone into the marriage primarily for the purpose of coming to Canada as a family class member; and

- the applicant lacked the intention to permanently reside with the sponsoring spouse.[10]

Consider the following case scenario:

Donna, a 53-year-old divorced Canadian citizen, goes on vacation to a Caribbean island with her girlfriends and meets Grant, a 30-year-old scuba instructor. She spends most of her time during the next two weeks with Grant and learns all about how difficult life is for him on the island. He asks for her help to immigrate to Canada and promises her a large sum of money, which he can get from his uncle. Donna had "the best time of her life" while on vacation but isn't looking for a long-term commitment. She doesn't know anything about immigration to Canada but, from what Grant tells her, the system seems unfair to men like Grant. She figures, what harm is there in helping out such a young, talented, good-looking guy as Grant? Together they work out a scheme to get married so that Grant can come to Canada as her spouse and she can make a little bit of money to renovate her house: a win– win situation. They marry on the eve of Donna's return to Canada.

In assessing Grant's application for permanent residence under the family class, the visa officer will consider the following issues as set out in s. 12 of "OP 2: Processing Members of the Family Class" in CIC's operations manual *Overseas Processing (OP)*:

Officers may need to closely examine evidence that a marriage took place. Photographs or other documents used as evidence of a marriage can be altered. Marriage certificates and other documents may be fraudulent.

In some instances, home visits may be used to establish cohabitation in the case of a marriage or common-law relationship.

Some factors that may be considered and that are common to marriage, common-law relationships and conjugal partner relationships are as follows:

- Do the spouses, common-law or conjugal partners have a good knowledge of each other's personal circumstances, background and family situation?
- The immigration status of the applicant and the timing of the marriage, common-law relationship or conjugal partner relationship.
- Is there evidence that both parties have planned their immigration or immigration of the foreign born spouse/common-law partners or conjugal partner jointly and over a period of time?
- Is there a history of multiple marriages, divorces, common-law relationships or conjugal partner relationships?
- Have previous relationships clearly ended and does the period of separation seem reasonable in the circumstances?
- Do the applicants speak a common language?

In cases where the new relationship is not genuine, the sponsor and applicant may not share a common language and may have no plans to reside together. As well, one may have made some kind of payment to the other for the inconvenience.

Although Donna and Grant have a valid and legal marriage, their age difference, their quick marriage, and their lack of knowledge of each other's personal circumstances would certainly raise a red flag and be questioned by the immigration officer.

Officers are also warned to consider whether relationships have been dissolved in order to facilitate immigration. Section 12.5 of "OP 2" gives the following direction:

> In addition to persons who may enter into relationships of convenience for the sake of acquiring any status under the Act, officers must be conscious of persons who "conveniently" dissolve their marriages or conjugal relationships and then subsequently resume them for the sake of facilitating immigration—that is, persons in conjugal relationships who fraudulently declare that their conjugal relationship is dissolved in order to facilitate their own or other persons' immigration application and later attempt to sponsor that person. R4.1 [s. 4.1 of the IRP Regulations] provides officers the means to refuse applications where persons have dissolved a relationship in bad faith in order to acquire any status under the Act.

Although neither Donna nor Grant dissolved any marriages or conjugal relationships in this scenario, you can see how such circumstances would also attract in-depth investigation by the visa officer.

In the case scenario involving Gary and Ellie, where both partners were in previous relationships, the visa officer would not only be interested in the documentary evidence that Gary is divorced but also be interested in the duration of his relationship with Ellie. By looking at the timing of Gary's divorce together with the timing of his subsequent marriage to Ellie, as well as the long-term relationship that existed before the marriage, the officer would determine that the motive to marry was not purely for immigration purposes.

What follows is a general discussion of each category of a family member who may be sponsored and some of the particular considerations that apply to each in establishing the relationship to the sponsor.

Spouse

According to s. 117(9)(a) of the IRP Regulations, a *spouse* must be at least 16 years of age, legally married, and not otherwise married to someone else to qualify for sponsorship. A *marriage* that takes place outside of Canada must be legal in the country where it took place and also conform to Canadian law (s. 2 of the IRP Regulations). The onus of proving the marriage's validity rests on the applicant (s. 16(1) of the IRPA).[11]

A same-sex spouse who is a Canadian citizen or a permanent resident qualifies for family class sponsorship, provided that the marriage took place in Canada and within the time frame allowed for each particular province. For example, in Ontario, the marriage must have taken place on or after June 10, 2003.[12]

Telephone marriages (where one member of the couple is not physically present but participates by telephone), *proxy marriages* (where one member of the couple is not present and has named another person, to represent him or her as the proxy), and *tribal marriages* (marriages carried out according to tribal custom) are considered legal marriages for immigration purposes if these marriages are legally recognized according to the law of the place where they occurred.

In our example concerning Ellie, she must provide documentary evidence that she and Gary were free to marry and entered into a legal marriage. She would provide a certified copy of Gary's divorce decree as evidence that he is divorced, and a certified copy of Paul's death certificate to prove that she was widowed. Ellie would also provide a certified copy of her marriage certificate with Gary to show that their marriage was a legal marriage in the country where it took place.

Common-Law Relationship

A "common-law relationship" is defined in s. 1 of the IRP Regulations as "in relation to a person, an individual who is cohabiting with the person in a conjugal relationship, having so cohabited for a period of at least one year." Temporary absences notwithstanding, the year of living together must be a continuous 12-month period, and cannot be intermittent periods that add up to one year, in order for the person in the common-law relationship to qualify for sponsorship.

Common-law relationships may be either opposite-sex or same-sex. The relationship must be genuine and not for purposes of acquiring immigration status. The sponsor must not be subject to enforcement proceedings or a removal order, must have a valid passport or travel document, and must generally satisfy admissibility requirements. Note that there is one exemption to the admissibility requirements: persons who have a medical condition that would place excessive demand on health and social services are usually not inadmissible because of their condition.

The common-law partner must be separated from any spouse or previous common-law partner for at least one year, and must be able to prove this.

One of the key issues that arises in determining whether a relationship meets the common-law definition is whether the relationship is conjugal. Section 5.25 of "OP 2" describes a conjugal relationship as having the following features:

- a significant degree of attachment, both physical and emotional;

- an exclusive relationship;

- a mutual and continuing commitment to a shared life together; and

- emotional and financial interdependency.

"OP 2" provides a more detailed examination of the characteristics and assessment of conjugal relationships. Visa officers are directed on how to assess whether a couple may be considered to be in a conjugal relationship and cautioned to assess each case separately to take account of cultural differences and whether local laws or customs might discourage parties from freely admitting the existence of the relationship.

Applicants for permanent residence must provide documentation to prove they are known as a couple, such as documents showing that they have combined their affairs and set up their household together in one home. This could include the following:

- joint bank accounts or credit cards;

- joint ownership of a home;

- joint residential leases;

- joint rental receipts;

- joint utilities (electricity, gas, telephone);

- joint management of household expenses;

- proof of joint purchases, especially for household items; and

- correspondence addressed to either person or both people at the same address.

Conjugal Partner

Section 2 of the IRP Regulations defines a "conjugal partner" as: "in relation to a sponsor, a foreign national residing outside Canada who is in a conjugal relationship with the sponsor and has been in that relationship for a period for at least one year." This category was created for those who might have applied as common-law partners but who did not live together continuously for one year, usually because of legal or social obstacles. These obstacles include the following:

- an immigration barrier, such as where the applicant and/or sponsor were denied long-term stays in each other's country;

- a person's marital status, such as where one partner is married to someone else and living in a country where divorce is not possible; or

- a person's sexual orientation, where the partners are in a same-sex relationship but same-sex marriage is not permitted in the country of the applicant.

Canadian immigration policy on conjugal partners assumes that if a Canadian and a foreign national could get legally married or could live together and thereby establish a common-law relationship, this is what they would have done before submitting the sponsorship and immigration applications. In other words, this category is considered an exception that applies only when marriage or common-law partnership was not an option in the particular circumstances.

"Conjugal" is not defined in the IRPA or the IRP Regulations; however, CIC provides direction to visa officers in assessing the conjugal nature of a relationship. Officers must look beyond the presence of a physical relationship and consider the following:

- whether the relationship is monogamous;

- whether the relationship is of some permanence—namely, a minimum duration of one year; and

- whether mutual interdependence exists between the partners.

A conjugal relationship must be similar to a marriage-like relationship where the couple can demonstrate that, over time, they have exclusive and emotional ties to one another and have made a commitment to each other. Although no legal document such as a marriage certificate exists, the conjugal partners should be able to provide other types of evidence of their significant commitment to each other, such as the following:

- insurance policies or estates showing they have named each other as beneficiaries;

- documents showing they hold joint ownership of possessions; and

- documents showing they hold joint expenses or share income.

DEPENDENT CHILDREN

One of the major changes brought in by the *Immigration and Refugee Protection Act* was the raising of the age for a dependent child from 19 to 22. The definition of a "dependant" in s. 2 of the IRP Regulations is technical and should be read carefully. In summary, it means a biological child (provided that the child was not adopted by a person other than the spouse or common-law partner of the parent), or an adopted child of the parent, where the child is in one of the following situations of dependency:

- under age 22 and single (no spouse or common-law partner);

- a full-time student and substantially dependent on a parent for financial support since before age 22, or since becoming a spouse or common-law partner (if this happened before age 22); or

- financially dependent on a parent since before age 22 because of a disability.

Using our case scenario concerning Gary and Ellie, Ellie's daughters Amanda (aged 17) and Martha (aged 12) both meet the regulatory definition of a dependant. The lock-in age is on the day that the Case Processing Centre receives the sponsorship application and the required processing fees. The sponsorship process can be lengthy, so the ages of Martha and Amanda will be "frozen in time" for the full duration of the time that it takes to process the sponsorship and applications for permanent residence: starting on the day that Gary submits his sponsorship application in Canada to the date of the issuance of the permanent resident visas by the visa office.

Dependants over the age of 22 who may still qualify if they are substantially dependent on their parents for financial support must either be full-time students enrolled in an accredited postsecondary institution or have a physical or mental disability. Applicants must provide evidence to prove this, such as school or medical records. In assessing applications, visa officers are encouraged to raise questions such as the following:

- Is the schooling a dominant activity in the life of the student?

- What is the attendance record?

- What grades were achieved?

- Can the student discuss with some knowledge the subjects being studied?

- Has a genuine effort been made to assimilate the knowledge in the courses being studied?

Should the conclusion be reached that the primary purpose of undertaking the program of study is for immigration purposes, officers are directed to deny the application for that child (s. 14.2 of "OP 2").

The applicant must also demonstrate with supporting documentation the degree of dependence. Officers inquire into the costs of study and the living arrangement of the child. For a student living apart from the parents, the parents are expected to show payment of room and board. Students who pay a significant portion of their own educational and living costs, or who may be receiving student loans or financial assistance from another source, may not meet the definition.

ADOPTED CHILDREN

Under family class provisions of the IRP Regulations, a child must be related to the sponsor by a blood relationship or by adoption. An adoption by definition severs a child's legal relationship to the biological parents (s. 3(2)). Severance from the biological parents means that an adopted child may not later sponsor the biological parents or grandparents.

In all cases of adoption, the genuine and informed consent of the biological parents must be provided. If both parents are alive, both should give consent. In the event that only one parent gives consent to an adoption, visa officers must be satisfied that the second parent has no legal rights with respect to the child.

To sponsor an adopted child for permanent residence, there are two processes to complete:

- the adoption process, and

- the sponsorship process or citizenship process.

Adoption Processes and Criteria

There are separate adoption processes and conditions depending on whether the sponsor is adopting a child from outside or from within Canada and whether the child is over age 18.

Adoptions Outside Canada

International adoption is complex because of social welfare laws, immigration laws, and the laws of the child's country. The IRP Regulations provide for the adoption abroad of children both under 18 years of age and children over 18 years of age (if they also meet the definition of a dependant).

Adoptions of children under 18 years of age must be in the best interests of the child, according to s. 117(2) of the IRP Regulations. If the foreign adoption was not in the best interests of the child, the child shall not be considered a member of the family class. To meet the "best interests" test, the following requirements listed in s. 117(3) must be met:

- a competent authority conducted or approved a home study of the adoptive parents;

- before the adoption, the child's parents gave their free and informed consent to the child's adoption;

- the adoption created a genuine parent–child relationship, and not a relationship of convenience for immigration purposes;

- the adoption was in accordance with the laws of the place where the adoption took place;

- the adoption was in accordance with the laws of the sponsor's country of residence;

- if the sponsor lived in Canada at the time that the adoption took place, the competent authority of the child's province of intended destination stated in writing that it does not object to the adoption;

- if the adoption was subject to the Hague Convention on Adoption, the competent authority of the country where the adoption took place and the province of destination both stated in writing that they approved the adoption as conforming to the Convention; and

- if the adoption was not subject to the Hague Convention on Adoption, there is no evidence that the adoption is for the purpose of child trafficking or undue gain within the meaning of the Convention.

The "best interests of the child" principle is recognized by the international community as a fundamental human right of every child, and is also entrenched in article 3 of the United Nations Convention on the Rights of the Child. Article 1 of the Convention defines a child as any person under the age of 18, unless an earlier age of majority is recognized by a country's law.

Article 3 elaborates on the meaning of "best interests" and provides that signatory states, including Canada, must ensure such protection and care as is necessary for a child's well-being, taking into account the rights and duties of parents, legal guardians, or other individuals legally responsible, and, to this end, shall take all appropriate legislative and administrative measures.

The Convention on the Protection of Children and Co-operation in Respect of Inter-Country Adoption (the Hague Convention), referenced in the IRP Regulations, provides minimum standards and procedures for adoptions between countries. It is intended to end unethical adoption practices and promote cooperation between countries. The Hague Convention puts in place procedures that minimize the chance of exploitation of children, birth parents, or adoptive parents during the adoption process.

The Hague Convention requires the central adoption authority in both the child's destination country and country of current residence to agree to the child's adoption. Canada and all provinces and territories follow the requirements of the Hague Convention. If the child to be adopted is from a signatory state to the Hague Convention, the adoption must follow the Convention's rules. In other words, no private adoptions may take place for a child from a signatory state. In Canada, a CIC officer must approve the sponsorship before the adoption may be completed.

The Hague Convention requires that the authorities in the child's country of origin ensure that

- the child is legally free for adoption;

- the birth parents have consented to the adoption in the child's best interests and understand the consequences for their parental rights; and

- the decision to place a child for adoption is not motivated by any financial gain.

The Hague Convention requires that the authorities in Canada, namely, Human Resources and Social Development Canada (HRSDC), Child, Family and Community Division, ensure the following:

- the adoptive parents are eligible and suitable to adopt; and

- the appropriate authorities have decided that the child will be allowed to enter and live permanently in Canada.

The CIC website directs sponsors/adoptive parents to links to access a list of countries that are parties to the Hague Convention, and provinces and territories in Canada that have implemented the Convention. Canadian adoptive parents must also obtain the approval of the province in which they live. There are several specific requirements that must be successfully met by prospective adoptive parents, as follows:

1. **Home study.** A home study is an assessment of the prospective parents with respect to their suitability to adopt. It is undertaken by provincial or territorial authorities, and generally carried out by an accredited social worker. The home study is comprehensive, and an important precondition to an adoption. It is also required for immigration purposes under s. 117(1)(g)(ii) of the IRP Regulations.

2. **Letter of no-involvement.** A letter of no-involvement may be accepted instead of a home study where a private adoption takes place outside Canada and in a state that is not a signatory to the Hague Convention. It may also be accepted in cases where an adoption is finalized abroad prior to the adopted child's arrival in Canada. The purpose of the letter of no-involvement is to inform the visa office that an adoption order, which is in accordance with the laws of the jurisdiction where the adoption took place, will be recognized by the adopting parents' province or territory of residence.[13]

3. **Letter of no-objection.** A letter of no-objection is a written statement from the province or territory where the child will live, stating that the province or territory does not object to the adoption (ss. 117(1)(g)(iii)(B) and 117(3)(e) of the IRP Regulations).

4. **Letter (or notice) of agreement.** A letter or notice of agreement is required in Hague Convention adoption cases, indicating that the province and adoptive parents agree to the adoption (s. 117(1)(g)(ii) and ss. 117(3)(f) and (g) of the IRP Regulations). It is sent by the receiving provincial or territorial authorities to the visa office, with a copy to the central authority of the adopted child's country of residence.

Adoptions Inside Canada

For in-Canada adoptions, s. 117(1)(g) of the IRP Regulations sets out the following conditions for membership in the family class:

- the child must be under the age of 18;

- there must be no evidence that the adoption is for the purpose of acquiring any privileges or status under the IRPA;

- if the adoption was subject to the Hague Convention on Adoption, the competent authority of the country in which the child lives and the province of destination of that child must have stated in writing that they approve the adoption as conforming to the Convention; and

- if the adoption was not subject to the Hague Convention on Adoption, the child must have been placed for adoption in the country in which he or she lives or is legally available in that country for adoption and there must be no evidence that the adoption is for the purpose of child trafficking or undue gain within the meaning of the Convention, and the competent authority of the child's province of intended destination must have stated in writing that it does not object to the adoption.

Adoptions of Children over 18

Adopted children over the age of 18 must be considered a dependant as defined in the IRP Regulations. For an adopted child over the age of 18, in order to be considered a member of the family class, the following circumstances have to exist:

- the adoption must have been in accordance with the laws of the place where the adoption took place and, if the sponsor resided in Canada at the time of the adoption, the adoption must have been in accordance with the laws of the province where the sponsor then resided, if any, that applied in respect of the adoption of a child 18 years of age or older;

- a genuine parent–child relationship must have existed at the time of the adoption and existed before the child reached the age of 18; and

- the adoption must not have been primarily for the purpose of acquiring a status or privilege under the IRPA.

Regardless of whether the adoption is outside or inside Canada, or if the adoptee is older than 18 years, a visa officer must be satisfied the adoption creates a genuine parent–child relationship, and not a relationship of convenience entered into for the sole purpose of gaining permanent residence. Section 4 of the IRP Regulations refers to this kind of relationship as a bad-faith relationship, and excludes adoption where the relationship between the sponsor and the adopted child exists only for immigration purposes. The sponsorship will not be approved if a visa officer concludes that the purpose of the adoption is to gain admission to Canada.

Immigration (Sponsorship) Process

Adoptive parents may apply to sponsor their child for permanent residence if

- the adopted child is coming to Canada to live right after the adoption takes place; or

- one or both parents are Canadian citizens or permanent residents.

The adopted person does not meet the requirements for the immigration process if

- the adopted person is not going to Canada to live right after the adoption takes place; or

- the adopted person is an adult adoptee living outside Canada and not returning to Canada to live right after his or her application is approved.

Before a permanent resident visa under the family class is issued for an adopted dependent child or orphan,[14] the sponsor must provide a statement in writing confirming knowledge of information regarding any medical condition of the child or orphaned person. This is intended to safeguard against the abandonment of the child by prospective parents, by ensuring that they are aware of, and equipped to deal with, any health or medical conditions before the adoption is complete and the child is issued a permanent resident visa to travel to Canada (s. 118 of the IRP Regulations).

Citizenship Process

Until recently, a child adopted by Canadian citizens did not automatically become a Canadian citizen, but instead arrived in Canada with a permanent resident visa and was admitted as a permanent resident. The parents then had to apply for citizenship on behalf of the child.

However, a new process introduced on December 23, 2007 allows an adopted child to apply for Canadian citizenship without first becoming a permanent resident, if the adoption was by a Canadian citizen after February 14, 1977. Adoptive parents may apply for citizenship on behalf of their adopted child if all the following criteria are met:[15]

- at least one adoptive parent is, or was, a Canadian citizen when the adoption took place;

- the adoption severs (or severed) all ties with the adopted person's legal parents; and

- the adoption was or will be completed outside Canada (except for Quebec).

The adopted person does not meet the requirements for the citizenship process if any of the following factors exist:

- neither parent was a Canadian citizen when the adoption took place;

- the adoption took place before February 15, 1977;

- the adoption did not fully sever all ties with the child's legal parents;

- the adoption will be completed in Canada; or

- a probationary period is to be completed in Canada before a final adoption order is issued from the child's birth country.

GUARDIANSHIP

The intent of the guardianship provisions was to provide a mechanism to sponsor an orphaned or abandoned child who would not otherwise meet the criteria of a "member of the family class," and who lived in a country where adoption is unavailable.

However, the guardianship provisions of the IRP Regulations were not implemented when those regulations came into force in June 2002, but rather were delayed to allow the provinces and territories time to conduct feasibility studies. The result was that the provinces and territories informed CIC that they would not participate in the implementation of the guardianship provisions, making implementation impossible.

The regulations relating to guardianship were subsequently repealed in 2005, and amended such that CIC will continue to deal with immigration cases where children in need of care are brought into families through guardianships. Officers examine these situations case by case and, where humanitarian and compassionate reasons exist, use their discretion to allow these children into Canada.[16]

SPECIFIED ORPHANED RELATIVES

Siblings, including half and step siblings, nephews, nieces, and grandchildren, may also be admitted as sponsored relatives if they meet all the following criteria according to s. 117(1)(f) of the IRP Regulations:

- they are orphaned;

- they are not a spouse or common-law partner; and

- they are under 18.

Generally, the sponsorship for orphaned relatives who are under 18 years of age follows the same procedures as for adopted children under 18 years of age, provided they are unmarried and not in a common-law relationship. As in adoption cases, a visa officer must obtain the written consent of the appropriate authorities in the country of residence of the child, before the child may be removed from that country. Written consent of any legal guardians must also be obtained.

Officers are directed to counsel sponsors to obtain legal guardianship of the child upon the child's arrival in the province of residence to ensure that the sponsor has legal obligations toward the sponsored child, according to s. 73 of "OP 3: Adoptions," in the CIC operations manual *Overseas Processing (OP)*.

Under the provisions of the former Act, the Federal Court of Appeal held that a visa officer did not have to consider whether the biological father was alive or not, if he was not married to the mother and there had been no declaration of parentage.[17]

Applying for Permanent Residence Under the Family Class

SPONSORSHIP KITS AND APPLICATIONS FOR PERMANENT RESIDENCE

Sponsorship kits can be obtained online from the CIC website or from a CIC Call Centre. All kits come with extensive guides that describe the forms in each kit, the supporting documentation that must be submitted, and the addresses for mailing. There are specific sponsoring kits, tailored to different family situations, as described below.

Family Members Abroad

For a sponsor who is sponsoring family members who are abroad, there are two different types of kits. One is for sponsoring a "spouse, common-law partner, conjugal partner or dependent child," and the other is for sponsoring "any other family member," as follows:

1. Spouse, common-law partner, conjugal partner, or dependent child: There are three parts for this kit, namely:

   a. sponsorship application (Part A);

   b. application for permanent residence (Part B); and

   c. region-specific forms (Part C).

2. Any other family member: The kit for "any other family member" contains only the sponsorship application because CIC first assesses the sponsor's eligibility before sending the rest of the kit, which consists of an immigrant's guide and Application for Permanent Residence in Canada form (IMM 0008).

Both the sponsor and the applicant for permanent residence complete the required forms. The sponsor must sign the Sponsorship Agreement form and send it to the person being sponsored. The applicant/family member must also sign the Sponsorship Agreement and return it to the sponsor along with the Application for Permanent Residence in Canada form (IMM 0008), other forms, and supporting documents.

Temporary Residents

The sponsorship kit for temporary residents in Canada who are applying for permanent residence under the "spouse or common-law partner in Canada" class is slightly different. The sponsorship kit consists of one guide, and it is to be used by both the sponsor and the applicant, who submit a joint application. The joint application must include the following:

- an Application to Sponsor and Undertaking form (IMM 1344A);

- an In-Canada Application for Permanent Resident Status form (IMM 5002), including Schedule 1 of that form;

- other forms and supporting documents; and

- fees.

A Canadian or permanent resident sponsor under this class must meet the same requirements as a sponsor under the "spouse, common-law partner, conjugal partner or dependent child" class. A sponsor must sign an undertaking and the sponsorship agreement, promising to provide for the basic requirements of the partner. The person being sponsored—the applicant for permanent residence—must generally have legal, temporary resident status and must meet the criteria of "member of the family class" and not be inadmissible.

FEES

There are a number of expenses associated with a sponsorship application, including two fees payable to CIC:

- the application or processing fees for the sponsor and the applicant for permanent residence; and

- the Right of Permanent Residence Fee.

Fees can be paid online or at a designated financial institution, and the "fees receipt" form (IMM 5401) must accompany the application forms (s. 295 of the IRP Regulations). There are additional fees to cover the costs for medical examinations, police certificates, the issuing of documents, and travel.

Application (Processing) Fees

Processing fees are charged to assess applications and these fees are non-refundable. Both the sponsor and the applicant for permanent residence must pay processing fees. The following provides an example of the fees charged; however, these fees are subject to change, so check the CIC website for a current schedule of fees:

- Sponsor's Application Fee (approximately $75)

- application for permanent residence fee (approximately $500 for applicants over 22, and significantly less for children).

In our case scenario involving Gary and Ellie, the processing fees add up to $850, as shown in the table below:

Person	Type of application	Fee
Sponsor, Gary	Sponsorship application	$75
Principal applicant, Ellie (over 22 years of age, married to the sponsor)	Permanent residence application	$475
Accompanying family member, Amanda (under 22 years of age, not married or in a common-law relationship)	Permanent residence application	$150
Accompanying family member, Martha (under 22 years of age, not married or in a common-law relationship)	Permanent residence application	$150
Total processing fees:		**$850**

Right of Permanent Residence Fee

In addition to the processing fees, there is a Right of Permanent Residence Fee (RPRF). This fee can be paid at the same time as the application fees, or at any time during the process, but must be paid before a permanent resident visa is issued. The

RPRF must be paid for the principal applicant (the person being sponsored) and other family members. Certain members of the family class, however, are exempted from paying the RPRF, as follows:

- a dependent child of the sponsor or principal applicant;

- a child to be adopted by the sponsor; or

- an orphaned brother, sister, nephew, niece, or grandchild of the sponsor.

The Right of Permanent Residence Fee is subject to change: for example, the fee was set at $975 for years and then it was reduced to $490 in 2006. Check the CIC website for the current amount.

For our case scenario, the fee is $490, as shown in the table below:

Person	Right of Permanent Residence Fee
Ellie, principal applicant	$490
Amanda, dependant of principal applicant	$0
Martha, dependant of principal applicant	$0
Total Right of Permanent Residence Fee:	**$490**

Therefore, the processing and Right of Permanent Residence fees total is $1,340 ($850 + $490) for Gary, Ellie, and her daughters. These fees do not cover the cost of medical examinations, or any criminal or background checks.

Decisions on Applications for Permanent Residence Under the Family Class

The possible outcomes of CIC decisions with respect to both sponsorship applications and permanent resident applications, and the rights of appeal of sponsors and applicants, are described in this section.

The sections that follow describe the possible decisions of CIC officials on the application for sponsorship by the sponsor, and on the application for permanent residence by the principal applicant and dependants. These sections also explain rights of appeal.

SPONSORSHIP DECISIONS

In our example, Gary sends his Application to Sponsor and Undertaking form (IMM 1344A) to the centralized Case Processing Centre in Mississauga, Ontario for processing. A Canadian immigration officer assesses the sponsorship application to verify that Gary meets all the requirements, as follows:

- the sponsor meets the regulatory definition and is eligible to sponsor;

- the applicants for permanent residence are members of the family class; and

- the application for permanent residence is complete, including fees.

The immigration officer's decision will result in one of a number of possible outcomes, as follows:

1. *Sponsor is ineligible—elect to end processing.* If the immigration officer finds that Gary is ineligible, Gary may choose to end the process by checking in box 1 of the Application to Sponsor and Undertaking form "To withdraw your sponsorship." If he does so, all processing fees (less $75) will be repaid. The immigration officer will close the file. Gary has no right to appeal the immigration officer's decision.

2. *Sponsor is ineligible—elect to pursue application.* If the immigration officer finds that Gary is ineligible, Gary may choose to pursue the matter at the next level, by checking in box 1 "To proceed with the application for permanent residence." The immigration officer will then transfer the application for permanent residence and the negative decision (that is, the officer's finding of ineligibility) to the nearest visa office where Ellie, the principal applicant, resides. Gary has the right to appeal to the Immigration Appeal Division of the Immigration and Refugee Board.

3. *Sponsor is ineligible because sponsored person is not a member of the family class.* If the immigration officer finds that Gary is ineligible because Ellie, the principal applicant, is not a member of the family class, Gary may accept this finding and elect to discontinue processing. However, if Gary does not accept the finding and elects to pursue the matter, the officer will send her decision to the visa office. Gary's right to appeal to the Immigration Appeal Division of the IRB is maintained.

4. *Sponsor is eligible.* Finally, if the immigration officer finds that Gary is eligible, the immigration officer's written decision and Ellie's application for permanent residence are forwarded to the appropriate visa office for further processing.

SPONSORSHIP APPEALS

Appeal procedures are discussed in Chapter 10: "Enforcement Procedures." Below is a brief explanation of when sponsorship appeals are permitted.

Appeals Permitted by Sponsor

A sponsor who is found to be ineligible to sponsor may appeal to the Immigration Appeal Division. Sometimes a sponsor may be ineligible because he does not meet the eligibility criteria—for example, when he does not meet the LICO requirements to be a sponsor. Ineligibility is determined by an immigration officer in Canada. The sponsor may also appeal the decision of the visa officer abroad. However, if the applicant for permanent residence (the person being sponsored) is not eligible, for example, a visa officer abroad may find the application incomplete, that the relationship is one of convenience, or that the family member is inadmissible.

If the application for permanent residence is refused by the visa officer, a **refusal letter** is sent to the applicant setting out the reasons for the refusal. The visa office also mails a copy of the refusal letter, together with a Notice of Appeal, to the sponsor. The notice informs the sponsor of his right to appeal under s. 63 of the IRPA.

The refusal letter sets out the grounds for refusal—that is, the reasons why the application for permanent residence was rejected. If the sponsor chooses to appeal the refusal, a Notice of Appeal along with a copy of the refusal letter must be filed at the Immigration Appeal Division of the IRB no later than 30 days of the sponsor's being notified of the decision. The sponsor also has the right to be represented by counsel and must provide the tribunal with the counsel's contact information.

Appeals Not Permitted by Sponsor

Sponsorship appeals are not permitted in the following cases:

1. *Ineligible sponsor—spouse or common-law partner in Canada.* Appeal rights for "in-Canada" applications are different from those for appeals of sponsorship cases abroad. When a sponsor does not meet the requirements of the "spouse or common-law partner in Canada class," as defined in s. 130(1) of the IRP Regulations, then it follows that the applicant for permanent residence does not have an eligible sponsor. The application for permanent residence is therefore refused, and the applicant for permanent residence is advised by the Case Processing Centre of the reasons for the refusal and directed to leave Canada or risk removal action.

   In this case, neither the sponsor nor the applicant for permanent residence has a right to appeal to the Immigration Appeal Division. However, the applicant for permanent residence may apply for a judicial review within 30 days after the date of refusal.

2. *Inadmissible applicant.* There are no appeal rights for applicants for permanent residence if they are found inadmissible on the most serious grounds of inadmissibility. Sponsors generally do not have the right to appeal when a family member applicant is found to be inadmissible under s. 64 of the IRPA on the grounds of security, violating human or international rights, serious criminality, or organized criminality. (For a full description of these grounds, refer to Chapter 3.)

PERMANENT RESIDENCE DECISIONS

In processing applications under the Family Class program, a visa officer reviews the application for permanent residence to ensure that the applicants (Ellie and her daughters, for example) do indeed meet the regulatory definition as members of the family class and that they have an eligible sponsor. The visa officer also does the following:

- examines the supporting documents to ascertain the applicants' identity, age, and relationship to the sponsor and other family members (whether those family members are accompanying them to Canada or not);

- examines their passports or travel documents to determine whether they are valid; and

- determines whether the applicants are inadmissible (including family members, whether they are accompanying them or not to Canada), according to any of the grounds of inadmissibility, described in Chapter 3.

Ellie might be called to appear for an interview with a visa officer. However, although visa officers have the authority to interview applicants, they generally waive interviews unless there is a need to confirm the applicant's identity or the relationship to the sponsor, or to address questions related to admissibility.

If all the requirements are met, the visa officer issues a permanent resident visa to travel to Canada as a permanent resident. The names of non-accompanying family members are included on the visa of the principal applicant. (In our case scenario, Ellie does not have any other dependants.) Ellie and her daughters must travel to Canada before the expiry date on their visas, where they will be examined at the port of entry.

If one or more of the requirements are not met, and the application is refused, the visa officer issues a refusal letter to the applicant and sends a copy to the sponsor. This written record can then be used as the basis of an appeal.

ECONOMIC CLASS

Immigration under the economic class fulfills one of the stated objectives of Canadian immigration policy: to "permit Canada to pursue the maximum social, cultural and economic benefits of immigration" (s. 3(1)(a) of the IRPA). Foreign nationals who acquire permanent residence under an economic class category help to develop the Canadian economy and fill labour market shortages with their skills, knowledge, expertise, and other assets.

The majority of permanent residents are admitted under the economic classes. In 2005, 60 percent of the total number of permanent residents admitted to Canada came under the economic classes, including their spouses and dependants. Within this group, the majority were admitted as skilled workers.[18]

The legal basis for selecting foreign nationals as members of the economic class is their ability to become economically established in Canada, according to s. 12(2) of the IRPA.

The economic class is composed of three main streams:

- federal skilled workers (outside of Quebec)

- provincial and territorial nominees

- members of the business class (entrepreneurs, self-employed persons, and investors).

Separate rules apply to skilled workers who intend to reside in Quebec. Because of the Canada-Quebec Accord, Quebec has sole responsibility for determining the selection criteria and for integrating skilled workers. Skilled workers who are destined for Quebec must obtain a Certificat de sélection du Québec (Quebec certificate of selection) from that province. However, issues of inadmissibility and the issuance of the permanent resident visa remain federal responsibilities.

What follows is a closer examination of the requirements for each of the main economic classes, including an overview of the process for applying.

Federal Skilled Workers

Foreign nationals who apply for permanent residence as skilled workers are expected to have the education, skills, work experience, language ability, and other qualities needed to contribute to the Canadian labour market. Applicants must demonstrate that they intend to enter the labour market and can be self-supporting at the time they arrive in Canada.

A person applying as a skilled worker is called the "principal applicant." The principal applicant may include family members in the application for permanent residence as long as the visa officer is satisfied that the family members are, in fact, family members and they are not inadmissible.[19]

The following case scenario is used in the sections below to demonstrate how to apply for permanent residence as a skilled worker:

Sanjay Patel was born in Ahmedabad, Gujarat on the west coast of India in 1970. His mother tongue is Gujarati. He learned English at school and he speaks, understands, reads, and writes fluently. He was exposed to French briefly as a young boy when his parents worked in the kitchen at a French consulate, and he can still answer simple questions in French.

Mr. Patel attended primary school at the Municipal School Harda from 1975 to 1983, then attended Sadhana Higher Secondary School from 1983 to 1987. He worked in various restaurants as a dishwasher, busboy, and kitchen helper until 1991 when he decided to go back to school to become a chef. He enrolled in a four-year degree program to obtain a bachelor's degree in hotel and tourism management at the Gujarat Institute of Hotel Management. In 1995, he married Anita just after he graduated, and he has worked in the food service sector since that time. Anita completed a four-year bachelor's degree and worked as an English teacher until the birth of their son, Sanjit, in 1997. Two years later, Priya, their daughter, was born. Anita did not return to work.

Mr. Patel's first job after obtaining his degree was as a cook in a local restaurant. In his spare time, he also ran his own business, catering medium-sized business functions. His reputation for good quality food and service brought him to the attention of the great chef Maestro, who talked Mr. Patel into joining his prestigious restaurant, Saffron, in 1999. He trained there as a sous-chef for four years under the guidance of Maestro. Since 2003, Mr. Patel has worked in a supervisory capacity with the promise of rising to the position of Executive Chef.

In 2004, Mr. Patel escorted Maestro to a cooking competition hosted by the Canadian Culinary Institute of the Canadian Federation of Chefs and Cooks, in Vancouver, British Columbia. Although the competition was a gruelling two weeks of hard work, Mr. Patel got his first "taste" of Canada.

Paul Pierre, a famous Toronto chef, noticed Mr. Patel at the competition. Mr. Patel was invited to spend an additional week in Toronto to check out the restaurant scene with Paul Pierre. Paul Pierre offered Mr. Patel the posting of Executive Chef at his new restaurant, Taj. Mr. Patel fell in love with the cosmopolitan city and sees this as his chance to finally realize his dream and provide a good life for his family.

Mr. Patel does not know anything about immigrating to Canada but thinks he would have to apply under the federal skilled worker class.

Is Sanjay Patel a good candidate for immigrating as a permanent resident with his family? We consider this question in the sections below.

REQUIREMENTS FOR FEDERAL SKILLED WORKERS

"Skilled workers" are a class of persons selected "on the basis of their ability to become economically established in Canada and who intend to reside in a province other than the Province of Quebec," according to s. 75 of the IRP Regulations. In our case scenario, Sanjay Patel is destined for Toronto, Ontario.

To be successful in his application for permanent residence as a skilled worker, Mr. Patel, as the principal applicant, must meet the following work experience requirements:

- he must possess a minimum of one year of continuous full-time paid work experience within the past ten years in a management occupation or in an occupation normally requiring university, college, or technical training as set out under skill type 0 or skill level A or B of the National Occupational Classification (NOC) matrix (as described below); and

- his occupation must not be considered a restricted occupation.

If Mr. Patel meets these requirements, the visa officer then reviews the application for permanent residence to ensure that the applicant meets the following selection criteria:

- he has sufficient points to meet or exceed the pass mark under the point system (discussed below under the heading "Point System"); and

- he is self-supporting upon arrival (based on a job offer or sufficient settlement funds).

Finally, Mr. Patel and his family members must not be inadmissible, as described in Chapter 3, "Inadmissibility."

National Occupational Classification

The National Occupational Classification (NOC) is used by Citizenship and Immigration Canada to differentiate between occupations and skill levels, with respect to prospective immigrants in the skilled worker class.

The NOC is developed by Human Resources and Social Development Canada (HRSDC) in partnership with Statistics Canada and is used by a variety of technicians from economists and business analysts to career counsellors. It is a standardized system that provides formal definitions for more than 500 Canadian occupations. Each occupation is coded according to the type and level of skill required to perform the work. It is a tool for understanding the world of work by describing duties, skills, interests, aptitudes, educational requirements, and work settings.

WEBLINK

To view the complete NOC matrix online, including the list of occupations in each Major Group, visit the NOC website at: www5.hrsdc.gc.ca/noc-cnp/app/index.aspx and click on the Matrix menu item.

The NOC is organized in matrix format to show the relationship between skill types and skill levels. There are nine skill types (coded by the digits 1 through 9) that are listed across the top of the matrix, and a tenth skill type (coded with 0) that occupies the first row of the matrix. There are four skill levels (A through D) that appear on the left side of the matrix. To demonstrate the organization of the matrix, an outline of the matrix is shown below with only the skill types and skill levels included. To see the complete matrix, go to www5.hrsdc.gc.ca/noc-cnp/app/aboutnoc.aspx?lc=e.

Occupations at skill type 0 require a relevant university degree, professional designation, college diploma or other management training, and proven management experience.

The four skill levels refer to the type of education or training needed to perform the work, as follows:

- skill level A: university

- skill level B: college/technical school or apprenticeship training

- skill level C: high school/on-the-job training

- skill level D: short demonstration training.

Generally, each matrix cell is called a Major Group, and consists of a list of specific occupations. Under the skilled worker class, applicants for permanent residence must have at least one year of continuous full-time paid work experience within the last ten years that is either in the category of skill type 0 or in skill level A or B.

To assist applicants to find their occupation in the National Occupational Classification, CIC directs applicants to the HRSDC website, where applicants can view the complete NOC matrix and descriptions of specific occupations.

For example, consider the field "Paralegal and Related Occupations," found within Major Group 42 in the matrix and coded in the NOC as 4211. For "Paralegal and Related Occupations," the NOC provides a lead statement to describe the work performed, job titles in this occupational field (for example, independent paralegal, law clerk, legal assistant, and legal researcher), and duties, as well as the employment requirements.

Let's take a closer look at the NOC code. The first digit of an occupational code designates the *skill type*. Skill type refers to the type of work performed and the field of training or experience normally required for entry into the occupation, including the educational area of study and employment. The skill type is intended to identify employment sectors on the basis of the ten broad occupational areas from 0 through 9.

In our example of code 4211, the first digit in the code is 4, corresponding to skill type 4, "Occupations in Social Science, Education, Government Service and Religion."

The second digit of the occupational code indicates the skill level: 1 corresponds to skill level A, 2 corresponds to skill level B, and so on.

If a skilled worker applicant has work experience in the category of skill level A, this means that she has experience in a professional occupation, requiring a relevant university degree, professional designation, or two-year college diploma, and several years of directly related experience.

If a skilled worker applicant has work experience in the category of skill level B, this means that she has experience as a technician or technologist. Occupations at skill level B require two to five years of apprenticeship training and apprenticeship or trades certification, and several years of directly related work experience.

	1 Business, Finance and Administration Occupations	2 Natural and Applied Sciences and Related Occupations	3 Health Occupations	4 Occupations in Social Science, Education, Government Service and Religion	5 Occupations in Art, Culture, Recreation and Sport	6 Sales and Service Occupations	7 Trades, Transport and Equipment Operators and Related Occupations	8 Occupations Unique to Primary Industry	9 Occupations Unique to Processing, Manufacturing and Utilities
0 Management Occupations									
Skill Level A									
Skill Level B									
Skill Level C									
Skill Level D									

In our example of code 4211, the second digit in the code is 2, corresponding to skill level B, which requires college/technical school or apprenticeship training.

Recall our case scenario. Would Sanjay Patel meet the minimum work experience requirements of having at least one year of continuous full-time paid work experience within the last ten years of the date of application that is in the category of skill type 0, or skill level A or B, according to the National Occupational Classification? The easiest way to find out is to go to the HRSDC website at www5.hrsdc.gc.ca/NOC-CNP/app/AboutNOC.aspx?lc=e and click on the Occupational Descriptions menu item. Click on the link for the appropriate skill type, "6 Sales and Service Occupations," to search for Sanjay's job title. "Sous-chef" is not listed but "Chefs" is listed (code 6241). Then click on the link to read a description of the duties for jobs in that field. We find that Mr. Patel's job title is listed and the duties described are a match with the work he performed. We also know from the case scenario that he has been working full time as a sous-chef since 2003. He therefore exceeds the minimum requirement of work experience in an occupation that is listed in the NOC.

Point System

Canada has used a point-based system to assess skilled workers since 1967, when it was first introduced into immigration regulations. Under the *Immigration Act* of 1976, skilled workers were known as "independent applicants," because they were not financially reliant on sponsors or the government.

The point system was designed to improve consistency and fairness by reducing discretion and the potential for discrimination in selecting immigrants. Under the point system, immigration officers assign points up to a fixed maximum in each of several categories. The minister is authorized to set the pass mark, or "minimum number of points required of a skilled worker," under s. 76(2) of the IRP Regulations. Such authority allows the minister to amend the pass mark when there are changes in the Canadian economic and social landscape or when there are changing demands for prospective immigrants. The pass mark is the minimum required total out of a possible 100 points for six selection factors. The current pass mark is 67 points.

Skilled workers are assessed according to the following six selection factors set out in ss. 78 to 83 of the IRP Regulations:

1. Education—maximum 25 points

2. Language proficiency in English and French—maximum 24 points

3. Experience—maximum 21 points

4. Age—maximum 10 points

5. Arranged employment—maximum 10 points

6. Adaptability—maximum 10 points.

Points are allocated to the principal applicant with a view to identifying the applicant's ability to become economically established. The fact that 70 out of 100 possible points are spread over only three factors—education, language skills, and work experience—shows the importance of these factors in the selection of skilled workers.

A grid of the selection factors is part of the self-assessment worksheet that is provided to applicants in the CIC instruction guide *Application for Permanent Residence: Federal Skilled Worker Class* (IMM EG7000). Below is a brief description of each of the selection factors.

Education—0 to 25 Points

The visa officer awards points for education in a range from 0 points to 25 points, generally based first on the number of years of completed full-time or full-time-equivalent studies, and then second on the applicant's educational credentials.

The following terms are defined in the IRP Regulations as follows:

- **Full-time studies:** a program of study leading to an educational credential, consisting of at least 15 hours of instruction per week during the academic year.

- **Full-time equivalent:** in reference to part-time or accelerated studies, the period that would have been required to complete those studies on a full-time basis.

- **Educational credential:** any diploma, degree, or trade or apprenticeship credential issued upon completion of a program of study or training at an educational or training institution recognized by the authorities responsible for registering, accrediting, supervising, and regulating such institutions in the country of issue (s. 73).

Educational credentials are not measured according to Canadian standards; rather, visa officers assess how they are considered locally. Professional degrees, such as medical and law degrees, may be considered first-level degrees (bachelor's degrees) or second-level degrees (graduate degrees), depending on the country. For example, a bachelor of laws degree in the United Kingdom is a first-level degree, because students require no university credits to enter law school. The same degree in Canada is a second-level degree, because students require a minimum number of university credits before applying to law school. Officers are instructed to consider how local authorities consider professional degrees, in the CIC's *Overseas Processing (OP)* operations manual.[20]

How many points would Sanjay Patel score for education? The calculations for years of study are as follows:

8 years full-time: attendance at primary school from 1975 to 1983

4 years full-time: attendance at Sadhana Higher Secondary School from 1983 to 1987

4 years full-time: four-year degree (bachelor's degree in hotel and tourism management from 1991 to 1995)

Total: 16 years full-time studies

Because of Mr. Patel's four-year university degree, and because he exceeds the 14 years of full-time study requirement, he would probably be assessed as having 20 points.

Language Proficiency in English and French—0 to 24 Points

The ability to communicate proficiently in one or more of Canada's official languages is another quality that is highly valued in the selection of skilled workers. The principal applicant must first consider which of the two official languages, English or French, to select as his first official language on the application form. Unless the principal applicant provides acceptable proof of language proficiency, language testing at a Canadian approved institution will be required.

Visa officers do not assess language proficiency; they award points based either on language test results or other evidence provided by the applicant. According to s. 79(2) of the IRP Regulations, the applicant's proficiency is assessed on the basis of benchmarks referred to in *Canadian Language Benchmarks 2000* for the English language and *Standards linguistiques Canadiens 2002* for the French language, in four abilities: speaking, listening, reading, and writing.

It is important for the applicant to make the distinction between "first" and "second" official language because more points are awarded for proficiency in the first official language. A maximum 16 points are awarded for proficiency in the first official language, and a maximum 8 points for ability in the second official language, as shown in the tables below, which are based on ss. 79(2)(a), (b), and (c) of the IRP Regulations:

First Official Language

Proficiency	Benchmark	Ability			
		Speak	**Listen**	**Read**	**Write**
High	8 or higher	4	4	4	4
Moderate	6 or 7	2	2	2	2
Basic	4 or 5	1-2	1-2	1-2	1-2
No	3 or lower	0	0	0	0

Second Official Language

Proficiency	Benchmark	Ability			
		Speak	**Listen**	**Read**	**Write**
High	8 or higher	2	2	2	2
Moderate	6 or 7	2	2	2	2
Basic	4 or 5	1-2	1-2	1-2	1-2
No	3 or lower	0	0	0	0

Returning to our scenario, how many points would Mr. Patel score for language proficiency? Mr. Patel would select English as his first official language, because his English skills are stronger than his French. He is proficient in all four abilities with respect to English, and his score is therefore the highest possible: 16 points.

Mr. Patel can answer simple questions in French, which requires the ability to understand and speak, so he probably would receive 1 point each under the speak and listen categories, for a total of 2 points for French.

Therefore, Mr. Patel's total language score would be 18 points.

Experience—0 to 21 Points

The visa officer awards points based on the principal applicant's full-time or full-time-equivalent paid work experience that occurred within the last ten years of the date of the application for permanent residence. Full-time work means at least 37.5 hours of work per week, according to s. 80(7) of the IRP Regulations.

The applicant must show past performance of the main and essential duties of the occupation as described in the National Occupational Classification to meet the regulatory definition of work experience. Furthermore, that work experience must be in the category of skill type 0, or skill level A or B, according to the NOC. Therefore, the principal applicant must provide the four-digit NOC code that corresponds to the occupation indicated on her application form.

The visa officer awards up to a maximum of 21 points as follows (s. 80(1) of the IRP Regulations):

Years of experience within the ten years preceding the date of application

	Less than one	One	Two	Three	Four or more
Points	0	15	17	19	21

Finally, the work experience may not be in an occupation that is considered a *restricted occupation*. The minister has the authority to restrict an occupation on the basis of labour market demands and consultations with HRSDC, the provinces, and other organizations, according to s. 73 of the IRP Regulations. There are currently no designated restricted occupations.

How many points would Mr. Patel score for work experience? Mr. Patel performed the duties of chef (code 6241) on a full-time basis since 2003. This amounts to more than four years of experience. Therefore, he would probably be assessed with 21 points.

Age—0 to 21 Points

Points based on age are awarded according to s. 81 of the IRP Regulations. The visa officer may award a maximum of 10 points to a principal applicant who is 21 years of age but less than 50 years of age. For every year younger than 21 or every year older than 49, 2 points are subtracted, to a maximum of 10 points, as follows:

Years of age	Points
21 or older but less than 50	10
20 or 50	8
19 or 51	6
18 or 52	4
17 or 53	2
Less than 17 or 54 years of age or older	0

How many points would Mr. Patel score for age? Mr. Patel was born in 1970. He falls within the range for maximum points; therefore, he would receive the full 10 points.

Arranged Employment—0 or 10 Points

"Arranged employment" is an offer of employment in Canada for an indeterminate term, meaning that it is open-ended and not a fixed term like six months. The visa officer may award 10 points if the principal applicant provides proof of an approved offer of employment, according to s. 82 of the IRP Regulations. However, the occupation must be listed in skill type 0 or skill level A or B of the National Occupational Classification matrix. Furthermore, the officer will assess whether the applicant is able to perform and is likely to accept and carry out the employment.

Proof of a job offer is obtained from Human Resources and Social Development Canada. The 10 points are awarded if the applicant satisfies one of the following four conditions:

1. The applicant is already in Canada as a temporary resident, holds a valid work visa, is currently working in the job, and has a valid job offer for an indeterminate basis for that same job if the applicant is accepted as a skilled worker.

2. The applicant is already in Canada as a temporary visitor under one of the international treaties for business visitors (such as the North American Free Trade Agreement), is working in the job, and has a valid job offer for an indeterminate basis for that same job if the applicant is accepted as a skilled worker.

3. The applicant does not intend on working in Canada before becoming a permanent resident and has an approved job offer for an indeterminate basis if the applicant is selected as a skilled worker.

4. The applicant is already in Canada as a temporary resident, holds a valid work visa or is a temporary visitor under one of the international treaties for business visitors, and has a valid job offer for an indeterminate basis for another job if the applicant is accepted as a skilled worker.

How many points would Mr. Patel score for arranged employment? If Toronto chef Paul Pierre follows through with his job offer of Executive Chef, he must request an approval of the offer of employment from the HRSDC office. If the approval is obtained, Mr. Patel will be assessed as having an arranged employment, for a total of 10 points. Without the HRSDC approval, no points will be awarded.

Adaptability—0 to 10 Points

Adaptability encompasses a variety of factors that are likely to benefit the applicant's chances of successful integration into Canadian society. These may include education, previous work or study in Canada, and arranged work, as they relate to the applicant and/or the applicant's partner. If the applicant's partner is likely to integrate well into Canadian life, this will assist the applicant to do likewise. Other support networks such as relatives in Canada may also increase the applicant's chances of successful integration.

The five elements for which the applicant may accumulate up to a maximum of 10 points, according to s. 83 of the IRP Regulations, are as follows:

Element	Description	Points
1. Educational credentials of spouse or common-law partner	The visa officer evaluates the spouse or common-law partner's educational credentials as if that person were the principal applicant, as follows: ◆ if the spouse or common-law partner would receive 25 points, the principal applicant receives 5 points ◆ if the spouse or common-law partner would receive 20 or 22 points, the principal applicant receives 4 points ◆ if the spouse or common-law partner would receive 12 or 15 points, the principal applicant receives 3 points	3-5
2. Previous study in Canada	The principal applicant or his accompanying spouse or common-law partner completed a program of full-time study of at least two years' duration at a postsecondary institution in Canada, by the age of 17 or older under a study permit, whether or not the person obtained an educational credential	5
3. Previous work in Canada	The principal applicant or his accompanying spouse or common-law partner has at least one year of full-time work in Canada under a valid work permit	5
4. Family relationships in Canada	The principal applicant or his accompanying spouse or common-law partner is related to a Canadian citizen or permanent resident who is a parent, grandparent, child, grandchild, child of a parent, sibling, child of a grandparent, aunt/uncle, or grandchild of a parent, niece, or nephew	5
	The principal applicant's spouse or common-law partner is a Canadian citizen or permanent resident living in Canada	5
5. Arranged employment	If the principal applicant was awarded points under the arranged employment factor	5

How many points would Mr. Patel score for adaptability? The case scenario does not provide much information about Mrs. Anita Patel, but let's assume that her bachelor's degree was a four-year degree. Mr. Patel would receive 4 points under adaptability for the educational credentials of his spouse.

Neither of the Patels studied or worked in Canada, and there is no information about relatives in Canada. However, Mr. Patel arranged employment for himself, for an additional 5 points. Therefore, the total number of points earned by Mr. Patel for adaptability would be 9 points.

Mr. Patel's overall total number of points for all factors exceeds the pass mark of 67.

Settlement Funds

The applicant must show proof of sufficient *settlement funds*, unless employment has been arranged, according to s. 76 of the IRP Regulations. The settlement funds must be enough to support the applicant and any dependants, and are assessed according to the applicant's family size using 50 percent of Statistics Canada's most current LICO for urban areas with populations of 500,000 or more.

The easiest way to determine the requisite amount of funds is to consult the CIC website or to refer to the *Application for Permanent Residence: Federal Skilled Worker Class* instruction guide (IMM EG7000), which contains a grid outlining the minimum amount required to settle based on family size.

Because Mr. Patel arranged employment for himself, he would be exempt from the requirement of settlement funds. Without the job offer, he would have calculated the amount of settlement funds required for a family of four, including himself, his wife, and their two children.

APPLICATION PROCEDURES FOR FEDERAL SKILLED WORKERS

Foreign nationals interested in applying as skilled workers are encouraged to first use a self-assessment tool available on the CIC website, called the Skilled Worker Self-Assessment. The self-assessment identifies how the applicant's skills and experience would be evaluated on an actual application. Applicants who score below the passing grade can consider which areas they can most easily upgrade, such as education or language skills. The self-assessment tool can also help couples decide which of them should be the principal applicant, based on who has more points.

Generally, applicants mail their applications to a Canadian visa office located in their country of residence. However, only about 30 percent of cases are processed in two years or less, and many cases take five years or even longer to be resolved.[21] Consequently, applicants may be required to update their documents periodically while waiting for their applications to make their way through the system.

A new *simplified application process*, implemented in September 2006, is now available to many applicants. It enables them to complete a modified application form and secure a place in the immigration queue. Supporting documentation need not be sent until the visa officer requests it at a later date,[22] reducing or eliminating the need to update documents. This process is discussed below.

Regular Application Process

The regular application process is used by applicants who are

- provincial nominees (see the section "Provincial Nominees" below);

- selected by Quebec (Quebec has its own program); or

- eligible for points for arranged employment.

It is also used by applicants submitting their applications at the Canadian visa office in Buffalo who have either of the following:

- legal temporary resident status in Canada as a worker or a student; or

- legal status in the United States.

The regular application kit consists of a guide, several forms, and other information, as follows:

- the *Application for Permanent Residence: Federal Skilled Worker Class* instruction guide (IMM EG7000)

- an Application for Permanent Residence in Canada form (IMM 0008)

- a Schedule 1: Background/Declaration form (IMM 0008 Schedule 1)

- a Schedule 3: Economic Classes—Federal Skilled Workers form (IMM 0008 Schedule 3)

- an Additional Family Information form (IMM 5406)

- a Use of a Representative form (IMM 5476), if the applicant uses a representative to complete the application

- an Authority to Release Personal Information to a Designated Individual form (IMM 5475), to authorize CIC to release information to someone other than the applicant

- specific instructions from the visa office (instructions about where to send the application and how to pay fees).

If the application is deemed complete, a visa officer date-stamps it to initiate the process and sends the applicant a letter of receipt with the visa office file number so that the applicant can track the progress of the case online.

In our scenario, restaurant owner Paul Pierre had to formalize the offer of employment by going to HRSDC to obtain an approved letter of offer for Mr. Patel. With an approved letter of offer, Mr. Patel must apply using the regular application process.

Simplified Application Process

Applicants who do not fall into any of the categories listed above under the regular application process may use the simplified application process.

The simplified application kit consists only of a simplified three-page application form and proof of payment for processing fees, which are filed at the visa office. A visa officer acknowledges receipt of the application with a *letter of receipt* that provides a visa office file number and labour market information, so that the applicant can upgrade skills during the waiting period.

The simplified application kit consists of the following:

- the Application for Permanent Residence: Federal Skilled Worker Class, Simplified Application Process instruction guide (IMM ESAP 7000)

- an Application for Permanent Residence in Canada form (IMM 0008SW)

- a Use of a Representative form (IMM 5476), if the applicant uses a representative to complete the application

- an Authority to Release Personal Information to a Designated Individual form (IMM 5475), to authorize CIC to release information to someone other than the applicant

- specific instructions from the visa office (instructions about where to send the application and how to pay fees).

When the visa office is ready to assess the application, it contacts the applicant with a request for updated information together with supporting documents, such as the following:

- status and identity documents such as birth and marriage certificates;

- educational credentials;

- work history and letters from employers;

- language test results;

- police certificate;

- proof of medical exam; and

- proof of settlement funds.

Sometime thereafter, a visa officer may invite the applicant for a personal interview in order to finalize the assessment and render a decision regarding the application.

Fees

Fees are paid at a designated financial institution. The "fees receipt" form IMM 5401 must accompany the application forms (s. 295 of the IRP Regulations).

The two main types of fees are:

- application (processing) fees, and

- the Right of Permanent Residence Fee.

Application or processing fees must be paid for the principal applicant and any accompanying family members. These fees are non-refundable.

Right of Permanent Residence Fees

The Right of Permanent Residence Fee may be paid at the same time as the application fees, or at any time during the process, but must be paid before a visa for permanent residence may be issued. This fee must be paid for the principal applicant and other family members. Certain members of the family class are exempted from the right of permanent residence fee, as follows:

- a dependent child of the sponsor or principal applicant;

- a child to be adopted by the sponsor; and

- an orphaned brother, sister, nephew, niece, or grandchild of the sponsor.

DECISIONS

Federal skilled worker class applications are decided by visa officers, who examine supporting documents to ascertain the applicant's identity, age, educational and work credentials, language test results, relationship to family members, and passports or travel documents. Although visa officers have the authority to interview applicants, they generally waive interviews unless there is a need to clarify information or address questions related to admissibility.

Visa officers review the application to ensure that the minimum work experience requirements and selection criteria are met, and that the applicant and family members are not inadmissible. If the application is refused on the basis of selection criteria, the visa officer issues a refusal detailing the number of points awarded for each selection factor and the reasons for refusal. There are no appeal rights extended to a foreign national whose application for permanent residence as a skilled worker is rejected.

If all the requirements are met and the application is accepted, the visa officer issues a visa to travel to Canada as a permanent resident and a Confirmation of Permanent Residence card. The names of non-accompanying family members are also included on the visa of the principal applicant. The principal applicant and all accompanying family members must travel before the expiry date on their visas.

Upon arrival at the port of entry, the principal applicant and all accompanying family members present their Confirmation of Permanent Residence cards to an officer at the port of entry and are subject to examination. The applicant must also present two copies of a detailed list of all personal and household items brought, and the value of each item, and two copies of an additional list of items that are arriving later, and the value of each item.

Generally, the officer counsels the new permanent residents about their rights and responsibilities as permanent residents, advises them about obtaining provincial health insurance and social insurance numbers, and officially welcomes them to Canada.

Applicants who already reside legally in Canada, such as temporary residents with legal work authorizations, are directed to present themselves, with permanent resident visas and Confirmation of Permanent Residence cards, to a CIC location to finalize processing as permanent residents.

Provincial Nominees

The minister is authorized by s. 8 of the IRP Regulations to sign agreements with the provinces, and to coordinate and implement immigration policies and programs. Individuals who are nominated by a province "may become permanent residents on the basis of their ability to become economically established in Canada" (ss. 87(1) to (2)). Provincial nominee programs can generally provide quicker entry into Canada for qualified workers and experienced business professionals who wish to settle as permanent residents in a particular province.

This program provides the provinces with the benefits of targeted recruiting and selection of foreign nationals who can contribute to meeting the local labour market and economic needs of each particular province, such as filling a skills shortage, or attracting specialized occupational skills.

The province must first enter into an agreement with the federal government to establish a provincial nominee program, because the responsibilities are shared between these two levels of government according to s. 87 of the IRP Regulations. Recruiting and selection are the responsibility of the province, and evaluation and inadmissibility assessment are the responsibility of CIC.

To date, the following provinces have agreements and provincial nominee programs in place:

Province	Agreement	Nominee program
Alberta	Canada-Alberta Agreement on Provincial Nominees March 2, 2002 Extended: August 31, 2006 to December 30, 2006	Alberta Provincial Nominee Program (PNP)
British Columbia	Agreement for Canada-British Columbia Co-Operation on Immigration Original signed in May 1998. April 2004 to April 2009	British Columbia Provincial Nominee Program (BC PNP)
Manitoba	Canada-Manitoba Immigration Agreement Original signed in October 1996. June 6, 2003 to indefinite	Manitoba Provincial Nominee Program (MPNP)
New Brunswick	Canada-New Brunswick Agreement on Provincial Nominees Original signed in February 1999. March 29, 2005 to Indefinite	New Brunswick Provincial Nominee Program
Newfoundland and Labrador	Canada-Newfoundland and Labrador Agreement on Provincial Nominees September 1, 1999. Extended December 1, 2005 to December 31, 2006	Newfoundland and Labrador Provincial Nominee Program (NLPNP)
Nova Scotia	August 27, 2002 to July 1, 2007 Canada-Nova Scotia Agreement on Provincial Nominees	Nova Scotia Nominee Program (NSNP)
Ontario	Canada-Ontario Immigration Agreement November 21, 2005 to November 21, 2010	pilot Provincial Nominee Program (pending implementation at time of writing)
Prince Edward Island	Agreement for Canada-Prince Edward Island Co-operation on Immigration signed March 29, 2001 and extended on March 22, 2006 to March 29, 2007	Prince Edward Island Provincial Nominee Program (PNP)
Saskatchewan	Canada-Saskatchewan Immigration Agreement framework agreement signed in 1998 May 7, 2005 to indefinite	Saskatchewan Immigrant Nominee Program (SINP)
Yukon	Agreement for Canada-Yukon Co-operation on Immigration April 2, 2001 Extended: April 2, 2006 to April 2, 2007	Yukon Provincial Nominee Program (YNP)

Source: Adapted from Minister of Public Works and Government Services Canada, *Annual Report to Parliament on Immigration 2006*, 2006, Table 2: Federal-Provincial/Territorial Agreements Currently in Force, page 12.

APPLYING UNDER A PROVINCIAL NOMINEE PROGRAM

There are two applications involved when applying to be a provincial nominee:

- an application to the province for nomination; and

- an application to a federal visa officer for permanent residence.

The criteria for nomination varies from province to province. Each province has its own application package, which must be submitted with related documentation and appropriate fees. The province nominates the individual, together with any spouse or common-law partner and dependent children, for permanent residence on the basis of that person's ability to contribute knowledge and skills to become economically established in that province.

An applicant who meets the province's selection criteria is notified by letter, so that he may begin the second stage of the application process. The province also issues a *certificate of nomination* and notifies CIC officials at the appropriate visa office.

Each province has a time frame for submission of the application for permanent residence to the visa office. Generally, the nominated applicant follows the same steps as federal skilled workers using the regular application process, and submitting the appropriate fees to the visa office.

The application kit consists of a guide, several forms, and other information, as follows:

- the *Application for Permanent Residence: Guide for Provincial Nominees* instruction guide (IMM EP7000)

- an Application for Permanent Residence in Canada form (IMM 0008)

- a Schedule 1: Background/Declaration form (IMM 0008 Schedule 1)

- a Schedule 4: Economic Classes—Provincial Nominees form (IMM 0008 Schedule 4)

- an Additional Family Information form (IMM 5406)

- a Use of a Representative form (IMM 5476), if the applicant uses a representative to complete the application

- an Authority to Release Personal Information to a Designated Individual form (IMM 5475), to authorize CIC to release information to someone other than the applicant

- specific instructions from the visa office (instructions about where to send the application and how to pay fees).

A nomination by the province does not guarantee that the applicant will be granted permanent residence—the final decision rests solely with CIC.

DECISIONS

Applications for permanent residence by members of the provincial nominee class are decided by visa officers. The officer evaluates the nominated applicant's ability to become economically established in Canada, according to s. 87(3) of the IRPA, and also assesses inadmissibility.

Business Class

The third stream of permanent residence immigration in the economic class is the *business class*, which in turn comprises three subcategories:

- entrepreneurs;

- self-employed persons; and

- investors.

The business class allows for the immigration of experienced business persons who can stimulate economic development in Canada with their financial capital and business knowledge. The business class represents only a small part of overall immigration, and applications take a long time to process. In 2005, just over 5 percent of new permanent residents (and their spouses and dependants) were admitted as business immigrants.[23] The CIC website claims there is "a waiting list to come to Canada as a business immigrant. This means it may be several years before your application is processed."[24]

Business class applicants are selected primarily on the basis of their ability to create jobs for themselves and other Canadians. Requirements vary depending on the subcategory.

The entrepreneur and investor subcategories are the most similar to each other, as both require two years of *business experience*, a minimum net worth, and an agreement with CIC. After examining the definition of business experience and *qualifying business*, as provided in s. 88(1) of the IRP Regulations, and the basic point system applicable to all business class applicants, we explain the differences among the subcategories.

As with all immigrants, the usual admissibility requirements also apply to business class applicants and their family members.

DEFINITION OF BUSINESS EXPERIENCE

To satisfy the requirement of business experience, the entrepreneur or investor must show that she managed a qualifying business for at least two years in the previous five years.

A qualifying business is one with operating income (income from the sale of goods or services), rather than only passive investment income such as interest, dividends, or capital gains. Additionally, the applicant is required to present documentary evidence of any two of the following:

- the percentage of equity multiplied by the number of full-time job equivalents is equal to or greater than two full-time job equivalents per year;

- the percentage of equity multiplied by the total annual sales is equal to or greater than $500,000;

- the percentage of equity multiplied by the net income in the year is equal to or greater than $50,000; and

- the percentage of equity multiplied by the net assets at the end of the year is equal to or greater than $125,000.

A *full-time job equivalent* means two or more part-time jobs that add up to 1,950 hours of paid employment annually.

POINT SYSTEM FOR THE BUSINESS CLASS

The point system for the business class includes only five selection criteria, as set out in s. 102 of the IRP Regulations:

- age,

- education,

- language proficiency in English and French,

- experience, and

- adaptability.

Age, education, and language proficiency are all measured in the same manner as for skilled workers. However, assessments of experience and adaptability vary depending on whether the applicant is applying as an entrepreneur, self-employed person, or investor. All business class applicants, regardless of subclass, must achieve a score of at least 35 points out of 100.

ENTREPRENEUR CLASS

The Entrepreneur Immigration Program is intended to attract experienced business people who can operate and potentially grow their businesses here in Canada. The requirements for eligibility are therefore related to this objective.

To be eligible for the entrepreneur class, applicants must satisfy the definition of "entrepreneur" as set out in s. 88(1) of the IRP Regulations. According to this definition, applicants must meet the following requirements:

- two years of business experience, as defined above;

- net worth of at least $300,000; and

- agreement to follow the conditions for entrepreneurs after arrival in Canada (ss. 98(1) to (5) of the IRP Regulations).

The entrepreneur must demonstrate a net worth of at least $300,000 Canadian. The net worth is calculated by subtracting all debts and liabilities (including those of any spouse or common-law partner) from the fair market value of all assets (including those of any spouse or common-law partner).

The entrepreneur must also demonstrate that all net worth was accumulated through legal means, such as employment income, business income, investment income, and inheritance. It may be necessary to prove this with documents that trace the sources of the money, such as pay slips, income tax returns, and business financial statements. This provision is very important to prevent those involved in organized crime from setting up shop in Canada.

Conditions

To ensure that the entrepreneur follows through with plans to operate a business in Canada, the permanent resident status of the entrepreneur and any family members is subject to terms and conditions. The Entrepreneur Immigration Program is the only program of the three in the business class where conditions apply.

Within three years of becoming a permanent resident, the entrepreneur must own at least one-third of a business in Canada and actively manage it, for one year. Additionally, the entrepreneur must create at least one full-time job equivalent (1,950 hours of paid employment) for a Canadian citizen or permanent resident (other than the entrepreneur and dependants).

CIC provides counselling and monitoring to entrepreneurs to ensure compliance with the program. The entrepreneur is provided with a counselling and monitoring guide along with the visa for the principal applicant and each of the dependants. The guide provides the details for reporting requirements, a mail-in card used for the first reporting period, a form to vary or cancel the terms and conditions, and a list of federal and provincial business immigrant contacts who can help the entrepreneur comply with conditions.

The reporting requirements are as follows:

- First report period (within six months of becoming a permanent resident)—provide CIC with contact information, such as address and telephone number.

- Second report period (within 18 to 24 months of becoming a permanent resident)—provide evidence of efforts to meet the conditions.

- Third report period (final time, within three years of becoming a permanent resident)—provide evidence that the conditions were met.

The conditions are removed once the entrepreneur sets up a significant business venture, hires at least one employee, and provides evidence of being actively involved in managing the business.

Selection Factors/Points for Entrepreneurs

Applicants must receive a minimum total of 35 points out of a maximum of 100 to pass, as follows:

Selection factor	Maximum points
Age	10
Education	25
Language	24
Business experience[25]	35
5 years—35 points	
4 years—30 points	
3 years—25 points	
2 years—20 points	
Adaptability	6
Business exploration trip to Canada—6 points	
Participation in federal–provincial initiative—6 points	

INVESTOR CLASS

The Immigrant Investor Program (IIP) was first established in 1986 to allow applicants to gain permanent residence by making a substantial investment in the Canadian economy. Essentially, the investor provides an interest-free loan to the government of Canada. The investment is government-guaranteed, and is repaid in full, without interest, after five years.

To be eligible for the investor class, applicants must satisfy the definition of "investor" set out in s. 88(1) of the IRP Regulations. According to this definition, applicants must meet the following requirements:

- two years of business experience, as defined above;

- net worth of at least $800,000; and

- written agreement to invest $400,000.

Immigrant Investor Program Subscription Agreement

The investor enters into a legally binding contract called the Immigrant Investor Program Subscription Agreement with CIC. The agreement sets out the operation and administration of the program. The applicant must pay the $400,000 directly to the Receiver General of Canada before the permanent resident visa can be issued. The investment is non-refundable after the visa is issued and is locked in for five years.

The debt obligation is also called an *IIP Promissory Note*. It advises the investor of the provincial distribution of her $400,000 investment, and states that the redemption date will be sent to the investor upon allocation to the provincial funds. At the end of the five-year period, the investor presents the IIP Promissory Note for repayment of her investment.

Selection Factors/Points for Investors

Like all business class applicants, those in the investor class must receive 35 points out of 100 to pass. Points for investor applicants are allocated as follows:

Selection factor	Maximum points
Age	10
Education	25
Language	24
Business Experience[26]	35
5 years—35 points	
4 years—30 points	
3 years—25 points	
2 years—20 points	
Adaptability	6
Business exploration trip to Canada—6 points	
Participation in federal–provincial business immigration initiatives—6 points	

SELF-EMPLOYED CLASS

To be eligible for the self-employed class, applicants must satisfy the definition of "self-employed person" set out in s. 88(1) of the IRP Regulations. According to this definition, applicants must generally have relevant experience, and the intention and ability to be self-employed and make a significant contribution to specified economic activities in Canada.

Relevant Experience

"Relevant experience" is not the same as "business experience" (required for entre-preneurs and investors). Self-employed applicants must instead have experience that involves at least two years of the following:

- cultural activities;
- athletics; or
- purchase and management of a farm.

Citizenship and Immigration Canada's *Overseas Processing (OP)* operations manual provides the following examples to assist visa officers in assessing relevant experience in cultural activities or athletics: music teachers, painters, illustrators, film makers, freelance journalists, choreographers, set designers, and coaches and trainers. Management experience includes theatrical or musical directors and impresarios.[27]

Intention and Ability

The self-employed applicant must demonstrate the intention and ability to establish a business that will, at a minimum, create employment for himself and that will make a significant contribution to the Canadian economy. There are no conditions imposed to set up the self-employed business (unlike the entrepreneur class) and there is no minimum financial investment (unlike both the entrepreneur and investor classes).

Selection Factors/Points for Self-Employed

Like all business class applicants, those in the self-employed class must receive 35 points out of 100 to pass. Points for self-employed applicants are allocated as follows:

Selection factor	Maximum points
Age	10
Education	25
Language	24
Business Experience[28]	35
5 years—35 points	
4 years—30 points	
3 years—25 points	
2 years—20 points	
Adaptability	6
Education of spouse or common-law partner—3 to 5 points	
One year full-time work in Canada[29]—5 points	
Two years full-time postsecondary studies in Canada—5 points	
Family member in Canada—5 points	

APPLYING

Generally, applicants mail their applications to a Canadian visa office located in their country of residence. There are two application processes: regular and simplified.

The simplified application process was implemented in September 2006. It allows applicants to complete a simplified application form and secure a place in the immigration queue, and only send supporting documentation when requested to do so by the visa office at a later date.[30]

The two application processes are essentially the same as described in the previous section for the skilled worker class.

Regular Application Process

The regular application process must be used by applicants who are either

- selected by Quebec (Quebec has its own program); or

- submitting their applications at the Canadian visa office in Buffalo and have either legal temporary resident status in Canada for a period of at least a year, or legal status in the United States.

The application kit, which is available on the CIC website, consists of a guide, several forms, and other instructions, as follows:

- an *Applying for Permanent Residence: Business Class Applicants* instruction guide (IMM 4000)

- an Application for Permanent Residence in Canada form (IMM 0008)

- a Schedule 1: Background/Declaration form (IMM 0008 Schedule 1)

- a Schedule 6: Economic Classes—Business Immigrants form (IMM 0008 Schedule 6)

- an Additional Family Information form (IMM 5406)

- a Use of a Representative form (IMM 5476) if the applicant uses a representative to complete the application

- an Authority to Release Personal Information to a Designated Individual form (IMM 5475), to authorize CIC to release information to someone other than the applicant

- specific instructions from the visa office (instructions about where to send the application and how to pay fees).

If the application is deemed complete, the visa officer date-stamps it for the processing queue, and sends the applicant a letter of receipt with the visa office file number so that the applicant can track the progress of the case online.

Simplified Application Process

Applicants who do not fall into any of the categories listed above under the regular application process may use the simplified application process.

The simplified application kit consists only of a three-page simplified application form and proof of payment for processing fees, which are filed at the visa office.

A visa officer acknowledges receipt of the application with a letter of receipt that provides a visa office file number and labour-market information so that the applicant can upgrade during the waiting period.

The simplified application kit consists of the following:

- an *Application for Permanent Residence: Simplified Application Process Business Immigration* guide (IMM 4000)

- an Application for Permanent Residence in Canada form (IMM 0008BU)

- a Use of a Representative form (IMM 5476) if the applicant uses a representative to complete the application

- and Authority to Release Personal Information to a Designated Individual form (IMM 5475), to authorize CIC to release information to someone other than the applicant

- specific instructions from the visa office about where to send the application and how to pay fees.

Visa officers examine the application to ensure that the applicant meets the statutory requirements and selection criteria: they examine the person's business and financial background, evaluate the soundness of business plans in Canada, and make sure the applicant's wealth was not obtained illegally.

Fees

Fees can be paid online or at a designated financial institution. The fees receipt form (IMM 5401) must accompany the application forms (s. 295 of the IRP Regulations).

The two main types of fees are the following:

- the application (processing) fee; and

- the Right of Permanent Residence Fee (if the application is approved).

Application or processing fees are charged to process applications and are non-refundable.

The Right of Permanent Residence Fee can be paid at the same time as the processing fees, or at any time during the process, but must be paid before a visa for permanent residence can be issued. This fee must be paid for the principal applicant and accompanying family members. Consultants should periodically check the CIC website for changes to amounts of fees.

There are additional fees to cover the costs for medical examinations, police certificates, and language testing.

Settlement Funds

Business class applicants must show they have sufficient funds to support themselves and their family members, because they do not receive any financial support from the Canadian government. Generally, an applicant who has met the net worth requirements for the entrepreneur or investment categories will have sufficient settlement funds.

HUMANITARIAN AND COMPASSIONATE CONSIDERATIONS CLASS

Most applicants for permanent residence fall within either the family class or economic class; however, there are sometimes situations that "just don't fit" the criteria, yet are compelling cases for permanent residence. These exceptional cases may be considered under the class of humanitarian and compassionate considerations (H & C).

The H & C class provides the minister (or delegated immigration officer) with the discretion to grant permanent or temporary residence to applicants who would otherwise not be able to meet statutory and regulatory criteria.

Generally, those who apply in Canada under the H & C class are doing so as a final attempt to remain here, often after having made an unsuccessful attempt to gain refugee status.

The Canadian Council for Refugees, a non-profit organization that advocates for the rights of immigrants and refugees, claims that many of the H & C class applicants for permanent residence fall under the following categories:[31]

- refugees who were refused status because of flaws in the determination system;

- survivors of human trafficking;

- family members of refugees or permanent residents;

- stateless persons;

- victims of domestic violence who left a family sponsorship because of the violence;

- persons whose removal from Canada would involve a serious rights violation, such as lack of treatment for a serious medical condition;

- persons from countries to which Canada generally does not deport because of a situation of generalized risk (moratorium countries);

- persons who have been continuously in Canada for several years;

- persons who have integrated in Canada, socially, culturally, and with family;

- persons who have worked for some time on temporary worker programs, notably as seasonal agricultural workers.

H & C applications are one of the more subjective processes in immigration matters. Decision making is based solely on documentation submitted by the applicant, and the decision maker has broad discretion when considering the reasons and circumstances of the application. There are no definitions in the IRPA or its regulations for the terms "humanitarian" and "compassionate," so the minister or delegated officer must use discretion in deciding applications.

Moreover, an officer may exempt an applicant from the requirements of the IRPA and its regulations for inadmissibility except for reasons of health, serious criminality, human rights violations, organized crime, and security.[32] These discretionary provisions are intended to allow for the approval of deserving cases that were not specifically anticipated when the IRPA was drafted.

H & C applications are not meant as an alternative means of immigration, and are intended only for extraordinary cases: the processing of applications is lengthy and the success rate is minimal. Permanent residence applications made under H & C considerations are approved on an exceptional basis and their acceptance rate is low compared with other types of permanent residence applications. For example, only 2.54 percent (6,653) of H & C applicants were granted permanent resident status in 2005 and only 4 percent (10,223) were accepted in 2006.[33] It may take years before a decision is made and there is no right of appeal from an unsuccessful H & C application.

Bearing in mind that H & C cases are generally unique, complex, and favourably decided only on an exceptional basis, the purpose of this section is to provide a general overview of H & C cases. The examples provided are not conclusive as successful types of cases; they are merely examples used to help explain the information.

Section 25 Criteria

The H & C criteria as set out in s. 25 of the IRPA infuse a degree of flexibility into an otherwise rigid and bureaucratic system. Section 25 offers an opportunity to those whose failure to qualify under any other class is causing significant distress because of individual circumstances. This section allows the minister or delegate to use discretionary power to grant status to foreign nationals where there are strong humanitarian and compassionate reasons for doing so. This may apply to both those who wish to come to Canada, and those who wish to remain here, but who are inadmissible for technical, medical, or criminal reasons.

Specifically, s. 25(1) of the IRPA provides that upon the written request of "a foreign national who is inadmissible or does not meet the requirements of the Act," the minister may

> examine the circumstances ... and may grant ... permanent resident status or an exemption from any applicable criteria or obligation of this Act if the Minister is of the opinion that it is justified by humanitarian and compassionate considerations ... taking into account the best interests of a child directly affected, or by public policy considerations.

Consider the following examples where normal eligibility requirements are not met, and where a person might ask to be considered for H & C reasons:

- excluded family members, under s. 117(9)(d) of the IRP Regulations;

- non-biological children who are separated from their only family, which is in Canada;

- parents and siblings of child refugees in Canada;

- other family members of persons in Canada where there are specific humanitarian concerns (for example, a situation of generalized risk); and

- a person whose spouse, a Canadian citizen or permanent resident, can afford to sponsor the applicant; however, it would be an unusual and undeserved and disproportionate hardship for the person to leave Canada in order to apply for sponsorship under the family class.

Two criteria specifically requiring consideration in the determination of an H & C application, according to s. 25, are: the *best interests of a child* directly affected by the decision; and *public policy* considerations. Both are examined briefly below. It is important to keep in mind that it is the responsibility of the applicant to satisfy the officer that sufficient factors exist to warrant an exemption from the regular admission criteria. Officers will not return the application to ask for further information, so it is very important that all relevant evidence to support one or both of the two criteria is submitted initially.

CHILD'S BEST INTERESTS

The minister must consider the best interests of any child that is directly affected by the decision because of the child's relationship to the applicant. In determining the child's best interests, the minister must consider the following issues:

- the child's emotional, social, cultural, and physical welfare;

- the child's age;

- the child's level of dependency on the applicant;

- the degree of the child's establishment in Canada;

- the child's links to country of origin or previous residence;

- the child's medical issues or special needs;

- the child's educational needs; and

- matters related to the child's gender.[34]

This provision applies regardless of whether the child is a Canadian citizen or foreign national. In other words, the best interests of a child who has no right to be in Canada must also be considered, if such a child is directly affected by the decision regarding the applicant. For example, how is it in the best interests of the child to remain in Canada as opposed to being removed to her home country? Are there family members in the home country to return to or will the child be separated from relatives remaining in Canada? Are the living conditions, education opportunities, and health care better or worse in the home country?

PUBLIC POLICY

The minister has the authority to respond to public demands through the creation of new categories for permanent residence or "public policy" cases. Consider the following examples:

1. *Resumption of Canadian citizenship*: The resumption of Canadian citizenship is a class of permanent residence established specifically for former Canadian citizens who lost their Canadian citizenship inadvertently as minors, because a parent lost his or her citizenship.

2. *Vietnamese living in the Philippines*: Vietnamese living in the Philippines without status since the 1970s, with close family members in Canada, were recently admitted. In a news release dated March 7, 2008, the

minister of CIC explained that applications by members of this group received by December 31, 2007 were considered on a priority basis by immigration officers, who examined each on a case-by-case basis to decide whether the applications warranted exemption from the statutory requirements and qualified for humanitarian and compassionate considerations.[35]

Public policy cases differ from other H & C cases because once a new category is created, all cases that fit the category are likely to be accepted.

Applying Under the Humanitarian and Compassionate Class

Each application is assessed on its own merits: officers consider the humanitarian and compassionate considerations for each application on the individual basis of the applicant's personal circumstances.

A written request for an H & C exemption must accompany either an application to remain in Canada as a permanent resident, or, in the case of a foreign national outside Canada, an application for a permanent resident visa (s. 66 of the IRP Regulations). It must be made by the principal applicant and, where applicable, by the following family members:

- spouse or common-law partner (if that person is in Canada and is not a permanent resident or a Canadian citizen); and

- any dependent children who are 18 years of age or older and are not permanent residents or Canadian citizens.

A person who has a removal order against him may apply for permanent residence for humanitarian and compassionate considerations, but the application will not delay removal from Canada. The applicant must leave on or before the date stated in the removal order, while the application is in process.

The application guide provided by CIC cautions that it can take as long as several years to process an application in the H & C category. The onus is on the applicant to put forth any and all H & C factors and to satisfy the decision maker that there are grounds for an exemption. The guide therefore comes with a warning that CIC will not ask for additional information because the onus is on applicant to "list any and all factors you wish to have considered at the time you submit your application."

PLACE OF APPLICATION

Like other permanent residence applications, most H & C applications are made from outside Canada.[36] Generally, a foreign national does not have the right to apply for permanent residence from within Canada. However, policy allows for such an application if the applicant lives in Canada and would experience unusual and undeserved or disproportionate hardship if she were required to leave.[37]

The inconvenience of leaving an established life in Canada and moving elsewhere in order to apply for permanent residence in the normal manner is not considered an unusual and undeserved hardship. According to department policy, an "unusual and undeserved hardship" is a situation unanticipated by the IRPA or the regulations that results from circumstances beyond the applicant's control.[38]

"Disproportionate hardship" is defined as hardship that has a "disproportionate impact on the applicant due to their personal circumstances."[39] This may be the case, for example, if there is no home or support system to which to return in the applicant's country of origin.

STEPS

Generally, in-Canada H & C applications are assessed in the following order:

Step 1: An immigration officer (or visa officer in the case of applications made outside of Canada) assesses the eligibility of the applicant under the permanent resident category (such as family class or skilled worker) in which she applied.

Step 2: If the applicant does not meet the requirements, the officer must decide whether to exempt the applicant from the requirement of applying outside Canada for H & C considerations. For example, if an applicant did not have sufficient points to meet the selection criteria under the federal skilled worker class, and there was a written submission from the applicant for H & C considerations, the visa officer could, instead of rejecting the application, review the case to decide whether there are grounds to exempt the applicant from this requirement.

Step 3: If the applicant is exempted from the requirement to apply outside of Canada, CIC will issue a letter informing the applicant of this and setting out requirements such as a medical examination and criminality check.

Step 4: The application for permanent residence will be processed to assess admissibility on the basis of criteria such as financial, medical, criminality, prior misrepresentation, or inadmissible family member (ss. 36 to 42 of the IRPA). There are exceptions made for protected persons, who are not generally removed from Canada because of their special status.

Step 5: If the applicant is not found to be inadmissible, she will receive a notice to appear for a final interview, at which the immigration officer will review the application for H & C considerations to decide whether to exempt the applicant from the requirements of ss. 70(1)(a), (c), and (d) of the IRP Regulations. If the application is rejected, the applicant will receive a letter with instructions to confirm her departure, and removal proceedings will commence if necessary.

Decisions on applications made outside of Canada are made in a similar manner, but steps 3 and 4 are skipped.

APPLICATION KIT AND FORMS

Generally, applications made outside Canada do not require specific forms. The foreign national applies for a permanent resident visa under one of the existing three classes (that is, family class, skilled worker class, or business class), and submits a written request for consideration on humanitarian and compassionate grounds.

If the visa officer determines that the applicant does not meet the requirements of the class of permanent residence, the officer makes an H & C determination.

An exception is the public policy to facilitate immigration to Canada of certain members of the Vietnamese community in the Philippines who do not have permanent resident status but have close family members in Canada. There are forms for applicants and sponsors relating to this public policy, which are available from CIC.

Applications made inside Canada require substantially more paperwork, because the applicant has the additional burden of proving that unusual and undeserved, or disproportionate, hardship would result if he were forced to leave Canada in order to apply. An application kit can be obtained online from the CIC website at www.cic.gc.ca/english/information/applications/handc.asp or from a CIC Call Centre, and it includes the following:

- the *Applying for Permanent Residence from Within Canada: Humanitarian and Compassionate Considerations* instruction guide (IMM 5291)

- an Application for Permanent Residence from Within Canada— Humanitarian and Compassionate Considerations form (IMM 5001)

- a Supplementary Information—Humanitarian and Compassionate Considerations form (IMM 5283)

- an Instructions—Use of a Representative form (IMM 5561)

- a Use of a Representative form (IMM 5476)

- an Authority to Release Personal Information to a Designated Individual form (IMM 5475)

- a Document Checklist: Humanitarian and Compassionate Considerations form (IMM 5280).

The guide describes the required forms and supporting documentation that must be submitted for in-Canada applications. The key document for setting out humanitarian and compassionate grounds is the Supplementary Information form (IMM 5283). Completing this form with as much detail as possible is essential. It is relied on by the officer to decide whether there are grounds for exempting the applicant. Consider the following review of the relevant boxes in the Supplementary Information form, together with examples borrowed from MOSAIC:[40]

Box 7: "Explain the humanitarian and compassionate reasons that prevent you from leaving Canada."

Although box 7 is not very large, the applicant must provide as much detail as possible to demonstrate that she would suffer unusual and undeserved or disproportionate hardship if forced to leave Canada and return to the country of origin. Supporting written arguments and other documents, such as letters and medical reports, can be attached.

Examples of hardship where the applicant cannot return to the country of origin are the following:

- the government of the country of origin does not recognize the applicant as one of its citizens;

- there is a complete breakdown of the infrastructure in the country of origin and there is no government in charge;

- the applicant or a family member would suffer medical hardship and might die because medical treatment is not available in the home country; or

- in the case of a female applicant, she would face specific difficulties.

The cost and inconvenience of applying for permanent residence outside Canada is not considered a hardship.

Box 8: "[C]learly indicate in your application the specific exemption(s) you are requesting; and ... provide all details related to this request, including the reasons why you should be granted an exemption on humanitarian and compassionate grounds."

Where an applicant or family member is inadmissible, such as for criminality, misrepresentation, health, or financial reasons, the applicant must state the specific exemption sought, because CIC will not ask for this information.

Box 9: "If applicable, describe the circumstances of your family and other relationships that would support your humanitarian and compassionate application."

In addition to other factors, CIC also considers the willingness of a family member or close relative in Canada to sign an undertaking of assistance to support the applicant's application for permanent residence. This type of sponsorship may be used as an important consideration when the applicant is not self-sufficient in Canada.

In such cases, the applicant must also submit the following sponsorship forms with the application:

- an Application to Sponsor and Undertaking form (IMM 1344A)

- a Document Checklist—Sponsor form (IMM 5287).

Box 10: "If applicable, considering the best interest of the child, provide information on any child affected by this decision."

The immigration officer must consider whether the applicant's child or children would face hardship if they were to return to the applicant's home country. The child's ties to Canada will be considered, such as whether the child was born in Canada, attends school here, or has ever been to the applicant's home country.

The applicant can submit evidence in the form of an opinion letter to demonstrate how the child or children would be affected from having to leave Canada. Opinion letters about the negative mental or physical effects on children from experts such as school counsellors, health workers, physicians, social workers, or psychologists can help to support the application for humanitarian and compassionate considerations.

Box 11: "How have you established yourself in Canada?"

CIC officials consider the following examples as evidence of establishment in Canada:

- the amount of time lived in Canada
- language skills in English and/or French and efforts to improve them
- efforts to improve education and skills while in Canada
- the number of family members and relatives legally in Canada
- the amount of contact with family in Canada
- marriage to a permanent resident or a Canadian citizen
- Canadian-born children
- contacts in Canada, other than family
- community involvement (religious or non-religious) and volunteer work.

Evidence that does not show establishment in Canada, and that might instead demonstrate the opposite, includes the following examples:

- the amount of time spent collecting welfare
- the amount of contact with family in the applicant's home country (having many close relatives in the applicant's home country suggests no hardship upon return)
- assets abroad
- children still living in the applicant's home country.

Evidence that the applicant is financially self-supporting in Canada includes documents such as letters from past and present employers, pay stubs, income tax assessments, mortgage statements, and bank statements. The evidence should support the existence of a reliable income stream and all assets owned.

Box 13: "Indicate any other information you want to have considered in your application."

The applicant may provide positive reference letters affirming her integrity and responsibility, from employers, schools, volunteer organizations, the religious community, and others.

Those applying under the s. 25 public policy provision because they lost their Canadian citizenship as minors must use the Request for Exemption from Permanent Resident Visa Requirement form (IMM 5001).

All applications for permanent residence within Canada for H & C considerations, along with supporting documentation, must be sent to the CPC in Vegreville, Alberta.

EXPENSES AND FEES

The expenses and fees for applying for a permanent resident visa under H & C considerations are the same as those for applying normally for permanent residence. Expenses include the cost of medical examinations, legal fees, fees for police certificates, and fees to obtain documents. The two fees payable to CIC are the application or processing fee, which is non-refundable, and the Right of Permanent Residence Fee.

Loans may be available for the Right of Permanent Residence Fee, but not for the application fee, and the applicant must show an ability to repay the loan. Fees payable to CIC can be paid online or at a designated financial institution and the fees receipt (form IMM 5401) must accompany the application forms (s. 295 of the IRP Regulations). Because fees are subject to change, check the CIC website regularly to keep up to date.

Decisions on Humanitarian and Compassionate Applications

If an applicant provides sufficient evidence of H & C considerations to satisfy a visa officer, she may be exempted from the normal requirements for applying in a particular immigration class. However, before the permanent resident visa may be issued, the visa officer must be satisfied that the applicant is not inadmissible. If the applicant, or any family member, is inadmissible, the application must be rejected.

This may result in a catch-22: an applicant seeks H & C consideration because she would not otherwise be able to obtain a permanent resident visa, and although the application is accepted on the basis of H & C considerations, the application may ultimately be rejected because of inadmissibility. This explains, in part, why H & C applications take so long to process and why so few are successful.

Although the visa officer may exempt the applicant from eligibility criteria, the officer does not have the authority to waive inadmissibility. Only the minister may waive inadmissibility on grounds related to security, human or international rights violations, and organized criminality.

Reasons for a refusal are not automatically provided, because there is no statutory obligation to do so. However, an applicant may write to CIC to request reasons.

As mentioned above, applicants have no right to appeal refused applications for permanent residence on humanitarian and compassionate grounds. However, an application for leave for judicial review may be filed with the Federal Court within 30 days after the date of refusal.

APPENDIX

The boxes below summarize the relevant provisions in the IRPA and IRP Regulations for the three main classes of permanent residents discussed in the chapter.

Reference for Family Class

Provision	IRPA and IRP Regulations
Objective relating to family reunification	IRPA s. 3(1)(d)
Sponsor does not meet requirements	IRPA s. 11(2)
Selection of members of family class	IRPA s. 12(1)
Rights and obligations to sponsor a family member	IRPA s. 13(1)
Inadmissible family member	IRPA s. 42
Right to appeal family class refusal	IRPA s. 63(1)
Exception to excessive demand	IRPA s. 38(2) and IRP Regulations s. 24
Definitions	IRP Regulations ss. 1, 2
Relationships of convenience	IRP Regulations s. 4
Definition of a member of the family class	IRP Regulations s. 117
Adoptions	IRP Regulations s. 117
Who may sponsor	IRP Regulations s. 130
Sponsorship criteria	IRP Regulations s. 133

Reference for Humanitarian and Compassionate Classes

Provision	IRPA and IRP Regulations
H & C considerations	IRPA s. 25(1)
Public policy	IRPA s. 25(1)
Best interests of the child	IRPA s. 25(1)
Application in writing	IRP Regulations s. 66
Application outside Canada	IRP Regulations s. 67
Application in Canada	IRP Regulations s. 68
Accompanying family members	IRP Regulations s. 69

Reference for Skilled Worker and Business Classes

Provision	IRPA and IRP Regulations
Economic class	IRPA s. 12(2)
Skilled worker class	IRP Regulations: Part 6, Division 1
Minimum requirements	IRP Regulations s. 75(2)
Minimum points required	IRP Regulations s. 76(2)
Selection grid for skilled workers	IRP Regulations ss. 78 to 83
Settlement funds requirement	IRP Regulations s. 76
Business class	IRP Regulations: Part 6, Division 2
Entrepreneurs and self-employed persons	
Definitions	IRP Regulations s. 88
Selection criteria	IRP Regulations ss. 102, 78, 79, 81, 103, 104, 105
Minimum points to pass	IRP Regulations s. 108
Conditions—Entrepreneur	IRP Regulations s. 98
Self-employed person defined	IRP Regulations s. 102
Units of assessment, self-employed person	IRP Regulations ss. 78, 79, 81, 103(2)
Investors	
Definitions	IRP Regulations s. 88
Minimum requirements	IRP Regulations s. 91

NOTES

1. Citizenship and Immigration Canada, *Annual Report to Parliament on Immigration 2007*, 2007, www.cic.gc.ca/english/resources/publications/annual-report2007/message.asp.

2. Statistics and figures from Citizenship and Immigration Canada, ibid.

3. Canada also allows applications for permanent residence from individuals in Canada whose refugee claims have been accepted. These persons receive Convention refugee status or are recognized as persons in need of protection by the Immigration and Refugee Board. As well, applications for permanent residence are permitted for persons who have been granted protection by Citizenship and Immigration Canada through the pre-removal risk assessment program. Those who are protected through these programs may apply for permanent residence for themselves and their dependants or close family members (whether they are in Canada or

abroad). More information about these programs is provided in Chapter 9.

4. Under the former *Immigration Act* of 1976, permanent residents known as "landed immigrants" held an IMM 1000 document in their passports as proof of status. A person landed before June 2002 and under the former Act must now apply to CIC for a Permanent Resident Card.

5. Section 63(4) reads as follows: "A permanent resident may appeal to the Immigration Appeal Division against a decision made outside of Canada on the residency obligation under section 28."

6. There are separate application kits depending on the relationship to the sponsor and whether the applications are made in Canada or outside Canada.

7. For the purpose of sponsorship, a co-signer can only be the spouse or common-law partner of the sponsor to help meet income requirements of sponsoring members other than the spouse or common-law or conjugal partner by pooling resources; if the co-signer is a common-law partner, the relationship must have existed for at least one year to qualify.

8. For a list of applicable sexual offences and applicable offences that equate to family violence, see Citizenship and Immigration Canada, "IP 2: Processing Applications to Sponsor Members of the Family Class," in *Inland Processing (IP)*, appendix E, June 20, 2008, www.cic.gc.ca/english/resources/manuals/ip/index.asp.

9. Such debts include transportation, adjustment assistance, admissibility or Right of Permanent Residence Fee loan, a deposit or guarantee of performance of an obligation, and removal costs of a foreign national.

10. *Horbus v. Canada (Minister of Employment & Immigration)* (1985), 22 D.L.R. (4th) 600, [1985] 2 F.C. 359 (T.D.); *Bali v. Canada (Minister of Employment & Immigration)* (1987), 3 Imm L.R. (2d) 135 (A.B.); *Ahn v. Canada (Minister of Employment & Immigration)* (1987), 2 Imm. L.R. (2d) 23 (A.B.); *Jhinger v. Canada (Minister of Employment & Immigration)* (1987), 1 Imm L.R. (2d) (A.B.), at 221.

11. See *Dhillon v. Canada (Minister of Employment & Immigration)* (1990), 14 Imm. L.R. (2d) 138 (Ref. Bd.).

12. The time frames for the other provinces and territories are as follows, as set out in s. 5.40 of "OP 2": Quebec (on or after March 19, 2004); British Columbia (on or after July 8, 2003); Yukon (on or after July 14, 2004); Manitoba (on or after September 16, 2004); Nova Scotia (on or after September 24, 2004); Saskatchewan (on or after November 5, 2004); Newfoundland (on or after December 21, 2004); New Brunswick (on or after July 4, 2005); all other provinces or territories (on or after July 20, 2005).

13. Citizenship and Immigration Canada, "OP 3: Adoptions," in *Overseas Processing (OP)*, December 2002, www.cic.gc.ca/english/resources/manuals/op/index.asp.

14. A person referred to in s. 117(1)(f) or (g).

15. Citizenship and Immigration Canada, "International Adoption," December 19, 2007, www.cic.gc.ca/english/immigrate/adoption/index.asp.

16. Regulations Amending the Immigration and Refugee Protection Regulations, *Canada Gazette*, vol. 139, no. 2, January 8, 2005.

17. *Lindo v. Canada (Minister of Employment & Immigration)*, [1988] 2 F.C. 396, 91 N.R. 75 (C.A.).

18. Citizenship and Immigration Canada, *Annual Report to Parliament on Immigration 2006*, 2006, www.cic.gc.ca/english/resources/publications/index.asp.

19. See ss. 33 to 43 of the IRPA for all inadmissible classes.

20. Citizenship and Immigration Canada, "OP 6: Federal Skilled Workers," in *Overseas Processing (OP)*, s. 10.2, April 24, 2008, www.cic.gc.ca/english/resources/manuals/op/index.asp.

21. Citizenship and Immigration Canada, "Statistical Information: Applications Processed at Canadian Visa Offices—Skilled Workers: Federal," 2007, www.cic.gc.ca/english/information/times/international/02a-skilled-fed.asp.

22. According to the CIC website, this is approximately four months before the visa office is ready to assess the application.

23. Supra note 18.

24. Citizenship and Immigration Canada, "Entrepreneurs: How to Apply—Simplified Application Process," www.cic.gc.ca/english/immigrate/business/entrepreneurs/apply-how-simple.asp.

25. As defined in s. 88(1) of the IRP Regulations.

26. As defined in s. 88(1) of the IRP Regulations.

27. Citizenship and Immigration Canada, "OP 8: Entrepreneur and Self-Employed," in *Overseas Processing (OP)*, s. 11.3, August 7, 2008, www.cic.gc.ca/english/resources/manuals/op/index.asp.

28. As defined in s. 88(1) of the IRP Regulations.

29. Applies to the principal applicant, spouse, or common-law partner.

30. According to the CIC website, this is approximately four months before the visa office is ready to assess the application.

31. Canadian Council for Refugees, "Issues for Roundtable, 26-27 March 2006" (no date), www.ccrweb.ca/H&CMarch2006.html.

32. Citizenship and Immigration Canada, "IP 5: Immigrant Applications in Canada Made on Humanitarian or Compassionate Grounds," in *Inland*

Processing (IP), s. 4.2, May 12, 2008, www.cic.gc.ca/english/resources/ manuals/ip/index.asp.

33. Supra note 1.

34. Supra note 32, s. 5.19.

35. Diane Finley, "Government of Canada Welcomes Vietnamese People Living Without Status in the Philippines" (news release), March 27, 2008, www.cic.gc.ca/english/department/media/releases/2008/index.asp.

36. Unless the applicants are members of the live-in caregiver class, the spouse or common-law partner in Canada class, or the protected temporary residents class—see s. 72(2) of the IRP Regulations.

37. Supra note 32, s. 5.1.

38. Supra note 32, s. 6.7.

39. Supra note 32, s. 5.1.

40. MOSAIC is a multilingual non-profit organization that addresses issues affecting immigrants and refugees. These examples are taken from "A Guide to Humanitarian and Compassionate Applications," March 2004, www.mosaicbc.com/whats_new_publications.asp.

REFERENCES

Canadian Charter of Rights and Freedoms. Part I of the *Constitution Act, 1982.* R.S.C. 1985, app. II, no. 44.

Canadian Council for Refugees, Fact sheet for nationals of moratoria countries without permanent status in Canada. July 2007. www.ccrweb.ca/documents/ infosheetmoratoria.pdf.

Citizenship and Immigration Canada. *Annual Report to Parliament on Immigration 2007*, Table 13: New Permanent Residents in 2006, by Immigration and Gender. October 31, 2007. www.cic.gc.ca/english/ resources/publications/annual-report2007/index.asp.

Citizenship and Immigration Canada. "IP 8: Spouse or Common-Law Partner in Canada Class." In *Inland Processing (IP)*. October 16, 2006. www.cic.gc.ca/ english/resources/manuals/ip/index.asp.

Citizenship and Immigration Canada. "OP 2: Processing Members of the Family Class." In *Overseas Processing (OP)*. November 14, 2006. www.cic.gc.ca/ english/resources/manuals/op/index.asp.

Citizenship and Immigration Canada. "OP 4: Processing of Applications Under Section 25 of the IRPA." In *Overseas Processing (OP)*. July 28, 2008. www.cic.gc.ca/english/resources/manuals/op/index.asp.

Citizenship and Immigration Canada. "OP 6: Federal Skilled Workers." In *Overseas Processing (OP)*. April 24, 2008. www.cic.gc.ca/english/resources/ manuals/op/index.asp.

Citizenship and Immigration Canada. "Sponsoring Your Family: Spouses and Dependent Children—Who Can Apply." September 8, 2008. www.cic.gc.ca/english/immigrate/sponsor/spouse-apply-who.asp.

Human Resources and Social Development Canada. National Occupation Classification. June 8, 2008. www5.hrsdc.gc.ca/noc-cnp/app/index.aspx?lc=e.

Immigration and Refugee Protection Act. S.C. 2001. c. 27.

Immigration and Refugee Protection Regulations. S.O.R./2002-227.

United Nations General Assembly. Convention on the Rights of the Child. November 20, 1989. United Nations, Treaty Series, vol. 1577, p. 3. www.unhchr.ch/html/menu3/b/k2crc.htm.

REVIEW QUESTIONS

1. Family reunification has been a cornerstone of Canada's immigration policy for years. Canadians believe that people who immigrate to Canada will establish themselves more easily if their family supports them. Find the three objectives of the Family Class program as stated in the IRPA.

2. Define the following terms found in the IRPA:
   - family member
   - common-law partner
   - dependent child
   - marriage

3. Who may be a sponsor?

4. What are the obligations of sponsors?

5. What are the applicable fees for sponsorship?

6. What is an undertaking?

7. What is the Sponsorship Agreement and who signs it?

8. Provide an example of a condition or situation that would bar a person from being a sponsor or co-signer.

9. What does the acronym LICO stand for?

10. Who is exempt from the minimum income test?

11. What is the rationale behind business class immigration, from Canada's point of view?

12. What is a qualifying business?

13. In what way is the point system for the business class different from the point system for other classes of permanent entry?

14. What are the three subcategories of business class applicants?

15. Which subcategory of business class applicant must meet conditions? What are they?

16. Which subcategory of business class applicant could be considered "buying a ticket to Canada"? What are the pros and cons of this type of immigration?

17. How is the simplified application process different from the regular application process?

18. In the examples provided under the heading "Application Kit and Forms" on pages 192 to 195, discuss what factors could lead to successful outcomes on H & C considerations or why the applications would be rejected.

CHAPTER 6
Citizenship

LEARNING OBJECTIVES

After reading this chapter you should be able to:

- Assess whether a client is eligible to apply for Canadian citizenship.
- Explain to a client the steps that must be taken in order to obtain citizenship.
- Describe the methods of becoming a Canadian citizen.
- Complete the citizenship application form for a client who wishes to become a Canadian citizen.
- Describe how Canadian citizenship may be lost.

INTRODUCTION

Citizenship is an important element in the makeup and identity of Canadian society. The rules of citizenship are designed to make sure that all people recognized as citizens, and granted citizenship, have significant ties to Canada. Some controversy still exists about these rules, and proposals to amend them have been made over the past years.

Many Canadians are citizens as a result of being born here. Others are citizens because one of their parents is a Canadian citizen. Most of this chapter is about a third category of Canadians—those who were formerly foreign nationals, but have since acquired Canadian citizenship as the result of a process called **naturalization**. In 2006–7, 243,003 permanent residents became Canadian citizens. The top ten countries of origin of new citizens were India, the People's Republic of China, Pakistan, the Philippines, Iran, South Korea, Romania, Sri Lanka, Jamaica, and the United States.[1]

A person is not a citizen of Canada merely because he has lived here for an extended period of time. For example, a person born outside Canada to parents who were not Canadian citizens could enter Canada, either legally or illegally, as a two-year-old child, spend an entire lifetime in Canada, yet not be a Canadian citizen. In order to become a Canadian citizen, a foreign national must first be admitted to Canada as a permanent resident, spend several years in Canada, and then apply to become a citizen.

This chapter will describe how citizenship is conferred because of place of birth or parentage, and also how it may be actively sought by a foreign national. The process of acquiring citizenship is described in some detail. The chapter also discusses the process of renouncing citizenship and the situations in which citizenship may be revoked. Finally, the chapter examines recent amendments to the *Citizenship Act* in the areas of adoptions and restoration of citizenship.

INTERNATIONAL LAW

International law allows a sovereign country such as Canada the power to decide whom to recognize as citizens and as nationals. The term "national" is a broader term than "citizen." It may include persons who are not citizens, but who have rights and obligations such as those given to Canadian permanent residents. International law also permits countries to establish rules and requirements regarding how citizenship may be acquired by **foreign nationals**.[2] **Citizenship** endows a person "with the full political and civil rights in the body politic of the state."[3] These may include the right to vote and hold political office. Citizenship may also carry potential obligations, such as military service.

In Canada, permanent residents have a right to enter and remain in Canada as long as they maintain their permanent resident status, but unlike Canadian citizens, they are not permitted to vote or hold political office.

A **stateless person** is not recognized by any nation as being its national, and therefore such a person has no residency rights in any country. Statelessness is addressed in article 15 of the Universal Declaration of Human Rights, as follows:

1. Everyone has the right to a nationality.

2. No one shall be arbitrarily deprived of his nationality nor denied the right to change his nationality.

The objective of this article is to encourage nations to take responsibility for their people, and reduce statelessness.

Special rights of entry are accorded to anyone registered as an Indian under the *Indian Act*. Such a person may enter Canada, even if not a citizen or permanent resident, according to s. 19(1) of the *Immigration and Refugee Protection Act* (IRPA). This special status is granted in recognition of the fact that the traditional homelands of some North American First Nations groups straddle both the United States and Canada, and to protect the right of First Nations people to move freely on these traditional homelands.

LEGISLATIVE HISTORY

Canada's *Citizenship Act* (1977) defines who is deemed a citizen at birth, and how foreign nationals may acquire citizenship through the naturalization process. A person is a citizen if born in Canada, or born outside Canada to a parent who is a Canadian citizen.

However, prior to 1947, Canada did not have its own citizenship act and instead relied on British law. There was legally no such thing as Canadian citizenship. Both native-born and naturalized citizens were British subjects. The rules determining who was a British subject also applied in Canada to determine the equivalent of citizenship for Canadians. Since 1947, the law has evolved with a series of Canadian citizenship statutes.

In Canada, the three time periods of importance are the following:

- Pre-1947: British law applied

- 1947–1977: *Canadian Citizenship Act* in force[4]

- 1977–present: *Citizenship Act* (1977) enacted, replacing the *Canadian Citizenship Act*.

Our first citizenship act, the *Canadian Citizenship Act*, came into force January 1, 1947, and thus for applications after this date Canadian law applied and replaced British rules. Each time the law changed, the new rules applied only to future, prospective citizens, so the former law may be applicable for citizenship applications. An example of this is that under the 1947 *Canadian Citizenship Act*, Canadian citizens who were not "natural-born" lost their citizenship if they resided outside of Canada for a period of six consecutive years. ("Natural-born" Canadian citizens include those who are born either in Canada or outside Canada if, at the time of birth, one parent is a Canadian citizen.) This period was increased to ten years during the 1950s, and repealed altogether in 1967. However, some people had already lost their Canadian citizenship, in many cases unknowingly.[5] Recent amendments to the current *Citizenship Act* provide a remedy for such situations by restoring citizenship to people considered as "formerly lost Canadians."

The *Canadian Citizenship Act* was replaced, effective February 14, 1977, with a new *Citizenship Act*, which continues to govern citizenship applications. This new Act introduced several major changes including the recognition of dual citizenship for Canadians, and a reduction of the residency period needed to apply for citizenship.

CITIZENSHIP COMMISSION

The Citizenship Commission is an administrative tribunal within Citizenship and Immigration Canada (CIC) that consists of citizenship judges with offices across Canada. Citizenship judges' authorities and responsibilities are derived from the *Citizenship Act* and the Citizenship Regulations. **Citizenship judges** are quasi-judicial decision makers who have the authority to decide citizenship applications.

CIC provides the Citizenship Commission with administrative, financial, and human resources services; however, it maintains an arm's-length relationship on decision-making matters related to citizenship in order to ensure the independence of citizenship judges.

The Citizenship Commission is responsible for the following functions:

- deciding citizenship applications

- administering the oath of citizenship and stating the rights and responsibilities of Canadian citizenship to new citizens;

- maintaining the integrity of the citizenship process; and

- promoting citizenship by working with school boards, service clubs, multicultural groups, and other community organizations.

According to the *Citizenship Act*, there are four types of citizenship applications for which citizenship judges make decisions:

- grant of citizenship, involving the conferral of citizenship on a non-citizen (s. 5(1));

- retentions, involving confirmation of citizenship of children of a Canadian parent (s. 8);

- renunciations, involving the termination of citizenship (s. 9(1)); and

- resumptions, involving the recommencement of a terminated citizenship (s. 11(1)).

Most of these applications are decided by judges on the basis of a file review. However, when a judge finds that more information is required to make a decision, the applicant is invited to attend a hearing before that judge.[6]

ATTRIBUTES OF CITIZENSHIP

Right to Enter and Remain in Canada

Every citizen has a right to enter and remain in Canada, according to s. 19 of the IRPA and s. 6 of the *Charter of Rights and Freedoms*. This means that a Canadian border services officer may not refuse admission to Canada at a port of entry if the officer is satisfied that the person is a Canadian citizen. Also, a Canadian citizen generally cannot be subject to removal or deportation from Canada.

These rights of citizenship are subject to reasonable limits, such as the power of an officer to detain a Canadian citizen subject to an arrest warrant. Similarly, although Canada may not banish or exile citizens, it may apprehend and extradite a citizen to face criminal charges in another country, according to the *Extradition Act*.

The Supreme Court examined the process of extradition in the case of *United States of America v. Cotroni* and confirmed that the process is in compliance with s. 6(1) of the Charter. However, the Court provided the following caution:

> Of course, the authorities must give due weight to the constitutional right of a citizen to remain in Canada. They must in good faith direct their minds to whether prosecution would be equally effective in Canada, given the existing domestic laws and international cooperative arrangements. They have an obligation flowing from s. 6(1) to assure themselves that prosecution in Canada is not a realistic option.

Extradition powers are important to prevent Canada from becoming an attractive place for fugitives.[7]

Also, although Canada may not order citizens to leave the country, it may revoke a Canadian citizenship that was obtained by fraud, misrepresentation, or concealment of important facts. Once citizenship is revoked, removal from Canada may be ordered.

Multiple Citizenships

Canada has permitted **multiple citizenships** since the *Citizenship Act* was enacted in 1977. Canada allows a person who becomes a citizen of Canada to retain any previous citizenship. This is subject to the law of the other country, which may choose to revoke the citizenship of those who obtain citizenship elsewhere, such as in Canada.

Right to Vote and Hold Office

Every citizen of Canada has the right to vote in provincial and federal elections and to be qualified to be a member of Parliament or the provincial Parliament, according to s. 3 of the Charter. Like all Charter rights and freedoms, these rights are also subject to reasonable limits, such as minimum voting age requirements. Our *Citizenship Act* makes no distinction between persons who are born citizens and persons who acquire citizenship through naturalization (s. 6). A naturalized citizen has all the rights that a citizen who was born in Canada or born to Canadian parents has. However, not all countries extend full political rights to naturalized citizens. For example, a naturalized citizen of the United States is prohibited from becoming president—only people born in the United States may become president.

BECOMING A CITIZEN

The two most common principles of citizenship are the following:

- ■ *Jus soli*: *Jus soli* is citizenship based on the land of birth. At birth, a person is automatically granted citizenship of the country in which she was born.

- ■ *Jus sanguinis*: *Jus sanguinis* is citizenship based on blood ties. At birth, a person is automatically granted citizenship of the country where one of the parents is a citizen. If the parents are citizens of separate or multiple countries, the child is granted citizenship of both or all of those countries.

Countries tend to adopt one or both of these principles, or some variation, as the basis for conferring citizenship. Other approaches used by some nations are to grant citizenship to foreign nationals who marry one of their citizens.[8] In addition, most countries allow immigrants to apply for citizenship, through the process of naturalization.

The Canadian *Citizenship Act* allows for all three methods of becoming a citizen —namely, being born in Canada, being born outside Canada to a Canadian citizen, and naturalization. Each method is described below.

Being Born in Canada

Generally, any person born in Canada is automatically a Canadian citizen. This is according to s. 3(1) of the *Citizenship Act* (1977), and follows the principle of *jus soli*, or citizenship by soil. The rule applies even if neither parent is a Canadian citizen, and even if one or both parents are in Canada illegally.

Some locations outside of Canada are deemed to be in Canada for the operation of the rule, including Canadian ships and aircraft registered in Canada. Persons born on these vessels are Canadian citizens according to s. 2(2) of the *Citizenship Act* (1977).

An exception to the rule that birth in Canada confers Canadian citizenship applies to a person who, at the time of his birth, is the child of a foreign national who is in Canada as the representative of a foreign government or an international agency. Such persons are deemed not to be Canadian citizens, according to s. 3(2) of the *Citizenship Act* (1977).

Being Born Outside Canada to a Canadian Citizen

A person born outside Canada is a Canadian citizen if one parent was a Canadian citizen. This follows the principle of *jus sanguinis*, or citizenship by blood. The rule applies even if the baby's only connection with Canada is having a parent who is a Canadian citizen and even if the baby never resides in or even visits Canada. Often, such a baby is automatically a citizen of the country of birth as well. Canadian law allows such a person to retain Canadian citizenship unless she takes steps to renounce it.

This raises an issue with respect to the continuation of citizenship for second and subsequent generations born outside Canada. Canadian citizenship could potentially be passed on for generations, even when connection with Canada is nonexistent. Canada would be obliged to admit these persons to Canada automatically, and to offer them the assistance of Canadian overseas services such as embassies and consulates.

Changes to the *Citizenship Act* (Bill C-37, which came into force on July 25, 2008) remove the requirement to register and retain citizenship by age 28. People born before July 25, 2008, and who are second or subsequent generation Canadians born abroad, retain their existing Canadian citizenship, according to the new s. 3(4). They must still apply for a citizenship certificate because they are subject to the retention requirement. CIC will send a letter advising them that steps must be taken before their 28th birthday in order to retain Canadian citizenship. Effective January 1, 2007, as an additional reminder for these citizens to retain their citizenship, their certificates now include a date by which they must act to remain Canadians.

The new rule limits citizenship by descent to one generation for people born after the rule comes into effect. This means that a child born abroad to a parent who derived her citizenship from a Canadian parent who was also born abroad will no longer automatically become a Canadian citizen, according to the new s. 3(3).[9]

Retaining Citizenship for Second and Subsequent Generation Canadians Born Outside Canada

John Smith was born in Calgary, Alberta in 1958. He moved to Australia in 1978 because of a job, and lived the rest of his life there. His son Bob Smith, born in Australia in 1979, is a Canadian citizen because his father was a Canadian citizen. Bob Smith lived his entire life in Australia, and had no connection with Canada. His son Roger Smith was born in Australia in 2005. Roger is a Canadian citizen even though both he and his father have no connection with Canada.

Before recent amendments to the *Citizenship Act* (1977), second and subsequent generation Canadians born outside Canada on or after February 15, 1977 to a Canadian parent who was also born outside Canada had to apply to retain Canadian citizenship before age 28. Otherwise, the chain would be broken and Canadian citizenship would be lost. In our example, Roger Smith's citizenship would be extinguished when he turns 28, if he does not apply to have it retained. Furthermore, Roger is required to meet either of the following criteria:

- reside in Canada for at least one year immediately preceding the application; or

- establish a substantial connection with Canada.

A **substantial connection with Canada** may be established in one of the following two ways according to s. 16 of the Citizenship Regulations, 1993:

- by working in specific occupations for two of the four years proceeding the application; the qualifying occupations are: employment in the federal or provincial public service; employment in the Canadian military; and employment as a Canadian representative to the UN or one of its agencies; or

- by (a) demonstrating adequate knowledge of Canada and one of the official languages, and the responsibilities and privileges of citizenship, and (b) after the age of 14, residing in Canada for more than one year, with a relative or in attendance at a high school, university, or college.

Using our example, if Roger wishes to retain his Canadian citizenship, he has several options. The simplest is to live in Canada for one year immediately prior to making his application. There are no knowledge requirements, and Roger may spend his year doing as he pleases.

Alternatively, Roger may establish a substantial connection with Canada. This may be achieved by working for Canada as a public servant, in the military, or for a UN agency on behalf of Canada, for two of the four years immediately prior to making his application. If this does not interest Roger, he may choose to reside in Canada for at least one year, with a relative or in attendance at school. This final option also requires Roger to have adequate knowledge of Canada, either English or French, and the responsibilities and privileges of citizenship.

for According to the legislative summary on Bill C-37, an exception is provided

> people who are born to a Canadian parent working abroad in or with the Canadian Armed Forces, the federal public administration or the public service of a province, unless the parent is a locally engaged person, according to the new section 3(5). For such people, citizenship is automatic at birth even though the person is a second or subsequent generation Canadian born abroad."[10]

up to here Cutting off citizenship by descent after the first generation of Canadians born abroad will result in some offspring of Canadians born abroad in the future being stateless. Therefore, amendments include a provision for a mandatory grant of citizenship to a person who was born outside Canada after the provision comes into force and to a parent who was Canadian at the time of the person's birth if, at the time that the person applies for Canadian citizenship, the person

- is less than 23 years old;
- has resided in Canada for at least three years during the four years immediately before the date of the application for citizenship;
- has always been stateless; and
- has not been convicted of various listed national security offences.[11]

Naturalization

Naturalization is the legal process that transforms a permanent resident into a Canadian citizen. In order to be naturalized the permanent resident must apply for citizenship. Most of these applications are decided by judges on the basis of a file review. However, when a judge finds that more information is required to make a decision, the applicant is invited to attend a hearing before that judge.[12]

Permanent residents who wish to obtain Canadian citizenship must meet certain criteria. They must

- be admitted to Canada as a permanent resident;
- be at least 18 years old or be included with the application of a parent who is over 18 years old;
- make an application for citizenship;
- pay fees;
- provide photos;
- have lived in Canada for at least three years (1,095 days) out of the four years prior to applying for citizenship;
- not be under a removal order or declared to be a threat to security or a member of an organized crime group;
- show an adequate knowledge of English or French;
- demonstrate an understanding of the responsibilities of a citizen and pass the citizenship test; and
- take the citizenship oath.

An applicant who is physically or mentally unable to comply may have the following requirements waived for compassionate reasons:[13]

- the citizenship test;

- competence in English or French; and

- the citizenship oath.

In these circumstances, medical documentation must be provided that outlines the applicant's condition and how it prevents the applicant from fulfilling the obligations.

NATURALIZATION PROCESS

Numerous steps must be taken when applying for Canadian citizenship. Some steps, such as the payment of fees, are relatively straightforward. However, many applicants require advice and assistance with other steps in the naturalization process. For example, documents must be provided to support the application, and if the originals are not in English or French, they must be translated into one of those official languages. An affidavit must be sworn by the translator stating that the translation is a true one.[14]

Other steps, such as demonstrating sufficient time spent residing in Canada, may be complex and require legal advice and guidance from counsel.

Proof of Identity and Age

The applicant for Canadian citizenship must be 18 years of age or over. The applicant must provide proof of his identity and age. Specifically, the applicant must do the following:

- Present two identity documents, such as a passport, health insurance card, and Canadian driver's licence.

- Establish age by filing a birth certificate or other evidence that shows the date and place of birth.

- Disclose any version of his name that has been used. It is not unusual for permanent residents to use Canadianized versions of their names, and these names must be reported on the application.

Application Form, Fees, and Photos

The applicant must complete the approved citizenship application form, Form CIT 0002, which must not be postdated. After three months the form will be considered stale-dated, and will have to be redone.

An applicant must pay the fees fixed by regulation and provide photos that conform to the size and other dimensions specified by regulation.

The fees include a $100 processing fee and a $100 right of citizenship that is payable if the applicant is 18 years or older. There are no additional fees for children

WEBLINK

A list and the amount of the fees required for a citizenship application can be found on the CIC website at www.cic .gc.ca/english/ information/fees/fees .asp.

included in their parents' applications. Fees are paid either using a credit card online or through an approved financial institution such as a bank. If the application is rejected, the processing fee will not be returned.

Photos must be signed on the back by both the photographer and the applicant. The applicant's signature on the photograph must match the signature on the application. Head coverings must be removed for the photo unless for the purpose of religious observance.

Proof of Residency

To satisfy the citizenship judge that sufficient residency was achieved, the applicant must meet three conditions of residency, according to s. 5(1) of the *Citizenship Act*, as follows:

1. *Lawful admittance to Canada as a permanent resident.* The applicant must file her Canadian immigration record/paper (such as the Record of Landing (IMM 1000), Confirmation of Permanent Residence (IMM 5292), or Permanent Resident Card (PRC)), which was obtained from CIC when permanent residency was granted, and a copy of both sides of the Permanent Resident Card. This shows entitlement to enter Canada. (It is also important to establish accumulation of the required residency period in Canada.)

2. *No loss of permanent residency.* The applicant's permanent residency must not be invalidated by a failure to maintain the connection with Canada, or by an order to leave Canada. A connection with Canada is not maintained if the person is not resident in Canada for two years out of every five-year period (loss of permanent resident status is discussed in Chapter 5, "Permanent Entry"). Permanent resident status is also lost if a removal order is made because the person has become inadmissible and the appeals of that order have been exhausted (s. 28 of the IRPA). This could occur if the permanent resident engaged in criminal activity, for example.

3. *Residence in Canada.* Under s. 5(b) of the *Citizenship Act*, the applicant must prove residency in Canada for at least three years (1,095 days) in the last four years (1,460 days). Days spent in Canada as a temporary resident count as half days for satisfying the residency requirements. The IRPA and its regulations make it clear that certain periods of time spent in Canada may not be included in the period counted toward residency, including time spent: incarcerated in a penal institution or jail, on probation, or on parole, according to s. 21 of the *Citizenship Act* (1977).

The requirement of **residence in Canada** is complicated by the fact that the *Citizenship Act* does not specify whether actual physical presence in Canada is required or whether it is sufficient to establish a life in Canada and to treat Canada as a home base while spending time outside of the country.

Case law is divided as to whether actual physical presence in Canada is required. In many cases, judges have held that once a person is resident in Canada he may be absent from Canada for periods of time provided that the pattern and length of absences from Canada are not significant enough to show that Canadian residence has been abandoned. This allows time spent outside Canada for a vacation or business trip to count toward the requirement. Consider the court's reasoning in *Re Papado-giorgakis*, at 213-214:

> It seems to me that the words "residence" and "resident" in paragraph 5(1)(b) of the new *Citizenship Act* are not as strictly limited to actual presence in Canada throughout the period as they were in the former statute but can include, as well, situations in which the person concerned has a place in Canada which is used by him during the period as a place of abode to a sufficient extent to demonstrate the reality of his residing there during the material period even though he is away from it part of the time. ...
>
> A person with an established home of his own in which he lives does not cease to be resident there when he leaves it for a temporary purpose whether on business or vacation or even to pursue a course of study. The fact of his family remaining there while he is away may lend support for the conclusion that he has not ceased to reside there. The conclusion may be reached, as well, even though the absence may be more or less lengthy. It is also enhanced if he returns there frequently when the opportunity to do so arises.

The residency requirement was further explored in *Koo (Re) (T.D.)*, where the court identified the following indicia of residency:

- The applicant was physically present in Canada for a long period prior to absences, which occurred before the application for citizenship.

- The applicant's immediate family and dependants (and extended family) are resident in Canada.

- The applicant's pattern of physical presence in Canada indicates returning home rather than merely visiting.

- The extent of the physical absences was limited. (If an applicant is only a few days short of the 1,095-day total, deemed residence is more likely to be found than if those absences were extensive.)

- The applicant's physical absence is caused by a clearly temporary situation, such as a posting as a missionary abroad, a course of study abroad as a student, temporary employment abroad, or time spent accompanying a spouse who has accepted employment abroad.

- The quality of the connection with Canada is more substantial than that which exists with any other country.

Evidence to support residency includes the following:

- ownership of residential property in Canada

- bank accounts in Canada

- club or association memberships

- membership in provincial health insurance plan

- travel documents and receipts showing frequent return trips to Canada

- presence of family in Canada

- income tax returns filed in Canada

- car registration in Canada

- provincial driver's licence

- registered retirement savings plan

- payroll deductions.[15]

Other judges reviewing appeals of citizenship application cases have taken the position that actual physical presence in Canada is required and that the applicant must show that he has been physically present in Canada for at least 1,095 days during the past four years. The need for physical presence in Canada was described in *Re Pourgashemi*, at 260:

> It is clear that the purpose of paragraph 5(1)(c) is to insure that everyone who is granted precious Canadian citizenship has become, or at least has been compulsorily presented with the everyday opportunity to become, "Canadianized." This happens by "rubbing elbows" with Canadians in shopping malls, corner stores, libraries, concert halls, auto repair shops, pubs, cabarets, elevators, churches, synagogues, mosques and temples—in a word wherever one can meet and converse with Canadians—during the prescribed three years. One can observe Canadian society for all its virtues, decadence, values, dangers and freedoms, just as it is. That is little enough time in which to become Canadianized. If a citizenship candidate misses that qualifying experience, then Canadian citizenship can be conferred, in effect, on a person who is still a foreigner in experience, social adaptation, and often in thought and outlook.

The court attempted to reconcile these conflicting opinions in *Re Mui*, as follows:

> I agree in principle with some decisions of this Court which, given special or exceptional circumstances, do not require physical presence in Canada for the entire 1095 days. However, it is my view, that an extended absence from Canada during the minimum period of time, albeit temporary, as in the present case, is contrary to the purpose of the residency requirements of the Act. Indeed, the Act already allows a person who has been lawfully admitted to Canada for permanent residence not to reside in Canada during one of the four years immediately preceding the date of that person's application for Canadian citizenship.

The contradictory rules provided in these cases create a challenge for immigration officers and citizenship judges who must make decisions about citizenship applications. In an effort to provide some direction, the *Citizenship Policy (CP)* operations manual instructs immigration officers as follows:

> If you determine that all the absences of the applicant fall within the allowable exceptions, you must then assess if the applicant was outside of Canada, in total, for a longer period of time than he or she was in Canada.
>
> Given that the purpose of the residence requirement is to ensure that the applicant for citizenship can become familiar with Canada and become integrated into Canadian society, it follows that the longer the absences of the applicant, the more difficult it will be for the Minister to be convinced that the applicant meets

the residence requirement. This is true even if the reasons for the absences seem to fall entirely within the exceptional circumstances described above.

Another way to consider the "majority rule" is to keep in mind that, for citizenship purposes, a person can only have one residence at any given time. Therefore, if a person is spending a lot of time in another country (in effect, residing there), that person cannot, at the same time, "maintain residence in Canada." If the citizenship judge approves an application where the applicant has been outside Canada the majority of the time (in other words, has been outside Canada for more time than in Canada), the citizenship judge's complete file on the applicant must then be referred to Case Management Branch for possible appeal by the Minister. Include your analysis of why the applicant does not appear to meet the residence requirement.[16]

In other words, the officer refers cases for review and possible appeal where the applicant was granted citizenship despite being physically out of the country for more than half the time of residency. This rule applies even if the absences were deemed by the judge to fall within the six categories set out in the *Koo* case.

The CIC website provides a **residency calculator** so that applicants can ensure they are not submitting applications too early. To be eligible for Canadian citizenship, an applicant must meet residency requirements for the four years preceding the date of application. The applicant must have lived in Canada for at least three years (1,095 days) out of the four years (1,460 days) preceding the application. At least two years of this must be as a permanent resident.

When calculating time in Canada the following rules apply:

- only the four years preceding the date of the application are taken into account;

- each day spent in Canada before the applicant became a permanent resident counts as half a day, up to a year;

- each day spent in Canada after the applicant became a permanent resident counts as one day;

- generally, time spent serving a sentence for an offence in Canada is not counted.

In cases where there were fewer than 1,095 days of physical presence in Canada, only a citizenship judge may determine whether residency requirements were met. Consider the following case scenario:

Grant, a citizen of Germany, came to Canada on September 1, 2003 on a student visa for postsecondary studies. He met and married a fellow classmate, Faye, on September 1, 2005. He applied for permanent resident status from within Canada and received that status on September 1, 2006.

What is the first date that Grant can apply for Canadian citizenship? Keeping in mind that Grant became a permanent resident on September 1, 2006 and that Grant must have lived in Canada for at least three years (1,095 days) out of the four years (1,460 days) preceding the application, the calculation is as follows:

Each day that Grant lived in Canada as a student in the 2 years prior to his becoming a permanent resident counts for one ½ day, up to a maximum of one year:

September 1, 2004 to September 1, 2006 = 730 days × ½ = 365 countable days

Grant needs a minimum of 2 years as a permanent resident, so count forward 2 years from the date he became a permanent resident:

September 1, 2006 to September 1, 2008 = 2 years = 730 countable days

Total countable days: 365 + 730 = 1,095

The first day that Grant can apply is September 2, 2008.

Admissibility

An applicant for citizenship must not be under a removal order. (For information about contesting removal orders, see Chapter 10, "Enforcement Procedures.") An applicant must also not be a declared threat to security or a member of an organized crime group. For information about declarations as a security threat or a member of an organized crime group, see Chapter 3, "Inadmissibility."

If applicable, any such ground of inadmissibility must be disclosed. However, the citizenship judge may recommend to the minister that the discretion to grant citizenship in the face of these problems be exercised, according to s. 5(4) of the *Citizenship Act*, as follows:

> In order to alleviate cases of special and unusual hardship or to reward services of an exceptional value to Canada, and notwithstanding any other provision of this Act, the Governor in Council may, in his discretion, direct the Minister to grant citizenship to any person and, where such a direction is made, the Minister shall forthwith grant citizenship to the person named in the direction.

Before the citizenship judge will make such a recommendation to the minister, the judge will need to be convinced that either the case is one of special and unusual hardship or the applicant rendered services of exceptional value to Canada.

Language Test

The applicant for citizenship must demonstrate an adequate knowledge of one of Canada's two official languages. Applicants between the ages of 18 and 54 are expected to be able to carry out simple everyday conversations in either English or French, and to carry out basic activities such as shopping, banking, and taking public transit. Applicants who fail the written language test are given the opportunity for an oral interview with a citizenship judge, during which the applicant's ability to engage in a conversation will be directly assessed. The judge will consider whether the applicant can respond to instructions, fill out a simple form, and talk about personal experiences. Upon the recommendation of a citizenship judge, the minister may, under s. 5(3)(a) of the *Citizenship Act*, waive this requirement on compassionate grounds, and does so routinely for older persons.

Canada's Citizenship Week

In 2006 CIC launched the first Citizenship Week to promote citizenship. Citizenship Week is an annual event celebrating the value of citizenship, and promoting the privileges and responsibilities of being a Canadian citizen. Canada celebrated the 60th anniversary of Canadian citizenship in 2007. For more information about Citizenship Week, visit the CIC website at www.cic.gc.ca/english/celebrate/celebrate.asp.

Citizenship Test

The applicant for citizenship must display an adequate knowledge of Canada and of the rights and responsibilities of Canadian citizenship. Applicants are generally required to take a citizenship test measuring knowledge of Canada in the areas of history, politics, geography, the rights and responsibilities of citizenship including voting, running for political office, and Canadian election procedures. The test is waived for applicants over age 55 or under the age of 18. Consider the following examples of questions:

Section I. Questions About Canada

1. Who are the Aboriginal peoples of Canada?

2. What are the three main groups of Aboriginal peoples?

3. In which parts of Canada did the Aboriginal peoples first live?

Section II. Questions About Your Region

181. When did settlers from Europe first come to your region?

182. Who were the first settlers in the area where you live?

183. Why did the early Europeans come to your region in the 1600s, 1700s, 1800s or early 1900s?

To assist with preparations for the test, CIC sends the applicant the booklet "A Look at Canada." Information about the test is also available to applicants on the CIC website.

The applicant will receive a Notice to Appear for a Citizenship Test, indicating the date, time, and place of the test.

Citizenship Oath

When an applicant meets the basic requirements for citizenship and has passed both the language and citizenship tests, she receives a Notice to Appear to Take the Oath of Citizenship. The oath of citizenship is administered at a special ceremony presided over by a citizenship judge.

The citizenship oath as set out in the schedule to the *Citizenship Act* reads as follows:

I swear (*or* affirm) that I will be faithful and bear true allegiance to Her Majesty Queen Elizabeth the Second, Queen of Canada, Her Heirs and Successors, and that I will faithfully observe the laws of Canada and fulfil my duties as a Canadian citizen.

WEBLINK

To learn more about the citizenship test and to see more sample questions, visit the CIC website at www.cic.gc.ca/english/resources/publications/look/index.asp.

Historically, such an oath would be taken holding a Bible. In recognition of the rights of religious freedom enshrined in our legal system, this is no longer required. Applicants with a religious or other objection to swearing an oath are given the option of affirming rather than swearing the oath. Applicants who choose to swear the oath are given the option of holding the holy book of their choosing when taking the oath.[17]

Applications for Minors

According to s. 5(2) of the *Citizenship Act*, a citizenship application for a minor may be completed by the parents (biological or adoptive), legal guardians, or other persons legally entitled to have custody of the child. A minor is a person who is not yet 18. A minor child between 14 and 18 years of age is expected to also sign the application, unless he has a mental disability. In addition to the information provided in the application that accompanies an adult's application, the following additional items must be provided:

- Evidence establishing that the minor child is the child of a citizen. Acceptable documents include birth certificates showing the names of the parents, adoption orders, parents' passports showing the names of the children, and IMM 1000 forms listing parents' names for children who entered Canada as refugees.[18]

- If the applicant is not a birth or adoptive parent of a citizen, evidence establishing that the applicant has legal custody of the child. Acceptable documents include a court order or written agreement.

Steps After Application Submitted

Once the applicant has completed the application for citizenship, she must mail it to the Case Processing Centre (CPC) in Sydney, Nova Scotia, where the following steps[19] occur:

Step 1: The CPC reviews the application to ensure the following:

- it is complete,

- the fee is paid, and

- all information is included.

Step 2: The CPC reviews the documents submitted with the application—for example, the Record of Landing (IMM 1000).

Step 3: The CPC mails the applicant a confirmation letter and a copy of "A Look at Canada."

Step 4: The CPC forwards the application to the following for background checks to ensure admissibility:

- Immigration Canada (CIC), to check for an immigration record;

- the RCMP, to check for a criminal record; and

- the Canadian Security and Intelligence Service, to check for a security record.

Step 5: The CPC prepares and sends a package of information to the CIC office nearest to the applicant.

Step 6: The CIC office sends the applicant a Notice to Appear for a Citizenship Test.

Step 7: If necessary, an interview with a citizenship judge is arranged to review residency issues, literacy, or possible prohibitions.

Step 8: If the citizenship judge approves citizenship, the applicant is invited to a citizenship ceremony by way of a Notice to Appear to Take the Oath of Citizenship.

Step 9: A citizenship ceremony is held, where the applicant takes the oath of citizenship and receives the Certificate of Canadian Citizenship. (Any citizen of Canada may apply for a certificate of citizenship as proof of his Canadian citizenship, according to s. 12 of the *Citizenship Act*. In 2003/2004, CIC issued 49,552 proofs of Canadian citizenship, and this number rose to 59,873 in 2004/2005. The processing time to obtain a certificate of citizenship is approximately five to seven months.[20])

Step 10: The applicant's completed file is microfilmed and stored.

Step 11: If the citizenship judge refuses citizenship, the applicant may reapply or appeal to the Federal Court. Only a lawyer, not an immigration consultant, may represent an applicant at the Federal Court.

In 2006–7 the estimated time for obtaining a grant of citizenship was 10.3 months.[21]

RENOUNCING AND REVOKING CITIZENSHIP

For administrative efficiency, applications to retain, renounce, and resume citizenship are decided by the senior citizenship judge.

Citizenship may be lost only for the reasons specified in the *Citizenship Act*, namely, renunciation and revocation.

Renouncing Citizenship

Renouncing citizenship means that a citizen actively takes steps to terminate citizenship. A Canadian citizen who is no longer resident in Canada may renounce her Canadian citizenship. A person may be motivated to do this if Canadian citizenship prevents entitlement to an advantage or benefit in another country.

For example, the Canadian-born newspaper magnate Conrad Black, when he had the opportunity to become a British Peer and sit in the British House of Lords, actively sought to revoke his Canadian citizenship. Black wanted to be granted a peerage by the Queen of England, an honour that has been bestowed on other wealthy Canadian newspaper owners in the past. A constitutional convention prevented the Queen from granting such a peerage to a Canadian citizen without the approval of the prime minister of Canada. The prime minister refused permission, and his refusal was upheld by the Ontario Court of Appeal in *Black v. Canada (Prime Minister)*. However, Black, as a resident of England, was allowed to renounce his Canadian citizenship so that the Queen could grant the peerage.

A person may also need to renounce his Canadian citizenship if he wishes to become a citizen of another country that does not allow dual citizenship.

Note that Canadian citizenship may not be renounced by a resident in Canada for the purpose of avoiding an obligation falling on Canadian citizens, such as military duty in the event of a draft.

Revoking Citizenship

Revoking citizenship means that the Canadian government takes steps to remove a person's citizenship. Revocation is done by Cabinet through an order in council.

Revocation proceedings may be applied to citizenship granted by any method under the Act, if it comes to light that either the person's admission to Canada for the prerequisite period of residence or the citizenship application itself involved at least one of the following:

- fraud;

- false representation (misrepresentation); or

- knowing concealment of material circumstances.

For example, if it can be shown that a person's documents indicating place of birth or parentage were falsified in order to claim citizenship by place of birth, or through a birth parent, then the citizenship of that person could be revoked. Likewise, a person who applies to retain citizenship on the basis of having a substantial connection with Canada and who files false documents showing educational time spent in Canada could have her citizenship revoked.

Often, the cases dealing with revocation of citizenship do not clearly define which of the three reasons is the basis for the revocation. This is because the facts that give rise to revocation may be described as fraudulent, as well as a false representation, as well as a knowing concealment of material circumstances.

The operation of these provisions was illustrated in the case of Helmut Oberlander, in which the government revoked Oberlander's citizenship because he lied about his participation in war crimes when he applied to come to Canada. During the Second World War, Mr. Oberlander worked as a translator for a Nazi police unit that killed 23,000 persons in the Ukraine during the years 1941 to 1943, although there was no evidence he took part in the killings. He immigrated to Canada in 1954. This was considered a material issue because Canada was not admitting persons involved in atrocities during the Second World War. The government did not take action until 2001 almost 50 years after Oberlander entered Canada.

An example of citizenship being revoked because of fraud would be a case where an applicant with a criminal record forges documents to support the application.

The applicant could obtain and try to use forged certificates showing he had no criminal record.

The evidentiary requirements for proving fraud are stricter than those for proving false representation or knowing concealment of material circumstances, as was illustrated in *Minister of Citizenship v. Odynsky*. In order to establish fraud, it is not sufficient to simply show that a person did an action such as making a false statement—it must be shown that there was some mental element involved in the activity such as an intention to get around the restrictions in the system.

In the *Odynsky* case, the government could not prove fraud but was able to show both knowing concealment of a material circumstance and the making of a false representation. Odynsky was forced to act as a guard in a concentration camp during the Second World War. He did not reveal this fact when he applied to come to Canada in 1949, and he became a Canadian citizen in 1955. It was not proven that Canadian officials asked about his actions during the war when he made his application; therefore, his omission was not fraudulent. However, by omitting this fact, he rendered his application untrue, and thus it was a false representation. In addition, the circumstances were material because Canada would not have admitted him if he had admitted he was a concentration camp guard, and he knew he was not fully revealing this information.

Note that to prove knowing concealment of a material circumstance it does not have to be shown that the person knew the circumstances were material. Furthermore, the person does not have to know about the criteria being applied by the Canadian authorities in assessing his application.

The mere fact of making a false representation is sufficient even without the presence of a mental element. Thus, in the *Odynsky* case, the government did not have to prove that Mr. Odynsky intentionally did not reveal his service during the war in order to circumvent the application process. Once it showed that the statement was false, this was sufficient. Finally, the courts have indicated that the false statement cannot be merely a technical or minor error in order for citizenship to be revoked.[22]

AMENDMENTS: ADOPTION AND RESTORATION OF CITIZENSHIP

Policy decisions to amend immigration law rules, including rules relating to citizenship, are often very controversial. The decisions as to who will be recognized as a citizen of Canada involve fundamental policy choices about the nature of Canada. There have been a number of controversial issues with respect to the recognition of citizenship including the treatment of foreign children adopted by Canadian parents.

There are two bills that recently received royal assent to amend the *Citizenship Act*:

- Bill C-14, *An Act to Amend the Citizenship Act (adoption)*, which addresses adoptions (royal assent given on June 22, 2007); and

- Bill C-37, *An Act to Amend the Citizenship Act*, which gives Canadian citizenship to those who have lost or never had Canadian citizenship because of outdated provisions in existing and former legislation (royal assent given on April 17, 2008).

Although both bills came into force on July 25, 2008, the CIC website states, "The new law will take effect no later than April 17, 2009. Until the new law takes effect, the current law applies."[23]

Adoption: Bill C-14, An Act to Amend the Citizenship Act

Bill C-14 amends the *Citizenship Act* by eliminating distinctions in the way that the *Citizenship Act* treats foreign-born children adopted by Canadian citizens and biological children born abroad to Canadian citizens. Whereas a child born of Canadian parents outside Canada is automatically a Canadian citizen, a foreign child adopted by Canadian citizens did not automatically become a Canadian citizen upon adoption. Instead, an application had to be made for the child to become a permanent resident first, and only then could an application for citizenship be made. The amendments now allow a foreign-born child adopted by a Canadian citizen after February 14, 1977 to access citizenship without requiring that the child first becomes a permanent resident.

Section 3 of the *Citizenship Act* states that adopted children who attain citizenship without first obtaining permanent resident status are Canadian citizens. Citizenship may now be granted to a minor child who is being adopted by a Canadian citizen, or to an adopted child of at least 18 years of age, provided that the adoption satisfies the following conditions:

- it is in the best interests of the child,

- it creates a genuine parent–child relationship,

- it was not primarily for the purpose of acquiring citizenship or immigration status,

- it was legal in the place of adoption, and

- it was legal in Canada or the country of residence of the Canadian citizen if the Canadian citizen was not resident in Canada.

This same rule applies in the case of the legal adoption of a person 18 years of age or older, provided that a parent–child relationship was established prior to the child becoming 18, and the adoption was not primarily for the purpose of immigration.

Bill C-14 enables the governor in council to make regulations providing for the factors to be considered in determining whether these requirements have been met.

Section 5 of the *Citizenship Act* applies to adopted children who are minors and also to those who are at least 18 years of age; amendments provide that, subject to certain conditions, the minister shall grant citizenship to children who are adopted abroad after February 14, 1977. The adoption must satisfy the following conditions:

- a genuine parent–child relationship must be established before the person is 18 years old as well as at the time of adoption;

- the adoption was not primarily for the purpose of acquiring citizenship or immigration status;

- the adoption was legal in the place of adoption; and

- the adoption was legal in Canada or the country of residence of the Canadian citizen if the Canadian citizen was not resident in Canada.

There is also a special provision for adoptions that are under the jurisdiction of Quebec. Adoptions in Quebec are considered finalized when the child is physically in Quebec and residing with the adoptive parents. Under Quebec law, the authority responsible for international adoptions must confirm in writing that the adoption complies with Quebec law so that Canadian citizenship can be granted to children adopted abroad before the adoption is officially approved by the Court of Quebec.

Adoption is also discussed in Chapter 5, "Permanent Entry."

Restoration of Citizenship: Bill C-37, An Act to Amend the Citizenship Act

Under existing and former legislation passed by previous Parliaments, there are several reasons why people could have lost their citizenship or were never recognized as Canadians. Bill C-37 addresses these situations as follows:

- it permits certain persons who lost their Canadian citizenship for specified reasons to have their citizenship restored from the time it was lost;

- it permits certain persons who, born outside Canada to a Canadian parent, did not acquire Canadian citizenship for specified reasons to become Canadian citizens from the time of their birth;

- it provides that certain persons born outside Canada to a Canadian parent who was himself or herself born outside Canada do not acquire Canadian citizenship; and

- it provides for a grant of citizenship, on application, to persons who have always been stateless and meet other specified conditions."[24]

Bill C-37 also addresses the issue of "Lost Canadians." Lost Canadians are individuals who have been residing most of their lives in Canada and had a reasonable but mistaken belief they were Canadian citizens. They either ceased to be citizens at some point, or never were Canadian citizens. Generally, lost Canadians only discovered they were not Canadian citizens when they applied for a certificate of Canadian citizenship or other document. Under current law, a person who lost Canadian citizenship had to apply for a resumption of citizenship. Under Bill C-37, amendments allow for citizenship to be granted or restored retroactively to most, but not all, lost Canadians.

The amendments to the *Citizenship Act* give citizenship to the following kinds of lost Canadians:

- people naturalized to Canada who subsequently lived outside the country for more than ten years prior to 1967 and lost their citizenship; and

- people born abroad to a Canadian parent before the current *Citizenship Act* came into effect on February 15, 1977.

The amendments also give citizenship to "former lost Canadians":

- people who lost their citizenship between January 1, 1947 and February 14, 1977 because they or one of their parents acquired the nationality or citizenship of another country; and

- second and subsequent generation Canadians born abroad since the current *Citizenship Act* came into effect on February 15, 1977. Furthermore, relief is provided for the anticipated situations where these amendments will result in some offspring of Canadians born abroad being stateless.

NOTES

1. Citizenship Commission—Office of the Senior Citizenship Judge, *2006–2007 Annual Report*, www.cic.gc.ca/english/resources/publications/index.asp.

2. See general texts on public international law such as J.G. Castel, *International Law* (Toronto: Butterworths, 1976) and I. Brownlie, *Principles of Public International Law*, 6th ed. (Oxford: Oxford University Press, 2003).

3. G.H. Hackworth, *Digest of International Law* (Washington, DC: US Government Printing Office, 1942), vol. 3 at 1, cited in Castel, ibid. at 431.

4. This Act provided that persons born outside Canada to Canadian fathers were Canadian citizens, but persons born outside Canada to Canadian mothers had to naturalize. The overt sexism of this provision was overturned by the Supreme Court of Canada in the case of *Benner v. Canada (Secretary of State)*, [1997] 1 S.C.R. 358.

5. Penny Becklumb, Law and Government Division, Legislative Summary: Bill C-37: An Act to Amend the Citizenship Act, January 9, 2008, www.parl.gc.ca/39/2/parlbus/chambus/house/bills/summaries/c37-e.pdf.

6. Simard, Michel C., Citizenship Commission—Office of the Senior Citizenship Judge, *2005-2006 Annual Report*, February 22, 2007.

7. *Canada v. Schmidt*, [1987] 1 S.C.R. 500.

8. See Patrick Weil, "Access to Citizenship: A Comparison of Twenty-Five Nationality Laws," presentation given October 28, 2002 as part of the Metropolis Presents series, http://canada.metropolis.net/events/metropolis_presents/eu_speakers/weil2_e.htm.

9. Becklumb, supra note 5.

10. Ibid. at 10.

11. Ibid. at 10-11.

12. Simard, supra note 6.

13. *Citizenship Act*, s. 5(3) and Citizenship and Immigration Canada, "CP 7: Waivers," in *Citizenship Policy (CP)*, July 27, 2006, www.cic.gc.ca/english/resources/manuals/cp/index.asp.

14. Citizenship and Immigration Canada, "CP 12: Documents," in *Citizenship Policy (CP)*, June 16, 2008, www.cic.gc.ca/english/resources/manuals/cp/index.asp.

15. *Nakhjavani v. Canada (Secretary of State)* (1987), 13 F.T.R. 107, [1987] 2 Imm L.R. (2d) 241 and *Koo (Re)*, [1993] 1 F.C. 286 (T.D.).

16. Citizenship and Immigration Canada, "CP 5: Residence," in *Citizenship Policy (CP)*, at s. 5.10, August 2002, www.cic.gc.ca/english/resources/manuals/cp/index.asp.

17. Citizenship and Immigration Canada, "CP 15: Guide to Citizenship Ceremonies," in *Citizenship Policy (CP)*, s. 3.10, May 27, 2008, www.cic.gc.ca/english/resources/manuals/cp/index.asp.

18. Citizenship and Immigration Canada, supra note 14, s. 1.3.

19. Adapted from Citizenship and Immigration Canada, "CP 1: Citizenship Lines of Business," in *Citizenship Policy (CP)*, s. 2.15, May 18, 2007, www.cic.gc.ca/english/resources/manuals/cp/index.asp.

20. Citizenship and Immigration Canada, *Annual Report to Parliament on Immigration 2005*, 2005, www.cic.gc.ca/english/resources/publications/index.asp.

21. Citizenship Commission—Office of the Senior Citizenship Judge, supra note 1.

22. *Canada (Minister of Multiculturalism and Citizenship) v. Minhas* (1993), 66 F.T.R. 155 (T.D.).

23. "Am I a Canadian Citizen?," April 17, 2008, www.cic.gc.ca/english/citizenship/questions-citizenship.asp.

24. Becklumb, supra note 5.

REFERENCES

An Act to Amend the Citizenship Act. S.C. 2008, c. 14. Assented to April 17, 2008. Formerly Bill C-37. www2.parl.gc.ca/HousePublications/Publication.aspx?Docid=3437373&file=4.

An Act to Amend the Citizenship Act (adoption). S.C. 2007, c. 24. Formerly Bill C-14.

Black v. Canada (Prime Minister). (2001), 54 O.R. (3d) 215 (C.A.).

Canadian Charter of Rights and Freedoms. Part I of the *Constitution Act, 1982*, R.S.C. 1985, app. II, no. 44.

Citizenship Act. R.S.C. 1985, c. C-29.

Citizenship and Immigration Canada. "CP 2: Decision-Making." In *Citizenship Policy (CP)*. March 21, 2007. www.cic.gc.ca/english/resources/manuals/cp/index.asp.

Citizenship and Immigration Canada. "CP 3: Establishing Applicant's Identity." In *Citizenship Policy (CP)*. January 14, 2008. www.cic.gc.ca/english/resources/manuals/cp/index.asp.

Citizenship and Immigration Canada. "CP 4: Grants." In *Citizenship Policy (CP)*. March 20, 2007. www.cic.gc.ca/english/resources/manuals/cp/index.asp.

Citizenship and Immigration Canada. "CP 8: Appeals." In *Citizenship Policy (CP)*. N.D. www.cic.gc.ca/english/resources/manuals/cp/index.asp.

Citizenship and Immigration Canada. "CP 9: Loss, Resumption, Renunciation, Revocation." In *Citizenship Policy (CP)*. November 4, 2005. www.cic.gc.ca/english/resources/manuals/cp/index.asp.

Citizenship and Immigration Canada. "CP 10: Proof of Citizenship." In *Citizenship Policy (CP)*. January 28, 2005. www.cic.gc.ca/english/resources/manuals/cp/index.asp.

Citizenship and Immigration Canada. "CP 11: Search of Records." In *Citizenship Policy (CP)*. November 23, 2005. www.cic.gc.ca/english/resources/manuals/cp/index.asp.

Citizenship and Immigration Canada. "CP 13: Administration." In *Citizenship Policy (CP)*. January 17, 2008. www.cic.gc.ca/english/resources/manuals/cp/index.asp.

Citizenship and Immigration Canada. "CP 14: Adoption." In *Citizenship Policy (CP)*. April 4, 2008. www.cic.gc.ca/english/resources/manuals/cp/index.asp.

Citizenship Regulations. S.O.R./93-246.

Extradition Act. S.C. 1999, c. 18.

Immigration and Refugee Protection Act. S.C. 2001, c. 27.

Indian Act. R.S.C. 1985, c. I-5.

Koo (Re) (T.D.). [1993] 1 F.C. 286, 1992 CanLII 2417.

Kuruvila, Elizabeth, Law and Government Division. *Legislative Summary: Bill C-14: An Act to Amend the Citizenship Act (adoption).* May 29, 2006. Revised September 24, 2007. www.parl.gc.ca/39/1/parlbus/chambus/house/bills/summaries/c14-e.pdf.

Minister of Citizenship v. Odynsky. [2001] F.C.J. no. 286 (T.D.).

Re Mui. (1996), 105 F.T.R. 158.

Re Papadogiorgakis. [1978] 2 F.C. 208, 88 D.L.R. (3d) 243 (T.D.).

Re Pourgashemi. (1993), 62 F.T.R. 122, 19 Imm. L.R. (2d) 259.

Simard, Michel C. Citizenship Commission—Office of the Senior Citizenship Judge. *2005-2006 Annual Report.* February 22, 2007. Citizenship and Immigration Canada.

United States of America v. Cotroni. [1989] 1 S.C.R. 1469.

Universal Declaration of Human Rights. G.A. res. 217A (III), U.N. Doc A/810 at 71 (1948).

Waldman, L. Chapter 4 in *Immigration Law and Practice* (Toronto: Butterworths, 2004).

REVIEW QUESTIONS

1. List the three basic methods by which a person may become a Canadian citizen.

2. List and describe the requirements that must be satisfied for a person to become a citizen of Canada through the process of naturalization.

3. List and describe the reasons why a person may lose Canadian citizenship.

4. What are the functions of a citizenship judge?

5. In what situation will time spent in Canada not be counted toward satisfying the residency requirement for citizenship?

CHAPTER 7

Refugees and Protected Persons

LEARNING OBJECTIVES

After reading this chapter you should be able to:

- Identify relevant international treaties pertaining to refugees and human rights and describe the role of international agencies with regard to those treaties.

- Understand Canada's obligations toward refugee claimants.

- Identify relevant sections of the *Immigration and Refugee Protection Act* as they relate to refugees and persons in need of protection.

- Describe the inclusion, exclusion, and cessation elements of the definition of a Convention refugee.

- Understand the criteria for determining refugee status.

- Understand the criteria for granting protection to persons in need of protection.

INTRODUCTION

Millions of people around the world leave their home countries each year, driven by war, political or religious oppression, natural disaster, environmental destruction, and poverty. Are they all **refugees**? Do they all need protection? Does Canada treat people fleeing from humanitarian crises, such as the 1994 genocide in Rwanda, the same as victims of natural disasters such as those left homeless in South Asia by the tsunami that struck in December 2004? How do Canada's decision makers involved in the refugee claim process distinguish between those who are genuinely in need of protection and those who are in search of better living and economic conditions?

Spontaneous Arrivals

In previous chapters, you learned about how individuals are selected to come to Canada as permanent residents: the rigorous criteria and the complicated, expensive, and time-consuming application processes in order to meet statutory requirements.

Canada's immigration programs are managed so as to control the flow of immigration through such means as established immigration levels, application criteria, enforcement procedures, and admissibility criteria. Generally, we know who is coming to Canada before they arrive because they have had to seek prior approval from the Canadian government.

Unlike immigrants, refugees are not selected. Refugees arrive at our borders without having been subject to any immigration assessment processes and without prior approval. Thus, they are considered spontaneous arrivals. As well, the criteria for a successful refugee claim differ from those for an immigration claim in that the requirements for a refugee claim are unrelated to origin, ability to speak English or French, ability for self-sufficiency, future contribution to the economy, ability to integrate, or family ties.

Consequently, refugees are oftentimes portrayed as illegal migrants and abusers of the immigration process or are criticized for using the back door to gain entry. Some people have the perception that refugees are queue jumpers, bogus claimants, and a burden on our social support systems. No doubt there is some abuse of the system by illegal migrants and the human smugglers who help them get to Canada. And some foreign nationals who do not otherwise qualify for temporary or permanent residence do try to manipulate the refugee system to their advantage. But most of the people who seek refugee status are genuine refugees and their motivation or intent is rooted in suffering, rather than a desire for economic betterment. Unlike immigrants, who make a considered decision to leave their homelands, refugees do not have a choice: they are forced to flee because of some serious risk to their life or because they are victims of human rights abuses, and they cannot safely return home. The fundamental difference, therefore, between a refugee on the one hand and an immigrant or an illegal immigrant on the other is that a refugee needs protection, which is not provided by the government of the country of origin.

Generally, Canada allows strangers who ask for legal protection to enter the country, then extends basic civil and legal rights and will not return them until it is proved whether they need longer term protection.

Principle of Non-Refoulement

What is the **principle of *non-refoulement***? *Non-refoulement* means "no return." The principle of *non-refoulement* is a rule of international law that obliges countries to provide protection to refugees against return to the country where they face a risk of persecution, or where their life or freedom would be threatened on account of their race, religion, nationality, membership in a particular social group, or political opinion.[1]

Canada is committed to the principle of not returning a refugee to the country of origin where the individual's life or human rights are threatened unless an exclusion applies under international law (discussed below under the heading "Exclusions"). The protection against *refoulement* applies both to refugee claimants who are awaiting a decision, and to those whose claims have been accepted. Canada does not expel refugee claimants while their claims are in process, and claimants may stay until a decision is made about the claim.

Refugee Sur Place

What is a **refugee *sur place***? A refugee *sur place* is someone who did not flee her country as a refugee when she first left, but later requires legal protection. In this situation, the person becomes a refugee while in a foreign country as a result of a change in government while the person is away from home, or some other change in circumstance. International law, specifically the United Nations 1951 Convention Relating to the Status of Refugees (Refugee Convention), does not require that a person is a refugee at the time of leaving the country of origin. If an occurrence gives rise to a well-founded fear of persecution while the person is in another country, the person may be deemed a refugee *sur place*.

Canada's Commitment

Another part of our formal commitment to identifying and protecting refugees is Canada's legal obligation to respect the basic rights of refugee claimants by enabling them to live normal lives. Consequently, refugee claimants are provided with work authorizations and have access to financial, legal, and medical assistance if required. As well, their children are allowed to attend public school.

Finally, Canada's commitment includes a refugee determination system. The process for deciding who is and who is not a genuine refugee is complex and can be lengthy because each case must be decided individually and on its own merits. Until a decision is made about the claim, the individual is a **refugee claimant**.

This chapter introduces you to the principles of refugee law, the international agreements that protect refugees and describe Canada's role in refugee protection, and the refugee claim process. By the end of this chapter you will be able to answer the questions, "Who are Convention refugees and protected persons?" and "How do they receive Canada's protection?"

INTERNATIONAL CONVENTIONS

A **convention**, "covenant," or "treaty" is an agreement that obliges countries under international law to conform to its provisions. Countries bind themselves through **ratification** or signing of the agreement, which is a confirmation of the commitment to abide by the agreement. When a country ratifies or accedes to an agreement, it becomes known as a state party to the agreement and is thereafter legally bound to the obligations imposed by the agreement.

There are also provisions in UN agreements for independent monitoring bodies to supervise implementation of and compliance with the obligations and responsibilities of state parties. These monitoring bodies and the relevant international conventions are described below.

In Canada, the basis in law for determining refugee status is found in the following UN refugee treaties:

■ the 1951 Convention Relating to the Status of Refugees, and

■ the 1967 Protocol Relating to the Status of Refugees.

Canada is also a state party to treaties respecting human rights, and the following UN international agreements provide the basis in law for granting human rights protection:

■ the 1984 Convention Against Torture and Other Cruel, Inhuman or Degrading Treatment or Punishment, and

■ the 1966 International Covenant on Civil and Political Rights.

The United Nations High Commissioner for Refugees and the Refugee Convention

The United Nations High Commissioner for Refugees (UNHCR) was created in 1950 by the UN General Assembly to ensure the protection of refugees and provide assistance to them. The UNHCR is an international agency responsible for supervising the refugee determination process and safeguarding the rights of refugees.

The Refugee Convention, formally known as the 1951 Convention relating to the Status of Refugees, is the major legal foundation on which the UNHCR's work is based. It was originally intended to help the hundreds of thousands of people displaced in Europe after the Second World War, and future refugees—but for a limited period of time. The framers of the 1951 Convention did not expect refugee issues to be a major international problem on an ongoing basis, and consequently the UNHCR was only given a three-year mandate to help the post–Second World War refugees. It was hoped that it would then go out of business.

Instead, the refugee crisis spread—from Europe in the 1950s to Africa in the 1960s and then to Asia. In 1967 the UN General Assembly adopted the 1967 Protocol Relating to the Status of Refugees, to strengthen the 1951 Convention so that it would continue to operate to the benefit of future waves of refugees. The 1967 Protocol removed the earlier time limit of three years and the geographical restrictions that had limited the Convention's mandate to resettling European refugees uprooted by the Second World War.

The Convention and its Protocol provide the framework of principles for Canada's refugee determination system. These instruments define a Convention refugee, describe our legal obligations toward refugees, set out the basic procedures for refugee determination, and describe the basic entitlements and obligations of refugees as well as the role and authority of the monitoring body—the UNHCR.

In 1969, Canada ratified the 1951 Convention and 1967 Protocol, thus cementing the obligation to establish a refugee status determination system and upheld the principle of *non-refoulement*. Prior to 1969, Canada had no legal process in place for protecting refugees. After ratifying the Convention, Canada began accepting refugees on a number of special programs. However, it wasn't until the 1976 *Immigration Act* that Canadian law distinguished between the immigrant and refugee classes, and implemented a process to determine refugee status. With the enactment of the *Immigration and Refugee Protection Act* (IRPA) in June 2002, Canada expanded its protection to include "persons in need of protection"—those who are in refugee-like situations but for whom the Refugee Convention does not apply.

Today, the UNHCR still maintains its authority to supervise the refugee status determination process. In Canada, the UNHCR has a branch office located in Ottawa and employs legal officers in cities throughout the country to monitor compliance with international refugee law to ensure that refugee claimants' rights are protected. Some practical examples of the UNHCR's work in Canada include observing refugee protection hearings and making recommendations to the Canadian government on refugee issues.

In addition to providing international legal protection for refugees, the UNHCR promotes international refugee agreements and provides programs and funding to assist refugees with the following:

WEBLINK
For more information about the UNHCR, go to www.unhcr.org and click on the Basic facts menu item.

- **voluntary repatriation** (voluntary return to home country) if conditions improve there;

- integration in the country of refuge; or

- **resettlement** in a third country.

Human Rights Conventions

CONVENTION AGAINST TORTURE

Torture is an extreme human rights violation. The 1984 Convention Against Torture and Other Cruel, Inhuman or Degrading Treatment or Punishment (CAT) provides a definition of torture, bans torture, and makes it illegal under all circumstances—including under state emergency and external threats.

Signatories to this Convention agree to exercise the principle of *non-refoulement*: a host country may not expel, return, or extradite a person to another country where there are substantial grounds for believing that a person in need of protection would be in danger of being subjected to torture. As a signing state to the CAT, Canada has also agreed to take into account the human rights record of the person's country when making the decision to return him.

The CAT consists of 33 articles, which became effective in June 1987. Canada was one of the original 20 states to ratify this Convention. To monitor the implementation and compliance of the CAT, a ten-member Committee Against Torture was created. States that are party to the Convention must report to the committee one year from becoming signatories and must submit a report to the committee every four years thereafter, for review and recommendation.

INTERNATIONAL COVENANT ON CIVIL AND POLITICAL RIGHTS

The 1966 International Covenant on Civil and Political Rights (ICCPR) serves to codify a person's core human rights, which are non-derogable. **Non-derogable rights** are rights that must be respected and cannot be taken away from an individual or suspended for any reason, even in a time of crisis. These include the right to life and freedom from torture.

By contrast, **derogable rights** are those that may be temporarily suspended, as by a state during emergencies. For example, freedom of movement may be restricted during war or a natural disaster. The ICCPR permits a state to temporarily suspend derogable rights in cases of public emergency; however, it must not discriminate between groups. For example, Canada's internship of Japanese Canadians during the Second World War would not be permitted under this exception, because it singled out Canadians of Japanese descent.

The ICCPR provides for the inherent right to life; the right to recognition everywhere as a person before the law; and the right to freedom of thought, conscience, and religion, including freedom to have or to adopt a religion or belief of one's choice. It forbids torture or cruel, inhuman, or degrading treatment or punishment; involuntary servitude; and arbitrary arrest or detention.

The ICCPR is based on the Universal Declaration of Human Rights (UDHR), the first international statement to use the term "human rights." The ICCPR, the UDHR, and another international legal instrument, the International Covenant on Economic, Social and Cultural Rights (ICESCR), are known collectively as the International Bill of Rights. In March 1976, the ICCPR became international law. Two months later, it was ratified by Canada. The UN Human Rights Committee was established to monitor compliance.

Canada also became a party to the Second Optional Protocol to the International Covenant on Civil and Political Rights, Aiming at the Abolition of the Death Penalty in November 2005. The Second Optional Protocol has the objective of protecting the right to life through abolition of the death penalty and obliges state parties to take all necessary measures to abolish the death penalty within their jurisdictions.

The table below summarizes and compares the international conventions we have discussed in the chapter.

International Conventions on Human Rights

Legal instrument	Key feature	Supervised by	Year ratified by Canada	Refugee status	Protected persons
1951 Convention Relating to the Status of Refugees	Defines a Convention refugee	UNHCR	1969	√	
1967 Protocol Relating to the Status of Refugees	Removes timelines and geographical limitations of 1951 Convention	UNHCR	1969	√	
1984 Convention Against Torture and Other Cruel, Inhuman or Degrading Treatment or Punishment (CAT)	Defines torture and makes it illegal under all circumstances	Committee Against Torture	1984		√
1966 International Covenant on Civil and Political Rights (ICCPR)	Codifies non-derogable and derogable human rights	UN Human Rights Committee	1976		√
Second Optional Protocol to the International Covenant on Civil and Political Rights, Aiming at the Abolition of the Death Penalty	Abolishes the death penalty	UN Human Rights Committee	2005		√

CANADA'S PROGRAMS

The first step in making an application generally happens at a port of entry when the individual is examined by an officer and asks for asylum. In Canada, people who apply for such protection are called refugee claimants. The United Nations High Commissioner for Refugees defines asylum as "the right to be recognized as bona fide refugees and receive legal protection and material assistance."[2]

Canada offers protection to the world's displaced people through three distinct processes, which are described briefly below. A fuller explanation of these processes is given later in the chapter.

Refugee and Humanitarian Resettlement Program

Canadian officials from missions abroad work with the UNHCR and various non-governmental organizations (NGOs) to identify refugees and persons in refugee-like situations from abroad who are in need of resettlement. CIC is the federal department responsible for this program. Refugees who arrive in Canada under this program are given financial assistance by the government or are assisted through private sponsorship and become permanent residents upon arrival. The process is described in detail in Chapter 8, "Refugee and Humanitarian Resettlement Program."

Pre-removal Risk Assessment Program

Claimants in Canada who are unsuccessful in arguing their case for refugee status, and who claim to face a risk if they are returned to their country of origin, may apply to have that risk assessed. CIC is the federal department responsible for this program, and it conducts an evaluation of the risk of return. This program is discussed further in Chapter 9, "In-Canada Refugee Determination Process."

In-Canada Refugee Determination Process

The In-Canada refugee determination process is for refugees who make claims for refugee protection status at the Canadian border. The process includes the involvement of CIC, the Canada Border Services Agency (CBSA), and the Immigration and Refugee Board (IRB) through its Refugee Protection Division (RPD). The participation, role, and mandate of each of these organizations are very specific, and this partially explains why the process is so complex and often misunderstood. This program is discussed further in Chapter 9, "In-Canada Refugee Determination Process."

Before we navigate our way through these programs and processes in Chapters 8 and 9, we must first understand the basics of Canadian refugee protection law, discussed in the sections below.

SCOPE OF PROTECTION

The *Immigration Act* of 1976 created the legal basis for a refugee determination system in Canada. Prior to the enactment of the *Immigration and Refugee Protection Act* in June 2002, refugee claims were assessed only within the scope of the Refugee Convention's technical definition of a refugee. Decision makers had no jurisdiction to assess claims beyond that definition. Consequently, a claim could be rejected if the person did not fit the limited definition of a Convention refugee, even if the person faced a threat or risk of threat to life or freedom.

The IRPA significantly broadened the scope of refugee protection and filled in gaps in the Refugee Convention. The new statute did not eliminate the importance of the definition of a Convention refugee, but expanded its protection to foreign nationals to include "persons in need of protection" —that is, those who are in refugee-like situations but for whom the Refugee Convention does not apply. The IRPA authorizes three ways that protection can be provided to those in need (s. 95):

1. abroad, through the selection of foreign nationals who apply for permanent or temporary residence when they have already been determined to be a Convention refugee or a person in similar circumstances (s. 95(a));

2. in Canada, through the determination by the Refugee Protection Division of the Immigration and Refugee Board that a foreign national is a Convention refugee or a person in need of protection (s. 95(b)); or

3. in Canada, through a decision on an application to the minister in certain cases prior to removal (this refers to the pre-removal risk assessment program described in Chapter 9).

The IRPA provides a Canadian legal definition of each category of refugee in the following sections:

1. Convention refugees (s. 96);

2. persons in need of protection—that is, persons who require protection because of a danger of torture (s. 97(1)(a)) or because of risk to life, or cruel and unusual treatment or punishment (s. 97(1)(b)); and

3. persons for whom the minister has allowed an application for protection (s. 97(1)(c)).

The IRPA also provides for instances where refugee protection must not be conferred (s. 98): it is known as "exclusion."

Convention Refugee Status

In s. 96, the IRPA borrows from the 1951 Convention to determine who is a refugee. The Act defines a **Convention refugee** as follows:

> A Convention refugee is a person who, by reason of a well-founded fear of persecution for reasons of race, religion, nationality, membership in a particular social group or political opinion,

(a) is outside each of their countries of nationality and is unable or, by reason of that fear, unwilling to avail themself of the protection of each of those countries; or

(b) not having a country of nationality, is outside the country of their former habitual residence and is unable or, by reason of that fear, unwilling to return to that country.

This provision confirms Canada's international obligation to protect refugees under the 1951 Convention Relating to the Status of Refugees and the 1967 Protocol Relating to the Status of Refugees. Canada has adopted the three parts of the Convention refugee definition in the IRPA, with the following three clauses:

1. *Inclusion clause:* defines the criteria for who is a refugee, such as a well-founded fear of persecution by reason of religion (s. 96).

2. *Exclusion clause:* defines who is not a refugee, such as people who commit war crimes (s. 98).

3. *Cessation clause:* defines when a person no longer enjoys the protection of the Convention—that is, when refugee protection ceases (s. 108).

Refugee claimants who meet all the inclusion elements of the definition of a Convention refugee will be granted refugee status. Therefore, it is important to identify each of the elements of the definition and understand how they are used in the decision-making process. There are four elements that form the positive basis for meeting the criteria of inclusion, as follows:

1. alienage must be established,

2. a well-founded fear must exist,

3. persecution must exist, and

4. the persecution must fall under one of the five grounds set out in the IRPA.

A refugee claimant must meet all of the elements of inclusion in order for her claim to be accepted. What follows is a general explanation of the four inclusion elements.

1. ALIENAGE

First, the claimant must establish alienage. **Alienage** occurs when a person is outside the country of her nationality or citizenship. If a person cannot establish a nationality or has no citizenship, alienage occurs when the person is outside a country considered to be the former habitual residence. Generally, people have an expectation of protection from their government, and it is only when their government is either unable or unwilling to protect them that they need to seek protection from another country.

Furthermore, the Convention refugee definition requires that the claimant make a claim against the country of nationality, and if the claimant has citizenship in more than one country, then she must establish a claim against each of those countries. Consider the following scenario.

WEBLINK

The UNHCR's *Handbook on Procedures and Criteria for Determining Refugee Status* (1979, re-edited January 1992) is recommended reading for an in-depth study of these elements. Go to www.unhcr.org/publ/PUBL/3d58e13b4.pdf.

Ariana is a citizen of Bovoria, an impoverished country with no universities and few prospects for women. Ariana's father is a prominent businessman in Bovoria who wants more for his daughter, so he decides to send her outside Bovoria to study. Ariana pursues a degree in political science at the National University of Vonburg in the neighbouring country of Furtania. She is outspoken about student rights and is a regular contributor of cartoons to the student newspaper. She is detained by Furtanian authorities for three days for participating in an anti-government rally and is subsequently harassed for the publication of her cartoons, which have been deemed too political. When her cartoons are denounced by the government-run Furtanian press, Ariana fears for her life in Furtania and flees the country without completing her degree. She is seeking protection in Canada.

One of the first elements that Ariana must establish in making her refugee claim in Canada is the element of alienage. In seeking protection, Ariana must prove that she cannot avail herself of the protection of any of her countries of nationality (or former habitual residence). Ariana, like all other refugee claimants, must provide documentary evidence of her citizenship (or multiple citizenships), usually by providing a birth certificate, national identity card, or passport.

Ariana has Bovorian citizenship, so Furtania does not qualify as "a former habitual residence," despite her time spent there. Furthermore, Ariana is not a citizen of Furtania and has the protection of Bovoria, so she is not able to claim protection in Canada against Furtania. The element of alienage cannot be established and Ariana's claim would be rejected.

2. WELL-FOUNDED FEAR

In considering each refugee claim, the member of the Refugee Protection Division will assess whether the refugee claimant's fear is well founded. There is both an objective and subjective component to this test. The objective component considers whether the fear is reasonable in the circumstances, and considers the circumstance in which the fear arises, such as the conditions in the country of origin. The subjective component considers the personal perspective of the claimant—does the claimant actually experience fear? The following case scenario sets out two cases to show how the element of **well-founded fear** can be individualized.

Kairat and Ravil are both citizens of Zarkhanistan, a country where young males between the ages of 18 and 33 have been arbitrarily arrested and detained in the context of the "war on terror." Some detainees have disappeared and others have been sentenced to death and executed. Young men are typically targeted in the southern part of the country. Kairat arrived in Canada directly from Zarkhanistan six months ago just after a raid in the neighbouring village that resulted in a total sweep of unmarried males. A relative of Kairat's has been missing since the raid. Ravil arrived in Canada around the same time as Kairat; however, he has been out of Zarkhanistan for the last 12 years working on a cruise ship. His contract has now expired and he would like to settle down, but he is concerned about the unstable situation in his home country.

In the above scenario, both Kairat and Ravil will make refugee claims; however, the decisions in their cases will be made on the basis on their independent accounts and circumstances. It is possible that one claim may be accepted while the other is rejected, even though both claimants are from the same country. This is because each claim will be decided on its own merits. The outcomes may be different because each claimant, who will have the opportunity to present his own story both orally and in writing, will submit separate and individualized evidence to a member of the RPD. Furthermore, the members who hear the cases are independent of each other, and they will each consider both the objective and subjective basis of the claims. The outcomes will depend on the merits of each case, including whether the information that the claimants provide is credible and trustworthy.

Objective Component

To establish that a claim is well founded, there must be an objective component—a valid reason for the fear. Background country information establishes the objective basis for a claimant's fear. Therefore, a claimant should support his allegations with documentary evidence of the prevailing country conditions, as reported in reliable country-of-origin reports, human rights reports, newspaper articles, and other personal documentation, and as testified by witnesses.

In our example, Kairat and Ravil would likely present similar objective evidence about their country of origin, Zarkhanistan. The objective component requires that each claim be assessed in the context of the prevailing conditions in the country of origin. This requires research into the country conditions to provide current and credible information about the following:

- whether the country of origin is in the midst of political upheaval, war, or generally unsettled conditions;

- the country's human rights record; and

- whether the government is able and willing to protect its citizens.

The IRB develops country-of-origin information packages on a variety of countries and is recognized internationally as a leader in the research, collection, and production of country-of-origin information and national documentation packages. These packages are used by staff and decision makers to keep abreast of general country and human rights conditions. The IRB's research holdings and publications are available to the public and widely used by counsel, students, and governmental and non-governmental organizations around the world.

It is generally accepted that if a claimant has suffered persecution in the past, he continues to be at risk and therefore needs the protection of the Convention. However, it is not necessary for a claimant to have suffered past harm to fear it in the future. That is why the definition is forward looking—the decision maker must look to the future to predict whether there is a risk in returning the claimant to his country of origin. Is there a reasonable possibility that the claimant would risk persecution if returned today or tomorrow? Have the conditions in the claimant's country changed? Would Ravil, who has been out of Zarkhanistan for many years, face persecution if he were to return there? Does he fit the government's profile of a potential terrorist? Is he likely to be perceived to be a threat?

WEBLINK

For more information about research at the IRB, visit www.irb-cisr.gc.ca/en/research/origin.

Subjective Component

The subjective component of a well-founded fear concerns the claimant's individual state of mind and fearfulness. The subjective basis will depend on the claimant's own background and experiences, as well as those of family and close associates. To support the subjective basis for a refugee claim, the claimant must make a credible case for future risk, and should provide evidence of past persecution, if any, by submitting documentary evidence such as medical or psychological reports. In practice, it is not always possible to provide independent evidence; most often, it is the claimant's written and verbal statements that provide insight into his state of mind.

The subjective component is unique to each claimant. Let's suppose that Kairat's claim was accepted and Ravil's claim was rejected, even though the prevailing country conditions—the objective component—are the same. Why might the outcomes be different? The difference in their claims may owe in part to the subjective component of their alleged fear.

The member also assesses whether the claimant's fear is valid and will be interested in the chronology of events that led him to make a claim for protection. Did the claimant delay leaving his country of origin when the fear arose? Did he delay making a claim or did he make a claim at the first possible opportunity? In our scenario, Kairat shows evidence of a valid fear: he lived next to a village where men like him were arrested; one of his relatives "disappeared"; and he left and sought refuge immediately when danger was imminent. Ravil, on the other hand, left the country 12 years ago to seek work on a ship, and in all his travels he never sought protection until after his contract expired. This may raise a suspicion that he is not genuinely fearful, but instead is seeking better economic conditions.

3. PERSECUTION MUST EXIST

A refugee claimant's well-founded fear must relate to persecution. The term **persecution** is not defined in the 1951 Convention or in the IRPA; however, Canadian courts provide some parameters for defining it. Generally, to qualify as persecution, an act or series of acts must present a serious harm—a threat to life or physical freedom, or other persistent and serious violations of human rights.

Under the 1951 Convention, a refugee claimant is not entitled to protection from legitimate prosecution by his country of origin. However, for the prosecution to be legitimate, the laws and the legal process must not violate fundamental human rights. Someone who fled her country to avoid a trial and punishment for having committed a criminal act such as robbery or murder is not "persecuted," provided that she would have been given a fair trial and fair treatment.

However, if a claimant faces prosecution for committing an act that is protected by international human rights standards—for example, the practice of his religion—this may amount to persecution. In this case, the "crime" is the exercise of a fundamental right; therefore, the claimant is fleeing persecution. Even if the crime is legitimate, issues of persecution could be raised if the claimant was not given access to a fair and impartial trial, or if the punishment was unduly severe—such as torture, or execution for a minor offence.

In some cases, the refugee claimant's fear is based on acts of discrimination or harassment. Although an individual act of discrimination or harassment on its own would usually not substantiate a case for persecution, a series of acts taken cumulatively may amount to persecution. This could be the case if the acts are perpetrated by the government or by government agents, or if the acts are perpetrated by individuals outside of the government, and the government takes no steps to provide protection against them. Consider the following case scenario, where discrimination and harassment occurred with repetition and persistence, and amounted to persecution.

> *Mr. K is a 35-year-old male of the ethnic minority in his country. For much of his life he has been the victim of attacks. His teachers discouraged him and verbally abused him as a child, and he had difficulty finding employment— all because of his ethnic background. He eventually found work in a factory, where he endured physical assaults by co-workers. But his employer was not interested in his problems and the police refused to investigate, stating that it was a personal matter. He joined an organization that worked to improve the work and living conditions of his ethnic community; this organization, however, was perceived by the authorities as a threat to local peace. Since then, Mr. K has frequently been stopped by the police on his way home from meetings, taken into detention, beaten, and released. This has been going on for several years. The detentions have become increasingly frequent and longer, and the beatings more severe. The authorities are not interested in stopping the violence and are sometimes the perpetrators. Other members of Mr. K's ethnic community have similar complaints.*

To determine whether the element of persecution exists, the RPD looks at who the agents of persecution are. Agents of persecution are those individuals who carry out the acts of persecution. Authorities of the claimant's country of origin are **state agents**, such as the police or members of the military, and their acts are generally sanctioned or authorized by the government or by legislation. Discrimination and harassment by state agents amounts to persecution if these actions are persistent and serious.

Members of the militia who violate human rights, or members of the majority ethnic or religious groups, rebels, guerrillas, drug or warlords, etc., who commit serious acts of discrimination or other targeted harmful acts are known as **non-state agents**. When persecution is carried out by non-state agents, the claimant must prove that the government is unwilling or unable to provide effective protection from those acts.

In the case of Mr. K, the agents of persecution were both state agents (the police) and non-state agents (teachers and co-workers). The police refused to assist Mr. K when he reported physical assaults by co-workers; therefore, these assaults amounted to persecution.

4. PERSECUTION UNDER ONE OF THE FIVE GROUNDS IN THE IRPA

Much like Canadian human rights legislation prohibits discrimination based on particular grounds, the IRPA sets out five grounds of persecution. The five grounds are enumerated in the definition of a Convention refugee and are as follows:

a. race,

b. religion,

c. nationality,

d. membership in a particular social group, and

e. political opinion.

To determine whether the persecution falls under the Act, the RPD considers the following questions: Does the persecutor perceive the claimant to be a member of a certain race, nationality, religion, or particular social group or to hold a certain political opinion? Is there a reasonable chance of persecution because of that perception? It is not necessary that the perception be accurate, only that the persecutor may act on it. Therefore, it is important for the claimant to provide as much information as possible about the context of the persecution.

a. Race

A claimant may have a well-founded fear of persecution on the basis of his race, which is understood to mean his ethnic group. Examples may include discriminatory hiring practices by government, exclusion from public education, segregation, and discriminatory taxation. The claimant must establish that persecution was suffered as a result of race. Evidence should include examples of how the claimant was targeted, what harm was suffered, whether the claimant's race is a minority group, and the general treatment of members of that group.

b. Religion

Claimants may be persecuted on the basis of religion because they are members of a religious minority or sect. The laws of the country may prohibit joining or worshipping in a particular religious community. In that case, the claimant must establish that he is a member of the particular religious group by detailing such things as whether he is a practising or non-practising member, whether his religious group is legally recognized in his country, and how members of that religious group are generally treated.

Alternatively, a country may prohibit the practice of any religion, and ban any religious instruction or practice. In that case, even members of a majority religion may be persecuted.

c. Nationality

Nationality encompasses not only a person's citizenship, but also a person's ethnic or linguistic group, and so may sometimes overlap with race. Examples of persecution based on nationality include genocide, torture, rape, and discrimination against members of a minority or low-caste clan.

d. Membership in a Particular Social Group

A particular social group "normally comprises persons of similar background, habits or social status," according to the UNHCR.[3] The Supreme Court of Canada in *Canada (Attorney General) v. Ward* classified "particular social group" as consisting of three distinct categories of groups:

■ "groups defined by an innate, unchangeable characteristic" (which might include claims based on a person's gender, linguistic background, sexual orientation, family, or caste);

- groups "whose members voluntarily associate for reasons so fundamental to their human dignity that they should not be forced to forsake the association" (which might include claims from members of human rights organizations or trade union activists); and

- groups "associated by a former voluntary status, unalterable due to its historical permanence" (which expresses the idea that "one's past is an immutable part of the person").

Some examples of persons suffering persecution on the basis of membership in a particular social group include women who face rape or other forms of violence by government agents, women who face female genital mutilation or forced marriage, homosexuals who face violence, and members of trade unions who face violence.

e. Political Opinion

A person may express a political opinion by words or actions—for example, by participating in anti-government demonstrations, distributing literature, or speaking out in public. However, a person who does not articulate a political opinion may still be identified by the government as an opponent—for example, by failing to attend pro-government rallies or join a government party. To prove the case, the claimant has to explain the significance of his actions or inactions, whether he was identified by the government, and how the government would likely react if he were returned to his country of origin. In assessing the claim, the RPD member asks: Does the government consider the claimant's actions to be political?

If a claimant belongs to a political party or group, it is important that he provide evidence of how his membership, activities, and opinions brought him to the attention of authorities or are the basis of a future risk. The claimant should be able to explain why the government would perceive the failure to do something, such as join a political party, as a political act. Documentary proof such as membership cards may also be useful.

IRPA—Persons in Need of Protection

The implementation of the IRPA extended the scope of refugee protection beyond the Convention refugee definition to **persons in need of protection**. The RPD now has jurisdiction to decide a person's claim if it can be established that the person faces one of the following:

- a danger of torture; or

- a risk to life, or a risk of cruel and unusual treatment or punishment.

A refugee claimant who is found to be a person in need of protection enjoys the same rights as those claimants who are granted protection under the Refugee Convention, including the right to apply for permanent residence.

The definition of "person in need of protection" in s. 97 of the IRPA confirms Canada's international obligation to protect refugees under the 1984 Convention Against Torture and Other Cruel, Inhuman or Degrading Treatment or Punishment, and the 1966 International Covenant on Civil and Political Rights. Section 97 reads as follows:

(1) A person in need of protection is a person in Canada whose removal to their country or countries of nationality or, if they do not have a country of nationality, their country of former habitual residence, would subject them personally

(a) to a danger, believed on substantial grounds to exist, of torture within the meaning of Article 1 of the Convention Against Torture; or

(b) to a risk to their life or to a risk of cruel and unusual treatment or punishment if

(i) the person is unable or, because of that risk, unwilling to avail themself of the protection of that country,

(ii) the risk would be faced by the person in every part of that country and is not faced generally by other individuals in or from that country,

(iii) the risk is not inherent or incidental to lawful sanctions, unless imposed in disregard of accepted international standards, and

(iv) the risk is not caused by the inability of that country to provide adequate health or medical care.

(2) A person in Canada who is a member of a class of persons prescribed by the regulations as being in need of protection is also a person in need of protection.

The elements of this definition are considered in more detail below.

COUNTRY OF NATIONALITY OR OF FORMER HABITUAL RESIDENCE

Similar to the concept of alienage for the Convention refugee definition, it is generally accepted that nationality refers to citizenship. A refugee claimant must prove that there is a risk of torture (or risk to life or cruel and unusual treatment or punishment) upon return to the country of citizenship. If the claimant has more than one nationality, the claimant must prove that there is a risk of torture upon return to any of those countries of citizenship. If the claimant does not have a country of citizenship, then a claim must be established against the country of former habitual residence.

RISK

Even if there is current and credible information to establish that torture is practised in the refugee claimant's country of origin, the refugee claimant must nevertheless demonstrate that, on a **balance of probabilities**,[4] she would be personally subjected to a danger of torture if returned. The claimant must present evidence of this personal risk—it will not be enough to establish that widespread torture occurs in the country.

The claimant may also be denied refugee status under the IRPA under the following conditions:

■ refuge exists within some parts of the country;

■ the risk is part of lawful sanctions, such as punishment for a crime; or

■ the risk is due to inadequate health or medical care.

Refugee status is intended for the truly desperate; therefore, claimants who are able to find safe haven in pockets of their own country are expected to go there. The IRPA also denies refugee status in circumstances where the floodgates would open up to large populations—such as where all citizens of a country are at risk of torture, or where poverty on a national scale precludes health or medical care. Under those conditions, other types of interventions such as diplomatic, military, and humanitarian aid are considered more appropriate.

GROUNDS

The two grounds for claiming to be a person in need of protection are: danger of torture (s. 97(1)(a)) and risk to life or of cruel and unusual treatment or punishment (s. 97(1)(b)).

Danger of Torture

Torture is considered an extreme violation of human rights. A major principle articulated in article 5 of the Universal Declaration of Human Rights is that people should be free from torture or cruel, inhuman, or degrading treatment or punishment.

Article 1 of the Convention Against Torture and Other Cruel, Inhuman or Degrading Treatment or Punishment sets out the definition of torture as follows:

> For the purposes of this Convention, the term "torture" means any act by which severe pain or suffering, whether physical or mental, is intentionally inflicted on a person for such purposes as obtaining from him or a third person information or a confession, punishing him for an act he or a third person has committed or is suspected of having committed, or intimidating or coercing him or a third person, or for any reason based on discrimination of any kind, when such pain or suffering is inflicted by or at the instigation of or with the consent or acquiescence of a public official or other person acting in an official capacity. It does not include pain or suffering arising only from, inherent in or incidental to lawful sanctions.

There are three essential elements to this legal meaning of torture,[5] which answer the questions "what," "who," and "why," as follows:

- What was done? Did the act result in severe physical or psychological pain or suffering?

- Who did it? Was the act intentionally inflicted by a state agent or public official, such as state police or secret security forces?

- Why was it done? Was the act carried out for the purpose of intimidation, deterrence, coercion, control, revenge, punishment, or information gathering?

The refugee claimant must prove, on a balance of probabilities, all three of these elements. For example, if a claimant could prove that physical pain was inflicted for the purpose of intimidation, but could not prove that the government was behind it or turned a blind eye to it, the claimant would be denied refugee status on the basis of torture. Consider the following case scenario:

WEBLINK
You can find an in-depth discussion of torture and some examples in *The Torture Reporting Handbook* at www.essex.ac.uk/ torturehandbook/ handbook.

Ms. W was a journalist for a national newspaper and wrote a critical piece about election fraud that exposed the criminal activities of top elected officials. She was arrested by the Secret Service shortly after her story was released. Ms. W was detained in a darkened cell, placed in metal restraints, and subjected to beatings and electric shock treatment during prolonged periods of interrogation about her sources, which she refused to name. She was extremely weakened by the time her interrogators dumped her by the roadside one night with a warning to stick to "fashion and entertainment reporting" or her children would "disappear." Shortly afterward, Ms. W, her husband, and her children fled the country. She continues to suffer from her physical injuries and post-traumatic stress disorder. She is making a refugee claim under s. 97 on the basis of having been tortured and the future risk to her life and the lives of her family.

The Canadian Centre for Victims of Torture

WEBLINK

For more information, see the Canadian Centre for Victims of Torture at www.ccvt .org.

The Canadian Centre for Victims of Torture (CCVT) provides services to immigrants and refugees who have experienced torture. These services include language training, job search assistance, referrals to other professionals and agencies, translation, and counselling. The CCVT is a non-profit, registered charitable organization and is considered a pioneer in the rehabilitation of survivors of torture. Based in Toronto, the centre works with the community to help survivors integrate into Canadian society and to raise awareness of the continuing effects of torture and war.

Under the Convention definition of torture, all three elements of torture were met: Ms. W suffered severe physical and psychological pain as a result of the incident; it was intentionally inflicted by state agents; and the purpose was punishment and intimidation.

Risk to Life or Risk of Cruel and Unusual Treatment or Punishment

The terms **risk to life** and **risk of cruel and unusual treatment or punishment** are not defined in the IRPA. However, these terms are customarily understood to refer to ill-treatment causing suffering that is less severe than torture. These acts are intentional and intended to cause significant physical, mental, and psychological pain or suffering. Consider the following case scenario:

Mr. X was a journalist for a major independent newspaper in his home country. He was investigating a story about international monetary transactions and uncovered a corruption scam by senior government officials. On several occasions (on his way home from work; on his way to the market; and on his way to a friend's house, within a block from his home), Mr. X has been attacked and threatened by thugs in masks. He claims they are members of the national intelligence service, which he says is attempting to censor him. It is well documented that journalists have been unlawfully detained for their critique of corrupt government officials, some of whom were Mr. X's colleagues. The attacks against newspaper publishers and journalists have started to escalate. Mr. X believes there is a risk to his life or a risk of cruel and unusual treatment or punishment even if he were to move to another city or the countryside, so he has fled his country.

Mr. X was the victim of acts that were intentional and intended to cause significant physical and mental suffering, so a claim under s. 97(1)(b) on the basis of risk to life or of cruel and unusual treatment or punishment is appropriate. Note, however, that the harm suffered by Mr. X was less severe than that suffered by Ms. W and that it is less clear whether the masked thugs were state agents, so a claim under s. 97(1)(a) would be less likely to succeed.

EXCLUSIONS

Even where a refugee claimant meets all the elements of the refugee definition in s. 96 of the IRPA, or all the elements of a person in need of protection in s. 97 of the IRPA, he may nevertheless be returned to the country of origin if any of the following exclusions apply:

- the claimant has protection elsewhere;

- the claimant is likely guilty of persecuting others;

- the claimant is likely guilty of a serious non-political crime; or

- the claimant is likely guilty of acts contrary to the purposes and principles of the United Nations.

These exclusions are set out in ss. E and F of article 1 of the Convention Relating to the Status of Refugees, which are included in a schedule to the IRPA. The sections are reproduced below:

> E. This Convention shall not apply to a person who is recognized by the competent authorities of the country in which he has taken residence as having the rights and obligations which are attached to the possession of the nationality of that country.
> F. The provisions of this Convention shall not apply to any person with respect to whom there are serious reasons for considering that:
> (a) He has committed a crime against peace, a war crime, or a crime against humanity, as defined in the international instruments drawn up to make provision in respect of such crimes;
> (b) he has committed a serious non-political crime outside the country of refuge prior to his admission to that country as a refugee;
> (c) he has been guilty of acts contrary to the purposes and principles of the United Nations.

These exclusions apply to refugee claimants under both ss. 96 and 97 of the IRPA as provided in s. 98, which states the following:

> A person referred to in section E or F of Article 1 of the Refugee Convention is not a Convention refugee or a person in need of protection.

Claims for refugee status are to be made only as a last resort, by those who have no other options, and by those who are innocent victims. Drafters of the Convention, and of the IRPA, were mindful of the potential for misuse of refugee laws by those who wish to emigrate for economic or personal reasons. They also wished to prevent refugee laws from offering protection to those who actually perpetrated acts of torture against others. Under some circumstances, such as civil war, atrocities are often committed by individuals on each side of the conflict. Refugee laws are not intended to offer asylum to anyone guilty of such acts.

Protection of Another Country

Article E of the exclusion clause refers to a refugee claimant who has taken residence in another country or territory and has the protection of that country or territory. In that case, the claimant is not in need of Canada's protection. If a claimant has the option of living safely elsewhere, even if it is economically difficult and not the claimant's preference, she is expected to do so.

War Crimes and Crimes Against Humanity

Article 1F(a) refers to a refugee claimant for whom there are serious reasons to believe that he has committed war crimes or **crimes against humanity**, such as crimes relating to genocide, slavery, torture, apartheid, or terrorist activities. Such a person is considered undeserving of the protection of the Refugee Convention, and should be tried in an international court for the alleged crimes, not awarded safe asylum in a host country such as Canada. There are also practical concerns with respect to how such a person might behave in Canada, and whether he would facilitate or perpetrate those crimes within Canadian borders.

Serious Non-Political Crime

Article 1F(b) refers to a refugee claimant for whom there are serious reasons to believe that she has committed serious **non-political crimes**. Again, such a person is considered undeserving of the protection of the Refugee Convention, and admitting her would raise practical concerns about criminal behaviour in Canada that could endanger Canadians. Although there is no list of serious crimes in the Refugee Convention, a serious non-political crime is understood to be an act committed for personal reasons or gain with no political end or motive involved. Generally, this would encompass the more serious crimes included in the Canadian *Criminal Code*, such as assault, murder, theft, and fraud. Petty crimes such as shoplifting and trespassing would likely not qualify as "serious" enough to justify the exclusion of an otherwise legitimate refugee claim.

Acts Contrary to United Nations Principles

Article 1F(c) refers to a refugee claimant for whom there are serious reasons to believe that he is guilty of committing acts that breach the purposes and principles of the United Nations. Such a person is considered undeserving of the protection of the Refugee Convention. The Charter of the United Nations lists the four purposes of that organization[6] as follows:

1. to maintain international peace and security;

2. to develop friendly relations among nations based on respect for the principle of equal rights and self-determination;

3. to achieve international cooperation in solving international socioeconomic and cultural problems; and

4. to harmonize the actions of nations in the attainment of these common ends.

For example, a refugee claimant who engages in acts of international terrorism that constitute a threat to international peace and security would be excluded from *non-refoulement* protection under article 1F(c) because such acts are contrary to the purposes and principles of the United Nations. The UNHCR, in its *Guidelines on International Protection: Application of the Exclusion Clauses—Article 1F of the 1951 Convention Relating to the Status of Refugees*, cautions the following in guideline 17:

> Given the broad, general terms of the purposes and principles of the United Nations, the scope of this category is rather unclear and should therefore be read narrowly. Indeed, it is rarely applied and, in many cases, Article 1F(a) or 1F(b) are anyway likely to apply. Article 1F(c) is only triggered in extreme circumstances by activity which attacks the very basis of the international community's co-existence. Such activity must have an international dimension. Crimes capable of affecting international peace, security and peaceful relations between States, as well as serious and sustained violations of human rights, would fall under this category. ... [I]t would appear that in principle only persons who have been in positions of power in a State or State-like entity would appear capable of committing such acts. In cases involving a terrorist act, a correct application of Article 1F(c) involves an assessment as to the extent to which the act impinges on the international plane—in terms of its gravity, international impact, and implications for international peace and security.

CESSATION OF PROTECTION

Refugee protection is not intended to be permanent. Article 1C of the United Nations Convention Relating to the Status of Refugees includes a **cessation clause**. This clause provides the framework for when protection may lawfully cease under s. 108 of the IRPA.

Section 108 provides that a claim for refugee protection shall generally be rejected, and a person is not a Convention refugee or a person in need of protection, where that person has done any of the following:

- voluntarily "reavailed" herself of the protection of the country of nationality—for example, by returning to live there;

- voluntarily reacquired her nationality—for example, by applying for a passport;

- acquired a new nationality and is enjoying the protection of the country of that new nationality; or

- voluntarily re-established herself in the country of former habitual residence on which the claim to refugee protection was based (where the refugee has no country of citizenship).

The cessation clause also provides that a person is not a refugee if the reasons for the claim in the first place have ceased to exist, such as when the country conditions in the country of origin have stabilized. Section 108 does provide one exception to this, in the rare cases where a refugee has been so traumatized by her experiences that she refuses to trust the protection of the country of origin when it is offered. To satisfy this exception to the cessation criteria, the refugee must establish compelling reasons arising out of previous persecution, torture, ill-treatment, or punishment for refusing to return home after conditions have improved.

Where refugee status has previously been granted, the burden of proof is on the minister to show that the protection should cease. Under rules 29 and 57 of the Refugee Protection Division Rules, the minister must apply in writing to the RPD, and must disclose any evidence to the refugee. At the hearing into the application for cessation, the minister is usually represented by a CIC officer called a Hearings Officer.

NOTES

1. Convention Relating to the Status of Refugees, 189 U.N.T.S. 150 (entered into force April 22, 1954), article 33(1).

2. United Nations High Commissioner for Refugees, "Basic Information About UNHCR: Refugees by Numbers 2006 Edition," 2006, www.unhcr .ch/cgi-bin/texis/vtx/basics/opendoc.htm?tbl=BASICS&id=3b028097c.

3. *Handbook on Procedures and Criteria for Determining Refugee Status Under the 1951 Convention and the 1967 Protocol Relating to the Status of Refugees* HCR/IP/4/Eng/REV.1, re-edited, Geneva, January 1992, UNHCR 1979.

4. *Li v. Canada (Minister of Citizenship and Immigration)* (2005), 249 D.L.R. (4th) 306 (F.C.A.).

5. Camille Giffard, *The Torture Reporting Handbook*, Human Rights Centre, University of Essex, 2000, www.essex.ac.uk/torturehandbook/handbook.

6. See Charter of the United Nations, 24 October 1945, U.N.T.S. XVI, chapter I, article 1, for the full text of these purposes.

REFERENCES

Canada (Attorney General) v. Ward, [1993] 2 S.C.R. 689, 103 D.L.R. (4th) 1, 20 Imm. L.R. (2d) 85 at 692 and 739.

Canadian Heritage. "Background Information, International Covenant on Civil and Political Rights." November 2005. www.pch.gc.ca/progs/pdp-hrp/docs/ iccpr/facts_e.cfm?nav=2.

Convention Against Torture and Other Cruel, Inhuman or Degrading Treatment or Punishment. G.A. res. 39/46, annex, 39 U.N. GAOR Supp. (no. 51) at 197, U.N. Doc. A/39/51 (1984), entered into force June 26, 1987.

Criminal Code. R.S.C. 1985, c. C-46.

Department of Justice. "Canada's accession to the United Nations Second Optional Protocol to the International Covenant on Civil and Political Rights, aiming at the abolition of the death penalty." November 2005. http:// canada.justice.gc.ca/en/news/nr/2005/doc_31756.html.

Human Rights Web. *A Summary of United Nations Agreements on Human Rights.* Created July 8, 1994. Last edited January 25, 1997. www.hrweb.org/legal/ undocs.html.

Immigration and Refugee Protection Act. S.C. 2001, c. 27.

Immigration and Refugee Protection Regulations. S.O.R./2002-227.

International Covenant on Civil and Political Rights. G.A. res. 2200A (XXI), 21 U.N. GAOR Supp. (no. 16) at 52, U.N. Doc. A/6316 (1966), 999 U.N.T.S. 171, entered into force March 23, 1976.

Legal Services, Immigration and Refugee Board. *Consolidated Grounds in the Immigration and Refugee Protection Act: Persons in Need of Protection— Danger of Torture.* May 15, 2002. www.irb-cisr.gc.ca/en/references/legal/ index_e.htm.

Legal Services, Immigration and Refugee Board. *Consolidated Grounds in the Immigration and Refugee Protection Act: Persons in Need of Protection—Risk to Life or Risk of Cruel and Unusual Treatment or Punishment.* www.irb-cisr .gc.ca/en/references/legal/index_e.htm.

Legal Services, Immigration and Refugee Board. *Interpretation of the Convention Refugee Definition in the Case Law.* December 31, 2005. www.irb-cisr.gc.ca/ references/legal/rpd/crdef/index_e.pdf.

Refugee Protection Division Rules. S.O.R./2002-228.

United Nations High Commissioner for Refugees. *Guidelines on International Protection: Application of the Exclusion Clauses—Article 1F of the 1951 Convention Relating to the Status of Refugees.* HCR/GIP/03/05. 4 September 2003. www.unhcr.org/publ/PUBL/3f7d48514.pdf.

United Nations High Commission for Refugees. *Handbook on Procedures and Criteria for Determining Refugee Status Under the 1951 Convention and the 1967 Protocol Relating to the Status of Refugees.* HCR/IP/4/Eng/REV.1. Re-edited, Geneva, January 1992, UNHCR 1979. www.unhcr.org/publ/PUBL/ 3d58e13b4.pdf.

United Nations High Commissioner for Refugees. *Refugee Status Determination: Identifying Who Is a Refugee—Self-Study Module 2.* September 1, 2005. www .unhcr.org/publ/PUBL/43144dc52.pdf.

Universal Declaration of Human Rights. G.A. res. 217A (III), U.N. Doc A/810 at 71 (1948).

RECOMMENDED READING

Canadian Heritage. Human Rights Program. www.pch.gc.ca/progs/pdp-hrp/docs/iccpr/facts_e.cfm. Describes the UN human rights system, UN instruments, and how Canada is involved in this area; provides a glossary of specialized terms and weblinks to related sites.

Office of the United Nations High Commissioner for Human Rights. www.ohchr .org.

Statutes of the Office of the United Nations High Commissioner for Refugees:

- Convention Relating to the Status of Refugees. 189 U.N.T.S. 150, entered into force April 22, 1954. www.unhchr.ch/html/menu3/b/o_c_ref.htm.

- Protocol Relating to the Status of Refugees. 606 U.N.T.S. 267, entered into force October 4, 1967. www.unhchr.ch/html/menu3/b/o_p_ref.htm.

- Convention Against Torture and Other Cruel, Inhuman or Degrading Treatment or Punishment. Can. T.S. 1987 no. 36; G.A. res. 39/46 (annex, 39 U.N. GAOR Supp. (no. 51) at 197, U.N. Doc. A/39/51 (1984)). www.unhchr .ch/html/menu3/b/h_cat39.htm.

- International Covenant on Civil and Political Rights. G.A. res. 2200A (XXI), 21 U.N. GAOR Supp. (No. 16) at 52, U.N. Doc. A/6316 (1966), 999 U.N.T.S. 171, entered into force March 23, 1976. www.unhchr.ch/html/menu3/b/a_ccpr.htm.

- Universal Declaration of Human Rights. G.A. res. 217A (III) U.N. Doc. A/810 at 71 (1948). www.un.org/Overview/rights.html.

Human Rights Organizations

Amnesty International. www.amnesty.org. An international organization whose mission is to conduct research and promote action to prevent human rights abuses.

Canadian Council for Refugees. www.ccrweb.ca. A non-profit umbrella organization that promotes the rights and protection of refugees, both in Canada and internationally. Composed of organizations that aid in the settlement, sponsorship, and protection of refugees and immigrants.

Human Rights Watch. www.hrw.org. An organization dedicated to protecting the human rights of people around the world and investigating human rights violations.

Country-Specific Sources for Research Purposes

Amnesty International Report 2008. http://thereport.amnesty.org.

Human Rights Watch Country Reports. www.hrw.org/countries.html.

US State Department Country Reports on Human Rights Practices. www.state .gov/g/drl/rls/hrrpt.

REVIEW QUESTIONS

This chapter was divided into six sections, each setting out key issues related to refugees and protected persons. The headings below correspond to those in the chapter. You should now be able to answer the questions under each heading.

Introduction

1. What is the fundamental difference between an immigrant and a refugee?

2. Describe in your own words the principle of *non-refoulement*.

3. What is a refugee *sur place*?

International Conventions

1. Name the two international instruments that are the basis for determining refugee status in Canada.

2. Name the two international human rights instruments that are the basis for protecting persons in need of protection in Canada.

3. List the ways that the UNHCR, as the main agency offering international legal protection for refugees, helps the world's uprooted peoples.

Canada's Programs

1. Which refugee protection programs are managed exclusively by CIC?

2. What is the name of the IRB division that has exclusive jurisdiction to hear and decide refugee claims in Canada?

Scope of Protection

1. What are the three clauses of the Convention refugee definition that have been adopted in the IRPA?

2. What are the five grounds of persecution contained in the definition of a Convention refugee?

3. Under what sections of the IRPA can a refugee claimant ask for protection when the Refugee Convention definition does not fit the claimant's situation?

Exclusions

1. On what grounds may a person be excluded from *non-refoulement* protection?

Cessation of Protection

1. In what situations does refugee protection cease to apply under the IRPA?

DISCUSSION QUESTION

Discuss why refugee protection is not intended to be a permanent status.

CHAPTER 8

Refugee and Humanitarian Resettlement Program

LEARNING OBJECTIVES

After reading this chapter you should be able to:

- Understand Canada's role in the resettlement of refugees.

- Identify the organizations involved in refugee resettlement.

- Define the different classes of refugees under the resettlement program.

- Describe the eligibility criteria for applying for resettlement.

- Describe the inadmissibility assessment that forms part of the resettlement application process.

- Understand the role and obligations of different types of sponsors of refugees.

- Describe the kinds of assistance available to refugees who apply for resettlement.

INTRODUCTION

Canada offers protection to the world's displaced people through the Refugee and Humanitarian Resettlement Program. The program is intended to protect refugees and people in refugee-like situations for the following purposes:

- to address humanitarian needs,

- to meet international responsibilities, and

- to respond to international crises.

The Refugee and Humanitarian Resettlement Program applies only to those refugees who are located outside of Canada, such as those who have sought temporary refuge in camps across the border from their war-torn country. The program is managed by Citizenship and Immigration Canada (CIC). Canadian officials from missions abroad work with the United Nations High Commission for Refugees (UNHCR) and various non-governmental organizations (NGOs) to identify refugees and persons in refugee-like situations who are in need of resettlement.

Note that the Refugee and Humanitarian Resettlement Program does not apply to refugee claimants seeking a status determination while already inside Canada. Refugee claimants who have found their own way here are subject to different procedures, which are examined in Chapter 9, "In-Canada Refugee Determination Process."

The program is part of a broader international effort led by the United Nations to find durable solutions for refugees. A **durable solution** is a lasting solution, and in the context of refugee law generally means one of the following:

- *voluntary repatriation*—voluntary return to the home country because it is safe to do so;

- *local integration*—integration in the country of refuge; or

- *resettlement*—resettlement in a third country such as Canada.

Dumo Akuak's husband was killed a year ago by a land mine, and she was left with five young children to support. One night, she was awakened by the screams of neighbours. She smelled fire and could make out flames in the dark. Was the village under attack by soldiers? Rebels? Dumo was not sure because both sides had been involved in a conflict in this region of Solaria for the past year. Dumo shouted out to her children and together they fled into the night wearing only light sleepwear. The family hid in the bush and waited until dawn. There was nothing left of their home. She tried to shield her children's eyes from the hacked-up bodies that lay on the side of the road. Dumo and her children set out for the border of a neighbouring country, hoping to find safety. They walked for days, and along the way met others who had lost their homes, parents, spouses, and children. By the time they reached the border, Dumo and her family had not eaten in days; the children were so weak they did not even cry anymore. Somehow Dumo found her way to a temporary camp: it soon filled up. Dumo waited in line for hours to register for shelter; life had become one long lineup for water, food rations, and news. The family lived in limbo, with no status in the new country; they could not work legally and the children were not allowed to attend school. Life was on hold as they spent the next year living in a temporary tent city as refugees. The family waited for the day when they could safely return home.

When a refugee does not have the option, in the foreseeable future, of either returning home or integrating into the country fled to, the only durable solution for a safe and viable new life is resettlement in a third country. Resettlement offers protection to those who need it, and Canada shares in the burden of resettling refugees for whom resettlement is the appropriate durable solution.

Canada has been providing humanitarian assistance to people fleeing persecution in their homeland and to people displaced by conflicts since the Second World War. From 1996 to 2005, Canada resettled over 285,000 Convention refugees and persons in refugee-like situations.[1] In 2007, Canada ranked 2nd out of the 14 countries that reported the admission of resettled refugees to the UNHCR, just behind the United States.[2] Canada has a history of accepting large numbers of persecuted and displaced persons, including refugees from the following countries:

- Hungary, in the 1950s;

- Czechoslovakia, in the 1960s;

- Chile, Uganda, and Vietnam, in the 1970s;

- the former Yugoslavia, in the late 1990s;

- Sudan and Somalia, in 2003; and

- most recently, the Karen refugees (from Myanmar), in 2006.

Refugees who resettle to Canada need a lot of support to adapt to their new home and become self-sufficient. A significant feature of the Refugee and Humanitarian Resettlement Program is that it allows private groups to sponsor refugees. Sponsorship is an important feature of the program, which provides financial and other resources to refugees. Generally, refugees who are resettled in Canada become permanent residents upon their arrival. This chapter provides an overview of Canada's Refugee and Humanitarian Resettlement Program, including the various types of sponsorship and settlement assistance available.

IMPORTANT ORGANIZATIONS

There are many organizations, agencies, and people who assist refugees in their quest for a durable solution. Three of the most important organizations are described below.

United Nations High Commissioner for Refugees

A person seeking to apply to resettle in Canada is required under s. 150(1) of the Immigration and Refugee Protection Regulations (IRP Regulations) to provide an **undertaking** or a referral from a recognized referral organization. Currently, the only referral organization recognized by the Canadian government is the UNHCR. The UNHCR's responsibilities include finding solutions to refugee problems, and the UNHCR is involved in resettling refugees in Canada. The role of the UNHCR is to assess each refugee's situation and identify those cases to CIC for which resettlement is the only durable solution. UNHCR provides a letter or document to a Canadian visa office, which serves as documentary proof of the referral.

Citizenship and Immigration Canada

Citizenship and Immigration Canada is the federal department responsible for the selection process for refugees and persons in refugee-like situations from abroad (with the exception of Quebec, which has its own organization). Visa officers receive referrals from the UNHCR or from private sponsors as well as applications for resettlement from those in need of resettlement. They assess, evaluate, and decide the outcome of the applications on the basis of whether they meet Canadian statutory eligibility and admissibility requirements.

Refugees in need of resettlement must apply for permanent residence under the program at a Canadian high commission, embassy, or consulate outside their home country. The Canadian government sponsors some refugees and works closely with non-governmental organizations, such as refugee groups, religious communities, and ethnic associations, in selecting refugees for resettlement in Canada.

In assessing applications, visa officers place emphasis on the following principles, which are articulated in the objectives of s. 3(2) of the *Immigration and Refugee Protection Act* (IRPA):

- to recognize that Canada's refugee program is about saving lives and offering protection to persecuted and displaced persons;

- to facilitate rapid refugee family reunification;

- to develop relationships with partners, such as sponsors; and

- to accelerate the processing of urgent and vulnerable protection cases.

At the same time, applicants for resettlement must meet the criteria for permanent residence set out in s. 139 of the IRP Regulations unless they qualify for an exemption. These criteria include the requirement in s. 139(1)(g) that,

> if the foreign national intends to reside in a province other than the Province of Quebec, the foreign national and their family members included in the application for protection will be able to become successfully established in Canada.

Exemptions are made in special needs cases, discussed below under the heading "Special Needs Cases."

CIC works with the International Organization for Migration (IOM) to coordinate the refugee's travel and resettlement arrangements.

International Organization for Migration

Established in 1951, the **International Organization for Migration (IOM)** is an intergovernmental organization that assists in the resettlement of displaced persons, refugees and migrants and works closely with governmental, intergovernmental, and non-governmental partners. Canada is a founding member and a full member of the IOM and works with the organization in resettlement cases.

The IOM organizes and makes arrangements for the transfer of refugees, displaced persons, and other individuals in need of international migration services to receiving countries. It also arranges medical examinations for refugees. In several locations around the world, the IOM assists refugees in the integration process before they arrive in Canada through an in-depth Canadian Orientation Abroad (COA) program.

CLASSES OF REFUGEES

There are two main classes of refugees covered by the Refugee and Humanitarian Resettlement Program: the Convention refugees abroad class; and the humanitarian-protected persons abroad class. The second class is further divided further into the country of asylum class and the source country class. The definitions and criteria for each are provided in the IRP Regulations.

Convention Refugees Abroad Class

As the name suggests, refugees under the Convention refugees abroad class must first meet the criteria of the Convention refugee definition, as explained in Chapter 7, "Refugees and Protected Persons." Refugees must apply for resettlement outside of Canada, and it must be established that no other durable solution other than resettlement is viable.

To qualify for resettlement as members of the Convention refugees abroad class, individuals must have the necessary financial resources. Those who do not have the financial means to support themselves and their dependants may receive support through government assistance, private sponsorship, or the Joint Assistance Sponsorship program, described later in this chapter.

Humanitarian-Protected Persons Abroad Class

The humanitarian-protected persons abroad class includes persons who are not Convention refugees but who are in refugee-like situations. This class is divided into two classes: the country of asylum class and the source country class. To qualify as a humanitarian-protected person, the person must meet the criteria of one of these subclasses.

COUNTRY OF ASYLUM CLASS

The country of asylum class deals with persons who have fled their countries and who are the victims of war or massive violations of human rights. Section 147 of the IRP Regulations defines members of the country of asylum class as individuals who "have been, and continue to be, seriously and personally affected by civil war, armed conflict or massive violation of human rights." In this context, "seriously and personally affected" refers to a sustained and effective denial of basic human rights. Additionally, to qualify as refugees under this class, individuals must

- be outside all of their countries of nationality and/or habitual residence,

- apply for resettlement outside of Canada, and

- be in need of resettlement as no other durable solution other than resettlement is viable for them.

To be permitted resettlement as a member of the country of asylum class, refugees must have a private sponsor or have their own financial means to support themselves and their dependants. In certain situations, they may qualify for a joint assistance sponsorship if they also qualify as a special needs case, described below.

SOURCE COUNTRY CLASS

The source country class comprises persons who remain in their country of citizenship or habitual residence and who are the victims of war or violations of fundamental civil rights or who would meet the Convention definition had they fled their country. For a person to be considered under the source country class, his country of nationality or habitual residence must appear on schedule 2 of the IRP Regulations, which lists the countries for source country classification.

The schedule is revised on a regular basis and is developed in consultation with a number of the department's partners. At the time of writing, there were six countries on the source country list:

- Colombia

- El Salvador

- Guatemala

- Democratic Republic of Congo

- Sierra Leone

- Sudan.

To be members of the source country class, individuals must reside in a country that is still listed in schedule 2 at the time that the visa is issued and for which there is no possibility of a durable solution other than resettlement in Canada.

To qualify under this class, individuals must also meet the following criteria. It must be shown that they

- have been and continue to be seriously and personally affected by civil war or armed conflict;

- have been or are being detained or imprisoned with or without charges, or subjected to some other form of penal control, as a direct result of an act committed outside Canada that would, in Canada, be a legitimate expression of freedom of thought or a legitimate exercise of civil rights pertaining to dissent or trade union activity; or

- are unable or unwilling to avail themselves of the protection of any of their countries of citizenship or habitual residence, because of a well-founded fear of persecution for reasons of race, religion, nationality, political opinion, or membership in a particular social group.

To be permitted resettlement as a member of the source country class, individuals must have a private sponsor or have the financial means to support themselves and their dependants. Alternatively, they may receive financial assistance from the government or may qualify for a joint assistance sponsorship if they also qualify as a special needs case.

SPECIAL NEEDS CASES

All types of special needs refugees must be members of the Convention refugees abroad or humanitarian-protected persons abroad classes. The label "special needs" means that there is special consideration of these cases, including priority processing and a deviation from the routine assessment eligibility criteria. Three categories of special needs cases are provided for in s. 138 of the IRP Regulations: urgent protection cases; vulnerable persons cases; and women at risk cases. These cases are given special consideration because they involve refugees in greater need of protection or in more immediate danger.

In assessing applications for special needs cases, the visa officer gives more weight to the need for protection than to the refugee's ability to settle in Canada. In these cases, the criteria are not applied as strictly, and individuals may be accepted despite having limited settlement prospects, because the overriding concern is their safety. All special needs cases are exempt from the requirement under s. 139(1)(g) of the IRP Regulations to successfully establish.

Special needs cases usually require expedited processing. The visa officer issues a temporary resident visa in situations like these to allow the refugee to travel to Canada prior to the completion of the admissibility assessment process. The admissibility assessment, regarding medical, security and criminality concerns, as discussed in Chapter 3, "Inadmissibility," is completed after the refugee is in Canada. If it is successful, the refugee may then apply for permanent residence from within Canada.

Urgent Protection Program

A person in **urgent need of protection** is defined in s. 138 of the IRP Regulations as someone whose life, liberty, or physical safety is under immediate threat and who, if returned to the country of nationality or former habitual residence, is likely to be killed or subjected to violence, torture, sexual assault, or arbitrary imprisonment.

When the UNHCR identifies an emergency case to a visa office where a refugee is in need of urgent protection because of immediate threats, the Urgent Protection Program (UPP) allows Canada to respond. Resettlement in urgent protection cases is undertaken as a priority where there is no other way to guarantee the security of the person concerned.

Vulnerable Cases

The term "**vulnerable**," as defined in s. 138 of the IRP Regulations, describes a person with a greater need of protection than other applicants for protection abroad, because of the person's particular circumstances that give rise to a heightened risk to their physical safety.

For example, a visa officer may identify as vulnerable a female refugee who is at risk of rape or sexual abuse because she does not have the protection of a family or support network. Similarly, victims of torture who are in need of medical treatment may be deemed vulnerable.

Women at Risk Program

The UNHCR identifies refugee women who are in dangerous situations and refers them for resettlement. The **Women at Risk program** is designed to offer resettlement to women who are members of the Convention refugees abroad or humanitarian-protected persons abroad class so that they may be admitted to Canada even if they do not meet the normal regulatory standard of "ability to establish" themselves. Furthermore, although inadmissibility on the grounds of security risk, violating human or international rights, serious criminality, organized criminality, and health risk or burden is still assessed, policies and procedures are in place to assess these grounds less stringently. For example, in the assessment of inadmissibility on criminality grounds, it is a matter of policy that officers do not require refugees to submit police certificates or certificates of no criminal conviction from their home country because of the risk of alerting authorities in the country of alleged persecution. Instead, officers may request police certificates from countries of temporary asylum. Also, under s. 38(2) of the IRPA, women at risk are exempted from inadmissibility on the ground of creating excessive demand on Canada's health care system.

In times of conflict, it is often civilian women who suffer violence, abuse, and exploitation. Women in these circumstances generally require additional assistance re-establishing themselves. They often are unable to meet the eligibility requirement of having the potential to become self-sufficient in the short or medium term. Women refugees face special, gender-based problems and can be at risk for a multitude of reasons, including the following:

- *They are alone.* A woman may have lost her husband, may not have the protection of a male relative or family members, and may be isolated because of the stigma of being raped or abused.

- *They lack basic skills.* A woman may be illiterate, and may lack the knowledge or experience necessary for dealing with local authorities.

- *They face health concerns.* A woman and her children may face exacerbated health problems due to living in refugee camps or as a result of conflict, famine, war-related injuries, or lack of medical attention.

- *They are vulnerable.* A woman and her children may be vulnerable to violence, sexual abuse, and sexual exploitation, and may have experienced harassment by local authorities or even by members of her own community.

- *They face barriers to resettlement.* A woman may have a minimal level of education, limited job skills, or heavy child-care responsibilities.

A woman who has been identified as "at risk" requires help in starting a new life. Generally, a woman who is resettled under this program requires a joint assistance sponsorship, described below, and needs a longer period to become integrated and established in Canada.

THE APPLICATION FOR REFUGEE RESETTLEMENT

An application for refugee resettlement must be accompanied by a referral from the UNHCR or by an undertaking for private sponsorship. Applications are submitted to a Canadian high commission, embassy, or consulate outside the refugee's home country. For refugees destined to Quebec, they require a Certificat de sélection du Québec[3] along with the required documentation.

Copies of documents must be translated and certified. In situations where the refugee applicant cannot provide all the necessary documentation, such as if the documents are not available from her homeland or don't exist, an explanation is required. Failure to explain why documents are missing will result in rejection of the application as incomplete.

There are no application or processing fees for refugees applying for permanent residence under this program, and the refugee applicant receives a letter of confirmation with a file number once the visa office receives the application.

The refugee applicant must meet the statutory requirements for admissibility to Canada, which apply to almost all new immigrants, and the statutory requirements for eligibility under the Refugee and Humanitarian Resettlement Program.

Eligibility

The refugee applicant must be eligible for resettlement under the Refugee and Humanitarian Resettlement Program, which means they must

1. be referred by the UNHCR[4] or sponsored (s. 150(1) of the IRP Regulations); and

2. meet the regulatory definition of one of the following:

    ■ a member of the Convention refugees abroad class;

    ■ a member of the country of asylum class; or

    ■ a member of the source country class.

A Canadian visa officer decides whether the applicant falls into one of the classes of refugees and is eligible under the program, which includes meeting selection criteria and not being inadmissible. If the applicant is found to be ineligible, the application is rejected.

Admissibility

There are a number of grounds for inadmissibility that apply generally to anyone entering Canada. Inadmissibility is described in detail in Chapter 3, "Inadmissibility." The visa officer considers the information and the documents provided in the application and the interview, and determines whether the refugee applicant is inadmissible. Refugee applicants do not have to meet the normal requirement for being self-sufficient as they are exempted from financial inadmissibility by the IRP Regulations at s. 139(3).

The following is a very brief overview of four of the grounds of inadmissibility as they relate to this program:

1. *Medical inadmissibility.* Canada normally bars someone who is inadmissible for health reasons because of a health condition that is likely to be a danger to public health; a health condition that is likely to be a danger to public safety; or a health condition that might reasonably be expected to cause excessive demand on health or social services. Refugee applicants, however, are exempted from the "excessive demand" grounds by the IRP Regulations at s. 139(4). Nevertheless, all refugee applicants must undergo medical examinations for health and public safety reasons. The refugee applicant must pass a medical examination to ensure that no medical condition exists that is likely to be a danger to Canadian public health or safety. The examination is carried out by a **designated medical practitioner** (a local physician), who is authorized by the Canadian government.

   If a refugee applicant cannot afford to pay for the medical examination, a loan may be issued under the provisions of the Immigration Loans Program, described below. In countries where the IOM is arranging travel for the refugees, the IOM may also arrange and prepay medical examinations. The IOM usually covers the cost of medical examinations for those refugees who are referred by the UNHCR. Canada later reimburses the IOM for costs incurred on behalf of refugees resettled to Canada.

2 & 3. *Serious criminality grounds* and *criminal checks.* The refugee applicant is not required to submit a police certificate from the country from which he is fleeing, and Canada does not contact organizations or individuals that could place the refugee applicant or family members in danger. However, a police certificate may be requested from any country that granted the applicant temporary asylum.

4. *Security or violation of human or international rights.* A refugee applicant can be inadmissible on security grounds because of her own activities or those of an organization to which she belongs outside of Canada, where the activities are related to espionage, subversion, and terrorism or are considered to be a danger to the security of Canada or which might endanger the lives or safety of persons in Canada. An applicant can also be found inadmissible if she has been convicted of, or has committed, crimes against humanity (for example, extermination, enslavement, imprisonment, torture, sexual violence, or persecution committed against any civilian population), genocide, or war crimes. Applicants who held positions with the government or military of regimes that participated in war crimes or crimes against humanity are inadmissible as a risk to security. Likewise, individuals who belong to organizations that espouse violence, such as terrorist groups, are also inadmissible.

If an applicant is found inadmissible, the application is rejected.

Selection Factors and the Admissibility Interview

Refugees who seek protection when already in Canada cannot be subjected to immigration selection criteria, unless they are first sent back to their country of nationality or former habitual residence. Obviously, this would not be an appropriate response to those claiming to have fled persecution and violence. However, applicants for permanent residence under the Refugee and Humanitarian Resettlement Program are not yet in Canada, and a process of selection is necessary to ensure that the number of refugees admitted does not exceed the resources available for their absorption in Canada.

There are a number of methods of selection, such as by order of application ("first come, first served"), by need, or by ability to become self-sufficient. The Refugee and Humanitarian Resettlement Program first emphasizes need and the ability to become self-sufficient, although once applicants are in the system, they are processed in the order received. Need may take priority over other considerations when an applicant falls within one of the special needs categories of urgent protection, vulnerable cases, or women at risk. For example, the selection factors with respect to self-sufficiency are not applied as strictly in cases identified by a visa officer as special needs because the overriding concern is protection.

Applicants that do not fall within a special needs category are assessed on the basis of their ability to become self-sufficient within three to five years of arrival in Canada. To determine the likelihood of the applicant's attaining self-sufficiency, the visa officer considers a modified version of the factors measured by the formal point system of skills and adaptability that is applied to skilled workers in the economic class. Refugees are interviewed as part of the selection process, and the following factors are considered:

- education,

- work experience and qualifications,

- language abilities in English or French, and

- suitability factors such as a support network of family connections or a sponsor.

Although these factors are similar to those used in the formal point system, the threshold for refugees is much less onerous. Also, CIC's guidelines for assessing refugee applicants instruct the visa officer to assess the refugee's qualities that "assist in integration" such as personal characteristics of "initiative, resourcefulness, ingenuity, perseverance or other characteristics."[5]

To illustrate the process by which the selection factors are evaluated, we return to our example of Dumo Akuak, an Inka refugee from Solaria:

The UNHCR came in contact with Dumo and her family in a refugee camp located in a neighbouring country to Dumo's. A UNHCR protection officer assessed Dumo's situation and determined that resettlement was the only durable solution. Furthermore, because Dumo is a single woman with five children, the officer concluded that hers was an urgent case.

A Refugee Referral Form would then be sent to a Canadian visa office, to serve as documentary proof of the UNHCR's referral. The form includes the refugee claim and information about the family. The family would then submit an application for permanent residence, along with their referral, to the Canadian embassy located in the capital of the host country.

In the host country, a Canadian visa officer would assess Dumo's application. In some cases, visa officers travel to camps to interview refugee applicants, and in other cases interviews are held at the embassy or consulate.

> *In Dumo's case, the interview was held in person at the visa office to determine the family's admissibility and the appropriate refugee class, and to assess Dumo's ability to become self-sufficient in Canada as a permanent resident. An interpreter was provided at the interview.*

The interview is used to establish identity, settlement plans, and the ability to be self-supporting. When assessing Dumo, the visa officer would ask many questions and consider many factors.

> *The visa officer determined that Dumo and her family were not personally subjected to persecution in their country of origin and therefore did not meet the regulatory definition of persons under the Convention refugees abroad class. However, because of their ethnic and religious background, there was a reasonable chance, given the genocide in their country of origin, that they were at risk should they be returned there.*
>
> *The visa officer also determined that even if the Akuak family were not Convention refugees, they met the requirements for the country of asylum class of the humanitarian-protected persons abroad class. They had fled their country as a result of war and human rights violations. They had been seriously and personally affected—their home was destroyed and their lives threatened. Although their country of origin was included on the source country list in schedule 2, Dumo and her family were outside of Solaria at the time of their application, so the appropriate class would be the country of asylum class.*

Before permitting Dumo to resettle in Canada as a member of the Convention refugees abroad class, the visa officer would consider the following criteria:

- *No other durable solution.* The host country was not willing or able to take Dumo and her children permanently, and they would be at risk if returned to their home country. Resettlement was the only viable and durable solution.

- *Self-sufficiency.* Normally, Dumo would have had to demonstrate to the visa officer that she had the potential to become self-sufficient within three to five years, and not burden Canada by depending on social assistance after that time period. To assess Dumo's earning potential, the visa officer asked about her level of education, work experience and training, language skills, and whether she had any family in Canada. Dumo had a grade eight education, and her work experience was limited to fieldwork for a neighbouring farm and her own small garden. She spoke broken English, and had no known family in Canada. Furthermore, she would have to take care of a large family on her own. However, the visa officer was impressed by the speed at which Dumo was learning English and by her resourcefulness in taking care of her five children under such terrible circumstances.

■ *Private sponsor or financial means.* Dumo had neither a private sponsor nor the financial means to support herself and her five children.

■ *Inadmissibility.* The visa officer also found that Dumo was not inadmissible to Canada on security and criminality grounds.

Dumo had come this far, but might have been rejected by Canada. Fortunately for her, the visa officer determined that she qualified for government assistance as a special needs case. The UNHCR referral identified her for the Women at Risk program as a woman alone, without the protection of a male relative, and particularly vulnerable because of her five young dependent children. As a result, her poor outlook for self-sufficiency in three to five years was given less weight, and she was entitled to a joint assistance sponsorship. She was also able to defer medical examinations for her and the children, necessary to confirm their admissibility, until after they arrived in Canada.

Because Dumo and her family were destined to a country very different from their own, the officer believed she was a good candidate for the **Canadian Orientation Abroad program** to help her integrate into Canadian society. This program is conducted in partnership with the IOM and consists of learning modules that last from one to five days. Topics include an introduction to Canada, the settling-in period, employment, rights and responsibilities, climate, finding a place to live, living in a multicultural society, cost of living, family life, education, communications, and adaptation to Canada. She would attend the sessions before travelling to Canada.

Forms and Documents

An Application for Permanent Residence in Canada form (IMM 0008) is the generic form used to apply for permanent residence. Each refugee applicant over 18 years of age must also submit the following additional forms:

■ Schedule 1 Background/Declaration form (IMM 0008 Schedule 1),

■ Schedule 2 Refugees Outside Canada form (IMM 0008 Schedule 2), and

■ Use of a Representative form (IMM 5476).

Other forms that may also be required, depending on the circumstances, are the following:

■ Military Service Details form (IMM 5579)

■ Supplementary Information form (IMM 5550).

WEBLINK

All forms are available on the CIC website at www.cic.gc.ca/english/information/ applications/conref.asp, as are general guidelines for completing them—see the guide entitled *Application for Permanent Residence in Canada: Convention Refugees Abroad and Humanitarian-Protected Persons Abroad* (IMM 6000) at www.cic.gc.ca/english/pdf/kits/guides/6000e.pdf.

There are many additional documents that applicants must also provide with their application forms, as follows:

1. six photos of each refugee applicant

2. identity and civil status documents for each refugee applicant:

   - copy of birth certificate

   - copy of marriage, divorce, annulment, or separation certificates

   - copies of death certificates of family members

   - children's information—copy of birth certificate, adoption papers, proof of custody papers, etc.

3. background documents for each refugee applicant (where applicable):

   - completion of military service card and military records

   - membership cards (for social, political, vocational, and cultural organizations)

   - educational certificates, diplomas, school-leaving certificates

   - trade/apprenticeship certificates

   - letters of reference from past employers

4. travel documents for each refugee applicant

   - copy of passport

   - copy of national identity document

   - copy of UNHCR registration card or national refugee registration document

5. proof of settlement funds (if self-supporting) including financial statements, and proof of assets

6. copy of the UNHCR referral or sponsorship undertaking (if privately sponsored).

There may be other documents required that are case or country specific. Many visa offices require that documents be translated into English or French.

Decision

The final decision as to whether to accept or reject a refugee applicant is made by the visa officer, after a consideration of both the admissibility and eligibility criteria. Those accepted as refugees are generally granted permanent resident status upon arrival in Canada. They enjoy the same rights accorded to all permanent residents, and are eligible to apply for Canadian citizenship.

Applicants who are refused admission to Canada as refugees are informed of this decision, and sent a letter outlining the reasons for the refusal. The IRPA does not specifically provide for a direct appeal of the visa officer's decision. However, the refused refugee applicant may seek leave for judicial review before the Federal Court of Canada.

TARGETS

The minister of CIC reports on the number of refugees who have resettled in the prior year, in the annual **immigration resettlement plan**. As we learned in Chapter 2, the minister tables this plan every year, and includes the number and types of foreign nationals who can come to Canada as permanent residents. Included in this plan are the targets for resettlement by class of refugee, either members of the Convention refugees abroad class or members of the humanitarian-protected persons abroad class, and whether they are government-assisted or privately sponsored refugees.

These targets are established through consultations both within the CIC and between the CIC and provincial governments, Canadian non-governmental organizations, and the UNHCR. Funding is then allocated to visa offices on the basis of projected resettlement needs.

Generally, Canada commits to resettle 7,500 government-assisted refugees and to process between 3,000 and 3,500 privately sponsored refugees each year. There is no **target number** (limit) for those refugees who are self-supporting and not in need of assistance.

WEBLINK

For this year's resettlement targets, consult the *Annual Report to Parliament on Immigration*, found on the CIC website at www.cic.gc.ca, usually under the Publications menu item.

FINANCIAL AND RESETTLEMENT SUPPORT

Refugees and their families who are in need of resettlement and who do not have sufficient resources of their own may obtain support from a number of sources, as follows:

- the Canadian government, through the Government-Assisted Refugee Program;

- Canadian citizens and permanent residents, individually or in groups, through the Private Sponsorship of Refugees Program; or

- both the Canadian government and private sponsors, through the Joint Assistance Sponsorship program.

The **Government-Assisted Refugee (GAR) Program** applies only to the sponsorship of members of the Convention refugees abroad and source country classes, including special needs cases that fall under these classes. Private sponsorship applies to all categories of refugees.

Government-Assisted Refugee (GAR) Program and Resettlement Assistance Program (RAP)

As the name suggests, government-assisted refugees are sponsored or supported by the Canadian or Quebec governments, generally through the Resettlement Assistance Program (RAP). Immigration loans and temporary health care may also be available.

Each year, the government of Canada plans for the resettlement of a number of refugees from abroad, and supports these refugees through the **Resettlement Assistance Program (RAP)**.

The RAP provides both financial and immediate essential services to government-assisted refugees, who require help integrating in their new community on their road to self-sufficiency and independence. Consider the following types of assistance available:

- *Financial assistance.* The refugee's personal assets, as described in the application, are considered when assessing the need for financial assistance. The amount of income support is guided by provincial social assistance rates for food and shelter, and covers the most basic needs for up to 12 months after arrival in Canada, or up to an additional 24 months for refugees identified as special needs cases. This money may be used for food, clothing, accommodation, basic household goods and furniture, and incidentals, such as soap and toothpaste.

- *Settlement assistance.* Unlike refugees who are privately sponsored, government-assisted refugees have no integration assistance from members of the community. Therefore, from the moment they arrive, they will require assistance and so will be provided with reception at the airport, transportation, temporary accommodation and meals, and winter clothing if needed. They receive assistance locating permanent housing and are provided with household furnishings and basic necessities. They receive help completing essential paperwork, such as that concerning medical insurance, social insurance numbers, and child tax benefits. Furthermore, they receive language training, employment training, and vocational training, which are usually administered by Human Resources and Social Development Canada.

   Settlement services are delivered by service provider organizations (SPOs), which consist of individuals, non-profit organizations, agencies serving immigrants, community groups, businesses, provincial and municipal governments, and educational institutions that receive funding from CIC.

Other Government Programs

IMMIGRATION LOANS

The **Immigration Loans Program (ILP)** is a special federal fund available to indigent refugees and immigrants who qualify by demonstrating both the need for the loan as well as the potential to repay it after arrival in Canada. Under the ILP, loans may be available to cover the cost of transportation to Canada, travel documents, immigration medical examinations, the Right of Permanent Residence Fee, and assistance loans to cover expenses such as housing rental and utilities.

Interest is charged at a rate set each January by the Department of Finance. However, members of the Convention refugees abroad and humanitarian-protected persons abroad classes may have a period of one to three years during which they will not be charged interest on their ILP loans. Also, under certain circumstances loan repayment may be deferred for up to two years, and special needs refugees (urgent protection, vulnerable cases, and women at risk) may be granted financial assistance in the form of a contribution that does not have to be repaid.

INTERIM FEDERAL HEALTH PROGRAM

Refugees are eligible for provincial health coverage, generally within 90 days after arrival in the province in which they reside. In the interim, the federal government provides essential and emergency health care coverage to refugees in need of assistance through the **Interim Federal Health Program**, administered by CIC.

Private Sponsorship Programs

Private individuals often agree to sponsor relatives or members of their own communities. However, sometimes individuals or groups wish to help others. Consider the following scenario:

Kim-Ly was only four when she, her parents, and two brothers fled the oppressive communist regime in Vietnam and arrived in Canada in 1980. She was one of 9,000 Indochinese "boat people" sponsored under Canada's newly created private sponsorship program. Kim-Ly's family settled in a small town in Ontario, the same community as the local church group that had sponsored her family. They were safe and in a new land now. They were the only Vietnamese family in town but that didn't matter to the community: they welcomed her family into their parish and their hearts. Kim-Ly recalls there were always people around to help the family learn the intricacies of the English language, ensure they had the proper clothes for chilling winters, and take them to local fairs, Thanksgiving dinners, and pancake breakfasts. Kim-Ly's father, a former schoolteacher, eventually opened his own vegetable and flower shop in town. He became what people today would refer to as "independent" or "self-sufficient." Kim-Ly's mother stayed home to care for Kim-Ly, her two brothers, and a sister born here. Kim-Ly started junior kindergarten shortly after her arrival; eventually she earned a college diploma and then moved to the city to pursue a career in fashion.

On one of her recent visits to her parents' home, Kim-Ly became curious about her homeland and what led to her family's departure. Her parents had refused to speak about atrocities they suffered and witnessed. She doesn't have any memories of "back home"—Canada is the only home she knows. However, Kim-Ly did have frequent, horrible nightmares as a child and sometimes still wakes at night for no apparent reason. There is a great sadness behind her father's eyes that no one ever talks about. She remembers that her mother used to cry often. She probably suffered from bouts of depression from missing her relatives who were killed. Kim-Ly knows that her life was saved by the kind people who sponsored her family. She laments to her mother that there seem to be so many people in the world today who deserve the same help that she and her family received. Her mother peers over her glasses at Kim-Ly and says, "So why don't you sponsor a refugee? One at a time you can make a difference, Kim-Ly." Her voice trails off. Could she, Kim-Ly, really do that? Sponsor someone? She is excited … but where to start?

The private sponsorship of refugees is the hallmark of Canada's refugee resettlement program, because it opens the door to a greater number of refugees and helps them to adapt to their new community. Sponsorship is considered a three-way commitment among the Canadian government, the sponsor, and the refugee.

Sponsors enter into a legal contract, called an undertaking, with the Canadian government, whereby they agree to be responsible for finding accommodation and basic household items for the refugees they are sponsoring. Sponsors help the family adjust to their new community, and orient them to resources and services available in the community. This may involve assistance with basic activities such as banking, registering children for school, taking public transportation, shopping, and searching for a job. Sponsors may also help enrol adult refugees in English or French language classes, and with anything else that needs to be done to promote self-sufficiency as soon as possible within the first 12 months of their arrival.

TYPES OF PRIVATE SPONSORSHIP

Although sponsoring one refugee or an entire family can be rewarding, it requires some effort and there is much to do before the refugee arrives. In our example, Kim-Ly may or may not know whom to sponsor or from which part of the world. There are two ways to identify whom to sponsor for resettlement, as follows:

1. *Sponsor-referred cases.* The sponsor may know of a particular refugee or refugee family from contacts abroad or in Canada, and can identify them to CIC. For this reason, sponsor-referred cases are also known as **named cases**.

    Sponsors may know refugees through friends, relatives, or religious and community organizations. Often these cases involve refugees with relatives in Canada. Sponsor-referred sponsorships are meant to promote and facilitate family reunification, where refugee applicants meet the eligibility criteria of one of the refugee classes.

2. *Visa office-referred cases.* The sponsor may not personally know a refugee or a refugee family, and instead may be matched up by the visa office. For this reason, visa office-referred cases are also known as **unnamed cases**. Instead of identifying a specific refugee, the sponsor submits to CIC a Request for a Refugee Profile, and CIC refers the request to the CIC Matching Centre. The sponsor then receives from CIC information that includes a description and profile about the refugee's family, community affiliation, language and work skills, and any special needs to determine whether the match is suitable for the sponsor.

Would-be sponsors must also determine their level of involvement in the sponsorship. Kim-Ly must decide whether she wants to be solely responsible for the sponsorship, or whether she would prefer to join a community group and share the responsibilities. Perhaps she would prefer to forgo responsibility altogether and simply donate money to an organization with experience in sponsoring refugees. CIC provides a Refugee Sponsorship Training Program to groups that are seriously interested in private sponsorship of refugees in need of resettlement. The following is an overview of the three types of private sponsorship groups and their general requirements.

Group of Five

Kim-Ly may decide to form a Group of Five (G5) with four or more other people she knows. Any group of five or more individuals, each from at least five different households, may join together to sponsor one or more refugees, provided that each member also meets the following requirements. Each member must

- be at least 18 years of age;

- be a Canadian citizen or permanent resident;

- live in the community where the refugees are expected to settle;

- not be in default on any other sponsorship undertaking; and

- have the necessary resources, such as financial, material, and social, to guarantee support for the full duration of the sponsorship, usually up to a 12-month period.

G5 sponsors are usually one-time sponsors who get together to respond to a special situation. In our example, Kim-Ly could form her group with friends, co-workers, or members of her family who belong to different households.

The five households must show that they can afford to support the refugees they intend to sponsor through a financial assessment and by providing a detailed plan for the refugees' settlement in the community. The individual members of the G5 act as guarantors: they ensure that the necessary support is provided for the full duration of the sponsorship, usually the refugee's first 12 months in Canada.

If Kim-Ly chooses to form a Group of Five, she will need to assess the financial resources of each potential member. Once the group is formed, they must start saving or raising funds. Kim-Ly's group then applies to CIC using the Group of Five sponsorship application kit: they should start the process by reading the *Refugee Sponsorship Application—Group of Five*. They will then complete a Sponsor

Assessment form and an Undertaking/Application to Sponsor—Groups of Five form. The G5 will also have to research and write a settlement plan and financial plan.

Community Sponsors

Community sponsor sponsorship is open to organizations, associations, and corporations that meet the following requirements. They must

- demonstrate the financial capacity to fulfill the sponsorship, raising funds if necessary;

- demonstrate the ability to provide necessary emotional and social supports, organizing members to take on various roles; and

- be based in the community where the refugee family is expected to live.

Kim-Ly may join an existing community sponsor, or may initiate the formation of a new group interested in sponsoring refugees. Generally, these groups are formed because a person in the community knows of a refugee, such as a relative, who needs to be resettled. That person approaches a community or faith-based organization to request its participation in the sponsorship. Several groups may come together as co-sponsors to form the sponsorship group. For example, if Kim-Ly belongs to a church near her home, regularly attends the local Vietnamese cultural centre, and is a member of her college's women's alumni association, she could approach one or more of these organizations to solicit their participation.

The composition of the community sponsor group will depend on a number of factors: the amount of money that the group can raise; how much each potential member can commit to donate; and how much each potential member can assist in the settlement of the refugees for the full duration of the sponsorship. All members of the community sponsor group are named in the undertaking with the minister of CIC; therefore, all members are held legally responsible for the sponsorship. One member, however, must be identified as the contact person. By signing the undertaking, the members are subject to any collection action by CIC should they breach the conditions of their financial obligations.

Sponsorship Agreement Holders and Their Constituent Groups

In contrast to community sponsors, **sponsorship agreement holders** (SAHs) are established, incorporated organizations. They have signed a Sponsorship Agreement with the minister of CIC (or with the Quebec government) to facilitate the sponsorship process. There are many SAHs across Canada ranging from religious organizations to ethnocultural groups and other humanitarian organizations. SAHs may undertake sponsorships on an ongoing basis and are completely responsible for managing sponsorships under their agreements.

Examples of organizations that have signed Sponsorship Agreements with the minister of CIC include national faith-based organizations, such as the Salvation Army, the Canadian Unitarian Council, and the Presbyterian Church in Canada, and ethnocultural groups such as the Afghan Women's Organization.

SAHs may sponsor refugees directly, or sponsorships may be undertaken indirectly through a local **constituent group (CG)**, which sponsors the refugees under the SAH agreement. For example, a local congregation of a national faith-based organization may apply to its head office to become recognized as a CG so that it can sponsor a refugee.

Each SAH sets its own criteria for recognizing CGs, and is responsible for managing and training any CGs belonging to it. A CG must be authorized in writing by the SAH to act on its behalf to sponsor refugees for resettlement. CGs are usually located in the community where the refugees are destined.

In our example, Kim-Ly might find that her local parish or congregation is already a CG, has experience sponsoring refugees, and is already in the process of sponsoring a family. Kim-Ly could therefore approach the organization and volunteer to raise funds, serve as a greeter, or provide some other ongoing assistance to the refugee after arrival in Canada.

OBLIGATIONS OF REFUGEE SPONSORSHIP

Refugees are responsible for becoming self-sufficient in 12 months or less from the date of arrival. This is a relatively short span of time, considering that many refugees come here with limited or no ability to speak, read, or write in English or French, minimal education, and psychological issues due to trauma suffered in their homeland. In exceptional circumstances, the length of the sponsorship may be extended up to 36 months, but only with the consent of the sponsor.

The obligations of sponsors are also onerous. The sponsorship application, together with the sponsorship undertaking, comprise a legal, binding contract between the sponsor and the minister of CIC. The minister of CIC can collect the financial obligation should the signees default in their undertaking and may refuse any future applications for sponsorship. Sponsoring groups undertake to work alongside refugees in order to ensure that they have the necessary support to integrate into life in Canada and to become independent. Consider the following examples of the responsibilities of sponsors:

- *Reception services.* Meeting the refugee upon arrival in the community and giving them an orientation to the community and life in Canada, which includes providing information about public transit, community resources, libraries, and volunteer and settlement agencies.

- *Accommodation.* Locating suitable accommodation, basic furniture, and other household essentials.

- *Access to education.* Arranging language training such as that provided by the Language Instruction for Newcomers to Canada program, or other basic training, and enrolling children in school or day care.

- *Employment.* Assisting with resumé writing, skills training, and job searches.

- *Financial orientation.* Explaining where and how to shop, bank, budget, etc.

- *Financial support.* Arranging for payment of rent, utilities, telephone, groceries, local transportation, clothes, and household supplies.

- *Assistance and support.* Completing forms, such as health insurance, social insurance, and child tax benefits forms; helping them understand the rights and responsibilities of being a permanent resident; explaining local laws; helping them find a physician and dentist; and providing ongoing friendship and emotional support.

The commitment to sponsor a refugee may be substantial in terms of both financial resources and time and energy. Fortunately, potential sponsors may choose from the several options described above, depending on what they have to give—money or time—and the degree of commitment they are comfortable making.

Settlement Plan

A **settlement plan** details the sponsor's commitment to provide the sponsored refugees with the following:

- basic financial support, such as money for lodging and food; and

- care, such as showing them how to register their children in school and providing a network of support and orientation.

The settlement plan is the framework for facilitating the newcomer's independence. It serves as a guide to members of the sponsoring group, and allocates responsibilities for each of the many tasks involved. The settlement plan must be submitted with the sponsor's application.

Joint Assistance Sponsorship (JAS)

There are certain types of refugees who are not likely to become independent after only 12 months of living in Canada. Consider the following examples:

- women at risk

- refugees who are severely traumatized by torture

- large families of refugees

- refugees who lived in refugee camps for extended periods

- refugees with medical conditions.

The **Joint Assistance Sponsorship (JAS) program** was designed to accommodate these kinds of situations. It is a sort of hybrid of the Government-Assisted Refugee Program and private sponsorship programs. The JAS program extends the normal sponsorship commitment of 12 months up to 24 months for special needs refugees, or 36 months in exceptional cases because of the extra care required for special needs cases.

Under the JAS program, the responsibilities for sponsorship are shared between CIC and private sponsors. CIC provides the financial assistance necessary to meet basic resettlement costs, such as food, shelter, clothing and essential household goods. The private sponsor provides the human contact of ongoing guidance, orientation to the community, help with language skills and job searches, and friendship.

Sponsorship Application Process

Anyone interested in becoming a sponsor should begin by reading the *Guide to the Private Sponsorship of Refugees Program*, available on the CIC website at www.cic .gc.ca/english/pdf/pub/ref-sponsor.pdf. It provides information about sponsorship opportunities and processes.

If the sponsor does not have a particular refugee in mind, a match form may be requested from CIC, and the sponsor will be provided with the following documents:

- *Request for a Refugee Profile* guide (IMM 5496)
- Request for a Refugee Profile application (IMM 5438)
- Use of a Representative form (IMM 5476).

There is a separate sponsorship application kit for each type of private sponsorship, namely, Group of Five, community sponsor, and SAH/CG. Generally, the sponsoring group must submit the application, an undertaking, and a financial and settlement plan to its local CIC branch. The following are a list of the different guides and forms included in each of the sponsorship kits:

1. Group of Five

   - *Refugee Sponsorship Application—Group of Five* guide (IMM 5414)
   - Undertaking/Application to Sponsor—Groups of Five form (IMM 5373)
   - Sponsor Assessment form (IMM 5492)
   - Settlement Plan and Financial Assessment—Group of Five form (IMM 5373A)
   - Financial Profile—Group of Five form (IMM 5373B)
   - Document Checklist—Group of Five form (IMM 5437)
   - Use of a Representative form (IMM 5476).

2. Community Sponsors

   - *Refugee Sponsorship Application—Community Sponsors* guide (IMM 5513E)
   - Undertaking/Application to Sponsor—Community Sponsors form (IMM 5514)
   - Settlement Plan and Financial Assessment—Community Sponsors form (IMM 5515E)
   - Sponsor Assessment form (IMM 5492)
   - Document Checklist—Community Sponsors form (IMM 5517)
   - Use of a Representative form (IMM 5476).

3. Sponsorship Agreement Holders or Constituent Groups

- *Refugee Sponsorship Application—Sponsorship Agreement Holders and Constituent Groups* guide (IMM 5413)

- Undertaking/Application to Sponsor Sponsorship Agreement Holders and Constituent Groups form (IMM 5439)

- Settlement Plan—Sponsorship Agreement Holder or Constituent Group form (IMM 5440)

- Sponsor Assessment form (IMM 5492)

- Document Checklist—Sponsorship Agreement Holders and Constituent Groups form (IMM 5441)

- Use of a Representative form (IMM 5476).

The sponsorship application is assessed by CIC, to determine whether the applicant for sponsorship meets the eligibility criteria, and to ensure that there is no bar to the applicant's becoming a sponsor, such as default of a child support obligation, or certain criminal offences and immigration violations, as described in s. 156(1) of the IRP Regulations. If the applicant for sponsorship is approved, CIC sends an approval letter to the sponsor, and provides information about how long it will take to process the refugee's application.

The refugee application is then processed. As explained earlier, this begins with an assessment by a visa officer, involving an interview, medical examination, and criminal and security checks. If the refugee application is approved, the refugee receives a visa to travel to Canada for permanent residence. Travel arrangements are generally made through the IOM. The sponsor receives a **Notice of Arrival** with information about the refugee's arrival in Canada.

NOTES

1. Citizenship and Immigration Canada, *Facts and Figures 2007: Immigration Overview—Permanent and Temporary Residents*, 2008, www.cic.gc.ca/english/resources/statistics/facts2007/index.asp.

2. United Nations High Commissioner for Refugees, *2007 Global Trends: Refugees, Asylum-seekers, Returnees, Internally Displaced and Stateless Persons*, June 2008, www.unhcr.org/statistics.html.

3. This certificate is issued to an applicant who meets Quebec's provincial selection criteria.

4. In exceptional cases, a person can have direct access to the program, through self-referral, when the minister has identified a specific geographic area as having a high number of refugees. For example, recent programs include the resettlement of Karen refugees living in remote camps in Thailand, beginning in 2006, and the resettlement of up to 5,000 Bhutanese refugees beginning in 2008.

5. Citizenship and Immigration Canada, "OP 5: Overseas Selection and Processing of Convention Refugees Abroad Class and Members of the Humanitarian-Protected Persons Abroad Classes," in *Overseas Processing (OP)*, s. 13.13, August 4, 2006, www.cic.gc.ca/english/resources/publications/index.asp.

REFERENCES: LEGISLATION AND REGULATIONS

Immigration and Refugee Protection Act

Immigration and Refugee Protection Act. S.C. 2001, c. 27.

Part 1: Immigration to Canada—Division 4—Inadmissibility, ss. 34 to 38.

Part 2: Refugee Protection—Division 1—Refugee Protection, Convention Refugees and Persons in Need of Protection, ss. 95(1)(a), 99(1) and (2) (governed by Part 1: ss. 11(1), 12(3), 13(2) and (3)).

Immigration and Refugee Protection Regulations

Immigration and Refugee Protection Regulations. S.O.R./2002-227.

Part 8: Refugee Classes—Division 1—Convention Refugees Abroad and Humanitarian-Protected Persons Abroad:

Definition—general, s. 138

Definition—Convention refugees abroad class, ss. 144 and 145

Definition—humanitarian-protected persons abroad class, s. 146

Member of the country of asylum class, s. 147

Member of the source country class, s. 148 and schedule 2 of the Immigration and Refugee Protection Regulations (list of source countries)

Application procedures, referral, s. 150

Part 8: Refugee Classes—Division 2—Convention Refugees Abroad and Humanitarian-Protected Persons Abroad.

Sponsorship, ss. 152, 153, and 156

"Special needs," defined, s. 157

REFERENCES: GENERAL

Citizenship and Immigration Canada. *Annual Report to Parliament on Immigration 2007*. 2007. www.cic.gc.ca/english/resources/publications/index.asp.

Citizenship and Immigration Canada. *Facts and Figures 2006: Immigration Overview—Permanent and Temporary Residents*. 2007. www.cic.gc.ca/english/resources/publications/index.asp.

Citizenship and Immigration Canada. *Guide to the Private Sponsorship of Refugees Program*. 2003. www.cic.gc.ca/english/pdf/pub/ref-sponsor.pdf.

Citizenship and Immigration Canada. *Refugee Sponsorship Application—Community Sponsors*. May 2008. www.cic.gc.ca/english/pdf/kits/guides/5513e.pdf.

Citizenship and Immigration Canada. *Refugee Sponsorship Application—Group of Five*. May 2008. www.cic.gc.ca/english/pdf/kits/guides/5414e.pdf.

Citizenship and Immigration Canada. *Refugee Sponsorship Application—Sponsorship Agreement Holders and Constituent Groups*. May 2008. www.cic.gc.ca/english/pdf/kits/guides/5413e.pdf.

Citizenship and Immigration Canada. *Request for a Refugee Profile*. May 2008. www.cic.gc.ca/english/pdf/kits/guides/5496e.pdf.

REVIEW QUESTIONS

1. What is the role of the UNHCR in refugee resettlement to Canada?
2. Briefly describe the Convention refugees abroad class.
3. Briefly describe the country of asylum class.
4. Briefly describe the source country class.
5. Find and list the countries on the source country list in schedule 2 of the IRP Regulations.
6. How does a refugee apply for resettlement?
7. The Government-Assisted Refugee Program is for special needs refugees. Briefly describe the types of special needs cases that qualify and describe the features of the program.
8. Who are private sponsors and how can they sponsor a refugee? What are their responsibilities?
9. What is the Joint Assistance Sponsorship program?

CHAPTER 9

In-Canada Refugee Determination Process

LEARNING OBJECTIVES

After reading this chapter you should be able to:

- Identify the main federal organizations involved in the in-Canada refugee determination process.
- Describe front-end processing and the application eligibility criteria.
- Be aware of important timelines in the refugee determination process.
- Work with the Personal Information Form and other forms.
- Describe a refugee claimant's rights and responsibilities.
- Understand the role and responsibilities of participants in the refugee hearing process.
- Know about the pre-removal risk assessment program.
- Understand post-determination options for the refugee claimant.

INTRODUCTION

By now you should have an understanding of the legal basis for providing refugee protection in Canada. You know the difference between someone who has a choice to leave her homeland and someone who is forced to flee. You also know that a person must have the legal permission to enter Canada by either having a right to enter and remain, such as a Canadian citizen or permanent resident, or have authorization to enter temporarily as a temporary resident, such as a visitor, business visitor, or student.

What happens when a person arrives at the border who does not fit into one of these categories, and who alleges to have been forced to flee her homeland? Refugees are not selected: people come to Canada seeking protection from being returned to a country where they are at risk. If protection is granted, this may lead to granting the right to remain permanently in Canada.

Refugee claimants are known as "spontaneous arrivals" because they have not gone through any immigration assessment processes and have no prior approval from Canadian authorities: protection is granted *later* without regard to the refugee's origin, ability to speak English or French, ability for self-sufficiency, future contribution to the economy, ability to integrate, or family ties. Consequently, refugees are oftentimes portrayed as illegal migrants and abusers of the immigration process or criticized for using the back door to gain entry. Some people have the perception that refugees are "queue jumpers" or "bogus claimants" or "illegal refugees" and "a burden on our social systems." The motivation or intent of genuine refugees who arrive at our borders is rooted in a desire to escape human rights violations rather than just a desire for economic betterment. Unlike immigrants who make a considered decision to leave their homelands, refugees do not have a choice: they are forced to flee because of some serious risk to their life or because they are victims of human rights abuses and cannot safely return home. The fundamental difference, therefore, between an "illegal migrant," "immigrant," or "economic migrant" and a refugee is that a refugee needs protection.

In this chapter we examine the process for making a claim for refugee protection. More specifically, we provide an overview of the steps that a refugee claimant takes during the determination process, the decision that is made about the claim, and, more importantly, the decision about whether or not the person is allowed to stay in Canada. This process involves many players and organizations, including the following:

- Citizenship and Immigration Canada (CIC) and its officials, whose role in the process is primarily related to immigration;

- the Canada Border Services Agency (CBSA), whose role in the process is primarily related to enforcement and security functions;

- the Immigration and Refugee Board (IRB), which processes the refugee claims and makes the determination about refugee status; and

- the participants, such as the refugee claimant and counsel.

As you learn about the process, you will no doubt be able to refer to exceptional cases where "failed refugee claimants" years later are still fighting removal or where some refugees have long waits to stabilize their status. It is beyond the scope of this text to describe every possible circumstance; therefore, the processes in a typical case are described. In a typical case, the following processes are used:

- front-end process and the refugee application (CIC, CBSA)

- refugee determination processes (IRB, CIC)

- post–determination processes (CIC, Federal Court).

FRONT-END PROCESS

Consider a refugee who flees his homeland because his life is at risk. Somehow he chooses Canada—he might have relatives or friends here, he might have heard that it is a safe haven, he may have paid a smuggler and "ended up here." Or he may have come here as a temporary resident and then learned that the conditions in his country of origin changed, causing him to fear returning (in which case he is a refugee *sur place*).

The people who make refugee claims in Canada have different motivations for doing so: there are those who are seeking protection, as in the cases above, those who are trying to improve their situations, and even those who are evading legal immigration processes. Although the port of entry officials do not decide the legitimacy of a refugee claim, they do have the authority to manage access to the refugee determination process: not every person is allowed to make a claim to protection in Canada.

The front-end process serves to screen people early in the determination process to control who may have his claim heard by the IRB's Refugee Protection Division (RPD) and who shall be denied access; furthermore, it serves to filter out potential security and criminal cases. CIC officials assess admissibility and eligibility and decide who should have access to the RPD. Security screening is initiated at the time that a claim is made. CBSA officials work with the Canadian Security Intelligence Service (CSIS) to conduct security screening and criminality checks. How does the process of making a refugee claim begin?

Initial Application

In all cases, the process of making a refugee claim begins with an initial **application**, which must be accepted by an officer. Unlike many of CIC's application processes that are done through mail-in services, the refugee determination process must be initiated in person. Refugee claimants apply at a port of entry or at an inland office to provide information to an officer in one of the following manners:

- orally, in an interview;

- in writing, by application form; or

- through a combination of oral interview and written application form.

To prevent the refugee system from being used by non-refugees as a last-ditch effort to avoid removal, a refugee claim may not be initiated after a removal order is made. However, a claim may be made at any point in the immigration process up to the time that a removal order is made, in either of the following ways:

- at a port of entry—for example, land border or airport; or

- by notifying an immigration officer at an inland immigration office.

Generally, at the port of entry, the application process commences at the time of the primary examination by an officer (oral interview). The purpose of the "application" (interview and/or application form) is to provide basic personal information, such as name, date of birth, country of origin, telephone number, address, language spoken, and detailed background information.

If the claimant does not speak English or French, the officer will attempt to find an interpreter so that the refugee claimant will be able to understand and communicate during the officer's examination. Generally, refugee claimants are not represented by counsel[1] at this stage of the process.

In the following case scenario, Mr. M makes an oral application at a port of entry, an airport.

Mr. M arrives by air at one of Canada's international airports on a cold day in February. He hasn't slept in 48 hours—he's too nervous, too afraid he will be sent back. From his window in the airplane, he could see that the ground was covered in white but it wasn't sand like back home; the ground staff wore ear muffs and large mitts—he could see their breath. He was confident he knew what he was doing; leaving was the only way to save his life. Soon, he hopes he can send for his wife and children. He practised for hours the only words he knows in English: "Please give me asylum. I am a refugee." Mr. M follows the passengers off the plane, finally arriving in a large room where line-ups form in front of officials in booths. Mr. M suddenly feels weak and begins perspiring. He clutches the passport he bought from some man named Samir, who got it from someone else; it cost nearly a month's wages. When it is his turn at the booth, he hands the passport, the customs declaration card, and his ticket stub to the official, a woman in a dark uniform. The woman looks at Mr. M then back at the photo; she doesn't smile; she says something but Mr. M doesn't understand. A woman, he thinks, what does she know? I need to talk to a man. The officer is staring at him coldly now, so Mr. M moves in closer and quietly says, "Please, asylum, refugee." The woman is talking again; she doesn't smile. Mr. M just shakes his head, not understanding; he wonders whether he should give her some money; he has a little. Then he notices that she is directing him to another official. He is escorted to a bright, windowless room.

In Mr. M's case, after all his information has been taken by the officer, his application will be considered complete. The process starts when the "application" is received by the officer (s. 99(3) of the *Immigration and Refugee Protection Act*).

The process may vary at an inland office. A person may be a legal visitor or may be without any legal status when she appears at the CIC office to make a claim for protection. Generally, the refugee claimant is provided with forms and may be interviewed or asked to report back to the office at a later date with the completed forms.

In both situations, after the application is completed, the officer has three days to determine eligibility.

In our case scenario, Mr. M will undergo an examination by the officer to determine the following:

- his identity,

- his admissibility; and

- his eligibility.

The officer creates a file and assigns a Client ID number. The Client ID number must be used when communicating with CIC about any matter related to the file.

Generally, at the port of entry and during the interview, the officer considers both admissibility and eligibility at the same time. The claimant, such as Mr. M, is photographed and fingerprinted. The officer conducts a search in various databases for information (for example, previous immigration file, criminality checks, and outstanding warrants for arrest) as a part of the background and criminality checking process. Mr. M must surrender all identity documents, including passport, travel documents, and birth and baptismal certificates. He will receive certified copies.

Criteria

ADMISSIBILITY

Typically, when a refugee claimant makes a claim at a port of entry, he is considered inadmissible because he came to Canada with the intent of remaining in Canada without permanent resident status. Therefore, an inadmissibility report, titled A44(1) admissibility report, is prepared and a **conditional removal order** is issued (for more information about inadmissibility see Chapter 3, "Inadmissibility").

When a claim is made inland, however, the officer must consider whether the claimant is inadmissible or still *in status*, meaning that the refugee claimant may be in Canada as a temporary resident. The conditional removal order comes into effect in any of the following circumstances:

- the claim is refused and all further steps have been exhausted;[2]

- the claimant abandons the claim; or

- the claimant withdraws the claim.

The conditional removal order may also specify terms and conditions (such as a requirement to report a change of address or to appear for all hearings and other matters, or a prohibition against working). The removal order is "conditional" upon the outcome of the claim for protection. When the refugee claimant is granted protected status, the conditional removal order has no force or effect. Should the claimant be refused protection, the removal takes effect and the claimant must leave Canada.

The officer also considers whether to detain a refugee claimant, generally when the claimant does not have any identity documents or when there are "reasonable grounds to believe" that the claimant is inadmissible because of serious criminality or security reasons. A refugee claimant who is detained must be advised of the right to counsel. If the officer decides to detain Mr. M—for example, because the officer believes that his passport is not legitimate or his identity is in question—it is at this point that he would be informed of his right to counsel.

According to s. 103 of the IRPA, if there are allegations that a refugee claimant is inadmissible because of criminality or security risk, the case is "suspended" either because the allegations need to be argued before a member of the Immigration Division or because the officer considers it necessary to await a decision of a court. (See Chapter 10: "Enforcement Procedures," for further details about the ID hearing process.)

ELIGIBILITY

Determination of eligibility answers the question, "Will this claim be considered?" It is not a decision about whether the claim is valid or whether the claimant is in need of protection. The officer only has authority to decide whether the claimant may seek a hearing before the Refugee Protection Division. As in all immigration matters, the refugee claimant is duty bound to answer all questions truthfully and produce all documents and information as requested (ss. 16 and 100(4) of the IRPA).

Mr. M's claim would be referred to the Refugee Protection Division once the officer finds that he is "eligible." Under the IRPA, officers have three working days to make their eligibility decision; otherwise, the claim is deemed to be referred to the RPD.

A claim is ineligible to be referred to the Refugee Protection Division under the following criteria listed in s. 101 of the IRPA:

- the claimant has been determined to be inadmissible on grounds of security, violating human or international rights, serious criminality, or organized criminality;

- the claimant has been recognized as a refugee under the 1951 Convention Relating to the Status of Refugees (Convention refugee) by a country other than Canada and can be sent or returned to that country;

- the claimant came to Canada through a third country designated by the regulations as a "safe third country";[3] or

- the claimant made a previous refugee claim in Canada and that claim was either accepted, rejected, deemed ineligible, withdrawn, or abandoned.

As in all immigration matters, the refugee claimant is duty bound to answer all questions truthfully and produce all documents and information as requested (ss. 16 and 100(4) of the IRPA).

Refugee claimants whose claims are ineligible will not be referred to the Refugee Protection Division. For example, if Mr. M is found to be inadmissible on grounds of security, violating human or international rights, serious criminality or organized criminality, this would preclude him from eligibility according to the criteria above and he would not be permitted to take his case for refugee status to the Refugee Protection Division.

When a claimant is found to be ineligible, the immigration officer issues an *ineligibility notice* and provides the refugee claimant with a conditional removal order. The officer also decides whether the refugee claimant is entitled to a pre-removal risk assessment (see below under the heading "Pre-removal Risk Assessment" for further discussion).

Although few refugee claimants exercise this right, in some circumstances claimants may apply to the Federal Court for judicial review of an unfavourable eligibility decision, on the basis of procedural unfairness.

Returning to our scenario, if Mr. M is found to be eligible, he would be referred to the Refugee Protection Division to have his case for refugee status heard. Refugee claimants who are found eligible or deemed eligible (automatic after three working days) are referred to the Refugee Protection Division. The immigration officer issues the "eligibility notice" and provides the refugee claimant with a number of documents such as the following:

- a copy of the admissibility report (A44(1) report)

- a copy of the removal order, along with any conditions

- a copy of the officer's interview notes

- certified copies of any travel or identity documents that were seized and a "seizure" form

- a Notice to Appear at the RPD

- medical forms and instructions (to complete medical examinations)

- an Interim Federal Health letter and instructions.[4]

The claimant is also given an information package related to preparing for the refugee hearing, which includes the following:

- a Personal Information Form (PIF) with instructions for the refugee claimant to complete and send it to the RPD within 28 days;[5]

- a list of immigrant and community services; and

- a list of non-governmental organizations (NGOs) that assist refugee claimants.

These documents are provided to the refugee claimant in English or French, except possibly for the lists of services and NGOs, which may be produced in some regions in foreign languages.

Occasionally, after the claim has been referred to the RPD, CIC will become aware of information that would have made the claimant ineligible to proceed with the claim. In such cases, proceedings before the Refugee Protection Division are terminated, or, if a determination has already been made, it is nullified (s. 104(2) of the IRPA).

SAFE THIRD COUNTRY AGREEMENT

The Safe Third Country Agreement rests on the general principle that a refugee claimant should make a claim in the first safe country in which she is physically present, unless she qualifies for an exception to the Agreement. The United States is the only country to be designated as a **safe third country** for the purposes of the IRPA (s. 101(1)(e)). This is because Canada and the United States signed the Agreement Between Canada and the United States of America for Cooperation in the Examination of Refugee Status Claims from Nationals of Third Countries on December 5, 2002. (Final Canadian regulations were published in Part II of the *Canada Gazette* on November 3, 2004.)

The Agreement covers refugee claimants who are seeking entry to Canada from the United States at Canada–US land border crossings by train or at airports (for example, if the person is a failed refugee claimant in the United States who is in transit through Canada and had been deported from the United States).

As a result, most refugee claimants who pass through the United States on their way to Canada are not eligible to make a claim in Canada.[6] Instead, they must make their claim in the United States. CBSA officers have a primary role in carrying out the provisions of the Agreement.

On November 29, 2007, the Federal Court ruled that the December 2004 Safe Third Country Agreement between Canada and the United States violated refugee rights and made an order quashing the designation of the United States as a safe third country. On January 31, 2008, the Federal Court of Appeal granted a stay of the order while the Canadian government appeals the case. In the interim, there is no change in policy or procedures at the border—the safe third country rules continue to apply.

Security Screening

Security screening is conducted for all refugee claimants. Front-end security screening is used to identify people who pose potential security and criminal risks to Canada and restrict their access to the refugee determination system. In our example, Mr. M is fingerprinted and photographed and his travel and other identity documents are seized: this is part of the security screening process.

Security screenings are conducted in partnership with the CBSA and CSIS. The CBSA is responsible for coordinating and informing the IRB when security screenings are completed.

Although the RPD's mandate is to schedule and finalize refugee hearings as quickly and fairly as possible, the RPD must defer a hearing up to one year from referral unless the CBSA confirms that front-end security screening is completed. At the time of writing, the screening was completed for most refugee claimants within 54 days of referral.

Referral of the Claim to the Refugee Protection Division

Recall that under the IRPA, officers have three working days to make their decision whether or not to refer a claim. If the officer takes no action, after the three days pass, the claim is deemed to be referred. According to rule 3 of the Refugee Protection Division Rules, the officer must notify the RPD about the date that the PIF was provided and provide copies of the refugee claimant's identity and travel documents as well as a copy of the interview notes. These documents form the basis of the file with the RPD.

Let us suppose that Mr. M has been referred to the RPD, where he will have the opportunity to explain why he needs protection. Mr. M will be provided with an information package containing the Personal Information Form. This may be given to him personally, if the decision to refer him was made in person, or by mail. The Notice to Appear will contain the RPD file number.

Accommodation, Work, and Study

The next step is to find accommodation. If the refugee claimant does not have a place to live with relatives or community members, the officer will make a referral to local social service agencies. Refugees without funds are entitled to social assistance.

Most refugee claimants want to work; however, to be authorized to work they must be in need of a job—that is, they must not be economically self-sufficient—and they must meet the following criteria:

- complete and pass medical examinations;

- file the Personal Information Form, on time, with the RPD;

- comply with all notices; and

- apply for authorization to work as described in Chapter 4, "Temporary Entry."

Refugee claimants who wish to study must apply for a student authorization; they are not exempt from the obligation to have a study permit, even for a short-term course or program of study. To obtain the study authorization, the claimant must obtain a letter of acceptance from the educational institution and apply as described in Chapter 4.

REFUGEE DETERMINATION PROCESSES

There are a number of different types of proceedings before the RPD, each with a different purpose. The refugee claimant may need to participate in one or more of the following proceedings:

- **Conference.** At a conference, the claimant (and/or counsel) meets with the RPD member prior to the hearing, to discuss issues, relevant facts, and any other matter for the purpose of making the hearing more fair and efficient.

- **Application.** On an application before the RPD, prior to or during the main hearing, the claimant (or counsel) asks the RPD to make a decision on a specific matter—for example, on a request for additional time to complete the PIF or to change the date or time of a hearing.

- **Hearing.** A hearing is a process whereby the claimant appears in person before a member of the Division (with or without counsel) to present evidence and testimony and to answer questions related to his claim.

- **Interview.** The interview is part of the fast track process whereby the claimant appears before a refugee protection officer, rather than a member, to answer questions related to his claim. It is less formal and more expeditious than a hearing.

The refugee determination process begins when the RPD receives a Notice of Referral from CIC. This referral gives the RPD the jurisdiction to hear the claim and starts the clock for counting the days that the case is with the RPD. In our scenario, the RPD must also wait for notification from the CBSA that Mr. M has been cleared by the front-end security screening process, before it schedules his case for a hearing.

After the referral, the RPD creates a file and issues a file ID number that is unique to the claimant. The RPD file number is the reference to be used in all communications with the RPD about matters related to the case. Note that the RPD file number is not the same as the Client ID number issued by CIC. Always use the appropriate number when communicating with CIC or the RPD on behalf of the refugee claimant.

Rules and Policies

The chairperson has the authority, as provided in s. 161 of the IRPA, to make rules related to the RPD's activities, practices, and procedures, in consultation with the deputy chairpersons and the director general of the Immigration Division, subject to the approval of the governor in council. These rules are binding, and it is important to know them well. Failure to comply with the rules may have severe consequences to claimants and their counsel.

Sometimes a flexible, non-binding approach is more appropriate than rigid rules that must be followed in all circumstances. Policy instruments, as described in Chapter 1, "Introduction," serve this purpose by providing guidance to those who need it, while not demanding compliance. Counsel are wise to familiarize themselves with these policy instruments, despite their non-binding nature. An awareness of policies will better able counsel to serve clients efficiently and effectively.

REFUGEE PROTECTION DIVISION RULES

The Refugee Protection Division Rules[7] are regulations under the IRPA that define roles and responsibilities, and govern practices and procedures in matters brought before the RPD. The RPD Rules are a "how to" for processing a claim, from the time of referral to the resolution and closing of the file. There are 71 rules and two schedules governing practices and procedures. For example, the Rules require that applications and most communications be made in writing, within time limits, and usually with proof that all parties have been copied.

Immigration consultants who represent claimants in RPD proceedings must have a thorough knowledge of the Rules, in addition to the provisions of the IRPA that set out the jurisdiction of the IRB and the RPD to hear and decide cases for refugee protection. The Rules are listed in the IRPA's table of contents under "Related Regulations," and may be accessed at various websites including the IRB website, the Department of Justice website, and the CanLII website. An immigration consultant who is unsure about the meaning or application of a particular rule may direct questions and requests for clarification to the registrar's staff, such as the deputy registrar or case officer, at the nearest business office of the IRB. (See the Appendix for a list of IRB office locations.)

Compliance with the RPD Rules by everyone involved is intended to lead to fair and consistent resolution of matters before the RPD. However, when the Rules were drafted, it was not possible to predict every possible scenario that might arise in the future, so the Rules provide the RPD with the necessary flexibility to address new concerns. Consider the following examples:

- The RPD may do "whatever is necessary" to deal with a matter, according to rule 68.

- Members of the RPD may act on their own initiative to change a rule, to excuse a person from a rule, or to extend or shorten time limits, according to rule 69.

- Failure to follow a rule in a proceeding does not, in itself, make the proceeding invalid, according to rule 70.

In this way, the Rules attempt to strike a balance between the value of predictability and consistency, and the need to make adjustments to meet the particular needs of individual cases. Many rules are referenced within this chapter; however, many others are not. It is important to review and understand all the rules before representing a client before the RPD.

POLICY INSTRUMENTS

When circumstances arise that are not addressed by the *Immigration and Refugee Protection Act*, its regulations, or the RPD Rules, the board and its chairperson have authority under the IRPA to address these gaps through policy instruments. Policy instruments may relate to the following functions:

- adjudication—the decision-making process;

- operations and administration—the management of cases and procedures; and

- legal practices—the provision of legal support functions to the RPD.

There are several types of policy instruments that guide RPD procedures, in addition to the binding RPD Rules, such as chairperson's guidelines, policies, chairperson's instructions, policy notes, jurisprudential guides, and identified persuasive decisions. All policy instruments are available on the IRB website. Some policy instruments are general in application, and others are specific to the RPD. Familiarity with policy instruments will provide counsel with confidence when navigating RPD processes.

Chairperson's Guidelines

The chairperson's guidelines are a source of guiding principles for members to manage cases. They may have an adjudicative or operational content. The chairperson has the authority pursuant to s. 159(1)(h) of the IRPA to issue guidelines for the RPD related to the following:

- specific legal issues;

- questions of mixed fact and law;

- procedure; and

- the preferred approach to the exercise of discretion.

The chairperson has issued seven separate guidelines for the RPD, as follows, and which can be reviewed on the IRB website:

- Guideline 1—Civilian Non-Combatants Fearing Persecution in Civil War Situations

- Guideline 3—Child Refugee Claimants: Procedural and Evidentiary Issues

- Guideline 4—Women Refugee Claimants Fearing Gender-Related Persecution

- Guideline 5—Providing the PIF and No PIF Abandonment in the Refugee Protection Division

- Guideline 6—Scheduling and Changing the Date or Time of a Proceeding in the Refugee Protection Division

- Guideline 7—Concerning Preparation and Conduct of a Hearing in the Refugee Protection Division

- Guideline 8—Guideline on Procedures with Respect to Vulnerable Persons Appearing Before the Immigration and Refugee Board of Canada.

Guidelines are not binding and members are not specifically directed to follow the guidelines. This is important to preserve the independent nature of the member's role in making decisions. However, members are expected to consider the guidelines, and either apply them or provide a reason for not doing so.

Policies

Unlike the chairperson's guidelines, RPD policies are used to communicate with claimants and their counsel about initiatives of the RPD. Policies formalize administrative and operational procedures for the management of refugee claims, and the related responsibilities of members and staff at the RPD. Policies governing the practices of the RPD are as follows:

- Fast Track Policy: Hearings Process

- Fast Track Policy: Expedited Process

- Policy on the Transfer of Files for Hearings by Videoconference (Refugee Protection Division)

- Policy for Producing Country of Origin National Documentation Packages

- Policy on the Treatment of Unsolicited Information in the Refugee Protection Division

- Policy on Document Harmonization in Support of Jurisprudential Guides

- Reasons Review Policy.

Generally, a portion of the policy statement will contain a mandatory element (policy statement) while other parts will be flexible enough to accommodate differences among the regional business offices and allow the required exercise of discretion by decision makers.

Chairperson's Instructions

Chairperson's instructions are formal instructions to IRB personnel about a specific practice and/or organizational concern. There are currently three sets of instructions that direct the actions of the Refugee Protection Division:

- Instructions for Gathering and Disclosing Information for Refugee Protection Division Proceedings

- Instructions Governing the Management of Refugee Protection Claims Awaiting Front End Security Screening

- Instructions Governing Communication in the Absence of Parties Between Members of the Refugee Protection Division and Refugee Protection

Officers and Between Members of the Refugee Protection Division and Other Employees of the Board.

Policy Notes

A policy note is the same as a memorandum and it is generally issued by a single business office to communicate with the members, staff, and the public (claimants and counsel) about a particular operational matter in that local office.

Jurisprudential Guides

The chairperson has the authority to issue jurisprudential guides for the RPD, pursuant to s. 159(1)(h) of the IRPA. Jurisprudential guides are issued as a tool to build a source of jurisprudence, based on member decisions that the RPD considers well reasoned. Jurisprudential guides serve to assist the members in adjudicating cases that share essential similarities, and to encourage consistency in decision making. However, members are not bound by them. Although members are expected to provide an explanation if they choose not to follow these cases, they are not binding precedent.

Persuasive Decisions

Persuasive decisions are similar to jurisprudential guides. A decision that is designated as a "persuasive decision" is selected for its value to assist other members in a consistent application of questions of law, or of mixed law and fact. The difference is that members who choose not to follow these decisions are not required to provide a reason.

Before the Proceeding

INTERPRETER SERVICES

At the time of referral of the claim to the RPD, the claimant will be directed to community organizations, such as community legal clinics, and settlement and newcomer agencies, which provide referrals, advice, and language assistance. Many community organizations have interpreters on staff or as volunteers in order to assist with the variety of linguistic skills required by refugee claimants.

Most refugee claimants do not speak English or French, so unless counsel speaks the claimant's language, the interview should be conducted through an interpreter. It is preferable not to use a family member or friend for this purpose, because they will not likely understand the legal terminology, or the consequences of omitting or embellishing information, and they may paraphrase or put their own spin on the claimant's statements.

When meeting with the refugee claimant, counsel should ensure that the interpreter is not providing information to the claimant, but rather translating only the information being presented by counsel and interpreting it as accurately as possible.

In cases where the claimant has experienced a traumatic event such as rape, the presence of family members or friends may inhibit the claimant from describing the event. However, if a claimant wishes to have a friend or relative present for moral support, she may do so. It is important to reassure the refugee claimant that information will be kept confidential, that their case, including the file and hearing, are closed to the public, and that the RPD will not share the information with representatives of their country of nationality.

When an interpreter is used to help translate the PIF and documents for the refugee claimant, the interpreter must sign and date the "Interpreter's declaration" on page 13 of the PIF, according to rule 5 of the RPD Rules. The claimant identifies her language and dialect on the PIF and indicates whether an interpreter will be required at future proceedings.

If the refugee claimant's language and dialect are different from what is stated on the PIF, the RPD must be notified in writing no later than 20 days before the hearing, according to rule 14. This rule also requires that the RPD be notified if an interpreter will be required to enable a witness to testify on behalf of the claimant. At the beginning of a proceeding, the interpreter must take an oath or make a solemn affirmation to interpret the proceeding accurately, also according to rule 14.

INFORMATION PACKAGE

Upon referral of the claim to the RPD, an information package is sent to the claimant containing a letter explaining the referral, a blank Personal Information Form to be completed, and a copy of each of the following documents:

- a Notice to Appear at the RPD (this document will contain the claimant's RPD file number),

- a copy of the inadmissibility report A44(1),

- a copy of the removal order and conditions,

- a copy of the eligibility document,

- copies of the claimant's identity, travel documents, and any seized documents,

- the port of entry (POE) or CIC officer's interview notes, and

- a photocopy of any written declaration by the refugee claimant.

These documents are useful in completing the PIF, because they help to capture the complete history of the claim. The refugee claimant's document package should be reviewed as soon as counsel accepts the case in order to comply with important and often tight deadlines.

IMPORTANT DEADLINES

The RPD Rules require that certain activities occur within certain time limits. Before taking on a refugee case, counsel first must consider both the time requirements of the RPD and the time necessary to carefully go over the client's information. For example, Mr. M's counsel must consider the many issues to overcome, such as communication barriers and Mr. M's ability to relive events, before deciding to take on Mr. M's case.

Counsel is expected to comply with the filing provisions of 28 days, so it is important to determine when "the clock started" on the case—that is, the date of receipt of the blank PIF by the claimant. There are three immediate and important deadlines that must be met, as follows:

1. *10 days after receiving PIF—Claimant Contact Information Form.* The Claimant Contact Information Form must be filed with the IRB's registry no later than 10 days after the refugee claimant received the blank Personal Information Form. This ensures that the RPD is able to contact the claimant for any matter, including notices, interviews, and hearings.

2. *28 days after receiving PIF—Personal Information Form.* The original and two copies of the Personal Information Form must be filed within 28 days of the claimant receiving the form, according to s. 6 of the RPD Rules. Failure to file the PIF may result in the claim being declared abandoned, according to rule 58(1)(a) of the Refugee Protection Division Rules. However, if the PIF cannot be completed within the 28 days, an application may be made for an extension of time under rule 6(2).

3. *20 days before hearing—changes to PIF.* Any changes to the PIF must be submitted 20 days before the hearing, in three copies and underlined, according to ss. 6(4), 29(4), and 30 of the RPD Rules.

THE RECORD

The RPD opens a claimant's file with the Notice of Referral and adds copies of the port of entry or officer's interview notes as set out in schedule 2 of the Refugee Protection Division Rules. Documents are added to the file as they are received by the RPD, and comprise the **record**. The record is the part of the file that will be before the decision maker when the case is considered, and includes the following documents:

- Claimant Contact Information Form,

- change of address notifications, if any,

- Notice of Representation Without a Fee or Counsel Contact Information Form (from counsel),

- Personal Information Form,

- List of Claimant's Documents form,

- list of minister's documents form (from the minister's representative, if the minister is intervening in the case),

- copies of any notices sent by the RPD,

- copies of any other correspondence, and

- any documents disclosed.

Like Mr. M, many refugee applicants do not communicate well in English or French, and need help to understand the numerous forms and documents. One of the important roles of counsel is to take the time to explain the purpose and importance of the various documents and forms, especially the PIF—the most important form.

It is also counsel's role to identify those documents required as evidence to support the claims made, and to double-check facts as much as possible to ensure that they support the claims made.

The Personal Information Form

The Personal Information Form is the key document in the refugee determination process. It presents the RPD with the first glimpse at the claimant's case. In our example, Mr. M is required to complete the PIF and file it with the RPD before he can apply for a work or student authorization. The Division uses the information in the PIF to achieve the following objectives:

- identify the key issues in the case;

- make decisions about scheduling the claim (conference, interview, hearing);

- collect information about the claimant's country conditions;

- disclose any required information or documents to the minister of CIC; and

- provide information at the hearing.

Rule 3 directs an officer (either CIC or CBSA) to inform the RPD in writing about the method of service of the PIF to the claimant, and to provide the Division with copies of travel, identity, and other documents. It also compels the officer to provide information required by schedule 2, also known as *port of entry notes* or the *officer's notes*.

Rule 1 of the Refugee Protection Division Rules defines the PIF, and schedule 1 describes the content required for the PIF. This form is available online at www.irb-cisr.gc.ca (under the Forms tab) and may be completed electronically. As counsel, you will want to know when and how the PIF was provided to your client so that you can submit it on time to the RPD.

Refugee claimants already face language and cultural barriers; they are not expected to be experts on refugee law; and the PIF can be confusing for them. Consequently, counsel's help to complete the PIF can be invaluable to the refugee claimant. For example, Mr. M's counsel can help Mr. M to develop a complete background, including family history, education, employment, and military service; and a logical and chronological history of events that gave rise to his fear and flight, such as dates of activities, arrests, travel history within the country, departure, and travel outside of the country.

> *When Mr. M met with his counsel, he was resentful and impatient about having to provide such personal details. He couldn't understand why the people at the refugee board wanted to know the same information he'd already given the other officials at CIC. He was also worried about what the Canadian government officials would do with the information. Would it be shared with officials of his country?*

Mr. M's counsel should explain the purpose and importance of the PIF—that it tells his story and can help him through the hearing process that is to follow. It is worthwhile to spend the time necessary to make the PIF as complete, accurate, and persuasive as possible. Also, because refugee claimants will not necessarily understand that the Refugee Protection Division is separate and independent from other government departments and officials, it is important for counsel to reassure clients such as Mr. M about the confidentiality of the process.

When completing the PIF, there are some practical items to note, as follows:

Page 2:

- use the RPD file number found on the Referral Notice

- use the same name as the one on the Referral Notice; the RPD uses the name found on the Referral Notice in its records and in issuing other notices (to appear, decisions, etc.)

- include different spellings of the claimant's name

- provide information about the claimant's language and dialect; this information will be used for interpreting the proceedings (boxes 1(i), 1(j), and 1(k))

Page 9:

- identify at least one ground for establishing a fear of persecution

Page 10:

- number the lines on any additional pages that are added

Page 12:

- communicate any changes of address to the Refugee Protection Division.

The elements of the refugee definition should also be kept in mind when completing the PIF. These are the facts that must be proved. For example, with respect to alienage, there are a number of questions related to establishing the claimant's identity and the right to seek protection.

The narrative in box 31 provides the opportunity to demonstrate well-founded fear. It should set out the objective and subjective basis for the claim as clearly as possible in chronological order, in order to establish the element of well-founded fear. The narrative also provides the opportunity to detail the nature and scope of persecution, torture, or serious harm suffered or anticipated.

Information about relatives in Canada, such as their status, whether they made claims, and the outcome of those claims, can help to identify potential witnesses and identify any cases that should be heard together. Counsel should ask permission to review the PIFs of any relatives who are refugee claimants.

It is only necessary to prove a fear of persecution based on one of the grounds listed—not all. However, the decision maker is not limited to considering only those grounds selected by the claimant. The member of the RPD who considers the claim will determine which ground, if any, is applicable to the refugee claimant's fear of persecution on the basis of the evidence raised in the claim. Once the member has found that the claimant's fear of persecution is by reason of one of the grounds, other grounds will not be considered.

Counsel Information

Usually, a refugee claimant does not seek legal representation until after the referral to the RPD by CIC. Legal clinics may provide legal advice and assistance with such activities as completing forms, making calls, writing letters, or accompanying a claimant to meetings. Legal aid is also available to refugee claimants in British Columbia, Alberta, Manitoba, Ontario, Quebec, and Newfoundland and Labrador.

Counsel never directly communicates with the decision maker, but rather must follow rule 2. Rule 2 provides that all communication, both oral and in writing, and including questions about the process, documents, or a particular claim, must be made through the registry. This rule is very important to avoid suspicions of bias or influence. All parties must be aware of all information being passed on to the decision maker, so that they have the opportunity to respond. A listing of registries may be found in the Appendix at the end of this chapter.

The RPD must have the refugee claimant's and counsel's contact information in order to provide notices about proceedings and other matters. "Contact information" is defined in rule 1 as a person's name, postal address, telephone number, and fax number and electronic mail address, if any. This information is also required as part of the claimant's PIF. If the RPD cannot contact the refugee claimant directly or through counsel, there is a risk that notices will not be received, such as a Notice to Appear for a hearing, and consequently the claimant will fail to appear. This may lead the RPD to declare the claim abandoned.

Rule 4 requires that the refugee claimant provide personal contact information to the RPD no later than ten days after receiving the PIF as well as provide any changes to that information, such as a new address, without delay. The same rule requires the refugee claimant to advise the RPD of counsel's contact information and any changes thereafter. As counsel, you will take on this responsibility.

Counsel must inform the RPD that he has been retained to represent the client, or the RPD may consider the claimant as unrepresented. If counsel is charging a fee, the appropriate form to complete is the Counsel Contact Information form (IRB / CISR 687), available on the IRB website under the Forms tab. Counsel must provide the membership identification number of either the Canadian Society of Immigration Consultants or the provincial law society.

Any counsel who represents a claimant and is not charging a fee should use the Notice of Representation Without a Fee form (IRB / CISR 692), available on the IRB website under the Forms tab.

Counsel is deemed *counsel of record* according to rule 9, once a date for a proceeding is set. In some cases, counsel may wish to be removed from the record—for example, if the client refuses to pay or is very difficult. Rule 10 provides that counsel must seek permission from the RPD to be removed from the case, and permission may be withheld if it would prejudice the claimant.

Documents

Documents are important evidence at RPD proceedings. There are several kinds of documents, such as documents that show the identity of the claimant, documents that support claims made by the claimant, interview notes by the officer at the point of entry, and documents regarding conditions in the country that the client has left. Because of the importance of documents to a fair resolution of the case, there are rules regarding filing documents with the RPD, disclosing documents, and ensuring that everyone has a copy of the documents well before the hearing.

Types of Documents

Consider the following types of documents, which are important to establish the facts of the case and to support the testimony of witnesses:

1. **Identity documents.** Rule 7 requires that the claimant provide acceptable documents to establish identity and other elements of the claim, or provide a credible explanation as to why they are not available, and what steps were taken to obtain them. Identity documents may include the following:

   - birth certificate,

   - passport,

   - marriage certificate,

   - divorce certificate,

   - voter registration,

   - driver's licence,

   - social security card,

   - police records, and

   - university transcripts.

   The existence of these kinds of documents bolsters the claimant's credibility and helps to establish the claimant's identity.

2. **Corroborative documents.** Documents that corroborate a claimant's allegations are a boost to credibility, and may replace the need to relive traumatic events at the hearing. For example, if the claimant has been tortured, medical or psychiatric reports may be available to corroborate the claim. Examples of useful corroborative evidence that may be filed include the following:

   - references to the claimant or associates of the claimant in any high profile human rights reports;

   - newspaper references to the claimant's involvement in incidents or activities, such as demonstrations;

   - evidence of the claimant's membership in a political party, or social or religious group; and

   - objective evidence, including background research.

3. **Port of entry notes.** The officer's port of entry notes may be entered as evidence. The notes may undermine the credibility of the claimant if they contradict the claimant's PIF. On the other hand, if they are consistent with the PIF, this will indicate that the claimant's story has not changed.

4. **Country information.** Information on the country of reference, such as country-of-origin information, is provided by the RPD. This means that every case will have some basic documentary evidence, which becomes part of the exhibit list used at the hearing. Counsel may already be familiar with the country conditions and human rights violations in the country of origin, because they have represented other clients from the same place. Counsel should review the country information with the client, to address any inconsistencies with the client's own personal experience.

In our scenario, Mr. M's counsel will review his client's identity documents provided by CIC in the documents package. Does the claimant have any? If not, why? Can the claimant obtain identity documents such as a passport, birth certificate, voter registration card, or domicile registration card, without putting relatives at risk? If documents cannot be safely obtained, are there any witnesses who can testify as to the claimant's identity?

Counsel will review the officer's port of entry notes with Mr. M to recall what was said during the interview. Any inconsistencies or discrepancies between the POE notes and the narrative of the PIF must be explained. Mr. M may have been exhausted, or fearful, or think it necessary to embellish his story. Counsel must insist that now is the time for Mr. M to be completely honest and forthcoming—counsel must not wait until the hearing to address inconsistencies, because they could further tarnish Mr. M's credibility. Counsel should make a list of any evidence needed to confirm the facts. It is crucial that counsel be prepared to deal with discrepancies between information given at the POE, in the PIF, and during Mr. M's testimony at the hearing.

Filing Requirements

As counsel you must use appropriate forms and follow the rules for filing documents. The rules concerning documents can be applied to any document, notice, or request, according to rule 31. Rule 32 sets out when documents must be provided to the registry, the minister's counsel, and the refugee claimant's counsel.

You will want to provide organized and professional-looking documents to the RPD. All documents intended for use at the hearing must comply with the following requirements:

- the documents must be submitted in either English or French, which may require translation (rule 28);

- the documents must be typewritten on one side of 21.5 cm by 28 cm ($8\frac{1}{2}''$ $\times$ 11") paper, with pages numbered (rule 27); and

- if the document is a photocopy, it must be clear and legible.

If the claimant files more than one document to be included in the record, a numbered list of all such documents must also be filed. The List of Claimant's Documents form (form RPD.05.1) should be used for this purpose, and is available on the IRB website under the Forms tab.

Disclosure and Provision of Documents

Documents are exchanged before the hearing to ensure that all participants have an opportunity to review them, and respond if necessary, in preparation for the hearing. To ensure that this happens, the RPD Rules require **disclosure** of documents, which is the release of documents to the opposing side, and impose requirements for providing copies of the documents to those entitled to have them.

Consider the following rules regarding disclosure:

- The time limits for disclosing documents, so that they are received before a proceeding, are set out in rule 25(4).

- Any documentary evidence to be used in support of a client's claim must be disclosed to the RPD by listing the documents on the List of Claimant's Documents form, and filed no later than 20 days before the hearing, according to rules 27(4) and 29(4).

- The RPD may refuse to use or allow documents that are not produced within the time limits according to rule 30.

- If the hearing has already started, an application must be made to the RPD to "provide documents after a hearing has started" so that the member can consider whether to allow admission of the documents, according to rule 37.

- When photocopies of documents are provided to the RPD, the originals must be provided for the hearing, according to rule 36. This rule also compels the officer who interviewed the refugee claimant for eligibility to provide the original identity and travel documents that were seized at that time.

Documents must be provided to the RPD and to the minister's counsel if she is intervening, to allow the opportunity to review and prepare the case. It would be unfair and inefficient if documents were withheld until the last minute. Because provision of documents is so important, it must generally be achieved by one of the following methods, pursuant to rule 33:

- by hand;
- by regular or registered mail;
- by courier or priority post;
- by fax (for documents no more than 20 pages long); or
- sometimes, by electronic mail.

Together with the copies provided to the Division, a written statement of how and when a copy was disclosed must be included. Documents provided under this rule must be received no later than 20 days before the hearing, or, if the document is provided to respond to another document provided by a party or the Division, no later than 5 days before the hearing.

Computation of time for receipt of a document is described in rule 34(2). Under this rule, when a document is sent by regular mail, it is considered received after 7 days. If day 7 falls on a Saturday, Sunday, or statutory holiday, the document is considered received on the next working day.

Types of Proceedings: Streaming

The RPD identifies the main issues that are central to the claim and records them on the RPD File Screening form. The issues determine the stream that will be used in scheduling the claim. Generally, the RPD uses two streams for hearing claims: the fast track process, and full hearings. The Notice to Appear identifies the stream.

FAST TRACK PROCESS

Claims assigned to the fast track process are further assigned to either the fast track expedited process or a fast track hearing.

Fast Track Expedited Process—Interview

Rule 19 of the RPD Rules allows for accepting a claim without a hearing. This is called the fast track expedited process, and, as the name suggests, it is a shorter process used to quickly decide claims. Rather than participating in a hearing, the claimant is interviewed by a refugee protection officer (RPO). The setting is informal—typically, an office consisting of a table and chairs, and the interview generally takes 30 to 90 minutes.

Claims that are assigned to this process are generally considered to be *manifestly founded* cases, where the RPD has a high acceptance rate for the country of reference. The fast track expedited process is used in the following circumstances:

- the claimant's identity is established;

- no issues of credibility arise from the PIF or POE notes;

- the minister is not intervening in the case; and

- the case is supported by known human rights conditions in the reference country.

Returning to our scenario, suppose that Mr. M received his Notice to Appear for an interview. He must appear at the scheduled time. At the interview, in addition to Mr. M and his counsel, there will be an interpreter and the refugee protection officer. The RPO, although generally a participant in the proceedings, is not a party or adversary in the interview. The RPO's role is defined in rule 1 of the RPD Rules, and duties are set out in rule 16. Pursuant to rule 19(2), the RPO interviews a refugee claimant in the expedited process; prepares a report based on the interview; and makes a recommendation to a member of the RPD to allow or disallow the claim without a hearing.

The member is not present for the interview. Instead, the RPO's file with notes and recommendation is forwarded to a member for a decision. If the member accepts Mr. M's claim, there is no need for a further hearing. The practice in some RPD offices is to inform the refugee claimant of the outcome and produce a Notice of Decision on the same day. If, however, Mr. M's claim is not accepted, the matter is scheduled for a full hearing so that he has the opportunity to present his case and be heard by a member.

Fast Track Hearings

Claims assigned to fast track hearings, also known as *short hearings*, are generally simple, single-issue claims that can be decided quickly. Typically, a member hears and decides the claim without the assistance of a RPO. These hearings are generally decided within a couple of hours.

FULL HEARINGS

Within the full hearings stream there are two different types of hearings, which were created by the RPD to manage its claim load, schedule appropriate hearing times, and allot the resources needed to hear the claim. The two hearing types are as follows:

1. **Regular full hearings.** Claims scheduled as regular full hearings usually involve more than two issues and require about a half day. A member hears and decides the claim, and generally the RPO is present to assist in questioning the refugee claimant.

2. **Complex full hearings.** Complex full hearings are held for claims that have multiple issues, and may include issues about the claimant's identity, credibility, or other serious matters.

Regardless of the hearing type, hearings are usually held in private and are conducted in an informal and non-adversarial manner. In a limited number of cases, the minister, represented by counsel, intervenes to argue against the claim—for example, because the minister believes that the claimant should be excluded from protection. The RPO is usually present to assist in questioning the refugee claimant. These cases may be scheduled for a half day or longer.

Adversarial hearings, where the minister intervenes to argue against the claim, may be conducted publicly in rare cases where the media takes an interest and brings an application for the hearing to be held in public.

Hearings

Before a hearing, counsel must be familiar with the RPD Rules, such as for disclosing documents, and also be familiar with the relevant legislation and case law. Counsel must have a clear understanding of the legal issues in the particular case. Common legal issues that frequently require hearings to resolve include the following:

- identity/nationality;
- existence of other claims;
- delay in making the claim;
- credibility assessment;
- nexus to the grounds (which grounds apply);

- the agents of persecution;

- objective evidence to support the claim; and

- what the claimant fears on return.

Counsel must be aware of all the pertinent facts of the case, and what to expect from witness testimony. If there are any discrepancies between the POE notes and the PIF, counsel must be ready to explain them. Finally, counsel must be able to apply the facts to the law, and formulate persuasive arguments to make at the hearing. For further information, see Guideline 7—Concerning Preparation and Conduct of a Hearing in the Refugee Protection Division at www.irb-cisr.gc.ca/en/references/policy/guidelines/index_e.htm.

Consider the experience of Mr. M, when he appears for his hearing and interacts with his counsel, his interpreter, and the RPD member:

Mr. M received a Notice to Appear for a hearing. On the day of his hearing, Mr. M arrives half an hour early to meet his counsel and go over last minute details. His counsel warned him not to be late because if the member was kept waiting for more than 15 minutes, she might conclude that Mr. M had abandoned his claim. This also gave him time to meet with the interpreter for his hearing, who asked him some questions to establish that they could understand each other. Mr. M bought a suit at a second-hand store for this day and he is very nervous. It was almost 18 months ago that Mr. M first stepped off the plane. It has been so hard living in this new country, and he has had difficulty making new friends; he misses his family. He reminds himself that this is his only chance to convince the decision maker that he cannot return home, and that he needs to get his family out of that country.

When it is time to start, Mr. M's counsel leads him down a hall and they stop at a hearing room. He recognizes the Canadian flag at the front of the room, behind a long desk. There are three long tables, each with a microphone: one on each side of the desk and one at the back of the room facing the desk. There are some chairs around the room's perimeter. Mr. M is seated next to the interpreter, sitting facing the desk. His counsel takes a seat at one table and a man he doesn't know takes a seat opposite his counsel—he is later introduced as the refugee protection officer.

The RPD member walks in from the front of the room a few minutes later, turns on the recording device, and introduces herself as the member in his case. From this point on, everything said in the room is translated into Mr. M's language so that he can understand, and everything he says is translated into English. Mr. M is given the choice of taking an oath or making a solemn affirmation at the beginning of the hearing. He hesitates, wondering what would please the lady member the most, and then decides he needs all the help of greater powers, so he chooses to swear on his holy book. The next part is confusing; he is feeling nauseous but tries to smile and nods when the interpreter asks whether he understands. The interpreter is translating something about "the order of the proceeding" and who will start questioning first.

GENERAL APPLICATIONS

There are many issues that may require resolution before the hearing can even begin, such as a change to the date or location of the hearing, reinstatement of a claim, or cancellation of a summons to witness. If a party wants a decision on such a matter, the general procedure set out in rule 44 must be followed. Applications must be provided to the RPD and in the following manner:

- in writing (although oral applications are sometimes accepted) and without delay;
- stating the outcome sought;
- providing the reasons for the request;
- stating (if known) whether the other party agrees to the application;
- including any evidence that the party wants considered, in an affidavit or statutory declaration; and
- with a statement of how and when a copy of the application was sent to the other party.

The opposing party may respond to the application no later than seven days after receiving a copy of the application, according to rule 45. The response must be provided in the following manner:

- in writing;
- stating the outcome sought;
- providing the reasons for the seeking of that outcome;
- including any evidence that the party wants considered, in an affidavit or statutory declaration; and
- providing a statement of how and when a copy of the written response was sent to the other party.

The applicant then has an opportunity to reply to the response according to rule 46. Generally, the applicant must do so within five days after receiving a copy of the written response.

SCHEDULING A HEARING

The RPD's objective is to schedule cases as early as practicable in order to complete them on a timely basis. The RPD will not set a date for a hearing until it either receives confirmation from the CBSA that security screening is complete, or one year has passed from the date of referral (whichever comes first). Generally, confirmation is received within two months for most claims.

Scheduling a hearing involves issues such as the date and time, the place, and whether the hearing will be open to the public. All these issues are addressed by the RPD Rules, which must be consulted frequently for changes.

Setting a Date

In setting a date for a proceeding, the RPD assesses its operational capacity—that is, the availability of decision makers and hearing rooms. Rule 21 allows the RPD to call scheduling conferences for the fixing of a date; however, the RPD is not obligated to consult counsel when setting a date for a proceeding. In fact, the Notice to Appear advises the refugee claimant that she must select counsel who is available on the scheduled hearing date, because the date will not be changed. It is important to check with the regional office, because scheduling procedures vary, and some offices will allow counsel to submit available dates. Refer to Guideline 6—Scheduling and Changing the Date or Time of a Proceeding in the Refugee Protection Division at www.irb-cisr.gc.ca/en/references/policy/guidelines/index_e.htm.

After the date has been set for a proceeding, a **Notice to Appear** for an interview, pre-hearing conference, or hearing is sent to the refugee claimant and counsel along with a copy of the RPD File Screening form. Rule 22 requires the RPD to notify the claimant in writing. After seeing the issues indicated on the RPD File Screening form, counsel is expected to notify the RPD as soon as possible of any issue to be added or deleted, and to provide an explanation.

Changing the Date

A request to change the date and time of a proceeding as specified in the Notice to Appear may be made by application to the RPD according to rule 48. This situation may arise if the claimant wishes to postpone a hearing to provide for more time to gather documents. The application must follow the general application procedures of rule 44, except that evidence need not be presented in an affidavit or statutory declaration. It must, however, be made no later than two working days before the proceeding. If that is impossible, the claimant must appear in person to make an oral application to change the date.

An application to change the date must provide at least six substitute dates and provide the reasons for the request. Rule 48 lists several factors that may be considered by the RPD when deciding an application to change the date or time of a proceeding, including the following:

- whether the party has counsel;
- whether counsel is knowledgeable and experienced;
- the time already afforded to the party to prepare;
- the party's efforts to prepare; and
- previous delays.

Changing the Location

A request to change the location of a proceeding as specified in the Notice to Appear may be made by application to the RPD according to rule 47. This situation may arise if the claimant wishes to transfer the case to another office. Like applications for changing the date, the application must follow the general application procedures of rule 44, except that evidence need not be presented in an affidavit or statutory declaration. It must, however, be made no later than 20 days before the proceeding. If the application is not allowed, the claimant is expected to appear for the proceeding at the fixed location.

Rule 47 provides several factors that may be considered by the RPD when deciding an application to change the location of a proceeding, including the following:

- whether the claimant is living in the same location as the proceeding;

- whether a change of venue would allow the proceeding to be full and proper; and

- whether a change would delay the proceeding.

Requesting a Public Hearing

Proceedings in the RPD are generally private and closed to the public. However, from time to time someone may wish to make the proceeding open to the public. This typically occurs when there is media interest in a claim.

Any person may make an application to have the hearing held in public, according to rule 51. The application must provide the following:

- a request for a public hearing;

- reasons why the RPD should agree to a public hearing; and

- any evidence that the applicant wants the RPD to consider in deciding the application.

The original application and two copies must be provided to the RPD, and a copy must be provided to each of the parties.

Refugee Claimant's Rights and Responsibilities

When working with refugee clients, it is important that counsel review the clients' rights and responsibilities. Clients must understand that they have the following rights:

- the right to counsel

- the right to an interpreter

- the right to present evidence and call witnesses

- the right to be present at their own case before an impartial and independent decision maker.

Clients must also understand that they have the following responsibilities:

- the responsibility to provide credible and trustworthy information and testimony

- the responsibility to meet the burden of proof—that suffering persecution upon return to their own country is probable, not merely possible.

PERSONS IN ATTENDANCE

There are a number of people who must be present at a hearing, such as the claimant and the RPD member. Other persons are likely to be present, such as the claimant's counsel, the refugee protection officer, and an interpreter. Still others may be present, such as witnesses, a designated representative, and the minister's counsel. Occasionally, a representative of the United Nations High Commissioner for Refugees may also be present.

Claimant

The claimant must be personally in attendance at the hearing.

Member

Generally, only one decision maker, a member of the RPD, has the authority to hear a refugee case. A member is actively involved in the RPD's inquiry process and has the authority to tell the hearing participants how to present their cases.

Case law has established that the RPD has control of its own procedures.[8] The Division decides and gives directions as to how a hearing is to proceed, including who will start the questioning. A member is a specialist in refugee law and is well informed about human rights abuses and other conditions and events in the country presented. Therefore, the member may inquire into anything considered relevant to establish whether a claim is well founded. The member will study the case file prior to a proceeding to become familiar with the issues that require resolution.

Claimant's Counsel

Counsel's role is essentially to protect the claimant's interests and right to a fair hearing. Counsel explains the process, provides advice, and presents the case in an efficient manner, within the limits set by the member.

The refugee claimant may choose to be represented by either an unpaid trusted adviser, such as a family member or clergy, or a paid consultant or lawyer. All paid counsel must be a member in good standing of a provincial law society or the Canadian Society of Immigration Consultants. Any counsel who represents the claimant for a fee must provide contact information in writing to the RPD and the minister, including the membership identification number for the relevant professional regulatory body.

Refugee Protection Officer

The role of the refugee protection officer is intended to be neutral. The RPO does not oppose or argue for the claim, and may or may not be present for the hearing. The RPO acts under the direction of the RPD, specifically the member presiding over the hearing, to help ensure that all relevant information is produced, according to rule 16. Prior to a proceeding, the RPO may be involved in gathering research for the case. If present, the RPO may present evidence and call and question witnesses, make representations, and do anything else that is necessary to ensure a full and proper examination of a claim or other matter.

Interpreter

Only **accredited interpreters** are used for hearings, which means they have undergone security checks and passed a language exam. They are not employees of the IRB (or RPD) as they are contracted on a case-by-case basis. They are permanently bound by their promise to interpret accurately once they take an oath or make a solemn affirmation to do so, according to rule 14. At the beginning of the proceeding, the interpreter confirms that she used a standardized script to ensure that she and the refugee claimant understand each other. The interpreter may not guide, provide advice, or offer an opinion to the claimant.

Witnesses

If counsel wishes to call a witness other than the claimant, he must fulfill the requirements of rule 38. The witness's contact information, counsel's reasons for calling the witness, and an estimate of the amount of time needed at the hearing for the witness's testimony must be provided in writing to the RPD and to the other party no later than 20 days before the hearing.

To reduce the risk of the witness failing to appear, it is prudent to request the RPD to issue a summons to order a witness to testify, according to rule 39. The summons must be provided to the summoned witness, and the RPD notified of this in writing. Witness fees and travel expenses are also the responsibility of the claimant. Should a summoned witness fail to appear, rule 41 sets out the process for making a request to the RPD to issue a warrant for that person's arrest.

Designated Representative

There are situations where the refugee claimant is not capable of making decisions, such as in the case of an unaccompanied minor or a person deemed mentally incompetent or unable to understand the proceedings.[9] In these instances, the Division appoints a person to act and make decisions on behalf of the claimant. The **designated representative** may be a relative or a professional, such as a lawyer or social worker. Counsel is permitted to take on the role of designated representative.

MINISTER'S COUNSEL

Although most refugee hearings proceed without intervention from the minister, the RPD is required to notify the minister when it has information (found in the PIF, for example) that might be of interest to the minister for the purpose of intervening in a case. Rules 23 and 24 require the RPD to give written notice to the minister when the RPD has this kind of information, and to provide the minister with the related information.

The minister may intervene to make arguments with respect to the following issues:

- credibility (issues about the honesty and accuracy of the claimant's statements and/or authenticity of documents);

- exclusion (for example, to exclude a refugee claimant because she already has protection according to article 1E of the Refugee Convention or article F of the Convention, which excludes those who have been in the role of persecutor from later being granted protection);

- inadmissibility (on grounds of security, violating human or international rights, serious criminality or organized criminality, or on the ground that there is an outstanding charge against the refugee claimant); or

- ineligibility (when the minister receives information after the claim has been referred and now wishes to argue that the claimant is ineligible according to the eligibility criteria provided at s. 101 of the IRPA or that there is misrepresentation according to s. 104(1)(c) or that the claim is not a first claim, as provided in s. 104(1)(d).

The hearing becomes adversarial when the minister's counsel, called a hearings officer, participates in the case to argue against the claim. Therefore, it is important that the RPD provide the claimant with a copy of the notice and the accompanying information that was provided to the minister. Should the minister decide to intervene in a case, either as a result of the RPD's notice or acting on the minister's own information, rule 25 requires the minister to give notice to the RPD of the minister's intention to intervene in a claim. The notice sets out how the minister will intervene, the minister's counsel contact information, and proof of notifying the refugee claimant. The notice must be given to the RPD no later than 20 days before the hearing. The minister must also serve the refugee claimant with a written copy of the notice of the minister's intention to intervene.

Representative of the United Nations High Commissioner for Refugees

A representative of the United Nations High Commissioner for Refugees is entitled to observe any refugee claimant's proceeding, according to s. 166(e) of the IRPA.

CONFIRMING ISSUES

What Mr. M probably doesn't understand is the process that the member uses to confirm the issues in the case. Generally, the member consults with the RPO and counsel about the issues and how long the hearing is expected to last. They reach agreement on limiting their questions to only those issues. The member also decides the order of questioning—whether the RPO or the claimant's counsel will ask questions first. In cases where the minister's counsel is present to intervene in a claim— for example, to argue exclusion—the minister's counsel may be directed to question first.

EVIDENCE

In this part of the hearing process, Mr. M answers questions about the information he provided on the PIF and about the documents he and his counsel disclosed. He is also given the opportunity to tell the member what he fears about returning to his homeland.

The RPD is not bound by any legal or technical rules of evidence and may base its decision on evidence that is considered credible or trustworthy in the circumstances, provided that the evidence is presented in the proceedings. The RPD must also deal with all proceedings that are before it, as informally and quickly as the circumstances and requirements of fairness and natural justice permit, according to s. 162(2) of the IRPA.

The RPD may take **judicial notice** of any generally recognized facts, or information or opinion within its specialized knowledge, providing that it gives notice to the refugee claimant that it is doing so, according to s. 170 of the IRPA. This means that it is unnecessary to bring evidence to prove a fact that is generally known. For example, it would not be necessary to prove that student protesters in Beijing's Tiananmen Square were massacred in June 1989 because this event is now generally known.

ORAL REPRESENTATIONS

After all questioning of Mr. M and any other witnesses is complete, and the member is satisfied that all the evidence has been heard, counsel has the opportunity to deliver **oral representations**—that is, make a final statement. Rule 60 requires counsel to be prepared for this at the end of a hearing. The member may direct the RPO to deliver or not to deliver representations, depending on whether the member considers representations necessary.

DECISIONS AND REASONS

The RPD member does not decide whether or not Mr. M would make a good permanent resident or citizen or whether he can remain in or must leave Canada. Rather, the member decides only whether Mr. M has established his claim under one of the following grounds:

- persecution under a Convention refugee ground;

- danger of torture; or

- risk to life or risk of cruel and unusual treatment or punishment.

There are four possible outcomes, as follows:

1. the claim is allowed because the claimant is found to be a Convention refugee;

2. the claim is allowed because the claimant is found to be a person in need of protection;

3. the claim is rejected because the claimant is not a Convention refugee and is not a person in need of protection; or

4. the claim is rejected because the claimant is not a Convention refugee and is not a person in need of protection and there is no credible basis.

Wherever practicable, the RPD member renders the decision and reasons orally at the end of the hearing. The Division is required by rule 61 to issue a written decision called a **Notice of Decision** to the claimant and to the minister, whether the minister intervened or not.

In the case of a rejected claim, written reasons for the decision must accompany the Notice of Decision. Furthermore, s. 107(2) of the IRPA stipulates that if the claim is rejected because there was no credible or trustworthy evidence, the member must include this finding in the reasons for rejecting the claim. The purpose of the "no credible basis" provision is to discourage frivolous and non-genuine claimants by providing for their speedier removal.

If the claim is successful, the claimant or the minister may request written reasons as long as the request is in writing and is made within ten days of notification of the decision, according to rule 62 and s. 169(c) of the IRPA.

POST-DETERMINATION PROCESSES

If Mr. M's claim is allowed, the conditional removal order issued by CIC during the front-end process does not take force. Now that Mr. M is a successful claimant, his next step, whether as a Convention refugee or as a person in need of protection, is to apply for permanent resident status. Mr. M's spouse and dependent children are also eligible to apply for permanent residence.

Application information will normally accompany the notice of decision from the IRB. According to s. 175 of the IRPA, the successful claimant has 180 days to apply for permanent residence using the In-Canada Application for Permanent Residence form (IMM 5202), available online from CIC. Applications are processed at the Case Processing Centre in Vegreville, Alberta. Although there is a processing fee for the application process, the Right of Permanent Residence Fee is waived for protected persons. In the interim, CIC issues a "protected person status document" (PPSD) to confirm the successful refugee claimant's status in Canada.

Mr. M may have to undergo security screening and medical examinations again, if the initial security checks and medical examinations have expired. Also, under ss. 114(3), 108, and 109 of the IRPA, a successful refugee claimant is not eligible to apply for permanent residence in any of the following situations:

- *A misrepresentation has been discovered.* If the protection was granted because of misrepresentation—for example, if the claimant provided false information—the claimant will be ineligible to apply for permanent residence.

- *Protection has ceased.* If the protection granted has ceased, such as because of a change in the country conditions as a result of a newly elected government in the claimant's country of origin, the claimant will be ineligible to apply for permanent residence.

- *Protection has been vacated.* If the protection granted was "vacated," such as when the RPD vacates its decision further to an application by the minister and nullifies refugee protection, the claimant will be ineligible to apply for permanent residence.

For each of the above situations, the minister must apply to the RPD to request a hearing into the matter to argue cessation or vacation. If Mr. M's claim is rejected, the removal order will come into effect. However, before removal takes place, the unsuccessful refugee claimant has the following options:

- leave Canada within 30 days from the date of the Notice of Decision;
- apply for leave for judicial review by the Federal Court within 15 days from the date of the Notice of Decision (the removal order may be stayed);[10] or

- apply to CIC for a pre-removal risk assessment (unless there was a "no credible basis" stipulation) within 15 days from the date of the Notice of Decision.

Instructions for applying for leave for judicial review, and for a pre-removal risk assessment, are sent to the rejected claimant by the RPD with the Notice of Decision.

Pre-removal Risk Assessment

The pre-removal risk assessment (PRRA) is a program intended for people who are about to be removed from Canada and who are desperate to stay, because one of the following exists:

- a well-founded fear of persecution, according to the Convention refugee definition; or

- a risk of torture, risk to life, or risk of cruel and unusual treatment or punishment, according to the Convention Against Torture.

The PRRA program is managed by CIC, and it is another example of Canada's commitment to the principle of *non-refoulement*. However, it is important to remember that the PRRA is not an appeal or review of a negative decision by the RPD. CIC has no jurisdiction to hear such appeals or conduct such reviews.

Generally, a successful PRRA applicant is granted Convention refugee status or protection, will not be removed, and may apply for permanent residence. However, a negative determination means removal arrangements proceed, and the applicant must leave Canada.

WHO MAY APPLY

The PRRA is for people who are **removal ready**, meaning that they are subject to a removal order that is in force, or that a security certificate has been issued against them (s. 112(1) of the IRPA), and they are in possession of a valid passport or travel document. There are several circumstances under which an applicant may generally apply for a PRRA, as follows:

- *ineligible to make refugee claim*—a person's claim was refused at the front end of the refugee determination process, and determined not eligible to be referred to the RPD;

- *repeat claim*—a person made a previous refugee claim and more than six months have elapsed since the person left Canada;

- *rejected, withdrawn, or abandoned refugee claim*—a person's refugee claim in Canada was rejected, withdrawn, or abandoned;

- *repeat PRRA applicant*—a person makes another PRRA application, as long as there is new evidence to present, which either did not exist at the time of the earlier application or was impossible or unreasonable to provide at that time; or

- *no previous claim for refugee protection*—a person applied for protection before removal from Canada and never made a previous claim for refugee protection.[11]

Even if an applicant falls within one of the categories listed above, she may nevertheless be denied access to the process. Section 112(2) of the IRPA bars a person from applying for a PRRA in the following situations:

- the person is subject to extradition under s. 15 of the *Extradition Act*;

- the person's claim to refugee protection was determined ineligible because she came directly or indirectly from a designated country, other than a country of her nationality or former habitual residence;

- in the case of a person who has not left Canada since the application for protection was rejected, the prescribed six-month period has not expired;[12] or

- in the case of a person who has left Canada since the removal order came into force, less than six months have passed since she left Canada after her claim to refugee protection was determined to be ineligible, abandoned, withdrawn, or rejected, or her application for protection was rejected.

There is another list of categories under s. 112(3) of the IRPA. Applicants for a PRRA who fall under the s. 112(3) restrictions are still entitled to have their application considered for a risk assessment on the grounds of the Convention Against Torture, but they will not be assessed against the Refugee Convention. They will not be granted refugee status in keeping with the principle of the definition's exclusion clauses, and they will not be able to apply for permanent residence.

A person who has been permitted to apply for a PRRA is allowed to remain in Canada until such time as the circumstances change—for example, there is a change in country conditions. Such changes would trigger a re-examination by the minister of the grounds on which the application was allowed and may lead to a cancellation of a stay, and the execution of the removal order. Until this happens, the applicant is allowed to remain in Canada in a kind of legal limbo: she cannot apply to sponsor family members; if she leaves Canada, she most likely will not be able to return; and although she is allowed to work, her work permit is issued for a short period of time.

In assessing the application, the PRRA officer must take into account whether the applicant is a danger to the public in Canada. Section 112(3) stipulates that refugee protection may not be granted to a PRRA applicant if the applicant

- is determined to be inadmissible on grounds of security, violating human or international rights, or organized criminality;

- is determined to be inadmissible on grounds of serious criminality with respect to a conviction in Canada punished by a term of imprisonment of at least two years or with respect to a conviction outside Canada for an offence that, if committed in Canada, would constitute an offence under an Act of Parliament punishable by a maximum term of imprisonment of at least ten years;

■ made a claim for refugee protection that was rejected on the basis of section F of article 1 of the Refugee Convention, because those who have been in the role of persecutor are excluded from later being granted protection; or

■ is named in a **security certificate** referred to in s. 77(1) of the IRPA; a security certificate is issued in exceptional circumstances where a person is deemed inadmissible for reasons of national security, for violating human or international rights, or for involvement in organized or serious crimes.

EVIDENCE CONSIDERED

The PRRA is an administrative process conducted by specialized CIC employees called PRRA officers. Although there are exceptions, generally PRRA officers process applications through a paper review of the application and assess whether there are any new facts or evidence to decide if there is a risk in removing and returning a person subject to a removal order. PRRA officers have the statutory authority to decide whether an oral hearing is warranted in exceptional cases. In rendering their decisions, the PRRA officers assess applications against the requirements of the Refugee Convention (for the granting of refugee status) and the Convention Against Torture (for the granting of protection as "a person in need of protection").

The PRRA provides the applicant with the opportunity to provide new evidence only—that is, evidence that could not reasonably or possibly have been provided at the refugee hearing. An example is a change in the applicant's country that puts the applicant at risk, such as a new political party coming to power, a new law being passed that seriously violates the applicant's human rights, or the outbreak of a civil war.

TIMELINES

The clock starts ticking on the date of a negative decision, whether it is a CBSA officer's decision that a refugee claimant is ineligible for consideration by the RPD, or a decision by the RPD to reject a claim. Where a negative decision is made at the front end of the process, the CBSA officer provides the claimant with the Advanced Information Notice that explains the PRRA process and allows the claimant to enter Canada to pursue the PRRA application. In the case of a claim rejected by the RPD, the claimant is notified about his options at the time of receiving the Notice of Decision. Those options include leaving Canada or applying for leave for a judicial review or for a PRRA.

At the point of receiving the Advanced Information Notice or Notice of Decision, the claimant has 15 days to complete the PRRA application form and send it to CIC. Once the application is submitted, the claimant cannot be removed until the PRRA officer makes a decision on the application. There is also an additional 15 days available for submitting evidence to support the application. Failure to submit the PRRA application by the 15-day deadline can result in the removal of the claimant.

DECISION

If the PRRA application is accepted, the applicant is usually granted refugee status or protection as a person in need of protection. Such applicants may then apply for permanent residence.

PRRA applicants who are successful in their request not to be removed, but who are ineligible for refugee determination (because of inadmissibility on grounds of security, violating human or international rights, serious criminality or organized criminality, or because they are named in a security certificate further to s. 77(1) of the IRPA), may not apply for permanent residence. Instead, the successful outcome of the PRRA application has the effect of a stay of the execution of the removal order, and the applicant is not removed from Canada. The person is allowed, however, to remain in Canada until such time as the circumstances change—for example, there is a change in country conditions. Such changes would trigger a re-examination by the minister of the grounds on which the application was allowed and may lead to a cancellation of a stay, and the execution of the removal order.

PRRA applicants who are rejected must generally be removed from Canada. There is, however, the possibility of applying to CIC to remain in Canada on humanitarian and compassionate grounds (see Chapter 5, "Permanent Entry").

The Refugee Appeal Division

The IRPA, in ss. 110 and 111, provides for an avenue of appeal to a new division of the Immigration and Refugee Board, called the Refugee Appeal Division (RAD). However, these sections have not yet been proclaimed into force, and the implementation of the RAD and its procedures continues to be delayed.

The RAD was legislated to create a forum for appeals by unsuccessful refugee claimants, or from the minister, against a decision of the RPD for refugee protection on questions of law, of fact, or of mixed law and fact. In addition, appeal rights are extended to the minister to appeal against the RPD's decisions to reject an application by the minister for a determination that refugee protection has ceased or to vacate a decision to allow a claim for refugee protection. There are no rights to appeal against decisions that refugee protection has been withdrawn or abandoned.

The appeal requires the appellant to serve the respondent with a Notice of Appeal within 15 days after the RPD issues its written reasons for the decision. The appeal process is envisaged to be a paper review—with no hearing. Members review the record of the RPD proceedings, along with any written submissions from the minister, the person who is the subject of the appeal, and sometimes a representative of the United Nations High Commissioner for Refugees.

As there is no RAD at this time, there are also no functioning rules of practice. Nevertheless, the IRB chairperson has proposed the Refugee Appeal Division rules vol. 135, no. 50, which were published in the *Canada Gazette*, part 1 on December 15, 2001.

Federal Court

Because the RAD has not yet been established, Mr. M cannot appeal the RPD's decision if his claim is rejected. However, he may apply for a judicial review by the

Federal Court. An applicant for judicial review must first seek leave of the Federal Court, requesting the court to hear the case. This must occur within 15 days from the later of the notice of the decision or the issuance of written reasons by the RPD. The application requirements (such as the use of Form IR-1) and the procedures for applying for leave are set out in the Federal Court Immigration and Refugee Protection Rules. Mr. M's application for leave must also be served on the minister, who may decide to oppose it.

In our example, Mr. M has a stay of the removal order that was issued against him, allowing him to remain in Canada pending the decision on his application for leave (s. 231(1) of the IRP Regulations). However, if Mr. M's claim was rejected with a finding of "no credible basis" for the claim, then he would not be entitled to a stay of removal (s. 231(2) of the IRP Regulations). If the Federal Court grants leave, the stay of the removal will be extended to allow Mr. M to remain in Canada for the judicial review.

A judicial review is not an appeal on the merits of a claim or a rehearing of the claim. There are six grounds set out in s. 18.1(4) of the *Federal Court Act* upon which a judge may grant a judicial review. For example, if there was an error of law or of fact in the decision of the RPD, or if there was a failure to observe a principle of natural justice. If an application for judicial review is allowed, the Federal Court will normally set aside the decision of the RPD and send the case back to the IRB to be reconsidered.

APPENDIX: IMMIGRATION AND REFUGEE BOARD REGIONAL OFFICES

The following are the business offices, also known as the "registries," for the purpose of contacting the Immigration and Refugee Board. All communication (oral or written) with the Board's divisions must be made through a registry.

Eastern Region

Montreal (Divisions: ID, RPD, IAD)
Registrar
Immigration and Refugee Board of Canada
200 René-Lévesque Boulevard West
Guy Favreau Complex
East Tower, Room 102
Montreal, Quebec H2Z 1X4
Tel.: (514) 283-7733
Fax: (514) 283-0164

Ottawa (Divisions: ID, RPD, IAD)
Registrar
Immigration and Refugee Board of Canada
Minto Place, Canada Building
344 Slater Street, 11th Floor
Ottawa, Ontario K1A 0K1
Tel.: (613) 943-8630
Fax: (613) 943-1550

Central Region

Toronto (Divisions: ID, RPD, IAD)
Registrar
Immigration and Refugee Board of Canada
74 Victoria Street
Suite 400
Toronto, Ontario M5C 3C7
Tel.: (416) 954-1000
Fax: (416) 954-1165

Niagara Falls (Division: ID)
Registrar
Immigration and Refugee Board of Canada
6080 McLeod Road
Unit #15
Niagara Falls, Ontario L2G 7T4
Tel.: (416) 954-1000

Western Region

Vancouver (Divisions: ID, RPD, IAD)
Registrar
Immigration and Refugee Board of Canada
Suite 1600, Library Square
300 West Georgia Street
Vancouver, British Columbia V6B 6C9
Tel.: (604) 666-5946
Fax: (604) 666-3043

NOTES

1. Counsel may be either legal counsel (lawyer or notary) or lay counsel; however, if lay counsel is representing the refugee claimant for a fee, counsel must be a member in good standing of the Canadian Society of Immigration Consultants.

2. After a claim is refused by the RPD, the claimant may not be immediately removed should she apply for a judicial review or a pre-removal risk

assessment (PRRA). The removal order only comes into effect if there is a negative PRRA decision or a finding that there is no credible basis for the claim.

3. Section 102 of the IRPA and s. 159.3 of the Immigration and Refugee Protection Regulations (IRP Regulations).

4. The Interim Federal Health letter provides coverage of emergency health services until the refugee claimant is eligible for provincial health coverage.

5. It is important to note the date when the refugee claimant receives the PIF because it is used by the RPD in calculating timelines.

6. Exceptions are outlined in the IRP Regulations (s. 159.5) and generally safeguard the principles of family reunification, the best interests of the child, and no return to a country to where a person faces the death penalty.

7. Published in the *Canada Gazette*, Part II, June 14, 2002, page 361. The Refugee Protection Division Rules came into force on June 28, 2002.

8. *Rezaei v. Canada (Minister of Citizenship and Immigration) (T.D.)*, [2003] 3 F.C. 421, which refers to the powers of administrative tribunals according to *Prassad v. Canada (Minister of employment and immigration)*, [1989] 1 S.C.R. 560.

9. Section 167(2) of the IRPA; rule 15 of the RPD Rules.

10. According to s. 231(2) of the IRP Regulations, if there is a finding of no credible basis, the claimant does not receive an automatic stay of removal for the purposes of court review. A stay is possible by application to the Federal Court; decisions are made on a case-by-case basis.

11. PRRA officers base their decisions on written evidence in the case of applicants for which there is no previous risk determination.

12. Section 112(2)(d) of the IRPA provides the six-month rule.

REFERENCES

Criminal Code. R.S.C. 1985, c. C-46.

Extradition Act. S.C. 1999, c. 18.

Federal Courts Act. R.S.C. 1985, c. F-7.

Federal Courts Immigration and Refugee Protection Rules. S.O.R./93-22.

Immigration and Refugee Board. "Instructions Governing the Management of Refugee Protection Claims Awaiting Front-End Security Screening." February 15, 2006. www.irb-cisr.gc.ca/en/references/policy/instructions/ securit_e.htm.

Immigration and Refugee Protection Act. S.C. 2001, c. 27.

Immigration and Refugee Protection Regulations. S.O.R./2002-227.

Legal Services, Immigration and Refugee Board. *Consolidated Grounds in the Immigration and Refugee Protection Act: Persons in Need of Protection—Danger of Torture.* May 15, 2002. www.irb-cisr.gc.ca/en/references/legal/rpd/cgrounds/torture/index_e.htm.

Legal Services, Immigration and Refugee Board. *Consolidated Grounds in the Immigration and Refugee Protection Act: Persons in Need of Protection—Risk to Life or Risk of Cruel and Unusual Treatment or Punishment.* May 15, 2002. www.irb-cisr.gc.ca/en/about/tribunals/rpd/cgrounds/life/index_e.htm.

Legal Services, Immigration and Refugee Board. *Interpretation of the Convention Refugee Definition in the Case Law.* December 2002. Addendum #1—December 2003.

Refugee Appeal Division Rules. *Canada Gazette*, vol. 135, no. 50. December 15, 2001. http://canadagazette.gc.ca/partI/2001/20011215/html/regle3-e.html.

Refugee Protection Division Rules. S.O.R./2002-228.

Security Intelligence Review Committee. *SIRC Report 2003-2004: An Operational Review of the Canadian Security Intelligence Service.* September 30, 2004. www.sirc-csars.gc.ca/anrran/index-eng.html.

United Nations High Commissioner for Refugees. Handbook on Procedures and Criteria for Determining Refugee Status Under the 1951 Convention and the 1967 Protocol Relating to the Status of Refugees. HCR/IP/4/Eng/REV.1 Reedited, Geneva, January 1992, UNHCR 1979.

RECOMMENDED READING

Canadian Heritage. Human Rights Program. www.pch.gc.ca/progs/pdp-hrp/docs/iccpr/facts_e.cfm. Describes the UN human rights system, UN instruments, and how Canada is involved in this area; provides a glossary of specialized terms and weblinks to related sites.

Hathaway, James C. *Rebuilding Trust: Report of the Review of Fundamental Justice in Information Gathering and Dissemination at the Immigration and Refugee Board of Canada.* Ottawa: Immigration and Refugee Board, 1993. Accompanied by "Action plan: Response of the Immigration and Refugee Board to the Report of Professor James Hathaway."

Hathaway, James C. *The Law of Refugee Status.* Toronto: Butterworths, 1991.

Hathaway, James C. *The Rights of Refugees Under International Law.* Cambridge, UK and New York: Cambridge University Press, 2005.

Office of the United Nations High Commissioner for Human Rights. www.ohchr.org.

Statutes of the Office of the United Nations High Commissioner for Refugees:

- Convention Relating to the Status of Refugees. 189 U.N.T.S. 150, entered into force April 22, 1954. www.unhchr.ch/html/menu3/b/o_c_ref.htm.

- Protocol Relating to the Status of Refugees. 606 U.N.T.S. 267, entered into force October 4, 1967. www.unhchr.ch/html/menu3/b/o_p_ref.htm.

- Convention Against Torture and Other Cruel, Inhuman or Degrading Treatment or Punishment. Can. T.S. 1987 no. 36; G.A. res. 39/46 (annex, 39 U.N. GAOR Supp. (no. 51) at 197, U.N. Doc. A/39/51 (1984)). www.unhchr.ch/html/menu3/b/h_cat39.htm.

- International Covenant on Civil and Political Rights. G.A. res. 2200A (XXI), 21 U.N. GAOR Supp. (No. 16) at 52, U.N. Doc. A/6316 (1966), 999 U.N.T.S. 171, entered into force March 23, 1976. www.unhchr.ch/html/menu3/b/a_ccpr.htm.

- Universal Declaration of Human Rights. G.A. res. 217A (III) U.N. Doc. A/810 at 71 (1948). www.un.org/Overview/rights.html.

Human Rights Organizations

Amnesty International. www.amnesty.org. An international organization whose mission is to conduct research and promote action to prevent human rights abuses.

Canadian Council for Refugees. www.ccrweb.ca. A non-profit umbrella organization that promotes the rights and protection of refugees, both in Canada and internationally. Composed of organizations that aid in the settlement, sponsorship, and protection of refugees and immigrants.

Human Rights Watch. www.hrw.org. An organization dedicated to protecting the human rights of people around the world and investigating human rights violations.

Country-Specific Sources for Research Purposes

Amnesty International Report 2008. http://thereport.amnesty.org.

Human Rights Watch Country Reports. www.hrw.org/countries.html.

US State Department Country Reports on Human Rights Practices. www.state.gov/g/drl/rls/hrrpt.

REVIEW QUESTIONS

This chapter was divided into four main sections setting out the process for making a claim for refugee protection in Canada and representing clients in the process. The headings below correspond to those in the chapter. You should now be able to answer the questions under each heading.

Introduction

1. What is a spontaneous arrival?

2. What separate government organizations are involved in the refugee protection claim process in Canada?

Front-End Process

Under what circumstances is a refugee claim ineligible to be referred to the Refugee Protection Division?

Refugee Determination Processes

1. Name the key document that the claimant must complete to tell her story. Outline the timelines and number of copies that must be filed at the Refugee Protection Division.

2. What is the potential consequence of failing to file this document?

3. Why is the Personal Information Form so important to the Refugee Protection Division?

4. As counsel, you should be able to explain the refugee determination process in full and prepare your client for a refugee hearing. Answer the following questions for your client:

    a. What forms and documents must be provided to the IRB?

    b. What is the nature of the proceedings?

    c. What are a refugee claimant's rights and responsibilities at a proceeding before the Refugee Protection Division?

    d. Who is present at a typical regular refugee hearing where the minister is not intervening? What are the roles of each person present?

    e. What are all possible determinations that a Refugee Protection Division member can make?

Post-Determination Processes

1. Explain the options available to the refugee claimant if his claim is accepted.

2. Explain the options available to the refugee claimant if his claim is rejected.

DISCUSSION QUESTION

Refugee claimants are duty bound to answer all questions truthfully and produce all documents and information as requested. Imagine someone who has fled for her safety, who is fearful of government officials, and who cannot understand or speak either of our official languages. Would that person trust the immigration officer in an interview and answer all questions truthfully? Discuss.

ACTIVITY

1. Find out what resources exist in your community to assist newcomer immigrants and refugees. Together with your classmates, compile a list of agencies and the services provided to refugees in your community.

2. The refugee claimant will be nervous on the day of the interview or hearing. Counsel can make the event more comfortable by managing the claimant's expectations. With a partner, assume the roles of counsel and client. As counsel, describe and explain to your client:

   - the physical layout of a hearing or interview room and the fact that counsel may not be sitting next to the claimant;

   - that the proceedings are private (generally closed to the public to protect the confidentiality of the claimant);

   - that the proceedings will be recorded;

   - that the proceedings will be held in English or French, although an interpreter will be provided;

   - the type of proceeding—will it be an interview (expedited), a pre-hearing conference, or a hearing?—as well as what to expect during the proceeding;

   - who will be present and what their roles are; and

   - that the proceedings will be non-adversarial unless the minister's representative is intervening.

CHAPTER 10

Enforcement Procedures

LEARNING OUTCOMES

After reading this chapter you should be able to:

- Identify the grounds of inadmissibility.

- Describe general control and enforcement activities.

- Distinguish among the various removal orders.

- Understand immigration enforcement proceedings.

- Understand the process of detention of foreign nationals.

- Understand the role of participants at immigration proceedings.

- Identify general Immigration Division rules.

INTRODUCTION

Managing permanent and temporary immigration to Canada is a difficult balancing act. On the one hand, immigration law and policy aim to facilitate immigration to attract a skilled workforce, reunite families, encourage students and visitors to stay on a temporary basis, and protect refugees and persons in need of protection. On the other hand, immigration law and policy must also deal with rules of exclusion and removal of inadmissible foreign nationals, such as controls to deny access to those who would pose a heavy burden on health and social services or a risk to the health, safety, and security of Canadians.

These competing goals are reflected in the stated objectives of immigration law, particularly ss. 3(1)(a) and (h) of the *Immigration and Refugee Protection Act* (IRPA):

(a) to permit Canada to pursue the maximum social, cultural and economic benefits of immigration;

(h) to protect the health and safety of Canadians and to maintain the security of Canadian society.

The task of balancing competing demands is reflected in the processing of applications of prospective permanent and temporary residents: an officer assesses a person's application to decide whether the applicant meets specific program criteria, and to determine whether there are reasons to find the person inadmissible, thereby refusing the application and denying access to Canada.

After arriving in Canada, temporary and permanent residents do not have an absolute right to remain here. A person who violates a Canadian law, such as the *Criminal Code* or an immigration law, may become inadmissible, triggering enforcement activities such as removal.

Since 2003, the Canada Border Services Agency (CBSA), which reports to the minister of Public Safety, has had the responsibility for border management and enforcement activities; it is the agency that is primarily responsible for the enforcement provisions of the IRPA. The Immigration Division (ID) of the Immigration and Refugee Board (IRB) also plays an important role by hearing and deciding immigration matters referred to it.

Key immigration enforcement and control activities include the following:[1]

- carrying out **interdiction** functions, or control activities that prevent illegal travellers and criminals from reaching Canada

- conducting background checks and other observations before visas are issued

- gathering information on activities such as human smuggling and illegal migration

- gathering intelligence on activities such as the creation, use, and distribution of fraudulent documents

- cooperating with other enforcement agencies, both domestic and international

- performing examinations abroad and at ports of entry

- conducting investigations and admissibility hearings

- issuing removal and exclusion orders

- creating and implementing measures to deal with dangerous criminals, security and safety risks, and war criminals

- arresting and detaining foreign nationals who pose a security or safety risk

- enforcing penalties for illegal activities

- streamlining the appeal process

- removing foreign nationals who are illegally in Canada.

The Immigration Division hears two types of immigration matters:

- **Admissibility hearings**. The ID has the authority under s. 45 of the IRPA to hear and decide whether permanent residents and foreign nationals alleged to have contravened the IRPA should be allowed to enter or remain in Canada, or should be ordered removed.

- **Detention reviews**. The ID has the authority under s. 54 of the IRPA to review the immigration detention of permanent residents and foreign nationals to decide whether to release them or whether there are sufficient reasons to continue the detention.

There are approximately 30 ID members across Canada who hear and decide immigration matters. In 2007, there were 2,519 admissibility hearings finalized, and 11,680 detention reviews held.[2]

Admissibility hearings and detention reviews are adversarial, and the ID member is expected to hear and decide the matter in an impartial and unbiased manner. There are two parties: (1) the *person concerned*, who may be a permanent resident, permanent resident visa holder, or a foreign national, and (2) the minister's counsel representing the minister of Public Safety and Emergency Preparedness (PSEP). The minister's counsel is called the *hearings officer*.

This chapter will help you understand how officers control admissions and enforce the IRPA and its regulations, including general enforcement procedures, and immigration hearings and detentions.

VISA APPLICATIONS AND EXAMINATIONS

Section 11 of the *Immigration and Refugee Protection Act* obliges all foreign nationals who wish to come to Canada, either permanently or temporarily, to apply prior to entering Canada. Foreign nationals must go through the application process to obtain a temporary or permanent resident visa, and undergo medical examinations and background checks for identity, criminality, and security. Temporary residence applicants from visa-exempt countries apply orally at the port of entry. Generally, foreign nationals whose applications are rejected because they are inadmissible are issued refusal letters explaining the basis for their refusal, and some have the right to a judicial review. The various grounds that bar a person from entering or remaining in Canada are discussed in detail in Chapter 3, "Inadmissibility."

Prior to Entry—Visa Applications

The purpose of requiring a visa is to stop those who are inadmissible from entering Canada before they travel, rather than waiting until they arrive at a port of entry and then incurring the expense of removal.

PERMANENT RESIDENT VISAS

Visa officers issue permanent resident visas for applicants under the various categories of permanent residence as a precondition to permanent entry (s. 21 of the IRPA). Successful applicants may travel to Canada but must undergo a further examination by an officer at the port of entry before being admitted and allowed to remain in Canada. (See Chapter 5, "Permanent Entry.")

TEMPORARY RESIDENT VISAS

Foreign nationals living in certain countries require a visa to enter Canada, even on a temporary basis. Visa officers issue **temporary resident visas (TRVs)** in three categories: visitors, students, and temporary workers, as described in Chapter 4, "Temporary Entry." Like the permanent resident visa, a temporary resident visa authorizes a person to board an airplane or ship to travel to Canada; however, the final decision to allow a person to come into Canada is made at the port of entry (s. 22 of the IRPA).

Port of Entry Arrival—Examinations

The events of September 11, 2001 refocused efforts on protecting the country against terrorists, at times lessening the openness and efficiency of cross-border movement that travellers previously enjoyed. These efforts are reflected in the functions of the CBSA. An agency of Public Safety Canada, the CBSA is responsible for managing and controlling Canadian ports of entry. CBSA officers decide who is allowed to enter Canada, whom to detain under the IRPA, and whom to remove. Section 18 of the IRPA authorizes the examination of all travellers at ports of entry, including Canadian citizens, registered Indians, permanent residents, permanent resident visa holders, temporary resident visa holders, and foreign nationals. Even travellers with appropriate visas must undergo examinations by an officer at the port of entry. The examining officer must be satisfied that a foreign national is not inadmissible in order to allow that person to come into Canada.

Ports of entry generally have two separate control points. If you have ever travelled outside of Canada, you experienced the interview at the first control point, or primary inspection line, upon your return to Canada. The primary inspection line is where CBSA officers conduct the initial interview of travellers and carry out a mix of immigration and customs activities. Here, they perform the basic duties of checking your identity and your immigration status, and asking about your travel and about any goods you may be bringing into the country.

CBSA officers attempt to balance their duty to prevent entry by problem individuals with the goal of allowing other travellers to move easily through the checkpoint. An officer may refer a person to a secondary examination if she believes that a more thorough interview is required. The purpose of the secondary interview is to confirm the identity of the traveller, verify documents such as passports and permits, and gather information to make an informed decision regarding admissibility.

PERMANENT RESIDENCE APPLICANTS

Permanent residence applicants seeking to establish permanent residence and any accompanying family members must have permanent resident visas and *Confirmation of Permanent Residence documents*. They must also show a valid passport and other essential documents, such as a list of all the household and personal items they are bringing into Canada, and proof of funds and assets.

A CBSA officer verifies whether there have been any changes since the issuance of the visa by the visa officer, and that the document holders are not inadmissible. For example, the CBSA officer confirms the applicant's identity, checks that medical examinations are still valid, and verifies that the applicant has enough money to cover living expenses (such as rent, food, clothing, and transportation) for a six-month period.

If the CBSA officer is satisfied that the applicant and any accompanying family members are not inadmissible, the officer is required to allow the person entry as a permanent resident. Conditions may be imposed, such as those required by the regulations for entrepreneurs and their family members under the business class, or a requirement that a medical condition be monitored. Non-compliance with conditions could result in inadmissibility and removal.

PERMANENT RESIDENTS

Permanent residents arriving at a port of entry who already have status (as compared with applicants who are seeking status) must undergo an examination to satisfy the CBSA officer that they have not lost their status or become inadmissible (s. 19(2) of the IRPA). An officer verifies the Permanent Resident Card and whether the residency obligation to live in Canada for two years in each five-year period was met, and checks for inadmissibility. If the officer is satisfied that the permanent resident has complied with the conditions of permanent residency and has not become inadmissible, then the officer must allow entry.

TEMPORARY RESIDENTS

Generally, in the case of temporary residents, a foreign national and any accompanying family members must have a temporary resident visa (unless exempt). They must also show a valid passport and other essential documents, such as proof of funds and assets, letter of confirmation for school, letter of invitation for visitors, and a return ticket.

Temporary residents must undergo an interview at the port of entry to confirm identity, verify admissibility, review any visa restrictions (such as expiration of a work permit or prohibition against work), confirm that medical examinations if required are still valid, and verify that they have enough money to cover living expenses for the duration of the visit. If the officer is satisfied that the foreign national and any accompanying family members are not inadmissible, then the officer is required to allow entry.

Conditions may be imposed—for example, the CBSA officer may confirm that a visitor may not work or study, and must leave before the temporary resident visa has expired. Admission as a temporary resident requires compliance with any conditions; non-compliance could result in removal.

Temporary Resident Permits

At times it is not workable to conduct an examination for inadmissibility right away. This may be due to circumstances such as lateness in the day or unavailability of an interpreter. In such cases, an officer may issue a **temporary resident permit (TRP)** and Notice to Appear, according to ss. 23 and 24 of the IRPA. This allows the person to enter Canada temporarily so that an examination or an admissibility hearing can be held at a later time.

The person is consequently allowed to enter Canada but is compelled to appear for her immigration proceeding, which may be an examination or a hearing. The temporary resident is permitted to move freely within Canada; however, Citizenship and Immigration Canada (CIC) must be notified of any change in address.

In some cases, a TRP may be issued to an applicant who has been found inadmissible. However, the TRP may be issued to an inadmissible applicant only where the grounds of inadmissibility are technical or medical, or where they concern the applicant's criminal history. Additionally, the officer must find compelling reasons to do so, while weighing the risk to Canada or Canadians.

For example, a person may be issued a temporary resident permit if there are sufficient humanitarian and compassionate grounds, such as the admission of a child to undergo life-saving surgery. Although the child would normally be found inadmissible for medical reasons, an exception may be made if the surgery is not available in the country of citizenship and if the medical bills are paid through charitable donations.

The cost of a TRP is $200 and may be issued for periods ranging from one day to three years.

INADMISSIBILITY REPORTS

An officer who believes that a permanent resident or foreign national who is already in Canada is inadmissible may prepare a report setting out the relevant facts for the minister, according to s. 44(1) of the IRPA.

The **inadmissibility report**, often referred to as a **s. 44(1) report**, sets out the grounds of inadmissibility alleged by the officer, with the related sections of the IRPA and the evidence in narrative form. The person may in some circumstances be detained under the IRPA pending a hearing.

Authority to Write Report

Generally, it is CIC officers who have the designated authority to write inadmissibility reports. However, if the grounds of inadmissibility are security, violations of human or international rights, or organized criminality, the cases are managed by the CBSA.

Discretion to Write Report

When an officer believes that a permanent resident has failed to comply with residency obligations and has lost permanent residence status as a result, the officer must write an inadmissibility report. However, in other cases, writing the report is at the discretion of the officer.

When the matter involves the more serious reasons for a finding of inadmissibility (that is, security, violations of human or international rights, serious criminality, or organized criminality), an officer will usually prepare an inadmissibility report, which initiates the removal process.

For matters involving less serious, non-criminal matters, an officer considers a number of options. For example, at a port of entry examination of a foreign national, an officer may take any of the following actions:

- inform the person that she is inadmissible and is allowed to leave Canada voluntarily—the person will be given an *Allowed to Leave Canada form (IMM 1282B)*;

- write the s. 44(1) report and detain the person pending an admissibility hearing; or

- write the s. 44(1) report and allow the person to enter temporarily to attend an admissibility hearing.

CIC's *Enforcement (ENF)* operations manual on writing s. 44(1) reports lists several factors that officers may consider when deciding whether to write a report:[3]

- the length of time the person has been in Canada and her status;

- the grounds of inadmissibility;

- whether the person is already the subject of a removal order;

- whether the person is already the subject of a separate inadmissibility report incorporating allegations that will likely result in a removal order;

- whether the officer is satisfied that the person is, or soon will be, leaving Canada, and if so, whether the imposition of a future requirement to obtain consent to return is warranted;

- whether there is a record of the person having previously contravened immigration legislation;

- whether the person was cooperative;

- whether a temporary resident permit was authorized;

- how long the person has been a permanent resident (for example, since childhood);

- whether the person was cooperative and forthcoming in providing information; and

- whether the person accepts responsibility and is remorseful.

Consider the following case scenario:

Eunice is a 22-year-old citizen of Jamaica. Eunice applied for and obtained a temporary resident visa as a visitor so she could visit her older sister, Nadine, and Nadine's family in Toronto. Eunice had not seen Nadine since Nadine left for Canada over ten years ago. She was happy to get reacquainted with her older sister and to become acquainted with Nadine's two school-aged children and husband. Eunice was provided with her own room in Nadine's home, shown around the city, and given new clothes (so she could face the Canadian cold). Eunice adored her niece and nephew and played with them often. This caught the attention of a next-door neighbour, who asked if

Eunice could watch over her children one day, while she went shopping. One of the neighbour's children was knocked down while playing with Eunice's nephew and got a bump on the head. This upset the neighbour, who thought Eunice too lenient about the ordeal. She also suspected that Eunice was an "illegal," seeing as she had been living next door for almost a year now. The neighbour, jealous about Nadine having the extra hands at home and offended by Eunice's attitude, decided to call police and falsely accused Eunice of hitting her child. After investigating the incident, the police determined that none of the children had been abused and did not charge Eunice. However, they informed immigration authorities. It turns out the neighbour was right about one thing: Eunice overstayed her temporary visa.

In this scenario, Eunice will be interviewed about her immigration status by an immigration investigator at the local immigration office. If the officer has reasonable grounds to believe that Eunice is inadmissible because her temporary resident visa expired and consequently no longer has authorization to be in Canada, the officer has no discretion and must write an inadmissibility report.

Contents of Report

The officer must complete the s. 44(1) report in writing and include the following information:

- the date of the report and place of issue;

- basic information about the person (full and correct name, date of birth, etc.);

- information about when the temporary resident visa was issued and when it expired;

- the allegation—in Eunice's case, that she failed to leave Canada by the end of the authorized period of stay;

- the exact section of the IRPA—in Eunice's case, s. 41(a) ("Non-compliance with the Act"); and

- the facts in the narrative of the report that amount to why the officer has reasonable grounds to believe that the person is inadmissible—in Eunice's case, the address where she is staying, the date and place her visa was issued, the date and place where she was admitted to Canada, the date her temporary visa expired, and any other details to support the allegation.

There is no information to support the neighbour's allegation that Eunice committed a crime, so the officer does not include this information in her report or base her finding of inadmissibility on criminal grounds.

The officer must address the report to the minister for review and sign the report.

Next Steps

If the minister, or the officer's supervisor (who is considered to be an officer with the delegated authority), is of the opinion that the report is well founded, the minister may issue a removal order in certain cases.

Alternatively, depending on the grounds of inadmissibility, the minister may refer the report to the ID for a hearing. In Eunice's case, the minister will refer the matter to the ID for a hearing because Eunice was already admitted to, and living, in Canada.

The officer will tell Eunice at the time of the interview that she is not under arrest and that there is no reason to detain her. She is free to return to Nadine's home to await her admissibility hearing. The officer explains that Eunice will be sent a Notice of Admissibility Hearing by mail, that Eunice must attend, and that she may make her case for staying in Canada. However, if the ID member finds that Eunice is inadmissible, an exclusion order will be issued and she will be required to leave Canada.

ADMISSIBILITY HEARINGS

Whereas reports regarding admissibility are called inadmissibility reports, hearings on the same subject are referred to as admissibility hearings. The inadmissibility report is used as evidence at the admissibility hearing.

Admissibility hearings are adversarial, in that the minister is represented by counsel, called the hearings officer. The hearings officer presents a case for the inadmissibility of the person whose admissibility is in question, called the person concerned. The person concerned may be represented at the hearing by an immigration consultant or lawyer. A member of the ID conducts the hearing, listening to both sides and rendering a decision.

Hearing Procedures

The hearing may be held in person or by means of live telecommunication—for example, a videoconference. The proceedings are recorded.

The ID member begins by making an opening statement. The member then has the parties and counsel identify themselves for the record, confirms that the person concerned can understand the interpreter if one is required, swears in the interpreter, and deals with other matters such as witnesses.

The hearings officer reads the inadmissibility report into the record and asks to file it as the minister's evidence. The member then explains the possible outcomes of the hearing to the person concerned.

Generally, the hearings officer then calls the person concerned, who is then sworn in and examined. The hearings officer files evidence and calls any other witnesses with information that supports the case for inadmissibility.

The person concerned (or her counsel) may then examine witnesses and file evidence. She may argue that the inadmissibility report is incorrect for technical, legal, or factual reasons. For example, she may argue that dates and names are wrong, signatures are missing, the grounds of inadmissibility do not apply, or the facts are inaccurate.

After all the evidence has been heard, counsel must be prepared to make a final oral statement, called representations, at the end of the hearing.

Onus of Proof

The onus of proof is the burden of proving facts, such as proving inadmissibility. In a criminal trial, the onus is on the prosecution to prove guilt. In a civil trial, the onus is generally on the plaintiff to prove that the defendant caused harm or breached a contract.

At an admissibility hearing, the onus of proof depends on whether or not the person concerned has legal status in Canada. If she was denied the right to enter Canada, and therefore has no legal status, the onus is on the person concerned to prove that she is not inadmissible.

However, if the person concerned was allowed to enter Canada and is alleged at a later time to have become inadmissible, then the onus is on the hearings officer to prove those allegations.

Standard of Proof

The standard of proof is the degree of proof necessary to satisfy the onus of proof. At an admissibility hearing, this means the degree or amount of proof necessary for a decision on inadmissibility to be made. It also applies to the decisions of a visa officer abroad or a CBSA officer at a port of entry.

REASONABLE GROUNDS

The standard of proof varies depending on the ground of inadmissibility at issue. However, in most cases the decision maker must have reasonable grounds for believing that some act has taken place, is taking place, or may take place that leads to the conclusion of inadmissibility.

Reasonable grounds involve more than a mere suspicion that a person is inadmissible; rather, there must be an objective basis for the allegation. The decision maker must have credible information that is sufficiently specific and reliable to support the allegation that a person is inadmissible.

Consider the following case scenario:

Frederico came to Canada on a student visa. Shortly after his arrival, Frederico discovered a Salvadoran restaurant owned by Antonio and Maria. Antonio was an old friend of Frederico's father from El Salvador, and Frederico often visited the little restaurant to get a "taste of home." When Antonio asked Frederico if he could help out a little on weekends, informing him that he would be paid cash "under the table," Frederico was only happy to help, even though he already had enough money to pay his tuition, books, accommodation, and food expenses. However, an ex-girlfriend of Frederico spotted him working there. Upset over the breakup, she informed immigration that he was working in a restaurant without authorization.

The IRP Regulations define "work" to mean "an activity for which wages are paid or commission is earned, or that is in direct competition with the activities of Canadian citizens or permanent residents in the Canadian labour market."

Frederico's case would not be easy for a hearings officer to prove at an admissibility hearing. Are there reasonable grounds for believing that Frederico "worked" without authorization and was therefore in non-compliance with the IRPA? What credible information is available to support the allegation? Would testimony from an ex-girlfriend who was angry with him be credible?

PROBABLE GROUNDS

The standard of proof is higher with respect to serious criminal acts that are committed outside of Canada, and which, if committed in Canada, would be punishable for a maximum term of at least ten years, according to s. 36(1)(c) of the IRPA.

For these cases, the decision maker must have probable grounds for believing that some act has taken place, is taking place, or may take place that leads to the conclusion of inadmissibility. In other words, the facts must be proven on a balance of probabilities. This means that the decision maker must believe that the allegations are more probable than not. In practice, the officer would attempt to obtain evidence such as the record of conviction; however, it is not always possible to do so.

INADMISSIBILITY ON SERIOUS GROUNDS

Canada is strictest about entry of persons who are inadmissible based on the most serious grounds, as follows:

- security;
- violating human or international rights;
- serious criminality; or
- organized criminality.

Where there is a finding of inadmissibility on one or more of these serious grounds, the person concerned has fewer rights. There is no right to appeal, and no right to make a refugee claim.

Right of Appeal

Where there is a finding of inadmissibility on any of the most serious grounds, there is no right to appeal. This may result in earlier removal, because there will be no delay to await the outcome of further immigration processes.

Refugee Claims

A person who is found inadmissible on any of the most serious grounds is barred from making a refugee claim, according to s. 101 of the IRPA.

However, there is a strict three-day time provision to process refugee claimants at the front end where an officer determines inadmissibility. As a result, it is not always possible to obtain the results of the security and background checks within this time-frame. Consequently, the deeming provisions take effect and refugee claims that otherwise should have been stopped may slip through.

In such cases, where information that the claimant is ineligible is received by the minister too late, after a claim was already referred to the RPD, the minister may choose to deal with the matter in one of two ways. The minister may suspend the refugee proceedings and hold an admissibility hearing, where issues of inadmissibility will be fully examined. (In this case, the RPD hearing will be held only if the claimant is successful at the admissibility hearing.) Alternatively, the minister may intervene and make arguments at the Refugee Protection Division.

SUSPENSION

The minister may serve notice to suspend the claim at the RPD, according to s. 103 of the IRPA. The matter of inadmissibility is then argued by a hearings officer at an admissibility hearing before a member of the ID. If the member finds the claimant inadmissible on security grounds, the claimant is consequently ineligible to make the refugee claim. Under s. 104 of the IRPA, the proceedings at the RPD are then terminated.

Officers must consider the alleged grounds of inadmissibility when opting to suspend refugee proceedings and hold an admissibility hearing, according to CIC's *Enforcement (ENF)* operations manual on ministerial interventions.[4] For example, cases involving security, criminality, or new trends in the movement of refugees, such as fraud and trafficking, are better suited to an admissibility hearing before the ID than ministerial intervention at an RPD hearing. This is because the ID member can issue the appropriate removal order at the end of the proceeding and then consider the issue of detention, both of which are immigration matters, not refugee matters.

MINISTERIAL INTERVENTION

The minister may choose to intervene at the refugee protection hearing, rather than suspend it. A ministerial intervention makes the RPD hearing adversarial: a hearings officer opposes the protection of the refugee claimant and argues that the exclusion clause of the definition of a Convention refugee under s. 98 of the IRPA applies to the case.

Exclusions are set out in ss. E and F of article 1 of the United Nations Convention Relating to the Status of Refugees and essentially bar a refugee claimant from refugee protection because of alleged war crimes, crimes against humanity, serious non-political crimes, or acts contrary to the United Nations Principles. (Exclusion is more fully discussed in Chapter 7.)

Cases involving credibility issues and the exclusion clause of the Convention refugee definition are better suited to a ministerial intervention because these issues are refugee matters related to the application of the Convention refugee definition.

REMOVAL

Canadian citizens are not subject to removal even if they become inadmissible (for example, for committing a crime). The only situation in which a citizen may be removed is if citizenship is first revoked. This may happen only in rare circumstances such as where citizenship was granted on the basis of a misrepresentation.

Foreign nationals and permanent residents who stay in Canada lawfully generally need not be concerned about removal. However, when a non-citizen is found to be inadmissible in Canada either at the port of entry or after being admitted (such as in the case of Eunice, above), the person may be ordered removed. A **removal order** may be made in either of the following circumstances:

- following an examination, in which case the minister issues the removal order; or

- at an admissibility hearing, in which case a member of the Immigration Division issues the removal order.

Any family members in Canada who are dependants of a person who is the subject of a removal order may also be included in the order as long as the family member is not a Canadian citizen or permanent resident 19 years of age or over (s. 227 of the IRP Regulations).

Removal from Canada is an important enforcement activity that is carried out by the CBSA and authorized under the IRPA. In some cases, people leave voluntarily after being issued a removal order; in other cases, CBSA officers must enforce removal orders by physically removing those persons. For the period from 2006 to 2007, the CBSA removed about 12,600 inadmissible persons, including about 1,900 criminals who posed a high risk to Canada.[5]

Timelines for Removal

Depending on the type of removal order, the person may be allowed time to prepare and arrange for leaving. The length of time allowed may vary. Or a removal order may be enforceable on the day that it is made when any of the following conditions exist, according to s. 49 of IRPA:

- the person has no right to appeal the order;

- the person has a right to appeal but has not appealed the order; or

- in the event of an appeal, a final determination has been made by the Immigration Appeal Division (IAD).

However, where refugee claimants and protected persons are subjected to a removal order, the removal is conditional upon the outcome of the claim. This is important because the consequences of removal may be life threatening. Generally, the order takes effect as follows:

- 7 days after a person is determined ineligible;

- 15 days after the claim has been decided by the Refugee Protection Division (RPD) and is rejected; or

- 15 days after the claim has been decided as withdrawn, abandoned, or terminated.

A removal order may be enforceable immediately in some cases. For example, when a foreign national arrives at a port of entry, the CBSA may issue a removal order against him and enforce it on the same day if he waives or exhausts any legal right to remain in Canada.

However, the removal process is not often such a simple process. After the removal order is issued, a person may seek a judicial review of the matter before the Federal Court of Canada and this decision may be appealed to the Federal Court of Appeal. In some cases, it may even reach the Supreme Court of Canada. The removal order takes effect when the person either does not pursue any further legal recourse or has exhausted these avenues.

Before the CBSA may carry out the removal order, however, there are a number of activities that must be attended to which may also prolong or further delay removal, especially if the individual being removed is not cooperative:

- instruct the individual for removal to ensure that he understands his responsibilities, such as the requirement to prepare for removal within the stipulated time-frame and the need to report to an immigration officer before leaving;

- confirm the identity of the person (who may conceal his identity to avoid being returned);

- obtain travel documents such as passports and visas from the person's country of destination (made more difficult if there is a situation of general unrest in the country or if the person is concealing his identity); and

- issue an immigration warrant for arrest and detention under the IRPA, if the person fails to appear for removal.

For the actual removal of a person, such as boarding the person on a plane destined for another country, the CBSA may assign escorts if any of the following concerns exist: the person will not obey the removal order, the person poses a risk of violence to himself or others, or the person poses a threat to the health or safety of other travellers. Generally, CBSA officers carry out removals but, in some cases, they may be assisted by the Royal Canadian Mounted Police (RCMP), if there are safety or security concerns, or by medical personnel, if there are health-related concerns. Furthermore, the airline may refuse to transport the person without an escort.

The function of removing a person from Canada is further complicated by the fact that the country of destination must be willing to allow the person to return. Generally, Canada removes persons to one of the following countries:

- the country from which they came to Canada;

- the country in which they last permanently resided before coming to Canada;

- the country in which they are a national or citizen; or

- their country of birth (s. 241 of the IRP Regulations).

However, if these countries are not willing to accept the person, the minister may select another country that is willing to allow the legal entry of the person.

Removal Costs

Removal costs may be paid by the person being removed (usually when the person leaves voluntarily), by the airline, or at the government's expense. In cases where the foreign national arrives at an airport and is not allowed to enter Canada, the airline must cover the cost. It is the airline's responsibility to ensure that travellers hold the proper documentation. If the airline transported the person without proper documentation, the airline is responsible for returning the person and also incurs the cost of an administrative fee.

A person who is removed at the expense of the government is not allowed to return to Canada until the removal costs are paid back. These costs are prescribed under s. 243 of the IRP Regulations, as follows:

- $750 for removal to the United States or St. Pierre and Miquelon; and

- $1,500 for removal to any other country.

Types of Removal Orders

There are three types of removal orders set out in s. 223 of the IRP Regulations, as follows:

- departure orders—reference s. 224

- exclusion orders—reference s. 225

- deportation orders—reference s. 226.

Each removal order has different consequences for the person against whom the order is made.

DEPARTURE ORDERS (SECTION 224)

A **departure order** generally requires a person to leave Canada within 30 days of the departure order coming into effect, and to obtain a certificate of departure as part of the criteria for removal (ss. 240(1)(a) to (c) of the IRP Regulations).

A departure order is usually issued for a less serious violation of immigration law. A person may successfully request a departure order at an admissibility hearing if voluntary compliance can be shown. As counsel you can prepare your client by providing proof of the client's ability and willingness to leave Canada; proof may include a valid passport or travel document, an ability to pay for travel arrangements with a return ticket, a letter of resignation from the employer, or arrangements to terminate a lease or the sale of a house.

A person who leaves Canada on a departure order may apply to return to Canada as long as a *certificate of departure* was obtained from CBSA officials at the port of entry just prior to departure. Although Canada does not have exit controls, the certificate of departure is a type of control that serves as proof that the person complied with the order by leaving for a country of destination that allowed lawful entry.

If a person fails to leave Canada within the 30-day time period, or leaves and fails to obtain a certificate of departure, the departure order is automatically deemed to be a deportation order, according to s. 224(2) of the IRP Regulations. This has serious consequences should the person wish to return to Canada.

Additionally, if immigration officials cannot locate the person, they may issue an *immigration warrant* for the person's arrest. The immigration warrant can be viewed in the Canada-wide Canadian Police Information Centre, a computerized information system that provides Canadian law enforcement agencies with information about crime and criminals. A person for whom an immigration warrant has been issued usually comes to the attention of CBSA or CIC officials after apprehension by police—for example, after being stopped by police for a minor traffic violation. When the person who has not left Canada is eventually arrested, he will likely be detained pending removal. It may be difficult for counsel to arrange for the person's release from detention given his previous failure to appear for removal.

Exceptions to the 30-Day Rule

There are several exceptions to the 30 days allowed for departure under a departure order, as follows:

1. **Conditional removal order.** A conditional removal order, or removal order with conditions, is a departure order with conditions attached. It is issued pending the outcome of a refugee claim referred to the RPD, for example.

2. **Stay of removal.** A stay of removal is an order that freezes the removal order temporarily, and allows the person to remain in Canada until the removal order becomes enforceable.

3. **Detention.** When a foreign national is detained within the 30-day period, such as for arrest on a criminal charge, the 30-day period is suspended until either the foreign national is released or the removal order becomes enforceable.

EXCLUSION ORDERS (SECTION 225)

The **exclusion order** differs from the departure order in that it bars a foreign national from returning to Canada for a specified period of time, either for one year or for two years.

The one-year ban is generally issued when a foreign national has committed a minor offence, such as trying to enter at the port of entry with incomplete documentation. The two-year ban is reserved for more serious offences. For example, if the person engaged in misrepresentation, an exclusion for two years must be issued (s. 225(3) of the IRP Regulations).

A person against whom an exclusion order has been issued may not return to Canada for the duration of the ban without the written authorization of an officer. The person must apply for an *Authorization to Return to Canada.*

DEPORTATION ORDERS (SECTION 226)

The **deportation order** permanently bars a person from future admission to Canada unless that person obtains the written consent of the minister. A deportation order may be issued in the following circumstances:

- the person has been found inadmissible to Canada on serious grounds;

- the person has committed a serious violation of Canadian law; or

- a departure order issued against the person has been turned into a deportation order.

If the deportation order is made against an accompanying family member of an individual who was found inadmissible, that family member may return to Canada without written authorization.

The following chart summarizes the grounds of admissibility and the related removal orders that can be made, by type of decision maker.

Types of Stays of Removal

Enforcement of a removal order may be stayed pending some other action or outcome. Specifically, there are five ways in which a removal order may be stayed, as follows:

- by the minister,

- by application for leave for a judicial review,

- by application for a pre-removal risk assessment (PRRA),

- by application for humanitarian and compassionate considerations, or

- by appeal to the Immigration Appeal Division.

Each of these is discussed below.

MINISTER'S STAY

The minister has discretion to stay a removal order in situations where the person would be sent to a country engaged in an armed conflict, or a country dealing with a serious environmental disaster or other situation that poses a risk to the civilian population there, according to s. 230(1) of the IRP Regulations.

However, the minister's discretion is limited by the need to protect Canadian society. The minister may not issue a stay where

- the person is inadmissible on grounds of security, violating human or international rights, serious criminality or organized criminality;

- the person is a refugee claimant who is ineligible because of section F of article 1 of the Refugee Convention (crimes against peace, war crimes, or crimes against humanity); or

- the person has consented in writing to her removal (s. 230(3) of the IRP Regulations).

A minister's stay is cancelled when the minister is satisfied that the circumstances in the country no longer exist and the person under removal order would not be at risk if removed to that country (s. 230(2) of the IRP Regulations).

STAY PENDING JUDICIAL REVIEW

An unsuccessful refugee claimant may obtain a stay of removal under s. 231 of the IRP Regulations if the claimant applied for a judicial review at the Federal Court within the permitted time limit unless the claim was rejected by the Refugee Protection Division with a finding of "no credible basis." This finding removes the claimant's appeal rights.

STAY PENDING PRE-REMOVAL RISK ASSESSMENT

The *pre-removal risk assessment (PRRA)* program is available to certain persons considered to be "at risk" who are about to be removed from Canada. The PRRA is a program intended for people who are desperate to stay. For a person to be eligible, one of the following conditions must exist:

- the person must have a well-founded fear of persecution in the country to which he would be returned, according to the Convention refugee definition; or

- if the person were returned to that country, one of the following risks would exist: a risk of torture, a risk to life, or a risk of cruel and unusual treatment or punishment, according to the Convention Against Torture.

This program and its procedures are discussed in Chapter 9, "In-Canada Refugee Determination Process." When a person applies for a PRRA within the appropriate time limits, and in accordance with s. 232 of the IRP Regulations, the removal order is stayed pending the decision on the application.

STAY PENDING HUMANITARIAN AND COMPASSIONATE CONSIDERATIONS

A removal order may be stayed if the minister is of the opinion that humanitarian and compassionate considerations or public policy considerations exist. The stay will be granted under s. 233 of the IRP Regulations until a decision is made whether to grant permanent resident status. Humanitarian and compassionate grounds are explored fully in Chapter 5, "Permanent Entry."

STAY PENDING APPEAL

Where the right to appeal exists, a person may appeal the removal order to the Immigration Appeal Division. The removal order may be stayed until the appeal is heard, pursuant to s. 68 of the IRPA, if the person satisfies the IAD member that, taking into account the best interests of a child, or humanitarian and compassionate considerations, the decision ought to be stayed.

A more detailed discussion about the IAD is provided in Chapter 11; however, it is important to note here that the IAD can impose certain conditions attached to decisions to stay removal orders.

Conditions and Review of a Stay

The removal order does not go away—in a sense it buys the person time to prove that he can stay out of trouble and comply with the IRPA. One way of ensuring this is through the imposition of conditions. Under s. 68(2)(a) of the IRPA, the IAD must impose mandatory conditions, such as the following set out in s. 251 of the IRP Regulations:

- provide current address information in writing;

- provide a copy of a valid passport or travel document;

- not commit any criminal offence;

- if charged with a criminal offence, immediately report to the CBSA or as instructed by the IAD in writing; and

- if convicted of a criminal offence, immediately report to the CBSA or as instructed by the IAD in writing.

The IAD also has the discretion to impose "any condition that it considers necessary" under s. 68(2)(a) of the IRPA, such as the following:

- report in person to the CBSA as determined by the IAD;

- submit to drug testing;

- attend meetings of Alcoholics Anonymous; or

- attend drug or alcohol rehabilitation programs or counselling.

The IAD does not monitor compliance with stay conditions. This is the responsibility of the CBSA (for example, for criminality cases) or CIC (for example, for monitoring compliance in entrepreneurial cases).

A *review of a stay* of a removal order may occur if there is a concern regarding compliance with the conditions. A person who breaches any condition must appear before the IAD to speak to the matter of the breach.

The IAD may on application by the minister, or on its own initiative, reconsider the appeal, pursuant to s. 68(3) of the IRPA. A *reconsideration of the appeal* is made to determine whether the person is complying with the conditions of the stay of the removal order. At the review, the IAD hears recommendations by the minister and makes a decision to do one of the following:

- maintain the stay for an additional amount of time, and maintain conditions or issue new or additional conditions;

- cancel the stay, dismiss the appeal, and order the removal to be enforced; or

- cancel the stay, allow the appeal, and quash the removal order (very unlikely if conditions have been breached).

However, in cases where a person who was inadmissible on the ground of criminality is subsequently convicted of a serious offence, the stay is cancelled by operation of law, and the appeal is terminated.

Removal Orders

Person against whom the removal order is made	Grounds of inadmissibility	Action taken by minister's delegate	Prescribed removal order
Refugee claimant	At the time the claimant makes the claim: ◆ reasons of health ◆ financial grounds ◆ non-compliance.	Issues removal order	Departure[1]
Foreign national	The foreign national is: ◆ an unaccompanied minor or ◆ a person unable to appreciate the nature of the proceedings. For any ground of inadmissibility (IRP Regulations s. 228(4)).	Refers case to ID	Order depends on ground of inadmissibility
Foreign national or permanent resident	Security risk (IRPA s. 34(1)).	Refers case to ID	Deportation
Foreign national or permanent resident	Violating human or international rights (IRPA s. 35(1)).	Refers case to ID	Deportation
Foreign national	Serious criminality in case where the evidence is straightforward and does not require extensive analysis or weighing (IRPA s. 36(1)(a) or 36(2)(a).	Issues removal order	Deportation
Foreign national	Serious criminality (IRPA s. 36(1)(b) or (c), or s. 36(2)(a), (b), (c), or (d)).	Refers case to ID	Deportation
Permanent resident	Serious criminality (IRPA s. 36(1)).	Refers case to ID	Deportation
Foreign national or permanent resident	Organized criminality (IRPA s. 37(1)).	Refers case to ID	Deportation
Foreign national	Health grounds (IRPA s. 38).	Refers case to ID	Exclusion[2]
Foreign national or permanent resident	Financial grounds (IRPA s. 39).	Refers case to ID	Exclusion[3]
Foreign national	Misrepresenting or withholding material facts (IRPA s. 40(1)(a)). Being sponsored by a person who is determined to be inadmissible for misrepresentation (IRPA s. 40(1)(b)).	Refers case to ID	Exclusion[4]

(The table is continued on the next page.)

Person against whom the removal order is made	Grounds of inadmissibility	Action taken by minister's delegate	Prescribed removal order
Permanent resident	Misrepresenting or withholding material facts (IRPA s. 40(1)(a)).	Refers case to ID	Exclusion
Permanent resident	Being sponsored by a person who is determined to be inadmissible for misrepresentation (IRPA s. 40(1)(b)).	Refers case to ID	Departure
Foreign national	On a final determination to vacate a decision to allow the claim for refugee protection by the permanent resident or the foreign national (IRPA s. 40(1)(c)).	Issues removal order	Deportation
Foreign national or permanent resident	On ceasing to be a citizen (IRPA s. 40(1)(d) and *Citizenship Act* s. 10)	Refers case to ID	Deportation
Foreign national	Non-compliance: ♦ failing to appear for an examination or an admissibility hearing.	Issues removal order	Exclusion
Foreign national	Non-compliance: ♦ failing to appear for examination (IRPA s. 41(a)).	Refers case to ID	Exclusion[5]
Permanent resident	Non-compliance: ♦ failing to comply with any conditions imposed under the regulations, or ♦ failing to comply with residency obligations (IRPA s. 41(b), 27(2), or 28).	Refers case to ID	Departure
Permanent resident	Non-compliance: ♦ failing to establish permanent residence (IRPA s. 41(a)).	Refers case to ID	Exclusion[6]
Foreign national or permanent resident	Non-compliance: ♦ failing to comply with any other section of the Act (IRPA s. 41(a))	Refers case to ID	Exclusion[7]
Foreign national	Non-compliance: ♦ failing to leave Canada by the end of the authorized period of stay (IRPA s. 41(a)).	Refers case to ID	Exclusion[8]
Foreign national	Non-compliance: ♦ failing to obtain the authorization to return to Canada (IRPA ss. 41 and 52(1)).	Issues removal order	Deportation

(The table is continued on the next page.)

Person against whom the removal order is made	Grounds of inadmissibility	Action taken by minister's delegate	Prescribed removal order
Foreign national	Non-compliance: ◆ failing to establish that they hold a visa (IRPA ss. 41 and 20).	Issues removal order	Exclusion
Foreign national	Non-compliance: ◆ failing to leave Canada by the end of the authorized period of stay (IRPA ss. 41 and 29(2)).	Issues removal order	Exclusion
Foreign national	Non-compliance: ◆ failing to comply with any conditions on the visa (IRPA ss. 41, 29(2), and 184).	Issues removal order	Exclusion
Permanent resident	Non-compliance: ◆ failing to comply with a residency obligation (IRPA ss. 41 and 28).	Issues removal order	Departure
Foreign national	Inadmissible family member (IRPA s. 42).	Issues removal order	Same removal order as issued to the inadmissible family member

Notes

The chart is based on ss. 228 and 229 of the IRP Regulations. For a complete list and explanation of exceptions, consult part 13 of the IRP Regulations.

1 Exception: Departure order is stayed and is conditional upon the outcome of the matter: the claim is ineligible; or has been decided by the RPD and is rejected; or is withdrawn, abandoned, or terminated.

2 Exception: A departure order to be issued for undecided refugee claims on health grounds and for persons who were previously removed for the same reasons, on health grounds.

3 Exception: A departure order to be issued for undecided refugee claims for financial reasons and for persons who were previously removed for the same reasons for financial reasons.

4 Exception: A departure order to be issued for persons who were previously removed for the same reasons of misrepresentation.

5 Exception: A departure order to be issued for undecided refugee claims for failing to appear for an examination and for persons who were previously removed for the same reasons of failing to appear for an examination.

6 Exception: A departure order to be issued for persons who are inadmissible for reasons of failing to establish permanent residence if the person was previously removed for failing to establish permanent residence.

7 Exception: A departure order to be issued for undecided refugee claims if inadmissible for reasons of failing to comply; or for persons who are inadmissible for failing to comply with the Act if the person was previously removed for the same reasons, or the person failed to comply with conditions under the previous Act, or the person has been convicted of a indictable offence or two offences in Canada, unless the grounds for removal are the convictions.

8 Exception: A departure order to be issued for undecided refugee claims if inadmissible for reasons of overstaying a temporary visa.

DETENTION

The Canada Border Services Agency has the authority under the IRPA for immigration arrest and detention of permanent residents and foreign nationals at a port of entry, or when the person is in Canada. Detention may also be ordered by a member of the Immigration Division at an admissibility hearing following submissions by an officer. Depending on the risk posed by the person in detention, she may be held at a local jail, a correctional facility, or a CBSA immigration holding centre.

When a person is arrested or detained, the *Canadian Charter of Rights and Freedoms* requires the officer to inform that person of her rights, including the following:

- the right to know the reason for the arrest and detention;

- the right to counsel; and

- the right to notify her government representative of the arrest or detention.

Another safeguard of rights is the requirement to obtain an immigration warrant for arrest where the person is a permanent resident or a protected person.

Detention of Children

Children under 18 should be detained only "as a measure of last resort," according to s. 60 of the IRPA. The best interests of the child must be taken into account generally when considering detention, as well as the following specific criteria from s. 249 of the IRP Regulations:

- the availability of alternative arrangements with local childcare agencies;

- the anticipated length of detention;

- where human smugglers brought the children to Canada, the risk of continued control by those smugglers;

- the type of detention facility that would be used;

- the availability for segregation of the children from adults; and

- the availability of educational, counselling, and recreational services.

Detention at the Port of Entry or Within Canada

At the port of entry or within Canada, an officer may arrest and detain a permanent resident or foreign national under s. 58 of the IRPA. The officer must have reasonable grounds to believe that the person has or may have breached immigration law, and one or more of the following criteria must also be met:

- the person is unlikely to appear for a future immigration matter (for example, examination, a hearing, or removal);

- the person is a potential danger to the public (for example, if the person is inadmissible on grounds of security or for violating human or international rights); or

- the person's identity has not been established.

Within 48 hours of a detention, an officer may review the reasons for the detention and may exercise her authority under s. 56 of the IRPA to release the person if the reason for detention no longer exists. Otherwise, the officer notifies the ID about the detention, without delay, so that a detention review hearing by the ID can be held (s. 55(4) of the IRPA).

Detention at Admissibility Hearings

A person appearing at an admissibility hearing may already be in detention, or may later be detained at the end of the hearing. For example, a hearings officer may make a submission to the ID member to order the detention of a person at the end of the admissibility hearing.

FACTORS

There are a number of factors that must be considered by the ID member when determining whether a person should be detained, according to s. 58 of the IRPA. The prescribed factors are set out in the IRP Regulations, in four categories, as follows:

- flight risk,

- danger to the public,

- identity not established, and

- other factors.

Consider the following case scenarios with respect to these factors:

*Shauna showed up for the admissibility hearing, but she has a history of staying in Canada after the expiry of her temporary resident visa. Five years ago, Shauna overstayed her visa and was brought before the ID; at that hearing, she cried on record, apologized, and claimed that she forgot about applying to extend her stay. She was issued a departure order and left Canada. This time, the evidence suggests that Shauna has done exactly the same thing: overstayed her status and failed to apply to extend the terms and conditions of her stay. After hearing the allegations, Shauna realizes their serious nature and asks for time to obtain counsel to assist her with her case. The hearing is adjourned; however, the officer wishes to ensure that Shauna will appear for the continuation of the proceeding. The officer is concerned that if Shauna is not detained, she may simply disappear. The officer will argue that Shauna is a **flight risk** and should therefore be detained.*

Jerome has several convictions for assault in another country and entered Canada illegally using an alias. He was arrested in a drug raid by Canadian police. It was only after he was fingerprinted that Jerome's true identity was discovered, along with information about his prior foreign convictions. Police believe that Jerome has ties to organized crime, and although the case is part of a larger, ongoing investigation, they were only able to charge him with a minor offence for which he was convicted. As soon as Jerome was released from jail, however, he was immediately detained by the CBSA as a risk to public safety. While he waits for his admissibility hearing, Jerome is brought before an ID member to review the reasons for his detention. Since Jerome's last review (the seven-day detention review), the officer has learned that Jerome may be wanted on outstanding charges back home. The officer is waiting for confirmation of this information from foreign authorities. This is Jerome's first 30-day review and the officer asks for the detention to continue. Jerome has no family in Canada.

With these scenarios in mind, we can now consider each of the prescribed factors in more detail:

1. *Flight risk.* There are a number of factors set out in s. 245 of the IRP Regulations that will be considered by the ID when determining whether a person is a flight risk, as follows:

   ■ Is the person a fugitive from justice in another country?

   ■ Has the person previously complied with a departure order, and appeared for any immigration hearing or criminal proceeding?

   ■ Has the person previously complied with any immigration conditions imposed when he was admitted to Canada, previously released from detention, or granted a stay of removal?

   ■ Does the person have a history of avoiding examination or escaping from custody, or attempting to do so?

   ■ Does the person have any involvement in people smuggling or human trafficking?

   ■ Does the person have strong ties to a community in Canada?

   In the case scenario involving Shauna, the officer will argue that Shauna is a flight risk because she did not comply with immigration conditions such as leaving Canada by the expiry of her visa, she did not extend her visa, and she has a history of overstaying. The officer could also seek alternatives to detention, such as the posting of a cash bond (see below under the heading "Release from Detention"), because although there are some factors of flight risk, they are not so great as to require detention. Shauna, on the other hand, does not wish to be detained. She will remind the ID member that she complied with a previous departure order and will promise to appear for the resumption of her hearing.

   Jerome's case is more complex and serious than Shauna's; the officer will do everything to make the case to keep Jerome in detention. Usually when an officer asks for the detention to be continued, it is for the same reasons as the original detention. In Jerome's case, the officer will also present the latest information. The officer will ask that detention be continued not only because Jerome is a danger to the public but also because he is a flight risk. To support the latter claim, the officer will point to the following facts:

- Jerome has prior convictions and may be fleeing prosecution. The officer will inform the ID member that he is still waiting to hear from foreign authorities about whether Jerome has any outstanding charges against him because of his ties to organized crime.

- Jerome entered Canada illegally and under an alias in an effort to avoid detection.

- The only ties that Jerome appears to have with Canada are with criminal elements, possibly an organized drug ring.

2. *Danger to the public.* Being detained as a danger to the public is serious because it means that the person has likely engaged in or will likely engage in serious criminal acts. The hearings officer will provide evidence related to the grounds of inadmissibility. A member of the ID will hear arguments from both parties when considering whether to order the detention to continue or to order release. The member considers the following factors as set out in s. 246 of the IRP Regulations, as follows:

- Is the person inadmissible on grounds of security, violating human or international rights, or serious criminality? Criminal convictions outside of or in Canada considered to be serious crimes include sexual offences, violent offences, weapons offences, and drug trafficking.

- Has the person engaged in people smuggling or human trafficking?

   In the case scenario involving Jerome, the officer will also renew the argument that Jerome is a danger to the public because

- he is alleged to be inadmissible on several grounds, including serious criminality;

- he has criminal convictions outside of Canada considered to be serious crimes including drug-related convicitons; and

- he is currently under investigation for engaging in organized crime.

3. *Identity not established.* There are a number of reasons why a person might conceal his identity from Canadian authorities. Consider the following examples:

- A person may be evading prosecution in his home country and be avoiding returning, such as in the case of Jerome.

- A person may have been previously deported from Canada.

   When the detainee is a foreign national whose identity is not confirmed or in situations where the person is uncooperative in proving his identity, the hearings officer will argue to keep the person in detention. In making a decision, the ID member will consider whether or not the person was cooperative in providing the following:

- evidence of his identity (to determine whether his identity documents are legitimate or false);

- information about his date and place of birth, as well as the names of his mother and father; and

- detailed information about his travel itinerary to Canada or in completing an application for a travel document, or in assisting to obtain evidence of identity.

Note that the above factors do not have an adverse effect on special considerations for minor children. Additional questions asked include the following:

- Has the person destroyed identity or travel documents, or travelled with fraudulent documents?

- Has the person lied or provided contradictory information about identity?

- Are there any documents that contradict information provided by the person about identity?

As a result of experiences with corrupt and violent government officials in their country of origin, many refugee claimants may be afraid to divulge personal information to government officials for the purpose of obtaining identity documents. They may also be reluctant to be completely candid with Canadian officials, because of a general distrust of authority. Although this may pose a challenge for immigration consultants, clients are required to cooperate in obtaining identity documents or information.

4. *Other factors.* Other factors to be considered are set out in s. 248 of the IRP Regulations, including the following:

- the reasons for detention;

- the length of time already spent in detention, in cases where the person was previously detained;

- whether there are any elements that can assist in determining the length of time that detention is likely to continue and, if so, that length of time;

- any unexplained delays or unexplained lack of diligence caused by the Department, the CBSA, or the person concerned; and

- the existence of alternatives to detention.

At the admissibility hearing, the ID member will ask the hearings officer to make a recommendation about any *aggravating circumstances* that the ID ought to consider, as s. 229(3) allows a deportation order to be made against a person instead of the prescribed removal order if the person concerned meets any of the following criteria:

- the person was previously subject to a removal order and is now inadmissible on the same grounds as in that order;

- the person failed to comply with any condition or obligation imposed under the IRPA or prior legislation, unless the failure is the basis for the removal order; or

- the person was convicted in Canada of an offence under an Act of Parliament punishable by way of indictment or of two offences under any Act of Parliament not arising out of a single occurrence, unless the conviction or convictions are the grounds for the removal order.

DECISION ON INADMISSIBILITY

Generally, the ID member delivers the decision at the end of the hearing, orally, following recommendations and oral representations. A decision rendered orally takes effect at the time that it is stated.[6] If the hearing is adjourned for a decision to be made in writing, the decision takes effect on the date that the member signs and dates the decision.

The ID member may make any of the following decisions, according to s. 45 of the IRPA:

- recognize the right of the person to enter Canada where the person is a Canadian citizen within the meaning of the *Citizenship Act*, a person registered as an Indian under the *Indian Act*, or a permanent resident;

- grant permanent resident status or temporary resident status to a foreign national if the member is satisfied that the foreign national meets the requirements of the IRPA;

- authorize a permanent resident or a foreign national, with or without conditions, to enter Canada for further examination; or

- make the applicable removal order (a) against a foreign national who has not been authorized to enter Canada, if the member is not satisfied that the foreign national is not inadmissible, (b) against a foreign national who has been authorized to enter Canada, or (c) a permanent resident, if the member is satisfied that the foreign national or the permanent resident is inadmissible.

If the decision is in favour of the person concerned, the member signs and dates a Notice of Decision and provides the minister's counsel with a copy. If the decision is unfavourable to the person concerned, the member must do the following, in accordance with rule 7(2) of the Immigration Division Rules (ID Rules):

- sign and date a Notice of Decision;

- issue a removal order, signed and dated; and

- advise the person concerned of the right to an appeal before the IAD or of the right to a judicial review by the Federal Court.

Counsel may make an oral request for written reasons at the end of the hearing, or later in writing, in accordance with rule 7(2), provided that the request is made within ten days of the date of the decision.

Detention Review

Counsel must be prepared to address the issue of detention at the end of an admissibility hearing, because detention pending removal may be ordered (s. 58 of the IRPA). The ID may also hold a hearing solely for the purpose of reviewing the reasons for detention. The CBSA provides to the ID a *request for detention review*, which generally contains the original grounds for detention and basic information about the person concerned.

TIMING OF DETENTION REVIEWS

There is no limit to the amount of time that a person may be in immigration detention as long as there is a periodic review. This principle was upheld by the Supreme Court of Canada when it stated that "extended periods of detention" are constitutionally valid so long as they are "accompanied by a process that provides regular opportunities" for "judicial review of the continued need for and justice" of the detention.[7]

The timing of reviews is set out in s. 57 of the IRPA. Reviews must be conducted

- within 48 hours after the person is detained;

- at least once during the seven days following the first detention review; and

- at least once during each 30-day period following each previous review.

Within 48 hours of a permanent resident's or foreign national's detention, an officer must review the reasons for the detention and has the authority under s. 56 of the IRPA to release the person if the reason for detention no longer exists. The officer may release the person with or without conditions, such as the payment of a deposit or the posting of a guarantee.

Detention reviews for permanent residents who are being held under a security certificate are conducted by the Federal Court under ss. 83 and 84 of the IRPA. Detention reviews for permanent residents must be conducted

- not later than 48 hours after the permanent resident is taken into detention;

- at least once in the six-month period following each preceding review; and

- at any other times that the judge authorizes.

The purpose of a hearing is to review the reasons for a continued detention. A party may make a written request for an early detention review, according to rule 9 of the ID Rules, if evidence to be produced could lead to release.

HEARING

A CBSA officer must bring the detainee to the ID or to a place specified by it, to argue and provide evidence why she should be released. This means that the person concerned might stay in the detention facility and be brought to a room with videoconferencing equipment, or alternatively be physically transported to the ID (s. 57(3) of the IRPA). The location will be specified in the Notice to Appear.

Detention reviews before the Immigration Division are adversarial hearings. A *hearings officer*, counsel for the minister, attends at the hearing to argue why the detention should be continued or to make recommendations about conditions for release. The detainee has the right to counsel, although the proceeding is not generally adjourned for this purpose. In some provinces, *duty counsel* may assist the detainee. Where the detainee has no counsel, the hearings officer will also provide information about the hearing process and rights. An interpreter is provided for the hearing by the ID, if required.

The ID member may make an opening statement, have the parties and counsel identify themselves for the record, confirm that the detainee can understand the interpreter if one is required, swear in the interpreter, and deal with other preliminary matters. The member explains the purpose of the detention review and the possible outcomes.

The hearings officer then begins by submitting facts and arguments concerning the detention. The hearings officer will also make a recommendation to continue detention or to release the person concerned with conditions. Counsel also has the opportunity to provide facts and arguments to have the client released. After all the evidence has been heard, counsel must be prepared to make a final oral statement, called oral representations, at the end of a hearing, according to rule 48 of the ID Rules.

DECISION ON DETENTION REVIEWS

The decision at a detention review hearing is usually rendered orally at the end of the hearing, in accordance with rule 11 of the ID Rules, and takes effect immediately. On rare occasions, the hearing may be adjourned for a decision to be rendered in writing, in which case it takes effect on the date the ID member signs and dates the decision. The member must do one of the following in accordance with rule 11(2):

- sign either an order for release or an order for detention, and provide a copy to the parties; or

- advise the person concerned of her right to a judicial review by the Federal Court (where the person concerned does not have appeal rights).

An order for release may contain conditions, such as the payment of a deposit or the posting of a guarantee for compliance with the conditions (s. 58(3) of the IRPA). Counsel may make an oral request for written reasons at the end of the hearing or later in writing, in accordance with rule 11(4) as long as the request is made within ten days of the date of the decision.

Release from Detention

A person may be released from detention, either by an officer or a member of the Immigration Division. Conditions may be imposed, including the payment of a cash bond and/or the posting of a *performance bond* (written guarantee).[8]

The cash bond may be paid by the detainee or by a third person. The amount of the bond is based upon the following, according to s. 45(2) of the IRP Regulations:

- the person's financial resources;

- the obligations that result from the conditions imposed;

- the costs that would likely be incurred to locate, arrest, detain, and remove the person; and

- in the case of a guarantee, the costs that would likely be incurred to enforce it.

If a third person or group acts as guarantor, it must, under s. 47 of the IRP Regulations, satisfy the decision maker of the following:

- it is not in default of another guarantee;

- it is a Canadian citizen or permanent resident;

- it is physically present and residing in Canada;

- it can ensure that the detainee obeys any conditions imposed; and

- it has the ability to fulfill the obligation if the person fails to comply with conditions imposed, and provide evidence of this ability (s. 47(2)).

Also, if there are reasonable grounds to believe that the guarantor's money was obtained illegally, it must be refused (s. 47(3)). Both the detainee and guarantor must notify the Department (CIC) or the CBSA, as directed, of any change of address and must appear for any matter as directed by an officer or the Immigration Division, according to s. 48. If any conditions are broken, the cash bond is forfeited. In the case of a guarantee, the signing person is required to pay the specified amount of money. The CBSA, and not the Immigration Division, is responsible for the administration and enforcement of cash bonds.

Consider again the example of Eunice:

The officer decided that a detention was not warranted, so when Eunice appeared for her admissibility hearing she was not "on immigration hold." Eunice chose to have legal representation at her admissibility hearing and felt well prepared; she knew there was a possibility that she could be detained after her hearing. But her counsel is confident he can show that Eunice is not a flight risk. Eunice does not have a criminal record outside of Canada and has not committed any crimes while in Canada, so she would not be considered a danger to the public. All of Eunice's identity and travel documents are in good order and Eunice has complied with police and immigration authorities, so her identity is not in question.

At the admissibility hearing, it was clear from the evidence presented by the hearings offficer that Eunice had, in fact, overstayed her visit. The ID member found Eunice to be inadmissible for "failing to comply" and issued an exclusion order.

After the order was made, the hearings officer made submissions that Eunice was a flight risk because she was close to her family members in

Canada and overstayed her visit to be with them. Eunice's counsel proposed, as an alternative to detention, that Nadine act as a bondsperson to ensure that Eunice leaves Canada. (Before Eunice's hearing, her counsel explained conditions of release and arranged for Nadine to attend the hearing just in case.)

The hearings officer recommended an appropriate sum as a deposit, which the member accepted. Nadine was able to answer questions to show she met the regulatory requirements of as a bondsperson. The member ordered Eunice's release with conditions. Before Eunice was free to go, Nadine posted the deposit. When Nadine paid the sum of money as a guarantee (to a CBSA official), she was given a copy of a Security Deposit form. She and Eunice were also required to sign an Acknowledgement of Conditions form as proof they both understood the conditions imposed.

Had Eunice's counsel not been adequately prepared for this situation, it is possible that Eunice would have been detained pending removal.

IMMIGRATION DIVISION RULES AND POLICIES

Immigration consultants who represent persons who are subject to a proceeding in the ID must have a thorough knowledge of the ID Rules, in addition to the provisions of the IRPA that set out the jurisdiction of the IRB and the ID to hear and decide matters. The Immigration Division Rules are the Division's regulations established to set out roles and responsibilities, and govern practices and procedures in proceedings before the ID.

Section 16(1) of the IRPA gives the chairperson of the IRB the authority to make rules related to the ID's activities, practices, and procedures, in consultation with the director general of the Immigration Division, subject to the approval of the governor in council. The ID Rules are binding, and it is important to know them well. Failure to comply with the Rules may have severe consequences to both clients and counsel.

The Rules are part of the regulations under the IRPA and may be accessed at various websites including the IRB website, the Department of Justice website, and the CanLII website. Requests for clarification about the meaning or application of a particular rule may be made to the registrar's staff, such as the deputy registrar or case officer, at the nearest business office of the IRB.

The Rules are divided into three parts:

- Part 1—Rules Applicable to Admissibility Hearings;

- Part 2—Rules Applicable to Detention Reviews; and

- Part 3—Rules That Apply to Both Admissibility Hearings and Detention Reviews.

In addition to the binding ID Rules, there are important policy instruments— namely, chairperson's guidelines and policy notes.

WEBLINK

For example, the Immigration Division Rules can be found on the Department of Justice website at http://laws.justice .gc.ca/en/I-2.5 under the heading "Related Regulations."

Policy Instruments

CHAIRPERSON'S GUIDELINES

The chairperson's guidelines guide ID procedures. Familiarity with the chairperson's guidelines will further provide counsel with confidence when navigating ID processes.

Although the majority of the chairperson's guidelines apply to the Refugee Protection Division, guidelines issued in December 2006 have a general application to all divisions, including the ID. For example, Guideline 2 deals specifically with detention, and Guideline 8 covers procedures with respect to vulnerable persons appearing before the IRB. Both may be useful for examining the issue of long-term detention and the basis for detention.

As explained in the first chapter, the guidelines are not binding and members are not specifically directed to follow them. However, they are a source of guiding principles. This is important to preserve the independent nature of the member's role in making decisions yet balance the need for consistency in the treatment of particular issues. The guidelines can be viewed on the IRB website.

POLICY NOTES

A **policy note** is a memorandum generally issued by a single business office to communicate with members, staff, and the public, including claimants and counsel, about a particular operational matter in that local office. However, the IRB issued policy notes in 2004 for all divisions, including the ID with respect to counsel, as follows:

- New Requirements for Counsel Who Charge a Fee for Their Services

- New Requirements for Counsel Who Charge a Fee for Their Services—Update.

These particular policy notes explain that the IRB will only recognize counsel (who are charging a fee) as an "authorized representative" if they provide their organization name and membership identification number for each case; and that such information is kept in the IRB's data-tracking system. If counsel information is not provided, the IRB will not consider the counsel to be an authorized representative, will not deal with the counsel on that case file, and will treat the subject of the proceeding as unrepresented.

Rules: Before the Proceeding

Compliance with the ID Rules by everyone involved is intended to lead to a fair and consistent approach. However, when the Rules were drafted, it was not possible to predict all potential scenarios that might arise in future cases, so rule 49 provides the ID with the flexibility to "do whatever is necessary to deal with the matter" should a procedural problem arise during a proceeding. Consider the following examples:

- ID members may act on their own initiative to change a rule, to excuse a person from a rule, and to extend or shorten time limits, according to rule 50; and

- failure to follow a rule in a proceeding does not, in itself, make the proceeding invalid, according to rule 51.

In this way, the Rules attempt to strike a balance between the value of predictability and consistency, and the need to make adjustments to meet the particular needs of individual cases. The following is an overview of those ID Rules that counsel will work with most often in a proceeding before the ID. However, it is important to review and understand all the Rules before representing a client before the ID.

DEFINITIONS

It is very important to know the meaning of key terms, which are defined in rule 1 of the ID Rules. Counsel demonstrate their professionalism when they understand and use relevant and appropriate terminology while presenting immigration cases.

For example, "detention review" is defined as a "forty-eight hour review, a seven-day review and a thirty-day review," and then each of these terms is further defined.

TIME LIMITS

The ID Rules require that certain activities occur within certain time limits. The time limits are included in the Rules for specific actions, as follows:

- holding detention reviews—rules 8(2) and 9;

- disclosing documents—rules 26(a) and (b);

- providing witness information—rule 32(2);

- making applications—rule 38(2);

- responding to applications—rule 39(3);

- responding to written responses—rule 49(3);

- making applications to conduct a proceeding in private—rule 45(4);

- making applications to conduct a proceeding in public—rule 46(4); and

- providing a notice of constitutional question—rule 47(4).

A document is considered received by the Division on the day that the document is date-stamped, according to rule 31(1). When counsel sends a document to the minister's counsel by regular mail, it is considered received seven days after the day it was mailed, according to rule 31(2). If day 7 falls on a Saturday, Sunday, or a statutory holiday, the document is considered received on the next working day.

SCHEDULING A HEARING AND NOTICE TO APPEAR

According to rule 21, the ID must "fix the date for a hearing and any other proceeding relating to the hearing." The ID may "require the parties to participate in the preparation of a schedule of proceedings by appearing at a scheduling conference or otherwise providing information."

The ID is responsible for notifying both the person concerned, and the minister, of the date, time, and location of a hearing, according to rule 22. This may be done orally—for example, at a proceeding—or in writing in a Notice to Appear document.

COMMUNICATING WITH THE DECISION MAKER

The parties and their representatives must never directly communicate with the decision maker, but rather must direct all communication through the registry, according to rule 2 of the ID Rules. This applies to all communication, both oral and in writing, including questions about the process, documents, or a particular proceeding.

It is very important that rule 2 be followed in order to avoid suspicions of bias or influence. All parties must be aware of all information being passed on to the decision maker, so that they have the opportunity to respond. Applications and other communications must be made in writing, within the time limits, and generally with proof that all parties have been served.

CONTACT INFORMATION

"Contact information" is defined in rule 1 of the ID Rules as a person's name, postal address, telephone number, and fax number and electronic mail address, if any.

Contact information for both the person concerned and counsel must be provided to both the ID and the minister. This is necessary to ensure that notices of proceedings and other matters can be communicated. Rule 12 requires the counsel of record to provide this information.

If notices, such as a Notice to Appear for a hearing, are not received because the ID does not have the proper address, the person concerned might fail to show up for the proceeding, leading to the issue of a warrant for the person's arrest. Changes to contact information must also be provided to the ID and the minister without delay, unless the person is detained, according to rule 4.

INTERPRETER SERVICES

If an interpreter is needed by the person concerned or any witness, the party must notify the ID of this, according to rule 17 of the ID Rules. Notice to the ID should be given as soon as possible in the case of a 48-hour or seven-day review or an admissibility hearing held at the same time, and in all other cases, at least five days before the hearing.

DOCUMENTS

Documents are important evidence at ID proceedings. There are several kinds of documents, such as documents that show the identity of the client, travel documents, documents that show the client's willingness to leave Canada, court documents, and conviction records. Because of the importance of documents to a fair resolution of the case, there are rules regarding filing documents with the ID, disclosing documents to the opposing side, and ensuring that everyone has a copy of the documents well before the hearing.

The rules concerning documents apply to any document, notice, written request, or application, according to rule 27 of the ID Rules. The timing for providing documents to the registry and parties is set out in rule 28. Any document provided to a party must also be provided to the party's counsel.

As counsel, you will want to provide organized and professional-looking documents to the ID. All documents intended for use at the proceeding must comply with the following requirements:

- *Format.* Documents must be typewritten using one side only of 21.5 cm by 28 cm (8½" × 11") paper, with pages numbered, according to rule 24. If the document is a photocopy, it must be clear and legible. If more than one document is filed, a numbered list of all the documents must also be filed.

- *Language.* Documents must be submitted in either English or French, which may require translation, according to rule 25.

- *Method of service.* Documents may be provided by a number of methods: by hand, by regular or registered mail, by courier or priority post, by fax (for documents no more than 20 pages long), and sometimes by electronic mail, according to rule 39.

Documents are exchanged before the hearing to ensure that all parties have an opportunity to review them, and respond if necessary, in preparation for the hearing. If counsel plans to provide documentary evidence at a client's hearing, the evidence must be disclosed to the opposing side before the proceeding.

The time limits for disclosing documents are set out in rule 26 as follows: as soon as possible, in the case of a 48-hour or seven-day review or an admissibility hearing held at the same time; and in all other cases, at least five days before the hearing.

Rules: Application Procedures

There are many issues that may require resolution before the hearing can even begin, such as a change to the date or location of the hearing. If a party wants a decision on such a matter, an application must be brought.

There are general procedures, which apply to all applications, and other procedures that apply for each kind of application. The general procedures are set out in rules 38 to 40 of the ID Rules and apply to all of the following matters:

- changing the location of a hearing—rule 42

- changing the date or time of a hearing—rule 43

- joining or separating hearings—rule 44

- making oral representations—rule 48.

Each type of application is also governed by its own rule, as shown above.

GENERAL PROCEDURES

Applications must be provided to the ID and in the following manner, according to rule 38 of the ID Rules:

- orally or in writing and as soon as possible or within the time limit in the IRPA or the ID Rules;

- stating the outcome sought;

- providing the reasons for the request;

- including any evidence that the party wants considered;

- including supporting evidence in an affidavit or statutory declaration, if the application is not specified in the ID Rules; and

- with a statement of how and when a copy of the application was sent to the other party.

The opposing party has the opportunity to respond to the application under rule 39, as soon as possible in the case of a 48-hour or seven-day review or an admissibility hearing held at the same time, and in all other cases, no later than five days. The response must be provided in the following manner:

- in writing;

- stating the outcome sought;

- providing the reasons for seeking that outcome;

- including any evidence that the party wants considered;

- including supporting evidence in an affidavit or statutory declaration, if the application is not specified in the ID Rules; and

- providing a statement of how and when a copy of the written response was sent to the opposing party.

The applicant then has an opportunity to reply to the response, according to rule 40.

SPECIFIC APPLICATIONS

Below is a description of the rules that apply to each type of application, in addition to the general procedures in rule 38 of the ID Rules, which also apply.

Change of Date and Time

A request to change the date and time of a proceeding as specified in the Notice to Appear may be made by application to the ID, according to rule 43 of the ID Rules. This situation may arise if, for example, the person concerned wishes to postpone or adjourn a hearing to provide for more time to gather evidence. Rule 43 also provides several factors that may be considered by the ID when deciding an application to change the date or time of a proceeding, including the following:

- when the application was made;

- whether the party was consulted about the date and time;

- the time already afforded to the party to prepare;

- the party's efforts to prepare;

- whether there have been exceptional circumstances;

- whether there are previous delays;

- the nature and complexity of the matter to be heard;

- whether the party has counsel;

- whether the time and date fixed for the hearing was peremptory; and

- whether allowing the application would unreasonably delay the proceeding or likely cause an injustice.

It is important for counsel to address these factors when arguing for a change of date or time, because they will be considered by the ID member when she makes her decision.

Change of Venue

A request to change the location of a proceeding as specified in the Notice to Appear may be made by application to the ID, according to rule 42 of the ID Rules. This may arise if the client wishes to transfer the case to another IRB business office.

Rule 42 also provides several factors that may be considered by the ID when deciding an application to change the location of a proceeding, including the following:

- whether a change of venue would allow the proceeding to be full and proper;

- whether a change would delay the proceeding; and

- whether the change would endanger public safety.

If the application is not allowed, the person concerned is expected to appear for the proceeding at the fixed location.

Public and Private Hearings

Proceedings before the ID that do not concern a refugee claimant are generally required to be held in public, according to s. 166(a) of the IRPA. Proceedings that concern a refugee claimant or protected person are generally held in private. From time to time someone may wish to make a public proceeding private, or a private proceeding public. In such a case, an application must be brought under rule 45 or rule 46 of the ID Rules, respectively.

Application for a Private Hearing—Rule 45

An application to make a public hearing private may be brought under rule 45 of the ID Rules in the following circumstances:

- there is a serious possibility that the life, liberty, or security of a person will be endangered;

- there is a real and substantial risk to the fairness of the proceeding; or

- there is a real and substantial risk that matters of public security will be disclosed.

A request to have the proceeding conducted in private must provide the following, according to rule 45:

- a statement of the desired outcome;

- reasons why the ID should agree to make the hearing private; and

- any evidence that the applicant wants the ID to consider in deciding the application.

Application for a Public Hearing—Rule 46

Although proceedings before the ID are generally held in public, matters concerning a refugee claimant or a protected person are generally held in private. From time to time someone may wish to make the private proceeding open to the public, such as when there is media interest in a claimant or protected person.

Any person may make an application to have the hearing held in public, according to rule 46 of the ID Rules. The application must provide the following:

- a request for a public hearing;

- reasons why the ID should agree to a public hearing; and

- any evidence that the applicant wants the ID to consider in deciding the application.

Non-Disclosure of Information—Rule 41

Occasionally, the minister may have information that must remain confidential because its disclosure could be injurious to national security or endanger the safety of any person. In such circumstances, s. 86 of the IRPA allows the minister to make an application for non-disclosure to exclude information from the person concerned.

Before the admissibility hearing or before a detention review, the minister must make the application for non-disclosure in accordance with rule 41 of the ID Rules. A member of the ID will hold a meeting with the hearings officer *ex parte*, meaning privately and in the absence of the person concerned and counsel, and before the immigration matter has commenced.

If the minister makes the application at the admissibility hearing or before a detention review, rule 41(2) requires the member to exclude the person concerned and counsel from the hearing room before hearing the application.

If the member decides that the minister's information is relevant to the matter and requires non-disclosure, the member writes a summary of the excluded material without disclosing it, a copy of which is provided to the person concerned and the minister, according to rule 41(3). The member may then consider all the non-disclosed information when determining the immigration matter.

Rules: At Hearings

The ID is not bound by formal rules of evidence and procedures, according to s. 162(2) of the IRPA. It may deal with matters more informally and efficiently than a court within the principles of natural justice.

Given the seriousness of the outcome of an immigration matter—namely, that the client can be removed—the client may have a high level of anxiety. To reduce the risk that this may interfere with the client's ability to answer questions clearly and credibly, it is important for counsel to prepare the client for the hearing by describing and explaining it and by answering any questions that the client may have. Below is a list of typical questions that clients may ask (or may want to know the answers to even if they do not ask), organized by topic. Selected sample answers are provided in parentheses.

- *Type of hearing.* What can the client expect during the hearing? What are the time-frames? Is it possible that the client will be removed immediately after the admissibility hearing? (No, this will not happen immediately.) What happens if the client is not released from detention? Is the matter expected to take all day? (We must arrange for alternatives to detention. Do you have someone who can post a bond?)

- *Hearing room.* What is the physical layout of the hearing room? Will the proceeding be held via videoconferencing, such as if the client is being held in a local jail or immigration holding centre? In that case, where will counsel be? (Counsel will be with the client.)

- *Public or private hearing.* Will the hearing be open to the public? (The proceedings are public, which means there could be observers.)

- *Hearing recorded.* Will the hearing be recorded? (Yes.)

- *Language.* In what language will the hearing be held? (The hearing will be held in English or French, and an interpreter will be provided if requested.)

- *Participants.* Who will be present and what is the role of each person? (The ID member, the hearings officer, counsel, the client, and possibly witnesses will be present.)

- *Nature of the proceeding.* Will the hearing be adversarial in nature? (Yes, the hearing is adversarial and involves the minister's counsel questioning the client and any witnesses, and arguing that the client should be removed or detained, depending on the type of hearing.)

- *Consequences to family members.* If the client is ordered to be removed, will her family members be removed as well? (Family members who are included in the inadmissibility report may be subject to the same removal order, if one is made.)

Clients who are being detained will have many questions about getting released or moved to a more comfortable facility, such as an immigration holding facility rather than a jail. It is also important to explain the difference between a criminal incarceration and an immigration detention.

JURISDICTION TO COMMENCE A PROCEEDING

Different rules apply to the commencement of each of the two types of hearing held by the ID, as outlined below.

Admissibility Hearings

The minister's referral under s. 44(2) of the IRPA gives the ID jurisdiction to hold an admissibility hearing. The document is a Request for Admissibility Hearing form (IMM 5245B). In addition to providing the inadmissibility report to the ID, as required by s. 44(1), the minister is compelled by rule 3 of the ID Rules to provide other specific information such as basic data about the person concerned (including name, contact information, date of birth, immigration status, and marital status), language of record and language of the interpreter if one is required, and other details.

Detention Reviews

The ID has jurisdiction to review the reasons for detention when it receives a request for a detention review by the minister. Rule 8 requires the minister to provide the date, time, and place of detention and the type of review (48-hour review, 7-day review, or 30-day review) as well as basic data about the person concerned (including name, contact information, date of birth, immigration status, and marital status), the language of record and language of the interpreter if one is required, and other details. Sections 57(1) and (2) of the IRPA set out specific time limits for detention reviews.

PERSONS IN ATTENDANCE

There are a number of people who must be present at an ID hearing, including the person concerned, the minister's counsel, and the ID member. Other persons are likely to be present, such as the claimant's counsel. Still others may be present, such as witnesses.

Person Concerned

The person concerned must be personally in attendance at the hearing.

Immigration Division Member

Each case is heard by only one member of the ID. The member has the authority to hear and decide immigration matters of inadmissibility and reasons for detention. The member will also hear and decide any applications that are made orally at the hearing.

Minister's Counsel

Minister's counsel is a public servant who works for the CBSA with the title of Hearings Officer. A hearings officer represents the minister of PSEP at ID proceedings. Prior to the hearing, the hearings officer reviews the report and prepares the case. At the hearing, the hearings officer examines and cross-examines witnesses and presents evidence.

Counsel

Counsel's role is to protect the interests and right to a fair hearing of the person concerned. Counsel explains the process, provides advice, and presents the case in an efficient manner, within the limits set by the ID member.

The person concerned may choose to be represented by either an unpaid trusted adviser, such as a family member or clergy, or a paid consultant or lawyer. An unpaid adviser who represents a client and is not charging a fee should use the Notice of Representation Without a Fee form (IRB / CISR 692), available on the IRB website under the Forms tab.

All paid counsel must be members in good standing of the Canadian Society of Immigration Consultants or a provincial law society. Counsel who represent a person concerned for a fee must provide their contact information in writing to the ID; otherwise, the ID may consider the client as unrepresented. If counsel are charging a fee, the appropriate form to complete is the Counsel Contact Information form (IRB / CISR 687), available on the IRB website under the Forms tab. Counsel must provide their membership identification number for either the Canadian Society of Immigration Consultants or the provincial law society to which they belong.

According to rule 13 of the ID Rules, counsel is deemed counsel of record once a date for a proceeding is set. In some cases, counsel may wish to be removed from the record—for example, if the client refuses to pay or is very difficult. Rule 14 provides that counsel must seek permission from the ID to withdraw from a case, and rule 15 provides for situations where the client wishes to remove the representative as counsel of record.

Interpreter

Only accredited interpreters are used for hearings, which means they have undergone security checks and passed a language examination. They are not employees of the ID but are contracted on a case-by-case basis. They are permanently bound by their promise to interpret accurately once they take an oath or make a solemn affirmation to do so. At the beginning of the proceeding, the interpreter confirms that she has used a standardized script to ensure that the interpreter and person concerned understand each other. The interpreter may not guide, provide advice, or offer an opinion to the person concerned.

Rule 17 requires that if a client or witness requires an interpreter, counsel must notify the ID in writing and specify the language and dialect needed as soon as possible for a 48-hour or seven-day review, and in all other cases at least five days before the hearing.

Witnesses

If counsel wishes to call a witness other than his client, he must fulfill the requirements of rule 32 of the ID Rules. Information such as the reason for calling the witness, the party's relationship to the witness, the amount of time required at the hearing for the witness's testimony, and whether the testimony is by videoconference or telephone must be provided in writing to the ID and copied to the other party. This must be done as soon as possible for a 48-hour or seven-day detention review or an admissibility hearing held at the same time no later than five days before the hearing.

To reduce the risk of the witness failing to appear, it is prudent to request that the ID issue a summons to order a witness to testify, according to rule 33, in writing or orally at a proceeding. The party is responsible for providing the summons to the summoned person by hand, to notify the ID in writing of this, and to pay witness fees and travel expenses. In the request, counsel must set out the factors to be considered in issuing the summons, such as the importance of the testimony of a witness and the witness's ability to provide such information.

A witness may apply to the ID to cancel the summons, according to rule 34. If the witness is unsuccessful with the application and subsequently fails to appear, a request may be made to the ID to issue a warrant for her arrest, according to rule 35.

The hearings officer may request that witnesses be excluded from the hearing room during the person concerned's testimony. A witness is not allowed to share any testimony given at the hearing with any other witness, according to rule 36.

Designated Representative

There are situations where the person concerned is not capable of making decisions such as in the case of an unaccompanied minor, or a person deemed mentally incompetent or unable to understand the proceedings (s. 167(2) of the IRPA). In these instances, rule 18 of the ID Rules provides that the ID appoint a person to act and make decisions on behalf of the person. Where counsel for either party believes that a designated representative is required, counsel must, without delay, notify the ID. The designated representative may be a relative, or a professional such as a lawyer or social worker. Alternatively, counsel may choose to take on the role of designated representative.

APPENDIX A

Reference for Enforcement Procedures

Provision	IRPA and IRP Regulations
Removals	IRP Regulations Part 13
Removal orders	IRP Regulations ss. 223 to 225 and 228 to 229
Removal orders stayed	IRP Regulations ss. 230, 231, 232
Removal orders—minors	IRP Regulations s. 249
Entry requirements	IRPA ss. 11, 16
Examinations	IRPA ss. 15, 18
Right of entry	IRPA s. 19
Temporary resident status and permits	IRPA ss. 22 to 24
Detention and release	IRPA ss. 54 to 61, IRP Regulations Part 14
Inadmissibility	IRPA ss. 33 to 43
Admissibility hearings	IRPA ss. 44, 45

APPENDIX B

The following table summarizes the various decisions that the minister or ID member can make for admissibility and detention review hearings, the provisions that grant jurisdiction, and the associated appeal rights to the Immigration Appeal Division.

NOTES

1. Office of the Auditor General of Canada, "Chapter 5: Citizenship and Immigration Canada—Control and Enforcement," in *2003 April Report of the Auditor General of Canada*, 2003, www.oag-bvg.gc.ca/internet/english/parl_oag_200304_e_1129.html.

2. Immigration and Refugee Board, "Admissibility Hearings and Detention Reviews," April 11, 2008, www.irb-cisr.gc.ca/en/media/infosheets/idfacts_e.htm.

3. Citizenship and Immigration Canada, "ENF 5: Writing 44(1) Reports," in *Enforcement (ENF)*, s. 8, August 10, 2007, www.cic.gc.ca/english/resources/manuals/enf/index.asp.

4. Citizenship and Immigration Canada, "ENF 24: Ministerial Interventions," in *Enforcement (ENF)*, s. 5.4, December 2, 2005, www.cic.gc.ca/english/resources/manuals/enf/index.asp.

5. Office of the Auditor General of Canada, "Chapter 7: Detention and Removal of Individuals—Canada Border Services Agency," s. 7.35, in *2008 May Report of the Auditor General of Canada*, May 6, 2008, www.oag-bvg.gc.ca/internet/english/parl_oag_200805_e_30714.html.

6. Section 169(a) of the IRPA; rule 7 of the Immigration Division Rules.

7. *Charkaoui v. Canada (Citizenship and Immigration)*, 2007 SCC 9 at paras. 110 and 123.

8. Section 58(3) of the IRPA and s. 45 of the IRP Regulations.

REFERENCES

Canada Border Services Agency. "Fact Sheet: Arrests and Detentions." March 2004. www.cbsa-asfc.gc.ca/media/facts-faits/007-eng.html.

Charkaoui v. Canada (Citizenship and Immigration). 2007 SCC 9.

Citizenship Act. R.S.C. 1985, c. C-29.

Citizenship and Immigration Canada. "ENF 1: Inadmissibility." In *Enforcement (ENF)*. August 8, 2008. www.cic.gc.ca/english/resources/manuals/enf/index.asp.

Citizenship and Immigration Canada. "ENF 2/OP 18: Evaluating Inadmissibility." In *Enforcement (ENF)*. May 24, 2006. www.cic.gc.ca/english/resources/manuals/enf/index.asp.

Admissibility Hearings

Decision makers and their powers	Essential features of the proceeding	Provisions granting jurisdiction	Nature of the proceeding	Decisions/Reasons	Possible outcomes	Appeal

◆ Director general (manager): authority as designated by the minister
 	
◆ ID member: public servant, employed in accordance with *Public Service Employment Act*. The ID member has the power and authority of a commissioner (*Inquiries Act*) to
  ◇ administer an oath
  ◇ issue a summons (rule 33 of the ID Rules).
	◆ Held to determine whether the person is inadmissible to and removable from Canada.
	
	◆ Inadmissibility and removal are assessed on the following grounds:
	  ◇ security: espionage, subversion, terrorism
	  ◇ human or international rights: war crimes, crimes against humanity
	  ◇ serious criminality convictions inside or outside Canada
	  ◇ criminality/ organized criminality
	  ◇ health grounds
	  ◇ financial reasons
	  ◇ misrepresentation
	  ◇ non-compliance with the IRPA.
		◆ The manager must "refer" the case to the ID under s. 44(2) of the IRPA. The ID member has jurisdiction to hear a matter when a referral for an admissibility hearing is received from the minister (rule 3 of the ID Rules).	◆ Quasi-judicial
			◆ Adversarial
			◆ Proceedings generally held in public
			◆ Parties are the subject of the proceeding and include
			  ◇ person concerned (PC);
			  ◇ counsel for the PC, who may be a lawyer or member of the CSIC, or other counsel if not paid;
			  ◇ hearings officer as the minister's counsel (PSEP/CBSA).
			◆ Conducted before a single member.
			◆ Not bound by any legal or technical rules of evidence.
			◆ Decision based on evidence considered credible or trustworthy.
				◆ The ID member must give reasons for her decision.
				◆ The decisions may be given orally or in writing.
				◆ At the request of the PC or the minister, the ID member must provide written reasons within ten days of the Notice of Decision.
					◆ Recognize right to enter Canada.
					◆ Grant permanent or temporary resident status.
					◆ Permit entry to Canada for further examination.
					◆ Make one of the following removal orders:
					  ◇ departure order
					  ◇ exclusion order
					  ◇ deportation order.
						◆ If the PC has the right to appeal, he may appeal to the Immigration Appeal Division.
						◆ If the PC has no right of appeal, he may file an application for judicial review to the Federal Court (IRPA s. 64).
						◆ The PC has no right to appeal to the IAD if he is inadmissible on one of the following grounds:
						  ◇ security
						  ◇ violating human or international rights
						  ◇ serious criminality (punished in Canada; imprisonment of at least two years)
						  ◇ organized criminality.

(The table is continued on the next page.)

Detention Reviews

Decision makers and their powers	Essential features of the proceeding	Provisions granting jurisdiction	Nature of the proceeding	Decisions/Reasons	Possible outcomes	Appeal
Same as above.	◆ Applies to most persons detained under the IRPA. ◆ Timing of detention reviews (IRPA s. 57): ◇ within 48 hours after the person is detained; ◇ at least once during the seven days following the first detention review; and ◇ at least once during each 30-day period following each previous review.	◆ A referral for detention review from the minister (IRPA ss. 57(1) and (2); rules 3 and 8 of the ID Rules).	Same as above.	◆ The decision may be given orally or in writing. ◆ The ID member must give reasons for her decision. ◆ At the request of the PC or the minister, the ID member must provide written reasons within ten days of the Notice of Decision.	◆ Release, with or without conditions. ◆ Continue detention on one of the following grounds: ◇ danger to public ◇ unlikely to appear ◇ flight risk ◇ identity not established ◇ other factors.	◆ The PC has the right to file an application for judicial review to the Federal Court.

Citizenship and Immigration Canada. "ENF 5: Writing 44(1) Reports." In *Enforcement (ENF)*. August 10, 2007. www.cic.gc.ca/english/resources/manuals/enf/index.asp.

Citizenship and Immigration Canada. "ENF 24: Ministerial Interventions." In *Enforcement (ENF)*. December 2, 2005. www.cic.gc.ca/english/resources/manuals/enf/index.asp.

Crimes Against Humanity and War Crimes Act. S.C. 2000, c. 24.

Criminal Code. R.S.C. 1985, c. C-46.

Immigration Division Rules. S.O.R./2002-229.

Vinokur, David. "An Introduction to the Immigration Division of the Immigration and Refugee Board." April 8, 2004. Notes from address at the Canadian Bar Association, Citizenship & Immigration Law Conference, IRPA: The Continuing Evolution, April 30 and May 1, 2004, Toronto, Ontario.

REVIEW QUESTIONS

This chapter covered removals, the admissibility hearings process, and detention reviews. You should now be able to answer the following questions:

1. List and briefly describe the three types of removal orders.

2. List and briefly describe the prescribed factors that must be considered for detaining a person.

3. What is the purpose of an admissibility hearing?

4. What are a person's rights and responsibilities at a proceeding before the Immigration Division?

CHAPTER 11

Immigration Appeal Division

LEARNING OBJECTIVES

After reading this chapter you should be able to:

- Identify the four types of immigration appeals.

- Understand the role of participants at immigration appeal proceedings.

- Identify general Immigration Appeal Division rules.

- Clarify the process of staying a removal order and reviewing a removal order.

INTRODUCTION

The Immigration Appeal Division (IAD) of the Immigration and Refugee Board (IRB) has jurisdiction to hear and decide certain types of appeals on immigration matters, according to s. 62 of the *Immigration and Refugee Protection Act* (IRPA). In this chapter we discuss who may appeal to the IAD, the different immigration appeal types, as described in s. 63 of the IRPA, how to initiate an appeal, and the related processes.

The parties to an appeal are the appellant and the respondent. The *appellant* is the party requesting that the appeal be heard, and the *respondent* is the party arguing that the lower decision should stand. In most cases, the minister is the respondent. A member of the IAD hears the appeal.

The right to appeal an immigration decision is not available in all cases, but only in circumstances described in s. 63 of the IRPA, as follows:

- sponsorship appeals by Canadian citizens and permanent residents, whose applications to sponsor close family members to Canada have been refused (s. 63(1) of the IRPA);

- removal order appeals by permanent residents, foreign nationals with a permanent resident visa, and protected persons who have been ordered removed from Canada (ss. 63(2) and (3) of the IRPA);[1]

- Loss-of-permanent-residence appeals (also called residency obligation appeals) by permanent residents who have been determined not to have fulfilled their residency obligation by an immigration officer outside of Canada (s. 63(4) of the IRPA);[2] and

- minister's appeals.

Usually, the appellant is an individual, such as a sponsorship applicant, the subject of a removal order, or a failed permanent resident applicant. However, the minister (of Public Safety and Emergency Preparedness, who has responsibility for the Canada Border Services Agency) may appeal a decision made by a member of the IRB's Immigration Division (ID) at an admissibility hearing (s. 63(5) of the IRPA).

A person may lose the right to appeal according to s. 64 of the IRPA if found inadmissible for serious reasons, such as security, violating human or international rights, serious criminality, or organized criminality. Loss of appeal rights for reasons of serious criminality requires that the person must have been sentenced in Canada to two years or more of imprisonment for a single sentence. Furthermore, a person loses appeal rights if found inadmissible for misrepresentation unless that person is the sponsor's spouse, common-law partner, or child.

However, if the appeal is granted, the appellant is accorded the same rights that she was given before the Refugee Protection Division—namely, the right to counsel, the right to an interpreter, the right to present and call witnesses, and the right be present at her own case before an independent and impartial decision maker.

IMMIGRATION APPEAL DIVISION RULES

The Immigration Appeal Division Rules (IAD Rules) are the Division's regulations established to set out the roles and responsibilities, and govern practices and procedures in proceedings before the IAD. The IRPA gives the chairperson of the IRB the authority under s. 161 to make rules related to the IAD's activities, practices, and procedures, in consultation with the deputy chairperson of the Immigration Appeal Division, and subject to the approval of the governor in council.

Immigration consultants who represent persons who are subject to a proceeding in the IAD must have a thorough knowledge of the IAD Rules, in addition to the provisions of the IRPA that set out the jurisdiction of the IRB and the IAD to hear and decide matters. The Rules are binding, and it is important to know them well. Failure to comply with the Rules may have severe consequences to clients and their counsel.

The Rules are part of the regulations under IRPA and may be accessed at various websites including the IRB website, the Department of Justice website, and the CanLII website. An immigration consultant who is unsure about the meaning or application of a particular rule may direct questions and requests for clarifications to the registrar's staff, such as the deputy registrar or case officer, at the nearest business office of the IRB.

WEBLINK

To access the Immigration Appeal Division Rules on the CanLII website, go to www.canlii.org/ca/sta/i-2.5 and click on the link "Associated Regulations."

The IAD Rules set out the applicable rules first by appeal type, such as sponsorship appeals or removal order appeals, then by rules that apply to all immigration appeals. There are 60 rules in all, governing practices and procedures before the IAD.

POLICY INSTRUMENTS

Chairperson's Guidelines

In addition to the binding IAD Rules, there are chairperson's guidelines that guide IAD procedures. Familiarity with chairperson's guidelines will further provide counsel with confidence when navigating IAD processes.

The chairperson of the IRB has the authority pursuant to s. 159(1)(h) of the IRPA to issue specific guidelines for the IAD, although none have been issued specifically for the IAD to date. However, some guidelines of general application may have particular relevance to an IAD procedure. For example, if the client is a vulnerable person, counsel should be aware of Guideline 8—Guideline on Procedures with Respect to Vulnerable Persons Appearing Before the Immigration and Refugee Board of Canada.

Guidelines are not binding and members are not specifically directed to follow the guidelines; however, they are a source of guiding principles for members to manage cases. This is important to preserve the independent nature of the member's role in making decisions. Guidelines can be viewed on the IRB website.

Policy Notes

A **policy note** is a memorandum generally issued by a single IRB business office to communicate with members, staff, and the public, including claimants and counsel, about a particular operational matter in that local office. However, the IRB occasionally issues policy notes for all divisions. For example, in 2004 the IRB issued the following two policy notes for all its divisions, including the IAD with respect to counsel:

- New Requirements for Counsel Who Charge a Fee for Their Services, and

- New Requirements for Counsel Who Charge a Fee for Their Services—Update

These important policy notes explain that the IRB will only recognize counsel as an "authorized representative" if he or she provides his or her organization name and membership identification number for each case.

NOTICE OF APPEAL AND TIME LIMITS FOR FILING APPEALS

In all cases, the process begins with a Notice of Appeal, generally filed at the registry (IRB business office) closest to the appellant's residence. The Notice of Appeal must meet the following criteria:

- it must be made by a person who has the right to appeal;

- it must be filed on time; and

- it must be filed in accordance with the rules of procedure specific to the type of appeal.

The IAD must then notify either the minister or the ID of the appeal so that the record can be prepared.

Time Limits for Filing Appeals

The time requirements for filing appeals are very important. If the Notice of Appeal is filed out of time, the minister may dispute the appellant's appeal right and make an application to dismiss the appeal on the basis that the IAD does not have jurisdiction to hear it.

SPONSORSHIP APPEALS

A refused sponsorship application may be appealed. The appellant must provide the Notice of Appeal to the IAD, together with the visa officer's written reasons for the refusal, no later than 30 days after the sponsor received the written reasons for refusal according to rule 3 of the IAD Rules.

REMOVAL ORDER APPEALS

Removal orders may be issued by a member of the Immigration Division at an admissibility hearing or by an officer at examination. The person against whom a removal order is made may appeal in either situation. The time limits for appeal in each situation are discussed below.

Decision at Admissibility Hearing

If the appellant is subject to a removal order made at an admissibility hearing, then rule 5 of the IAD Rules provides two options, as follows:

1. the appellant may provide the Notice of Appeal by hand at the end of the admissibility hearing to the member of the ID who made the removal order, in which case it is the ID member's responsibility to provide the Notice of Appeal to the IAD without delay; or

2. the appellant may provide the Notice of Appeal directly to the IAD, together with the removal order, no later than 30 days after the appellant received the removal order.

Decision at Examination

If the appellant is subject to a removal order made by an officer at an examination, rule 7 of the IAD Rules requires the person to provide the Notice of Appeal to the IAD together with the removal order, no later than 30 days after receiving the removal order. In this situation, the IAD must notify the minister of the appeal with the removal order, without delay.

RESIDENCY OBLIGATION APPEALS

A permanent resident outside of Canada may appeal an officer's decision that permanent residence status was lost. To do so, the appellant must provide a Notice of Appeal to the IAD along with the officer's written decision to the registry closest to where the appellant last resided in Canada, within 60 days after receiving the written decision, according to rule 9 of the IAD Rules.

The longer time limit for this type of appeal (60 days rather than 30 days) is intended to accommodate the fact that the appellant is located outside of Canada. The IAD must notify the minister of the appeal with the written decision, without delay.

If the appellant wishes to be physically present in Canada for the appeal hearing, this must be indicated in the Notice of Appeal and the appellant must formally make a request under rule 46 of the IAD Rules (see below under the heading "Return to Canada").

MINISTER'S APPEALS

The minister of Public Safety and Emergency Preparedness (PSEP), as a party to the admissibility hearing, also has the right to appeal the decision of a member of the ID. To initiate the appeal, the minister must provide a Notice of Appeal to the respondent (the subject of the admissibility hearing), to the ID, and to the IAD, in accordance with rule 11 of the IAD Rules, no later than 30 days after the ID decision was made.

THE APPEAL RECORD

After receiving a Notice of Appeal, the IAD verifies that it has jurisdiction to hear the matter. If the IAD is satisfied that the Notice of Appeal complies with all requirements, the IAD notifies the respondent (the minister or the ID, depending on the type of appeal), without delay. It is then the responsibility of the respondent to prepare and serve a group of documents, known as the *appeal record*, in accordance with the IAD Rules.

Time Limits for Serving the Appeal Record

The IAD may not commence a hearing until the appeal record is received. In the past, the time limitation afforded to the minister to prepare the record was problematic, generally because of operational demands such as heavy workload of visa offices and transfer of personnel. Consequently, appellants were kept waiting for lengthy periods for their appeal to be scheduled and heard. To shorten these delays, the IAD created rules to address situations where the record is not received on time. These are discussed below with respect to each type of appeal.

SPONSORSHIP APPEALS

Generally, the visa office is informed of a sponsorship appeal and this triggers the preparation of the appeal record by the officer who refused the sponsorship. The following documents comprising the record must be prepared according to rule 4 of the IAD Rules:

- a table of contents;

- the application for permanent residence that was refused;

- the sponsor's application and undertaking;

- documents that were considered in the application; and

- the written reasons for refusal.

The record must be provided to both the IAD and the appellant no later than 120 days after the minister is served with the Notice of Appeal.

If the record is not received within the 120 days, rule 4(5) compels the minister to explain the delay and provide reasons to wait for the record, or provides the IAD with the option to start the appeal hearing with a partial record or no record.

REMOVAL ORDER APPEALS

Decision Made at an Admissibility Hearing

The ID is responsible for preparing the appeal record, which is composed of the following documents in accordance with rule 6 of the IAD Rules:

- a table of contents;

- the removal order;

- the transcript of the admissibility hearing;

- documents admitted into evidence at the admissibility hearing; and

- the ID's written reasons for the removal order.

The record must be provided to the IAD, the appellant, and the minister no later than 45 days after the ID received the Notice of Appeal. Unlike sponsorship appeals, there is no rule dealing with non-receipt of the record, because the ID is a division of the same tribunal as the IAD and internal procedures are in place to meet the 45-day time-frame. Rule 6 is silent, however, on the issue of non-compliance from the ID for providing the record within this time-frame. The record in these situations is prepared by the registrar, who is responsible for providing support to both the ID and the IAD.

Decision Made at an Examination

For appeals relating to a decision made at an examination, the minister is responsible for preparing the appeal record no later than 45 days after the minister received the Notice of Appeal. In accordance with rule 8 of the IAD Rules, the record must consist of the following:

- a table of contents;

- the removal order;

- any document relevant to the removal order; and

- the written reasons for the minister's removal order.

The record must be provided to the IAD and the appellant. Rule 8(5) provides the IAD with a process for dealing with late receipt of the record: if the record is not received within the 45 days, the IAD may compel the minister to explain the delay and provide reasons to wait for the record, or it may start the appeal hearing with a partial record or no record.

RESIDENCY OBLIGATION APPEALS

The minister of Citizenship and Immigration Canada (CIC) is responsible for preparing the appeal record, which is composed of the following documents in accordance with rule 10 of the IAD Rules:

- a table of contents;
- any document relevant to the decision on the residency obligation; and
- the visa officer's written decision and reasons.

The minister must provide the record to the IAD and the appellant no later than 120 days after the minister received the Notice of Appeal. Rule 10(5) provides the IAD with a process for dealing with late receipt of the record: if the record is not received within the 120 days, the IAD may compel the minister to explain the delay and provide reasons to wait for the record, or it may start the appeal hearing with a partial record or no record.

MINISTER'S APPEALS

The ID is responsible for preparing the appeal record, which consists of the following documents in accordance with rule 12 of the IAD Rules:

- a table of contents;
- the removal order;
- the ID's decision;
- the transcript of the ID admissibility hearing;
- any document accepted into evidence at the hearing; and
- any written reasons for the ID's decision.

The ID must provide the record to the IAD, the respondent, and the minister, no later than 45 days after the ID received the Notice of Appeal.

BEFORE THE PROCEEDING—KNOWING AND FOLLOWING THE RULES

In the same way that the ID Rules attempt to balance consistency and fairness with flexibility, rule 57 of the IAD Rules provides the IAD with the flexibility to "do whatever is necessary to deal with the matter" should a procedural problem arise during a proceeding. Consider the following example:

- IAD members may act on their own initiative to change a rule, to excuse a person from a rule, and to extend or shorten time limits, according to rule 58; and

- failure to follow a rule in a proceeding does not, in itself, make the proceeding invalid, according to rule 59.

Although there are many other similarities between the ID Rules and the IAD Rules, it is important to review and understand all the IAD Rules before representing a client before the IAD. Some of the more important rules are described below.

Definitions

Important key terms are defined in rule 1 of the IAD Rules. Counsel demonstrates professionalism by understanding and using relevant and appropriate terminology while arguing appeal cases. For example, counsel must understand that a "proceeding" may refer to a hearing, a conference, an application, or an alternative dispute resolution process. It is also important that counsel be able to distinguish the terms "appellant" and "respondent" and understand what "contact information" entails. (The latter is discussed below under the heading "Contact Information.")

Scheduling a Hearing and Notice to Appear

Appeals are scheduled when the case is considered *ready to be heard*, meaning that the appeal record and required documents have been received, documents have been exchanged pursuant to the rules of disclosure, and witnesses are available.

Generally, the parties are required to participate in a scheduling conference, also known as *Assignment Court*, to set a hearing date according to rule 22 of the IAD Rules. This is a formal proceeding, which is recorded and presided over by a member of the IAD. Assignment Court is held so that the parties can speak to the matter of readiness to proceed. The parties have the opportunity to agree to a hearing date, or, alternatively, explain why they are not ready to proceed.

The IAD member presiding at Assignment Court can remind unrepresented appellants of their right to counsel, explain the hearing process, and describe what is expected of them. Where the record has not been received on time pursuant to the IAD Rules, or where there is reason to believe that one of the parties is delaying the hearing, the member may decide to proceed peremptorily by setting a date for a hearing.

The IAD is responsible for notifying both parties of the date, time, and location of a hearing according to rule 23. This may be done orally—for example, at Assignment Court or another proceeding—or in writing in a Notice to Appear.

COMMUNICATING WITH THE DECISION MAKER

As with ID procedures, the parties and their representatives must never directly communicate with the decision maker, but rather must direct all communication through the registry, according to rule 2 of the IAD Rules. This applies to all communication, both oral and in writing, including questions about the process, documents, or a particular proceeding.

It is very important that rule 2 be followed in order to avoid suspicions of bias or influence. All parties must be aware of all information being passed on to the decision maker, so that they have the opportunity to respond. Applications and other communications must be made in writing, within time limits, and generally with proof that all parties have been served.

Contact Information

Exactly like rule 1 of the ID Rules, rule 1 of the IAD Rules defines "contact information" as a person's name, postal address, telephone number, and fax number and electronic mail address, if any.

Contact information for both the appellant and counsel must be provided to the IAD, so that the IAD can serve notices about proceedings and other matters. Rule 13 requires counsel of record to provide this information.

If notices, such as a Notice to Appear for a proceeding, are not received because the IAD does not have the proper address, the appellant might fail to show up for the proceeding, leading to dismissal of the appeal. Changes to the appellant's or counsel's contact information must be provided to the IAD and the minister without delay, according to rule 13(4).

Counsel of Record Information

Unrepresented appellants who wish to be represented are expected to retain counsel without delay. If the appellant has already agreed to a hearing date, counsel should be chosen who is available to appear on that date.

Once retained, counsel must inform the IAD. Counsel is deemed counsel of record according to rule 14 of the IAD Rules once a date for a proceeding is set. In some cases, counsel may wish to be removed from the record—for example, if the client refuses to pay or is very difficult. Rule 15 provides that counsel must seek permission from the IAD to withdraw from a case. If, on the other hand, the client wishes to remove counsel, the client must provide written notice to the IAD, to counsel, and to the minister, in accordance with rule 16.

Any counsel who is charging a fee must complete the appropriate form, the Counsel Contact Information form (IRB / CISR 687), available on the IRB website at www.irb-cisr.gc.ca under the Forms tab. Counsel must provide his or her membership identification number for either the Canadian Society of Immigration Consultants or the provincial law society to which he or she belongs.

Any counsel who represents a client and is not charging a fee should use the Notice of Representation Without a Fee form (IRB / CISR 692), also available on the IRB website.

Interpreter Services

The appellant must choose a language of record, either English or French, no later than 20 days of filing a Notice of Appeal with the IAD, pursuant to rule 17 of the IAD Rules. If the appellant or any witnesses need the services of an interpreter, then the party must notify the IAD of this no later than 20 days before the proceeding, according to rule 18.

Documents

There are several kinds of documents relevant at IAD proceedings, such as financial statements or medical reports and documents that show the client's relationship to family members. As at ID hearings, documents are important evidence at IAD proceedings, and the rules are similar for both. Because of the importance of documents to a fair resolution of the case, there are rules regarding filing documents with the IAD, disclosing documents to the opposing side, and ensuring that everyone has a copy of the documents well before the hearing.

As counsel, you must use appropriate forms and follow the rules below for filing documents:

- all documents provided to the IAD must be provided to the registry, according to rule 32;

- any document provided to the minister must be provided to the minister's counsel, according to rule 33; and

- any document provided to a person who is subject to the appeal must be provided to that person's counsel if the person is represented, according to rule 33.

As counsel, you will want to provide organized and professional-looking documents to the IAD. All documents intended for use at the hearing must comply with the following requirements:

- *Format.* Documents must be typewritten using one side only of 21.5 cm by 28 cm (8½" × 11") paper, with pages numbered, according to rule 28. If the document is a photocopy, it must be clear and legible. If you file more than one document, a numbered list of all such documents must also be filed.

- *Language.* Documents must be submitted in either English or French, which may require translation, according to rule 29.

- *Method of service.* Documents may be provided by a number of methods: by hand, by regular or registered mail, by courier or priority post, by fax (for documents no more than 20 pages long), and sometimes by electronic mail, according to rule 34. Otherwise, a request must be made to provide it in an alternative format (or not at all) in accordance with rule 35.

- *Computation of time.* A document is considered received by the Division on the day that the document is date-stamped, according to rule 36. When counsel sends a document to the minister's counsel by regular mail, it is considered received seven days after the day that it was mailed. Or, if the document was mailed to or from outside of Canada, it is considered received 20 days after the day that it was mailed. If day 7 or day 20 falls on a Saturday, Sunday, or statutory holiday, the document is considered received on the next working day.

Documents are exchanged before the hearing to ensure that all parties have an opportunity to review them, and respond if necessary, in preparation for the hearing. If counsel plans to provide documentary evidence, the evidence must be disclosed to the opposing side before the proceeding, together with a copy to the IAD, and a written statement of how and when the copy was provided to the other party, according to rule 30. If a document is not disclosed before the hearing, the IAD may not use it at the hearing, according to rule 31.

Disclosure of documents must occur at least 20 days before the hearing, unless the documents are in response to another document provided by the other party, in which case disclosure must occur at least 10 days before the hearing.

There is a separate rule for the disclosure of medical documents related to an appeal based on inadmissibility on health grounds: these documents must be disclosed no later than 60 days before the hearing, unless the document is in response to another medical document, in which case the time limit is 30 days before the hearing.

APPLICATION PROCEDURES

There are many issues that may require resolution before a hearing can even begin, such as a change to the date or location of the hearing. If a party wants a decision on such a matter, an application must be brought. There are general procedures, which apply to all applications, and other procedures that apply for each kind of application. The general procedures are set out in rule 42 of the IAD Rules and apply to all the following matters:

- a request to return to Canada to appear for an appeal hearing—rule 46

- an application to change the location of a hearing—rule 47

- an application to change the date or time of a hearing—rule 48

- a notification to withdraw an appeal—rule 50.

Each type of application is also governed by its own rule, as shown above.

General Procedures

Applications must be provided to the IAD and in the following manner, according to rule 43 of the IAD Rules:

- orally or in writing and as soon as possible or within the time limit in the IRPA or IAD Rules;

- stating the outcome sought;

- providing the reasons for the request;

- including, if known, whether the other party agrees to the application;

- including supporting evidence in an affidavit or statutory declaration, if the application is not specified in the IAD Rules; and

- with a statement of how and when a copy of the application was sent to the other party.

The opposing party has the opportunity to respond to the application under rule 44, no later than seven days after receiving the application. The response must be provided in the following manner:

- in writing (if the application was made in writing);

- stating the outcome sought;

- providing the reasons for seeking that outcome;

- including supporting evidence in an affidavit or statutory declaration, if the application is not specified in the IAD Rules; and

- providing a statement of how and when a copy of the written response was sent to the opposing party (the applicant).

The applicant then has the opportunity to reply to the response according to rule 45, no later than five days after receiving the copy of the response.

Specific Applications

Below is a description of the rules that apply to each type of application, in addition to the general procedures under rule 43 of the IAD.

RETURN TO CANADA—RULE 46

A request to return to Canada to appear for an appeal hearing may be made to the IAD according to rule 46. This may arise if the client is appealing an officer's decision that he has lost his permanent resident status because he did not meet the residency obligation of residing in Canada for two years out of a five-year period. Documents must be provided to the IAD no later than 60 days after the Notice of Appeal was filed on the IAD. If the application is accepted and the IAD orders the person to physically appear for his hearing, CIC must issue a travel document for that purpose according to s. 175(2) of the IRPA.

CHANGE THE DATE AND TIME—RULE 48

A request to change the date and time of a proceeding as specified in the Notice to Appear may be made by application to the IAD according to rule 48 of the IAD Rules. This situation may arise if, for example, the person concerned wishes to postpone a hearing to provide for more time to gather evidence. The application must be received at least two working days before the proceeding, and must include at least six alternative dates. If the application is not allowed, the client is expected to appear for the proceeding at the fixed date and time.

Rule 48 provides several factors that may be considered by the IAD when deciding an application to change the date or time of a proceeding, including the following:

- whether the party was consulted about the date and time;

- when the application was made;

- the time already afforded to the party to prepare;

- the party's efforts to prepare;

- whether the party needs more time to obtain information and whether proceeding in the absence of such information would cause an injustice;

- the knowledge and experience of counsel representing the party;

- whether there have been previous delays;

- whether the time and date fixed for the hearing was peremptory;

- whether allowing the application would unreasonably delay the proceeding or likely cause an injustice; and

- the nature and complexity of the matter to be heard.

CHANGE OF VENUE—RULE 47

A request to change the location of a proceeding as specified in the Notice to Appear may be made by application to the IAD according to rule 47 of the IAD Rules. This situation may arise if the client wishes to transfer the case to another office. Documents must be provided to the IAD no later than 30 days before the proceeding. If the application is not allowed, the client is expected to appear for the proceeding at the fixed location.

Rule 47 provides several factors that may be considered by the IAD when deciding an application to change the location of a proceeding, including the following:

- whether the client is residing in the location where she wants the proceeding to take place;

- whether a change of venue would allow the proceeding to be full and proper;

- whether a change would delay or slow the proceeding;

- whether the change would affect the operation of the IAD; and

- whether the change of venue would affect the parties.

PUBLIC VERSUS PRIVATE HEARINGS—RULE 49

The IRPA requires that proceedings before the IAD be held in public (s. 166(a) of the IRPA). However, from time to time someone may wish to make the proceeding private. This typically occurs when

- there is a serious possibility that the life, liberty, or security of a person will be endangered;

- there is a real and substantial risk to the fairness of the proceedings; or

- there is a real and substantial risk that matters of public security will be disclosed.

A request to have the proceeding conducted in private must be made no later than 20 days before the proceeding. Any person may respond in writing to the request.

NON-DISCLOSURE OF INFORMATION

Occasionally, the minister may have information that must remain confidential because its disclosure could be injurious to national security or endanger the safety of any person. In such circumstances, s. 86 of the IRPA allows the minister to make an application for non-disclosure to exclude information from the person concerned.

Before the hearing, the minister must make the application for non-disclosure in accordance with the general application rules. A member of the IAD will hold a meeting with the hearings officer *ex parte*, meaning in the absence of the appellant and counsel, and before the appeal hearing has commenced.

If the minister makes the application at the appeal hearing, the IAD member adjourns the hearing before holding the *ex parte* meeting.

If the member decides that the minister's information is relevant to the appeal and requires non-disclosure, the member writes a summary of the information and gives it to the minister. If the minister agrees with the summary, the summary is provided to the appellant. The member may then consider all the non-disclosed information when deciding the appeal. Should the minister disagree with the summary, in whole or in part, the minister has the option of withdrawing the application or the information, and then the member's decision shall not take into consideration any of the information.

HEARINGS

Counsel can prepare the client for the appeal process by describing and explaining it and by answering any questions that the client may have. Below is a list of typical questions that clients may ask (or may want to know the answers to even if they do not ask), organized by topic. Selected sample answers are provided in parentheses.

- *Type of hearing.* What can the client expect during the appeal hearing? What are the time-frames? Is the matter expected to take all day? (The length of the hearing depends on the number of witnesses and other factors. It is important to set out which issues will be examined and cross-examined.)

- *Hearing room.* What is the physical layout of the hearing room?

- *Public or private hearing.* Will the hearing be open to the public? (The proceedings are public, which means there could be observers.)

- *Hearing recorded.* Will the hearing will be recorded? (Yes. The hearing will be recorded.)

- *Language.* In what language will the hearing be held? (The hearing will be held in English or French, and an interpreter will be provided if requested.)

- *Participants.* Who will be present and what is the role of each person?

- *Nature of the proceeding.* Will the hearing be adversarial in nature? (Yes. The hearing is adversarial and involves the minister's counsel questioning the client and any witnesses, and arguing against your appeal.)

- *New evidence.* Can new evidence be presented during the appeal hearing? (Yes. New information that wasn't presented or available at the time that the decision was made may be presented during the appeal hearing.)

Generally, after the appellant and any witnesses are sworn in, the appellant's counsel will begin the examination, followed by the minister's counsel.

Jurisdiction

IAD hearings are *de novo* (Latin for "anew") and therefore the IAD member is not limited strictly to reviewing the evidence that led up to the refusal or removal order, and must also consider any additional facts as they exist at the time of the hearing.

The IAD has jurisdiction to hear appeals from decisions of the Canada Border Services Agency (CBSA), CIC, or ID, and may consider whether the decision was wrong in law or wrong in fact, whether the decision was wrong in mixed law and fact, or whether there was a breach of natural justice.

For sponsorship appeals, the IAD may consider humanitarian and compassionate reasons as long as the sponsor meets the definition of "sponsor" and the person whose application was refused meets the definition of "member of the family class" as described in s. 65 of the IRPA.

Persons in Attendance

There are a number of people who must be present at an appeal, including the appellant, the minister's counsel, and the IAD member. Other persons are likely to be present, such as the appellant's counsel. Still others may be present, such as witnesses.

APPELLANT

The appellant must be personally in attendance at the appeal.

COUNSEL

Counsel's role is to protect the appellant's interests and right to a fair hearing. Counsel explains the process, provides advice, and presents the case in an efficient manner, within the limits set by the IAD.

The appellant may choose to be represented by either an unpaid trusted adviser, such as a family member or clergy, or a paid consultant or lawyer. An unpaid adviser who represents a client and is not charging a fee should use the Notice of Representation Without a Fee form (IRB / CISR 692).

MINISTER'S COUNSEL

Minister's counsel is a public servant who works for the CBSA with the title of Hearings Officer. A hearings officer may represent the minister of PSEP or the minister of CIC depending on the decision being appealed. For example, for sponsorship appeal or residency obligation appeal hearings, a hearings officer represents the minister of CIC; for any other appeal, the hearings officer represents the minister of PSEP.

At the hearing, the hearings officer's role is generally to defend the decision against which the appeal is made, such as a visa officer's refusal of a sponsorship application or the minister's or the ID member's decision to issue a removal order. However, a hearings officer may in some cases consent to allow the appeal, if the hearings officer agrees with the appellant that there was an error in law or fact or a breach of natural justice.

IMMIGRATION APPEAL DIVISION MEMBER

Generally, only one decision maker, a member of the IAD, has the authority to hear and decide appeals. The member will also hear and decide any applications that are made orally at the hearing.

INTERPRETER

If a client or witness requires an interpreter, rule 18 of the IAD Rules requires that counsel notify the IAD in writing and specify the language and dialect needed no later than 20 days before the hearing.

The IAD will arrange for an accredited interpreter to be present at the hearing. Interpreters have passed security checks and a language exam. They are not employees of the IRB or IAD; instead, they are contracted on a case-by-case basis. They are permanently bound by their promise to interpret accurately once they take an oath or make a solemn affirmation to do so, according to rule 18(2). The interpreter may not guide, provide advice, or offer an opinion.

WITNESSES

If counsel wishes to call a witness other than her client, she must fulfill the requirements of rule 37 of the IAD by informing the opposing party and the IAD in writing no later than 20 days before the hearing. The following information must be provided:

- the witness's contact information;

- the amount of time required at the hearing for the witness's testimony;

- the party's relationship to the witness;

- whether the testimony is by videoconference or telephone; and

- a signed report with qualifications and summary of evidence for any expert witness.

If counsel does not make the request in writing, she faces the risk that her witness may not be allowed to testify under rule 37(4).

To reduce the risk of the witness failing to appear, it is prudent to request that the IAD issue a summons to order a witness to testify, according to rule 38, in writing or orally at a proceeding. The party is responsible to provide the summons to the summoned person by hand, to notify the IAD in writing of this, and to pay witness fees and travel expenses. In the request, counsel must set out the factors to be considered in issuing the summons such as the importance of the testimony of a witness, and the witness's ability and willingness to provide such information. Under rule 39, the witness may apply to the IAD to cancel the summons.

Rule 40 sets out the process for making a request to the IAD to issue a warrant for the arrest of a summoned witness who fails to appear.

Witnesses testify following the appellant's testimony. While the appellant testifies, witnesses stay in the waiting room. A person is not allowed to share any testimony given at the hearing with any witness who was excluded from the hearing room, until after the witness has testified according to rule 41.

DESIGNATED REPRESENTATIVE—RULE 19

There are situations where the person concerned is not capable of making decisions, such as in the case of an unaccompanied minor, or a person deemed mentally incompetent or unable to understand the proceedings (s. 167(2) of the IRPA). If counsel for either party believes that a designated representative is required, counsel must notify the IAD without delay according to rule 19 of the IAD Rules. The IAD may then appoint a person to act and make decisions on behalf of the person concerned. The designated representative may be a relative, or a professional such as a lawyer or social worker. Alternatively, counsel may be permitted to take on the role of designated representative.

DECISIONS

A final disposition of an appeal is communicated to the parties by way of a **Notice of Decision**, according to rule 54(1) of the IAD Rules. Sponsorship appeals and any decision to stay a removal order also require written reasons for the decision. The decision may be one of the following:

1. *Appeal allowed.* The appeal may be allowed pursuant to s. 67 of the IRPA, if the appellant satisfies the IAD member that the minister's decision was wrong for any of the following reasons:

   - there was an error in law;

   - there was an error in fact;

   - there was an error in mixed fact and law;

   - there was a breach of the principles of natural justice; or

   - taking into account the best interests of a child or humanitarian and compassionate considerations, the appeal ought to be allowed.

   If the appeal is allowed, the original decision is set aside and the IAD may substitute its own decision, such as to admit the person to Canada, or refer the matter to the appropriate decision maker for reconsideration. For example, if the appeal of a decision in a sponsorship case is allowed, the sponsorship application may be returned for further processing and assessment.

2. *Stay of the removal order.* A stay of a removal order may be granted pursuant to s. 68 of the IRPA, if the appellant satisfies the member that, taking into account the best interests of a child, or humanitarian and compassionate considerations, the original decision ought to be stayed. If the member stays the removal order, conditions may be attached. Some conditions are mandatory as found in s. 251 of the IRP Regulations (discussed in Chapter 10 under the heading "Conditions and Review of a Stay").

3. *Dismiss the appeal.* The appeal may be dismissed pursuant to s. 69 of the IRPA, if the appellant does not satisfy the member that the appeal ought to be allowed or a removal order ought to be stayed.

The IAD is required to provide written reasons for all decisions regarding an appeal by a sponsor and for decisions that stay a removal order. For all other decisions, the person concerned or the minister must request written reasons within ten days after the day that person receives the decision, according to rule 54(2).

ALTERNATIVE DISPUTE RESOLUTION

Alternative dispute resolution (ADR) in the context of immigration appeals involves mediation and negotiation, as provided by rule 20(1) of the IAD Rules. In many cases it is successful at quickly resolving the appeal without a hearing.

ADR brings the parties together in an informal meeting to explore opportunities to negotiate and settle the appeal. The process is much shorter than a hearing, often lasting about an hour. Generally, sponsorship appeals are suitable for the ADR process.

In addition to the appellant and counsel, and the minister's counsel, a dispute resolution officer (DRO) attends the meeting to facilitate the process. The DRO is a specially trained tribunal officer or a member of the IAD, under rule 20(2) of the IAD Rules. The DRO is not a party and does not decide the outcome of the appeal. The DRO is neutral, and does the following:

- makes an opening statement;

- if desired, meets with the parties separately;

- asks questions about why the appeal should be allowed;

- provides an opinion about the strengths and weaknesses of the appeal;

- prepares a summary statement if the minister consents to allowing the appeal, or, if the appeal cannot be settled, prepares an objective assessment for consideration by the appellant in deciding whether to proceed to a hearing or to withdraw the appeal; and

- sets a date for a hearing, if required.

During the meeting, the parties may also ask each other questions, and provide information and evidence. The process is confidential. Possible decisions arising from the ADR meeting include:

- Appeal **allowed on consent**. The appeal may be allowed on consent, if the minister concedes to the appellant's position.

- Appeal **withdrawn**. The appeal may be withdrawn by the appellant, if the appellant concedes to the minister's position.

- Appeal referred to a hearing. The appeal may be referred to a hearing if it is unresolved—that is, if neither party is willing to concede.

Even when the minister consents to an appeal, a member of the IAD must approve the settlement. A Notice of Decision will be issued thereafter, and, in the case of a sponsorship appeal, the minister will advise the visa office to process the sponsorship application.

If the appeal cannot be settled, the appellant maintains the right to be heard by a member at a hearing or may withdraw the appeal. Under rule 20(4), any information, statement, or document that was used at the ADR meeting generally remains confidential and does not appear on the hearing file unless it is disclosed in accordance with the IAD Rules.

NOTES

1. There is no right to appeal a removal order if the person was found inadmissible on the grounds of security, violations of human or international rights, serious criminality, or organized criminality.

2. In Canada, a removal order is issued against a permanent resident who loses her permanent resident status; that person can appeal the minister's decision to issue the removal order. The difference is that there is no removal order made against a person outside of Canada who loses her status.

REFERENCES

Citizenship and Immigration Canada. "ENF 24: Ministerial Interventions." December 2, 2005. www.cic.gc.ca/english/resources/manuals/enf/index.asp.

Immigration and Refugee Board. "Tribunals." November 10, 2005. www.irb-cisr .gc.ca/en/about/tribunals/index_e.htm.

Immigration Appeal Division Rules. S.O.R./2002-230.

REVIEW QUESTIONS

This chapter covered the process for appealing immigration decisions. You should now be able to answer the following questions:

1. List and briefly describe the four types of immigration appeals before the Immigration Appeal Division.

2. What types of admissibility cases do not have a right to an immigration appeal?

3. Discuss the advantages and disadvantages of a scheduling conference.

4. What is the nature of a hearing before the Immigration Appeal Division?

5. What are the appellant's rights at a proceeding before the Immigration Appeal Division?

6. What are the advantages of alternative dispute resolution as an appeal process? What type of appeal is suited to this process?

Reference for the Immigration Appeal Division

Provision	IRPA and IRP Regulations
Removal orders stayed	IRP Regulations ss. 230, 231, 232
Removal orders—minors	IRP Regulations s. 249
Right to appeal	IRPA ss. 63 to 65
Decision on appeals	IRPA ss. 66 to 69

Provision	IAD Rules
Definitions	rule 1
Communicating with the Division	rule 2
Sponsorship appeal	rules 3, 4
Removal order appeals	rules 5 to 8
Residency obligation appeal	rules 9, 10
Minister's appeal	rules 11, 12
Contact information	rule 13
Counsel of record	rules 14 to 16
Language of record	rules 17, 18
Designated representative	rule 19
Alternative dispute resolution	rule 20
Conferences	rule 21
Scheduling	rules 22, 23
Stay of removal order	rules 26, 27
Documents	rules 28 to 36
Witnesses	rule 37
Applications	rules 42 to 50
Hearings	rule 49
Decisions	rules 53 to 56
General provisions	rules 57 to 59

CHAPTER 12

Regulation of Immigration Consultants

LEARNING OBJECTIVES

After reading this chapter you should be able to:

- Identify which level of government regulates immigration consultants.

- Describe how a non-lawyer can be authorized to act in immigration matters.

- Apply the rules for professional conduct of immigration consultants.

- Distinguish between professional misconduct and conduct unbecoming an immigration consultant.

- Apply the profession's rules of conduct to the operation of an immigration consultant's practice.

- Understand the process for dealing with a claim of misconduct against an immigration consultant and the discipline measures that may be taken.

INTRODUCTION

In other fields of law, non-lawyers who provide legal services are called *paralegals*. In the field of immigration law, non-lawyers who provide legal services are called *immigration consultants*. Paralegals and immigration consultants work independently, and must be distinguished from *law clerks*, who also provide legal services, but who are employed and supervised by lawyers.

In the past, there have been highly publicized instances of non-lawyers involved in immigration work committing frauds on their clients and the Canadian government, and engaging in shoddy work. As a result the government decided to regulate the profession of immigration consulting. Non-lawyers who practise immigration law must now be members in good standing of the Canadian Society of Immigration Consultants (CSIC), according to the Immigration and Refugee Protection Regulations (IRP Regulations).

The CSIC, which was created in 2003, is a self-regulating professional organization that determines the requirements for entry to practise, sets rules for the professional conduct of its members, and imposes discipline or other corrective measures if those rules are disregarded. Many of the unethical and prohibited activities addressed by the CSIC code of professional conduct were identified by the government in its reasons for imposing regulation of immigration consultants:

> Most representatives conduct their work in an ethical, professional and effective manner. However, there are persistent and credible reports that some unscrupulous immigration consultants, both in Canada and abroad, facilitate people smuggling and fabricate documents permitting foreign nationals to enter this country illegally. Certain consultants who hold themselves out as experts have no training or experience handling complex files. Others promise the impossible and fail to deliver, and charge exorbitant fees for their services. In a number of reported cases, consultants have charged fees for an unfulfilled promise to file immigration applications, while providing bogus file reference numbers and advising clients that the Canadian government refused the application.[1]

The Federal Court described the reasons for the creation of the CSIC as follows:

> There has been a long-recognized need to regulate immigration consultants in Canada. Unqualified and unscrupulous consultants have been known to take advantage of vulnerable prospective immigrants and refugees. This is detrimental, not only to the victims of these consultants, but also to Canada's international reputation, as well as her economic and national security interests.

Consider the following examples of the types of conduct engaged in by unscrupulous immigration consultants, found in the news media:

1. Gideon McGuire Augier was convicted of defrauding would-be immigrants because of his bogus scheme to get immigrants into Canada. Some of his clients lost their life savings. It is alleged that he cheated hundreds of people in Russia and the Ukraine. He sold desperate families the dream of job opportunities and new lives in Canada. He collected fees, in some cases $5,000, from people abroad by promising to expedite their work permits for Canada when often no application was made. He also charged families to be sponsored under a non-existent family sponsorship scheme. He also accepted consulting fees from people in Russia and the Ukraine, knowing their applications to enter Canada on humanitarian and compassionate grounds could not be made from outside the country. (*Hamilton Spectator*, May 21, 2006)

2. Mr. Zhang immigrated to Canada in 1991. He returned to China and married his high school sweetheart. He paid a $2,000 fee for an immigration consultant to help him sponsor his new bride and her son from a previous marriage into Canada. The consultant filed the application but did not complete the required documentation. The sponsorship application was dismissed and the consultant did not inform Mr. Zhang, so the time period for filing an appeal expired. As a result, Mr. Zhang had to engage in the lengthy process of getting the decision judicially reviewed. (*Toronto Star*, April 13, 2004)

3. An immigration consultant was charged with nine counts of fraud totalling $100,832. The consultant advised clients to pay between $3,000 and $28,000 to buy businesses or real estate because they were told such investments would improve their chances of being accepted as immigrants. These purchases had no impact on their applications. (*Toronto Star*, May 5, 1987)

There were many other reported instances of misconduct by immigration consultants, but it was many years before the profession was regulated. The failure of government to legislate was due in part to uncertainty as to whether the federal or provincial level of government had jurisdiction. This constitutional issue was resolved by the Supreme Court of Canada in 2001 in *Law Society of British Columbia v. Mangat*.

FEDERAL JURISDICTION: LAW SOCIETY OF BRITISH COLUMBIA v. MANGAT

The Supreme Court of Canada in the case of *LSBC v. Mangat* determined that the federal government and not the provincial government had jurisdiction to regulate immigration consultants. The *Mangat* case arose when the Law Society of British Columbia claimed that only lawyers could legally provide paid immigration services. Mr. Mangat, an immigration consultant, was charged with the provincial offence of conducting an unauthorized legal practice, because he was not a lawyer yet he provided immigration services to clients for a fee.

The services provided by Mr. Mangat included appearing on behalf of clients at the Immigration and Refugee Board (IRB), drafting immigration documents for clients, and giving clients advice about Canada's immigration laws. There was no evidence that the services he provided were below the standard that would have been provided by a lawyer.

The Supreme Court decided that because immigration was a federal matter according to the *Constitution Act, 1867*, it was the responsibility of the federal government, not British Columbia, to decide who may practise immigration law. The Court found that the provincial statute governing the practice of law in British Columbia did not apply to the practice of immigration law.

The *Immigration Act*, which was in force at the time, permitted representation by a barrister or solicitor or other counsel. This was broad enough to allow non-lawyers to act on behalf of clients on immigration matters. There were no restrictions on how immigration law was practised by non-lawyers. Anyone could open up a business and call themselves "immigration consultants." This total lack of regulation led to many instances of incompetence and fraud.

The *Mangat* case clarified that it was the federal government that had the power to restrict the practice of immigration law. The federal government chose not to prohibit practice by non-lawyers, as the BC government had attempted to do; instead, it set up a regulatory regime to ensure the ability and integrity of immigration consultants and the quality of their services.

AUTHORIZED PRACTITIONERS AND THE CSIC

In order to earn a fee for the practice of immigration law, a practitioner must be an *authorized representative* as defined in the IRP Regulations. This means that the practitioner must be either a lawyer and a member in good standing of a provincial law society, or a member in good standing of the CSIC. The federal government may make regulations, according to s. 91 of the *Immigration and Refugee Protection Act* (IRPA), to license immigration consultants. Section 13.1 of the IRP Regulations defines an authorized representative and prohibits any person who is not an authorized representative from acting for a fee.

A non-lawyer must be a member in good standing of the CSIC to carry out the following activities:

- represent paying clients at any IRPA proceeding; or

- advise or consult paying clients regarding any IRPA proceeding or application.

This requirement applies to all matters before the following decision makers:

- the minister responsible for Citizenship and Immigration Canada (CIC);

- the minister responsible for the Canada Border Services Agency (CBSA);

- immigration officers; and

- the Immigration and Refugee Board.

The CSIC governs all persons who complete immigration documents or provide advice on how to proceed on immigration applications, and is not limited to immigration consultants who act as advocates and appear before the IRB. However, the regulatory scheme does not extend to citizenship applications, because citizenship is governed by the *Citizenship Act* and not the IRPA.

Entry to Practice

The CSIC reported that as of June 26, 2008 it had 1,314 members in good standing.[2] These are immigration consultants who are permitted by law to advise, consult, and represent clients in immigration matters. Members in good standing of the CSIC are listed on that organization's website. To be admitted as a member of the CSIC, and thus be permitted to practise as an immigration consultant, an applicant must satisfy the following criteria:

- be a Canadian citizen, permanent resident, or registered Indian under the *Indian Act*;

- complete an immigration practitioner's certification program approved by the CSIC, take the mandatory Pre-admission Course, and pass the membership entrance examination;

- be of good character, as shown by a sworn statement and police certificates from all countries where the applicant spent at least six months during the ten years prior to the application, indicating no criminal convictions since the age of 18 (however, the CSIC has discretion to admit persons with past convictions in some cases, so any information regarding convictions should be provided);

■ show the ability to carry on business in English or French by successfully completing a language test;

■ obtain liability insurance, known as professional errors and omissions insurance, with $1,000,000 coverage;

■ pay an application fee consisting of a $500 non-refundable processing fee and a $225 liability insurance fee; and

■ pay a prorated membership fee.

Renewing members pay an annual fee, which consists of a membership fee of $3,097.50 and an extended errors and omissions insurance fee of $267.45. Both fees are payable each October 31 and include GST.

A person may not become a member of the CSIC in the following circumstances:

■ *When the person is a lawyer.* Lawyers are permitted to practise all aspects of immigration law and are regulated by their own professional association. Therefore, they are not permitted membership to the CSIC.

■ *When the person has been suspended.* Anyone removed or suspended by a regulatory authority for disciplinary reasons in the last ten years is not permitted membership to the CSIC. This prevents disbarred or suspended lawyers, as well as disciplined immigration consultants, from joining the CSIC.

■ *When the person has an unpardoned criminal conviction.* Anyone with an unpardoned criminal conviction, as an adult, from anywhere in the world, is not permitted membership to the CSIC where the admission of that person would bring the CSIC into disrepute. (The CSIC may admit people with criminal convictions where the conviction does not damage the reputation of the institution. For example, a conviction for fraud would likely bar entry, whereas a conviction related to use of motor vehicles might not.)

■ *When the person has declared bankruptcy.* Generally, anyone who has declared bankruptcy is barred from entry to the CSIC, although the CSIC has discretion to admit such a person.

■ *When the person has lied to or misled the CSIC.* Anyone who has lied to or misled the CSIC on an application is not permitted to join the CSIC.

A *transition period* was instituted at the time that regulation of immigration consultants was introduced. Unauthorized representatives were given a period of four years to complete work already commenced, provided that the work was for the same person and on the same application or proceeding. For example, an unauthorized representative representing a person on a refugee claim had four years to complete that claim but could not take on new applications for the person, such as a family class sponsorship, nor could she start a refugee application for another person. The four-year period ended April 13, 2008. Any uncompleted work after that date had to be transferred to a member of the CSIC or a lawyer.

A persistent but illegal practice is that of **ghost consulting**. In this practice a person who is not authorized to practise as an immigration consultant completes the application forms on behalf of a client but then has the forms submitted as if they were personally completed by the applicant. The unauthorized person then charges a fee for the work done. This is a breach of the IRPA and may be subject to an investigation by the Royal Canadian Mounted Police. Ghost consulting also carries a risk for the client. If a client has difficulties with a ghost consultant, he will have no access to the complaint procedures of the CSIC because the CSIC has no power to deal with the existence of ghost consultants.

Consider the following scenario:

Joe, a permanent resident from Mexico, is a paralegal licensed by the Law Society of Upper Canada (LSUC). He represents clients before a number of tribunals, such as the Landlord and Tenant Board, and helps fight traffic tickets.

Joe's childhood friend Manny visited Canada from Mexico in July, and wants to stay in Canada. He doesn't have much money and his ability to read and write in English is limited. Joe wants to help his friend, so he explains Canada's immigration laws and advises Manny that he should first apply as a student. Joe helps Manny fill out the forms but does not sign the application. In return for his trouble, Manny buys Joe dinner and a few beers.

If dinner and a few beers qualify as a "fee," Joe may be in violation of the rule against ghost consulting. Paralegals who wish to dabble in immigration law should seek qualification by the CSIC to avoid this problem.

Legal Challenges to the Creation of the CSIC

In its first few years of existence, the CSIC was challenged by immigration consultants who did not wish to be regulated, and by the LSUC, which would have preferred to take over that regulatory role itself.

In *Chinese Business Chamber of Canada v. Canada*, several organizations and some individuals challenged the power of the government to regulate and restrict immigration practice. They challenged the creation of a regulatory scheme that requires all immigration consultants to be members of the CSIC, and applied to the court for an order preventing CIC and the IRB from refusing to deal with immigration consultants who were not members of the CSIC.

The court rejected these claims and stated the following:

The immigration consultant regulations are aimed at the protection of vulnerable persons and the preservation of the integrity of the immigration process, both of which are clearly in the public interest. Indeed, all of the parties agree that regulation in this area is both necessary and long overdue.[3]

The court found that the applicants had failed to demonstrate that they would suffer irreparable harm as a result of regulation.

In *LSUC v. Canada (Citizenship and Immigration)*, the LSUC contested the CSIC's authority to regulate immigration consultants. The court confirmed that the CSIC did have authority: it is an independent body separate from CIC. It further found that delegation of regulatory powers to the CSIC was authorized by s. 91 of the IRPA and that investigation by the CSIC of complaints against consultants employed at law firms did not pose a risk of breach of solicitor–client privilege.

In its reasons, the court reaffirmed the importance of immigration consultants and the valuable role they play in helping individuals navigate the immigration system.

CSIC Structure

The CSIC is governed by an elected board of directors, at least two-thirds of which is composed of members in good standing of the CSIC. The remaining third (or less) consists of public interest members who are not immigration consultants.

The CSIC has enacted a set of Bylaws to govern the operation of the organization. These Bylaws include rules for the election of directors and conduct of directors' meetings, and rules to determine the conditions that must be satisfied for entry to practise as an immigration consultant.

RULES OF PROFESSIONAL CONDUCT

The CSIC's Rules of Professional Conduct are intended to protect the public from improper, unprofessional, or incompetent practice. An immigration consultant who fails to comply with the Rules may face disciplinary measures, including expulsion from the CSIC. Expelled members may not operate as immigration consultants.

The Rules provide guidelines on how to run an immigration consulting practice in a proper manner. It must be carefully noted that minimal compliance with the strict letter of the Rules may not be sufficient because a consultant is expected not only to comply with the minimum set of specific situations detailed in the Rules but to live up to the "spirit of the Rules," especially in situations that are not specifically dealt with under them.

Some of the topics specifically dealt with by the Rules include the following, with the part identified:

- competence and quality of service (Part 3)

- professional misconduct (Part 3)

- conduct unbecoming (Part 3)

- responsibility for actions of agents or employees (Part 3)

- proper advice to clients (Part 4)

- confidentiality and solicitor–client privilege (Part 5)

- avoiding conflict of interest (Part 6)

- dealing with clients' property (Part 7)

- proper advocacy (Part 8)

- retainer and fees (Part 9)

- ending the relationship with a client (Part 10)

- proper advertising (Part 11)

- consultants operating other businesses (Part 12)

- rules against discrimination (Part 13)

- liability insurance (Part 14)

- discipline (Part 15).

These topics are explained briefly below; however, immigration consultants should be familiar with the Rules of Professional Conduct in their entirety. The Rules are reproduced in the appendix at the end of this chapter, and are also available on the CSIC website at www.csic-scci.ca/content/professional_conduct.

Competence and Quality of Service

A consultant must be diligent, efficient, and conscientious. Unprofessional habits, such as poor record keeping, disorganization, shoddy work, or failing to respond to phone calls and correspondence, are unacceptable. Consultants must have an effective **tickler system** in place for reminding them of deadlines. Missing a deadline for the filing of information, where the consequences to the client may be severe, is a particularly serious transgression.

The standard of competence and quality of service demanded is objective—based on what could be expected of a reasonably competent immigration consultant in similar circumstances. The standard is not perfection—reasonable people are not perfect. However, it does not allow for personal circumstances or disability, such as addiction or depression, to excuse poor performance.

Professional Misconduct

Professional misconduct is any improper action of an immigration consultant during the course of conducting business. It is professional misconduct for an immigration consultant to fail to comply with any of the following:

- the Rules of Professional Conduct;

- the IRPA;

- the IRP Regulations; or

- the CSIC Bylaws.

It is also professional misconduct for a consultant to misappropriate or deal dishonestly with another person's money, including any of the client's money deposited with the consultant. This prohibition is so important that it is addressed again in Part 7: Preservation of Clients' Property and in Part 9: Retainer and Fees.

It goes without saying that an immigration consultant may not bribe or attempt to bribe a government official to ignore immigration rules or give preferential treatment to a client. It is also professional misconduct for a consultant to state or imply that he is engaged in this type of activity.

Consider the following case scenario:

Lara is a licensed immigration consultant. She has been working in this field for many years and is familiar with many immigration officials and tribunal members. When a prospective client comes into her office, she promotes herself by emphasizing that she "knows everyone in this business" and "knows how to get her clients through the red tape." "It is all about who you know and keeping them happy," she says.

Lara's statements could be interpreted as meaning that she knows how to get preferential treatment for her clients. Even if she has never actually bribed any official, intimating that she does constitutes professional misconduct.

Conduct Unbecoming

Conduct unbecoming refers to improper conduct that occurs outside the immigration consultant's practice. Generally, it does not directly affect a client. The rationale behind prohibiting such conduct is that any improper conduct by a person identified with the profession might discredit the profession in the eyes of the public. This could undermine the public's confidence in the integrity of all immigration consultants.

Examples of the types of conduct that are prohibited and will likely result in discipline include the following:

- participating in criminal activity that brings into question the consultant's honesty, trustworthiness, or fitness, such as fraud;

- engaging in conduct that falls short of a crime but that involves dishonesty, such as improperly claiming to have certain credentials or legal status;

- taking improper advantage of a person in a vulnerable situation, such as people who are young, ill, unsophisticated, poorly educated, inexperienced, or lacking in business savvy; and

- failing to abide by an order of the CSIC or a court as to the proper fee that should be charged to a client.

A purely private indiscretion on the part of a consultant that does not bring into question the consultant's integrity should not cause the CSIC to impose discipline, but it is left to the CSIC to determine the boundaries between conduct unbecoming and purely private conduct.

Responsibility for Actions of Agents or Employees

An immigration consultant may hire employees to perform tasks such as record keeping, reception, and interviewing clients. An immigration consultant may also hire agents to perform functions such as delivering documents. However, it is important that the duties of such employees and agents do not involve advising, consulting with, or representing clients, unless the agent or employee is also a member of the CSIC. It is not sufficient to have an accredited immigration consultant supervise an agent or employee who is not a member of the CSIC.

It is professional misconduct if the consultant knowingly assists or induces an agent or employee to violate any of the following:

- the Rules of Professional Conduct

- the IRPA

- the IRP Regulations

- the CSIC Bylaws.

Thus, a consultant cannot try to avoid the consequences of breaching the Rules of the CSIC by having someone else do the improper actions on their behalf. Consultants should also be aware that they may be held personally responsible for the actions of agents or employees, according to the principle of **vicarious responsibility**.

Proper Advice to Clients

Immigration consultants must provide *proper advice* to their clients, meaning they must be "honest and candid." A consultant must explain the case in a manner that the client understands, to enable the client to make appropriate decisions and give directions to the consultant. If the consultant does not speak the client's language, an interpreter should be used.

The Rules state that the consultant must be careful to never "knowingly assist in or encourage" dishonesty, omission of relevant information, provision of misleading information, fraud, crime, or illegal conduct. The consultant may advise a client on how to comply with immigration law and regulations, but must not advise on how to violate the law. For example, a client sponsoring a spouse who is a resident in a foreign country should be encouraged to collect and maintain all records of contact with the spouse, such as letters and phone records, but it would be improper to encourage the client to fabricate such records.

The consultant must be very cautious in providing services, especially when dealing with clients outside the country and when providing advice and completing documents based on documents produced outside the country. The IRPA makes misrepresentation an offence, and if the consultant suspects that the client's documents are false, they should not be used.

Confidentiality and Solicitor–Client Privilege

An immigration consultant is required to keep client information and communications confidential, and generally must obtain the client's permission before disclosing any such information. However, the consultant may be compelled by a court to disclose *confidential information* in a legal proceeding. For example, if a client is charged with an IRPA or *Criminal Code* offence, or there is a lawsuit against the client, the immigration consultant can be subpoenaed and required to attend court and answer questions related to the legal proceeding.

Also, the CSIC may demand information from an immigration consultant, according to bylaw 13. This obligation overrides the duty of confidentiality owed to clients. The CSIC may demand information regarding the following:

- the consultant's knowledge, skill, or judgment;

- whether the consultant is paying attention to the client's interests;

- the consultant's practice, including the records systems and procedures used; and

- any other aspects of the consultant's practice.

The consultant must respond to the request for information within the time limits set by the CSIC.

By contrast, client information and communications shared in the context of a lawyer–client relationship are protected by **solicitor–client privilege**. A court may not compel the disclosure of such information against the wishes of the client. This may be an important advantage to clients in some cases. Therefore, immigration consultants should explain their duty of confidentiality, and how it differs from solicitor–client privilege, at the time of the initial interview with the client. It is important that the clients of immigration consultants be aware that they are not protected by solicitor–client privilege, before they divulge information.

Avoiding Conflict of Interest

A **conflict of interest** occurs where a consultant represents clients with incompatible interests. In other words, the best course of action for one client may harm the interests of another.

A situation may also arise where there is a potential for a conflict, but no actual conflict. For example, a consultant may represent both an employer and a foreign worker that the employer wants to hire. In these circumstances the consultant must inform both the employer and foreign worker of the potential for a conflict of interest. Should an actual conflict arise, such as the foreign worker obtaining a job offer from another employer, the consultant must cease representation of one or both parties.

Dealing with Clients' Property

Immigration consultants must be very careful with property belonging to clients. Meticulous records must be kept, and a trust account designated so that client property does not find its way into the general business account. (For details, see bylaw 12 of the Bylaws of the CSIC.) Funds held in trust on behalf of a client should be limited to an amount reasonably necessary for payment of the consultant's fees and disbursements, any agent's fees, and CIC fees. Funds for other purposes, such as those required for entry under the investor class, should not be in the possession of the consultant.

Proper Advocacy

Immigration consultants may appear before the Immigration and Refugee Board to advocate for clients. The duty of an immigration consultant when appearing before the IRB is to resolutely and fearlessly raise every issue, and advance every argument, to support the client's position. However, the consultant must do so fairly and honourably. The consultant must act legally and ethically. For example, the consultant must not counsel a witness to lie, or make claims that are clearly unsupported or false.

Consultants must treat members of the IRB and government officials with courtesy, respect, candour, and fairness. The consultant has an absolute duty to abide by the rules of procedure of the IRB.

Retainer and Fees

A consultant may demand a *retainer* from a client, which is funds paid in advance of services. Retainers must be deposited in a separate trust account at a financial institution, and transferred into the business account only after services are rendered on the client's behalf and the client is billed.

The retainer agreement must indicate the reason that the consultant is being hired, and set out the fair and reasonable fees for services and *disbursements* (out-of-pocket expenses, such as photocopying) that will be charged by the consultant. Terms and conditions, such as a statement that interest will accrue on unpaid accounts, should also be specified. The agreement must also inform the client of how to contact the CSIC in the event of a disagreement over fees.

Ending the Relationship with a Client

Once a consultant has accepted a client, the consultant is generally obliged to maintain the relationship. There are exceptions that allow the consultant to terminate the relationship, and in a few circumstances the consultant is required to do so.

A consultant may terminate the client relationship only for a proper purpose and if it is not unfair or prejudicial to the client. Common reasons for ending the relationship with a client include the following:

- refusal to pay fees;
- abusive behaviour;
- lying to the consultant;
- failure to instruct the consultant; and
- refusal to take advice on a significant matter.

A consultant who wishes to terminate the relationship must ensure that the client has sufficient opportunity to seek the assistance of new counsel in time for any upcoming hearing dates. Terminating the relationship for the purpose of delaying a hearing to allow the client to stay in Canada longer is an improper purpose, even if it is the client's wishes.

A consultant must end the relationship with a client in the following circumstances:

- the client instructs the consultant to violate the law or contravene the Rules;

- the matter is too complex for the consultant; or

- the consultant will be placed in a conflict of interest by continuing to represent the client.

There are no restrictions on a client's ability to "fire" a consultant. The client may end the relationship at any time, without explanation. However, the client remains responsible for payment of any outstanding fees.

Once the relationship ends, the consultant must return the client's papers and information on the case, return any retainer funds held in trust (less the amount of any outstanding fees), account for fees and disbursements, cooperate with any new consultant hired by the client, and inform CIC and/or the IRB.

If you are taking over a case from another immigration consultant, it is prudent to contact the former consultant and confirm that she is no longer handling the case.

Proper Advertising

Advertising must be in good taste and not bring the profession into disrepute. It may not be false or misleading. In particular, advertising should not guarantee results or guarantee maximum times for completing processing of applications, nor should it be expressed or implied that the consultant has special connections with government officials or that the consultant is a lawyer. The consultant must be careful that any foreign credentials listed, such as a foreign law degree, do not suggest to the public that the consultant is a lawyer in Canada.

The CSIC has also provided detailed guidelines, called the Guidelines for Advertising, Solicitation and Making Services Available, to assist consultants in dealing with advertising issues. The Guidelines make it clear that all forms of advertisement are covered by the Rules, including letterhead and business cards, and newspaper flyers and the Internet. The consultant should communicate factual, accurate, and verifiable information through advertisement. A consultant may use the term "immigration consultant," advertise the fact of CSIC membership, and use the CSIC logo. The Guidelines prohibit the consultant from using testimonials in advertisements and from criticizing competitors.

Consultants Operating Other Businesses

An immigration consultant is allowed to operate other businesses as well as immigration consulting. For example, the immigration consultant may also be a licensed paralegal, accountant, real estate agent, financial adviser, or tax consultant.

An immigration consultant who juggles more than one business must ensure that competent service is maintained in the immigration consulting business. The consultant must also avoid conflicts of interest between the immigration business and any other business. For example, it would be a conflict of interest for a consultant also acting as financial adviser to steer the clients into investments that provide a greater payment to the consultant but which may not qualify in support of an application to enter Canada under the investor category.

Rules Against Discrimination

A consultant is not permitted to discriminate against clients on the basis of categories such as race and religion. Discrimination may include charging more or refusing to represent. Consultants will often target their marketing efforts at certain groups by noting that they are able to speak certain languages, by advertising in specific community newspapers, and by getting referrals from contacts within a certain community. This is acceptable and not considered to be discrimination. It is also possible, and in fact required, to refuse clients on the basis that the service requested is outside the area of expertise of the consultant. However, it is not permissible to refuse clients based on their ethnicity or indicate that you will only represent people of a particular religion, gender, or ethnic group.
Consider the following case scenario:

> Gita is a qualified immigration consultant and an immigrant herself. She has a law degree from her native country and she speaks four languages— English and three other languages from her country of birth. She is very connected to her ethnic community here in Canada, and her clients are exclusively from that community. Gita writes a column in her local ethnic newspaper, which lists her law degree and membership in the CSIC. Gita also advertises in this newspaper and sometimes includes words of praise from well-known members of her community who were former clients.

This scenario raises a number of issues. Gita must be careful when referencing her foreign law degree. She must not misrepresent herself as a lawyer in Ontario. There is nothing wrong with promoting herself to her own ethnic community, but she must be careful not to refuse service to a client who does not belong to her ethnic group. Finally, Gita's advertising is problematic because it includes testimonials, which are prohibited by the CSIC Guidelines.

Liability Insurance

Immigration consultants must purchase *liability insurance*, also called *errors and omissions insurance*. This insurance protects clients by providing funds for compensating clients for any successful professional negligence or fraud claim against an immigration consultant. For example, if an immigration consultant defrauds a client of $100,000 by telling him that the money will be used for a qualifying investment under the investor class, the insurer will pay the money back to the client. This is important, because the money may have disappeared, and not be retrievable.

Liability insurance also protects immigration consultants—without it, a consultant could be forced to use personal assets, such as a family home, to pay a damages award. Consider an immigration consultant who misses a deadline and thereby causes a client to expend an additional $60,000 in legal fees. The consultant would benefit from the insurer paying the amount of the damages award, rather than being required to cash in a registered retirement savings plan in order to pay it.

Discipline

If a claim is made against a consultant, the CSIC first investigates the claim. If it is groundless, no action will be taken. If the investigation discloses that the claim is credible, the CSIC will commence discipline procedures. The immigration consultant must be informed of the complaint and be given 30 days to respond to the allegations.

Certain complaints cannot be resolved by the CSIC because it has authority only to discipline a member for professional misconduct or for conduct unbecoming an immigration consultant. If the investigation discloses that the complaint relates to negligence, the matter may be referred to the errors and omissions insurance company or to the civil courts. If the consultant is not a member of the CSIC, the issue is referred to the police for prosecution pursuant to the IRPA (see ss. 126 and 127 for offences and penalties related to counselling and misrepresentation). In this case, the CSIC cannot resolve the issue; it is a matter for the courts.

If the consultant is a member of the CSIC, the following actions short of discipline could be taken:

- the consultant could be sent a note advising her of more appropriate steps to be taken in future practice;

- the consultant could be given advice and required to take training;

- the consultant could be warned and cautioned not to repeat the action that resulted in the complaint;

- the consultant could be asked to attend a meeting with the CSIC where appropriate conduct would be explained to her; or

- the consultant may be required to give a written promise that she will not take the same inappropriate actions again.

In serious cases, the CSIC will start a discipline hearing.

An unsatisfied client of an immigration consultant may submit a complaint in writing to the CSIC. The CSIC may address complaints by either attempting to mediate and resolve the dispute, or by investigating the complaint to determine whether the Rules of Professional Conduct or the Bylaws were violated. If the investigator finds a violation, the CSIC may impose discipline.

An investigator is expected to be fair and impartial, favouring neither the complainant nor the consultant. The investigator's job is to find facts, by reviewing documents and interviewing the parties, and to provide the CSIC with sufficient information on which it may make a decision about whether the Rules or the Bylaws were breached.

After completion of the investigation, the investigator prepares and submits a written report to the manager of complaints and discipline. The manager may choose any of the following options:

- issue a written reprimand to the consultant;

- provide advice to the consultant regarding better practice, including the need for additional training;

- issue a written caution;

- caution the consultant in person;

- require an undertaking to carry out certain actions to improve practice; or

- refer the matter to a discipline hearing.

A disciplinary hearing is a more formal process by which each party has an opportunity to present evidence and make arguments before an impartial decision maker. If a ruling is made against the consultant, discipline such as a suspension or revocation of membership may be ordered. The consultant may also be required to pay all or part of the costs incurred by the complainant.

There are a number of responses to a complaint that are not open to the CSIC. The CSIC is not permitted to do any of the following:

- address complaints about non-members (this is a matter for the police);

- determine reasonable fees (this is a matter to be negotiated between the consultant and client);

- determine whether a member was negligent and the extent of damages (this is a matter for the civil courts or for the consultant's liability insurer);

- provide immigration advice to the complainant (this is a matter for members of the CSIC, but not for the CSIC); or

- provide legal advice regarding liability or other issues (this is a matter for lawyers).

In other words, the CSIC's responsibility is limited to enforcement of the Rules and the Bylaws, and the remedies it may impose are limited to discipline and costs.

NOTES

1 Regulatory Impact Analysis Statement, *Canada Gazette* Extra, vol. 138, no. 4, PartII, April 14, 2004, http://canadagazette.gc.ca/partII/2004/20040414-x/html/sor59-e.html.

2 Canadian Society of Immigration Consultants, "CSIC Membership Surpasses 1300," June 26, 2008, www.csic-scci.ca/ann/show.html/10122.

3 *Chinese Business Chamber of Canada v. Canada*, 2005 FC 142; upheld 2006 FCA 178.

REFERENCES

Canadian Society of Immigration Consultants. Bylaws. April 11, 2006. www.csic-scci.ca/content/bylaws.

Canadian Society of Immigration Consultants. Guidelines for Advertising, Solicitation and Making Services Available. (N.D.). www.csic-scci.ca/content/advertising_guidelines.

Canadian Society of Immigration Consultants. Rules of Professional Conduct. (N.D.). www.csic-scci.ca/content/professional_conduct.

Constitution Act, 1867. (U.K.), 30 & 31 Vict., c. 3.

Immigration and Refugee Protection Act. S.C. 2001, c. 27.

Immigration and Refugee Protection Regulations. S.O.R./2002-227.

Law Society of British Columbia v. Mangat. [2001] 3 S.C.R. 113.

Law Society of Upper Canada v. Canada (Citizenship and Immigration). 2008 FCA 243.

REVIEW QUESTIONS

1. List the steps that a person must take to become a member of the CSIC.

2. What is the difference between an immigration consultant and a law clerk?

3. Compare and contrast professional misconduct and conduct unbecoming an immigration consultant.

4. What is ghost consulting and why would Canadian officials want this practice stopped?

5. Describe the types of advertising that are acceptable to the CSIC.

6. How should a consultant deal with money paid to the consultant in order to pay fees to CIC?

7. What is the obligation of a consultant acting as an advocate in a hearing before the IRB?

8. What organization can impose discipline on a consultant? What reasons will motivate that organization to impose discipline and what forms of discipline is that organization authorized to impose?

9. If a consultant operates more than one business, what must the consultant do in order to avoid improper practices?

10. What is a conflict of interest? How can a consultant avoid getting into a conflict of interest, or resolve a conflict of interest if one arises?

DISCUSSION QUESTIONS

1. Should the Canadian government require immigration consultants to be licensed or should it leave it to the marketplace and the general legal rules against fraud and negligence to deal with unscrupulous and incompetent immigration consultants?

2. Should the CSIC be concerned with the private conduct of immigration consultants or should it limit its rules to professional misconduct?

APPENDIX

Canadian Society of Immigration Consultants Rules of Professional Conduct

PART 1 INTRODUCTION

1.1 The Rules of Professional Conduct (the "Rules") establish the expected standard of professional conduct and competence for Immigration Consultants. The Rules also provide guidance to the profession, with the goal of protecting the public from unprofessional, improper or incompetent practice.

1.2 A breach of the Rules may result in an Immigration Consultant being disciplined. The Rules cannot address every situation of professional or ethical misconduct. Immigration Consultants shall endeavour to follow the spirit of these rules at all times.

1.3 A person who wishes to practice as an Immigration Consultant must be a member of the Canadian Society of Immigration Consultants.

1.4 The Canadian Society of Immigration Consultants is responsible for administering the Rules.

1.5 It is the duty of any person to whom the Rules applies to comply with its provisions.

PART 2 DEFINITIONS

"Agent"
means a person who:
    (a) represents an Immigration Consultant with respect to Clients;
    (b) solicits Clients on behalf of an Immigration Consultant; or
    (c) liaises with a Client with the intent to provide information to assist the Immigration Consultant in representing, advising or consulting with a Client.

> ***Commentary:***
>
>   1. An Agent is not an Immigration Consultant and may not represent, advise, or consult with a Client. Any person, either domestic or foreign, assisting Immigration Consultants with obtaining Clients or information regarding Clients, will be deemed to be an Agent.

"Board"
means the Immigration and Refugee Board, which consists of the Refugee Protection Division, Refugee Appeal Division, Immigration Division and Immigration Appeal Division.

"Canadian Society of Immigration Consultants"
means the corporation designated by the Minister pursuant to section 91 of the Immigration and Refugee Protection Act, S.C. 2001, c. 27, as amended, (the "IRPA") or subsequent provisions of the IRPA Regulations pursuant to IRPA section 91 to establish standards and regulate the conduct of Immigration Consultants.

"Client"
means a person on whose behalf an Immigration Consultant undertakes to represent, advise or consult with in respect of any proceeding or application before the Minister, an Officer, or the Board.

"Conduct Unbecoming an Immigration Consultant"
means conduct in an Immigration Consultant's personal or private capacity that tends to bring discredit upon the profession including, for example:

(a) committing a criminal act that reflects adversely on the Immigration Consultant's honesty, trustworthiness, or fitness as an Immigration Consultant;

(b) taking improper advantage of the youth, inexperience, lack of education, lack of sophistication, ill health, or un-businesslike habits of another;

(c) engaging in conduct involving dishonesty; or

(d) failing to abide by a fee dispute resolution either resolved by the Society or a court of competent jurisdiction.

> ### *Commentary:*
>
> 1. Dishonourable or questionable conduct on the part of an Immigration Consultant in either private life or professional practice will reflect adversely on the integrity of the profession and the administration of justice. If the conduct, whether within or outside the professional sphere, is such that knowledge of it would be likely to impair the Client's trust in the Immigration Consultant, the Society may be justified in taking disciplinary action.
>
> 2. Generally, however, the Society will not be concerned with the purely private or extra-professional activities of an Immigration Consultant that do not bring into question the Immigration Consultant's integrity.
>
> 3. An Immigration Consultant must abide by any fee dispute resolution of either the Society or a court.

"Designated Professional Body"
means a law society of a province or territory or the Chambre des notaires du Quebec.

"Employee"
means a person who is in an employee/employer relationship with an Immigration Consultant but does not include an Immigration Consultant.

> ***Commentary:***
>
> 1. An Employee is not an Immigration Consultant but assists an Immigration Consultant with respect to his or her duties as an Immigration Consultant. As such, an Employee may not represent, advise or consult with a person in respect of a proceeding or application before the Minister, an Officer, or the Board. An Employee may merely facilitate the Immigration Consultant in his or her practice.

"Immigration Consultant"
means any person who is a member of the Society who is thereby authorized to represent, advise or consult with a person in respect of a proceeding or application before the Minister, an Officer, or the Board.

"Minister"
means the Minister or Ministers responsible for the administration of IRPA. The Minister or Ministers are the members of the Queen's Privy Council designated as such by the Governor in Council.

"Officer"
means any person or class of person designated as Officers by the Minister to carry out any purpose of any provision of IRPA.

"Professional Misconduct"
means conduct in an Immigration Consultant's professional capacity that tends to bring discredit upon the profession including:

(a) (i) violating or attempting to violate one of the rules in the Rules or a requirement of the IRPA or its regulations or the by-laws of the Society;

(ii) undermining or attempting to undermine the Society's mandate and/or governing principles.

(b) (i) knowingly assisting or inducing another Immigration Consultant to violate or attempt to violate one or more of the Rules or a requirement of IRPA or its regulations or the by-laws of the Society;

(ii) knowingly assisting or inducing another Immigration Consultant to undermine or attempt to undermine the Society's mandate and/or governing principles.

(c) (i) knowingly assisting or inducing an Employee or Agent to violate or attempt to violate one or more of the Rules or a requirement of the IRPA or its regulations or the by-laws of the Society;

(ii) knowingly assisting or inducing an Employee or Agent to undermine or attempt to undermine the Society's mandate and/or governing principles.

(d) misappropriating or otherwise dealing dishonestly with a Client's or a third party's money or property;

(e) stating or implying an ability to influence improperly a government agency or official; or

(f) engaging in conduct that is prejudicial to the administration of justice.

"Society"
means the Canadian Society of Immigration Consultants.

PART 3 COMPETENCE AND QUALITY OF SERVICE

3.1 An Immigration Consultant owes the Client a duty to be competent to perform any services undertaken on the Client's behalf.

3.2 An Immigration Consultant should serve the Client in a conscientious, diligent and efficient manner, and should provide a quality of service at least equal to that which Immigration Consultants generally would expect of a competent Immigration Consultant in a like situation.

Commentary:

1. The quality of an Immigration Consultant's work reflects on the entire profession. While minor errors and omissions do not constitute professional misconduct, a pattern of shoddy work or unprofessional habits may amount to professional misconduct. To avoid claims of professional misconduct, an Immigration Consultant should endeavour:

   (a) to keep the Client reasonably informed;

   (b) to answer reasonable requests from the Client for information;

   (c) to not mislead the Clients as to steps to be taken;

   (d) to do all work in a professional manner without omissions or mistakes;

   (e) to not withhold information from the Client or mislead the Client about the position of a matter in order to cover up the fact of neglect or mistake; and

   (f) to make a prompt and complete report when the work is finished, or if a final report cannot be made, failure to make an interim report when one might reasonably be expected.

2. An Immigration Consultant will accept only assignments for which he or she is qualified and in which it is believed there may be real benefits to the Client. An Immigration Consultant will recommend that other professionals be retained whenever their special knowledge and skills may be needed by the Client. In particular, an Immigration Consultant has a positive duty to refer a Client to a competent lawyer where the legal issues are complex and require an analysis and interpretation of the applicable law by a lawyer, or where the matter clearly requires representation by a lawyer, such as a proceeding before the Federal Court of Canada.

3. An Immigration Consultant should not undertake representation of the Client before the Board unless the Immigration Consultant has the ability and capacity to deal adequately with the matters to be undertaken.

4. An Immigration Consultant will act responsibly and with due diligence in the handling of a Client's case and act within the bounds of the law to obtain the best results possible for the Client in the circumstances.

> 5. An Immigration Consultant may permit an Employee to act only under the supervision of the Immigration Consultant. The extent of supervision will depend on the type of matter, including the degree of standardization and repetitiveness of the matter, and the experience of the Employee generally with regard to the matter in question. The burden rests on the Immigration Consultant who uses his or her Employee to educate the latter concerning the duties that may be assigned to the Employee and then to supervise the manner in which such duties are carried out. An Immigration Consultant should review his or her Employee's work at sufficiently frequent intervals to enable the Immigration Consultant to ensure its proper and timely completion.

3.3 An Immigration Consultant will keep his or her knowledge and skills up-to-date in compliance with Continuing Professional Development requirements established by the Society.

3.4 An Immigration Consultant has a responsibility to adapt to changing professional requirements, standards, techniques, and practices.

3.5 An Immigration Consultant should assume complete professional responsibility for all work entrusted to him or her and should directly supervise Employees to whom particular tasks and functions are delegated.

3.6 Where Agents are utilized, the Immigration Consultant should ensure that all Agents are qualified for the task undertaken. An Immigration Consultant shall be responsible for the acts or omissions of his or her Agents. Agents must be made aware in writing of the requirements that the client's information be retained in confidence as more particularly described in Part 5.

Commentary:

> 1. If an Immigration Consultant utilizes an Agent, the Immigration Consultant is responsible for the activities of the Agent. An Agent includes not only someone who assists the Immigration Consultant but someone who directs clients to an Immigration Consultant or co-markets with an Immigration Consultant.

3.7 Except with the written permission of the Society, an Immigration Consultant may not employ or retain in any capacity having to do with the practice of Immigration law a person whose membership or registration has been removed or suspended by the Society or any Designated Professional Body or share space or be partner or associate with such a person.

3.8 An Immigration Consultant should seek help from colleagues and appropriately qualified professionals for personal problems that adversely affect his or her service to Clients, The Society or the profession.

3.9 An Immigration Consultant should avoid impugning the reputation of colleagues for personal motives; however, subject to the duty of confidentiality, he or she should report to the appropriate authority any unprofessional, illegal or unethical conduct by colleagues or others. Wherever possible, the Immigration Consultant should request an explanation from this individual to assist the consultant in determining whether there is any obligation to report this individual's conduct.

3.10 An Immigration Consultant should not engage in professional misconduct or conduct unbecoming an Immigration Consultant.

PART 4 ADVISING CLIENTS

4.1 When advising Clients, an Immigration Consultant must be both honest and candid.

4.2 When advising a Client, an Immigration Consultant must exercise due care and must never knowingly assist in or encourage any dishonesty, provision of misleading information, omission of any required relevant information, fraud, crime or illegal conduct, or instruct the Client on how to violate the law and avoid punishment.

4.3 When advising a Client who does not speak English or French, nor any other language in which the Immigration Consultant is fluent and proficient, it is imperative that the Immigration Consultant make every reasonable effort to engage the services of an interpreter when communicating with the Client.

4.4 An Immigration Consultant must advise the Client promptly and fully regarding any error or omission that has occurred in the matter for which an Immigration Consultant was retained, that is or may be damaging to the Client and cannot be readily corrected. The duty includes recommending that the Client seek independent advice regarding any rights that may arise out of the error or omission. An Immigration Consultant shall further advise the insurer promptly regarding any potential claim arising out of the matter.

Commentary:

1. An Immigration Consultant has a duty to give the Client competent advice based on sufficient knowledge of the relevant facts, sufficient appreciation and consideration of the applicable law, operational policies and practices, and an Immigration Consultant's own experience and expertise.

2. An Immigration Consultant should avoid overly bold and confident assurances to the Client, especially when the Immigration Consultant's employment may depend on advising in a particular way.

3. An Immigration Consultant must be aware of and refer Clients in appropriate circumstances to services or benefits for which the Client may be eligible, such as legal aid or legal clinic services.

4. An Immigration Consultant should be on guard against becoming the tool or dupe of an unscrupulous Client, Agent, or persons associated with a Client or Agent.

5. An Immigration Consultant must exercise due diligence to prevent the commission of an offence with respect to any proceeding or application before the Minister, an Officer, or the Board.

PART 5 CONFIDENTIALITY

5.1 An Immigration Consultant has a duty to hold in strict confidence all information concerning the personal and business affairs of the Client acquired during the course of the professional relationship, and should not disclose such information unless disclosure is expressly or impliedly authorized by the Client, is required by law, or is otherwise permitted by the Rules.

5.2 An Immigration Consultant shall take all reasonable steps to ensure the privacy and safekeeping of a Client's confidential information.

5.3 An Immigration Consultant shall not disclose the fact of having been consulted or retained by a person unless the nature of the matter requires such disclosure.

5.4 Subject to being compelled by law or legal process, an Immigration Consultant shall preserve the Client's confidential information even after the termination of the retainer, whether or not differences have arisen between the Immigration Consultant and the Client.

5.5 An Immigration Consultant should ensure that Employees and Agents maintain and preserve the Client's confidential information.

Commentary:

1. An Immigration Consultant owes a duty of confidentiality to every Client whether a casual or continuing Client. This duty survives the professional relationship and continues indefinitely even after the professional relationship has terminated, and regardless of whether there are differences between the Client and Immigration Consultant.

2. An Immigration Consultant is forbidden from ever using confidential information for his or her own benefit, for the benefit of a third party, or to the disadvantage of the Client.

3. Disclosure of confidential information may be permitted where expressly or impliedly authorized by the Client or where compelled by law or legal process. Disclosure may also be permitted where the fee or conduct of an Immigration Consultant has been called into question by the Client— but, in such cases, disclosure may only be permitted to the extent necessary to defend against such allegations.

4. An Immigration Consultant should avoid indiscreet conversations or gossip, and should not repeat gossip or information about a Client's affairs, even though the Client is not named or otherwise identified.

PART 6 CONFLICTS OF INTEREST

6.1 An Immigration Consultant shall not represent parties with potentially conflicting interests in an immigration matter, save after adequate disclosure to and with the consent of the parties, and shall not act or continue to act in a matter when there is or is likely to be a conflict of interest.

Commentary:

1. A conflicting interest is one that would be likely to affect adversely the Immigration Consultant's judgment or advice on behalf of, or loyalty to a Client or prospective Client.

2. Conflicting interests include, but are not limited to, circumstances where the Immigration Consultant and his or her Employees or family members have an undisclosed financial interest in a Client's affairs, including the receipt of undisclosed commissions, referral fees or other real or potential benefits.

3. In the case of an Investor Category (as defined in the IRPA) applicant or any Provincial Nominee Class Client (as defined in the IRPA) where the Immigration Consultant may receive referral fees or commissions from a financial institution or other company which may enter into an agreement with the Client, the Immigration Consultant shall disclose that he or she may receive fees or commissions and should encourage the Client to receive independent legal advice on any contract or agreement the Client may be entering into with said financial institution or company.

4. A conflict also exists where an Immigration Consultant acts for more than one Client and must favour the interest of one Client to the material detriment of another.

5. An Immigration Consultant who practices in association with, or in partnership with a lawyer is obligated to abide by the professional standards ascribed to by these rules.

6. This rule requires adequate disclosure to enable the Client to make an informed decision about whether or not to have an Immigration Consultant act for him or her despite the existence or possibility of a conflict of interest.

7. Generally speaking, in disciplinary proceedings arising under this rule the Immigration Consultant will have the burden of showing good faith and that adequate disclosure was made in the circumstances and that the Client's consent was obtained.

PART 7 PRESERVATION OF CLIENTS' PROPERTY

7.1 An Immigration Consultant owes a duty to the Client to ensure the safekeeping of the Client's property in accordance with the law and with the same care of such property as a careful and prudent owner would when dealing with property of like description.

Commentary:

1. With respect to the Client's money paid on account of services to be rendered, or on account of disbursements, an Immigration Consultant should maintain a proper trust account and adequate records so that at any time the Immigration Consultant may promptly account for and if necessary deliver such property to the Client.

2. It is generally improper for an Immigration Consultant to withhold from the Client immigration documents or other valuable property held on behalf of the Client as collateral for an unpaid debt.

PART 8 IMMIGRATION CONSULTANT AS ADVOCATE

8.1 When representing the Client before the Board, the Immigration Consultant should resolutely, and honourably, within the limits of the law, represent the Client's interest while treating the Board members, the Minister and Officers with courtesy and respect.

Commentary:

1. An Immigration Consultant as advocate must fearlessly raise every issue and advance every argument in advancing the Client's interests, but must do so fairly and honourably, without illegality, and in a manner consistent with the duty to treat Board members, Officials, and other practitioners with candour, fairness, courtesy and respect, and must abide by the procedural rules of the Board.

2. The duty to fearlessly raise every issue and advance every argument is limited by the concurrent duty of an Immigration Consultant to not abuse the immigration or tribunal process by pursuing manifestly unfounded or spurious applications or claims.

PART 9 RETAINER AND FEES

9.1 It is a mandatory requirement that the Immigration Consultant provide the Client with a written retainer agreement or engagement letter that clearly states the matter and scope of services for which the Immigration Consultant is retained, fully discloses the fees and disbursements being charged, such fees being fair and reasonable in the circumstances, any other remuneration being received as a consequence of the matter, and payment terms and conditions. The retainer agreement must disclose that the Immigration Consultant is a member of the Society and must

provide electronic, telephonic and address details as to how the Client may contact the Society.

9.2 An Immigration Consultant must not appropriate any money or property of a Client held in trust or otherwise under the Immigration Consultant's control for or on account of fees or disbursements without the express or implied authority of the Client.

9.3 An Immigration Consultant may not hold Client money, for the benefit of a third party except for money to pay the Immigration Consultant's fees, including Agent's fees, Citizenship and Immigration Canada's ("CIC") fees and disbursements related thereto. For greater clarity, the prohibition on holding Clients' money applies to money that the Client needs to qualify for any eligibility program under the IRPA.

Commentary:

1. Factors to be considered when determining whether a fee is fair and reasonable in the circumstances include: the nature of the services to be performed; the time required; the Immigration Consultant's experience, ability and the degree of responsibility assumed; and the benefits that accrue to the Client.

2. The Immigration Consultant must not receive hidden fees or commissions or other remuneration arising out of his or her representation of the Client unless possible receipt of the same has been disclosed in the retainer agreement or engagement letter.

3. Contingent fees can be appropriate, where the terms are fully disclosed in writing and understood by the Client.

4. An Immigration Consultant is not to hold money for a Client, aside from fees necessary to process the Client's application or filing fees for a proceeding. In particular, an Immigration Consultant must not take possession of money that the Clients are required to expend for any qualifying program authorized by CIC, including investor programs.

5. It is in keeping with the best traditions of the profession to provide services pro bono and to reduce or waive a fee where there is hardship or poverty or the Client or prospective Client would otherwise be deprived of adequate professional advice and representation.

6. An Immigration Consultant must issue receipts, proper statements of account and retain proper records for the safeguarding of, and timely reporting to the Client with respect to, payments received or funds held in trust.

7. Breaches of this rule and misunderstandings about fees and financial matters bring the profession into disrepute. The Immigration Consultant must try to avoid such conflicts and must be prepared to explain the basis of charges, especially if the Client is unsophisticated or uninformed about the proper basis and measurement for fees. Furthermore, the Immigration

Consultant is under a positive duty and should either in the retainer agreement or engagement letter, or upon an issue with respect to fees arising, advise the Client in writing that a procedure exists for reviewing the account on behalf of the Client by the Society.

PART 10 WITHDRAWAL FROM REPRESENTATION

10.1 Obligatory withdrawal—An Immigration Consultant shall sever the consultant-client relationship or withdraw as representative if:

(a) discharged by the Client;

(b) instructed by the Client to do something illegal or in contravention to any rules in the Rules;

(c) the Immigration Consultant's continued involvement will place the Immigration Consultant in a conflict of interest; or

(d) the Immigration Consultant is not competent to handle the matter.

10.2 Optional withdrawal—An Immigration Consultant may, but is not required, to sever the consultant-client relationship or withdraw as representative if there has been a serious loss of confidence between the Immigration Consultant and Client, such as where:

(a) the Client has deceived the Immigration Consultant;

(b) the Client has refused to give adequate instructions to the Immigration Consultant; or

(c) the Client has refused to accept and act upon the Immigration Consultant's advice on a significant point.

10.3 Residual right to withdraw—In situations not covered by rules 10.1 and 10.2, an Immigration Consultant may sever the consultant-client relationship or withdraw as representative only if the severance or withdrawal:

(a) will not be unfair to the Client; and

(b) is not done for an improper purpose.

Commentary:

1. Unfairness to the Client will depend on the circumstances of each case, but will normally include consideration of whether the severance or withdrawal will:

    (a) occur at a stage in the proceedings where the Client will have to retain another Immigration Consultant to do the same work, or part of it, again;

    (b) leave the Client with insufficient time to retain another Immigration Consultant; and

    (c) give the newly retained Immigration Consultant insufficient time to prepare to represent the Client.

2. Improper purpose will depend on the circumstances of each case, but will include severance or withdrawal in order to:

(a) delay any proceeding or application before the Minister, an Officer, or the Board; and

(b) assist the Client in effecting an improper purpose.

10.4 Withdrawal for non-payment of fee—Where, after reasonable notice, the Client fails to provide funds on account of disbursements or fees, an Immigration Consultant may withdraw unless serious prejudice to the Client would result.

10.5 Manner of withdrawal—When an Immigration Consultant withdraws, the Immigration Consultant should try to minimize expense and avoid prejudice to the Client and should do all that can reasonably be done to facilitate the orderly transfer of the matter to the successor Immigration Consultant. Upon discharge or withdrawal, an Immigration Consultant should:

(a) deliver to or to the order of the Client all papers and property to which the Client is entitled;

(b) give the Client all information that may be required in connection with the case or matter;

(c) account for all funds of the Client then held or previously dealt with, including the refunding of any remuneration not earned during the representation;

(d) promptly render an account for outstanding fees and disbursements;

(e) co-operate with the successor Immigration Consultant so as to minimize expense and avoid prejudice to the Client; and

(f) notify in writing Citizenship and Immigration Canada or the Immigration and Refugee Board where the Immigration Consultant's name appears as representative for the Client that the Immigration Consultant has withdrawn.

10.6 Duty of successor Immigration Consultant—Before agreeing to represent a Client, a successor Immigration Consultant should be satisfied that the former Immigration Consultant has withdrawn, or has been discharged by the Client.

PART 11 ADVERTISING, SOLICITATION AND MAKING SERVICES AVAILABLE

11.1 An Immigration Consultant should make professional services available to the public in an efficient and convenient manner that will command respect and instil confidence, and by means that are compatible with the integrity, independence and effectiveness of the profession.

11.2 An Immigration Consultant or his or her Agent shall not engage in false or misleading advertising or representations. In particular, an Immigration Consultant or his or her Agent shall not misrepresent or mislead a Client as to his or her qualifications, services, fees, available programs or benefits. In addition, an Immigration Consultant or his or her Agent shall not provide false or unrealistic expectations as to either results or processing times. Under no circumstances shall an Immigration Consultant or his or her Agent purport to have special access or influence with respect to the Minister, an Officer, or the Board.

11.3 In all instances, advertising should be in good taste and is not such as to bring the profession or the Society into disrepute.

Commentary:

1. Example of "purported special access or influence" includes but is not limited to; pictures with or letters received from employees or officials of the Canadian Government.

2. Use of the term "guarantee" when describing services or fees is inappropriate, and must be avoided. Wording such as "refund policy" or reference to contingent fee arrangements, if factual and supported in writing in a retainer agreement or engagement letter, may be appropriate.

3. An Immigration Consultant has a positive duty to promote the Society and Rules, and to prevent unregulated practice, and is encouraged where appropriate to educate the public at large regarding the Society and the regulatory system and safeguards with respect to Immigration Consultants.

4. Former government officials currently acting as Immigration Consultants must take special care to ensure representations regarding their qualifications and past employment are strictly factual, and must not promote the notion that they may have special access or influence since any suggestion of special access or influence regarding the immigration process brings the integrity of the immigration process into disrepute. Furthermore, former immigration officials must abide by and ensure they are in compliance with the Government's own post-employment rules.

5. An Immigration Consultant shall clearly distinguish his or her own credentials from those of a lawyer licensed to practise law in any province or territory, and shall not refer to any foreign credential or in any other way make representations that may reasonably lead to a misapprehension that the Immigration Consultant is a lawyer, provides legal services or has credentials as a lawyer when that is not the case.

PART 12 OUTSIDE INTERESTS

12.1 An Immigration Consultant who engages in another profession, business, or occupation concurrently while acting as an Immigration Consultant shall not allow such outside interest to jeopardize his or her professional integrity, independence and competence.

Commentary:

1. The term "outside interest" covers the widest range of activities such as, but not limited to: real estate agent; mortgage broker; financial advisor; tax consultant; and accountant. Where the outside interest is not related to the services provided as an Immigration Consultant, then there will likely be no issue of concern. However, there will be a concern if the outside interest compromises the Immigration Consultant's competency, either because [of] a conflict with a Client's interest or because too much time is spent on the "outside interest" resulting in a lack of attention to or preparation in a particular matter or in the failure to maintain professional standards.

PART 13 NON-DISCRIMINATION

13.1 No Client or anyone else with whom an Immigration Consultant interacts shall be discriminated against on such grounds as age, gender, sexual orientation, same-sex partnership status, marital status, family status, national or ethnic origin, ancestry, race, colour, religion, creed, citizenship, physical or mental disability, political affiliation, or socio-economic status. This does not abrogate the Immigration Consultant's right to refuse to accept a Client for legitimate reasons.

13.2 An Immigration Consultants shall respect the dignity and integrity of all individuals and ensure fair and equitable treatment in all aspects of the provision of immigration services.

PART 14 ERRORS AND OMISSIONS

14.1 Every Immigration Consultant shall maintain errors and omissions insurance in an amount as to be prescribed by the Society from time to time.

14.2 An Immigration Consultant must advise the Client promptly and fully regarding any error or omission that has occurred in the matter for which an Immigration Consultant was retained, that is or may be damaging to the Client and cannot be readily corrected. The duty includes recommending that the Client seek independent advice regarding any rights that may arise out of the error or omission. An Immigration Consultant shall further advise his or her insurer promptly regarding any potential claim arising out of the matter.

Commentary:

1. It is the responsibility of an Immigration Consultant to maintain the requisite minimum amount of errors and omissions insurance coverage. The Society does not establish the maximum insurance required by an Immigration Consultant. If an Immigration Consultant reasonably believes that more insurance coverage is needed, it is the obligation of that Immigration Consultant to obtain the necessary insurance.

PART 15 DISCIPLINARY AUTHORITY

15.1 An Immigration Consultant is subject to the disciplinary authority of the Society regardless of where the person's conduct occurs or where the person resides.

15.2 The Society may discipline an Immigration Consultant for Professional Misconduct.

15.3 The Society may discipline an Immigration Consultant for Conduct Unbecoming an Immigration Consultant.

15.4 An Immigration Consultant subject to discipline, may also be required to pay all or a portion of the costs associated with the investigation and hearing of the discipline proceeding.

PART 16 RESPONSIBILITY TO THE SOCIETY AND OTHERS

16.1 An Immigration Consultant shall immediately notify the Society and clients of any changes in contact information, including but not limited to home and business address, telephone, facsimile and electronic address.

16.2 An Immigration Consultant shall reply promptly to any communication from the Society.

16.3 An Immigration Consultant shall not in the course of a professional practice send correspondence or otherwise communicate with a complainant, another Immigration Consultant, or any other person in a manner that is abusive, offensive or otherwise inconsistent with the proper tone of a professional communication from an Immigration Consultant.

16.4 The Immigration Consultant shall not communicate with a complainant on a matter if the complainant has so requested.

16.5 An Immigration Consultant shall act toward the Society with respect and dignity.

16.6 An Immigration Consultant shall not bring discredit upon the Society by acting in such a way as to undermine or threaten to undermine the Society's mandate and/or governing principles.

Glossary of Terms

accredited interpreter an interpreter used in a refugee hearing who has undergone a security check and has passed a language exam

acquittal a finding of not guilty

administrative tribunal a specialized governmental agency established under legislation to implement legislative policy; for example, the Immigration and Refugee Board is an administrative tribunal established under the IRPA

admissibility hearing the hearing that is held at the Immigration Division when a person allegedly breaches Canadian immigration laws pursuant to s. 44 of the IRPA, where an officer is of the opinion that a permanent resident or foreign national is inadmissible

admission the granting of entry into Canada; a foreign national has been admitted if she passed through a port of entry (air, land, or sea) and is permitted to enter by border officials

agent of persecution *see* non-state agents; state agents

alien a term generally used in the United States to describe non-citizens

alienage being outside one's country of nationality or citizenship

alternative dispute resolution (ADR) in the case of the Immigration Appeal Division, a method of dispute resolution used in place of a hearing; involves a neutral third party (the dispute resolution officer) who tries to help the disputing parties reach a mutually agreeable solution

applicant a person who formally requests a government or legal action, such as the granting of permanent or temporary residence

application in the immigration and refugee context, a request that can be made orally or in writing to an officer or other decision maker by a person seeking a government action; for example, a person may make an application for permanent residence

arrest to take a person into legal custody

asylum the refuge or protection a country may grant to a person seeking protection from the authority who persecutes that person; the term is used internationally and is the equivalent to "refugee protection" in Canada

asylum seeker a person who is seeking protection or asylum, where the decision on a claim is still pending; this term is used internationally and is the equivalent to "refugee claimant" in Canada

balance of probabilities the standard of proof in civil matters, determined on the basis of whether a claim or a fact as alleged is more probably true than not true; this is a much lower standard of proof than that required in criminal court, where the evidence must establish "beyond a reasonable doubt" that an accused is guilty

blanket labour market opinion (LMO) an approval in principle issued to an employer by HRSDC, so that several foreign workers may be recruited at once

bona fide Latin for "in good faith"; made without fraud or deceit; sincere, genuine

burden of proof the duty of a party to a proceeding to prove a disputed assertion or charge; for example, the burden of proof is on an applicant for permanent residence to show that he is entitled to enter Canada and not inadmissible under Canadian legislation

business person a person who seeks entry to Canada through some sort of pre-arrangement, such as an employment contract or under NAFTA or GATS

business visitor under NAFTA, a citizen of the United States or Mexico who seeks admission to Canada to engage in certain international business activities, and whose primary source of remuneration remains outside Canada

Canada Border Services Agency (CBSA) an agency of Public Safety Canada responsible for the management and operation of Canada's borders, including arrests, detentions, removals, and port of entry functions

Canadian Orientation Abroad program one- to five-day program designed to help integrate refugees into Canadian society

Canadian Police Information Centre (CPIC) a Canada-wide computerized information system that provides Canadian law enforcement agencies with information on crimes and criminals, including immigration warrants

case law law created by courts and other adjudicators in their judgments; it includes the common law as well as the interpretation of statutes and regulations

certificate *see* security certificate

cessation clause provides the framework for when protection may lawfully cease under s. 108 of the IRPA

citizen a person who has the right to live in a country because she was born there or because she legally acquired the right

citizenship the full political and civil rights in the body politic of the state

Citizenship and Immigration Canada (CIC) the federal government department responsible for immigration, refugee, and citizenship matters

citizenship judge a quasi-judicial decision maker who has the authority to decide citizenship applications

claim generally refers to the application and assertion made to the Refugee Protection Division by a person seeking a determination of his refugee status; for example, a person whose claim for refugee protection is accepted will be granted refugee status

claimant a person who makes an application for refugee protection

codified formalized and clarified in writing in the form of binding legislation

common law body of legal principles and rules that trace back to Britain, and which are found in court judgments; a category of case law

common-law partner "in relation to a person, an individual who is cohabiting with the person in a conjugal relationship, having so cohabited for a period of at least one year" (s. 1 of the IRP Regulations)

community sponsors organizations, associations, and corporations that sponsor refugees

concurrent processing initiative policy that allows Canadian visa officers outside Canada to begin processing a foreign worker's permit application while the LMO is pending

conditional removal order a departure order with conditions attached; issued pending the outcome of a refugee claim

conduct unbecoming improper conduct that occurs outside the immigration consultant's practice

conjugal partner "in relation to a sponsor, a foreign national residing outside Canada who is in a conjugal relationship with the sponsor and has been in that relationship for a period of at least one year" (s. 2 of the IRP Regulations)

constituent group (CG) a group authorized by a sponsorship agreement holder to sponsor refugees on its behalf

Constitution the basic framework under which all other laws are created, establishing the basic principles to which all other laws must conform

convention an agreement that obliges countries under international law to conform to its provisions

Convention refugee a person who has been granted protection under the refugee definition in the 1951 Convention Relating to the Status of Refugees

Convention Relating to the Status of Refugees UN convention created after the Second World War to help displaced persons; today, it, together with its Protocol, provides the framework of principles for Canada's refugee determination system

country of habitual residence the country in which a person normally lives; temporary absences (for example, travel holidays, visits, and business) do not change a person's country of habitual residence

credibility (assessment of) assessment of an application in order to determine whether the information presented by the applicant is reliable and believable

crime against humanity any inhumane act or omission that is committed against any civilian population or any identifiable group

criminality domestic crime, as opposed to crimes against humanity or war crimes; the IRPA defines three categories of criminality: serious criminality under s. 36(1), criminality under s. 36(2), and organized criminality under s. 37

cross-examination in an immigration or immigration appeal hearing, the questioning of a witness by the opposing party after the examination-in-chief; the main purpose of cross-examination is to test the credibility of the witness and to assist the party that is cross-examining

customary international law customs and practice that take on the force of law over time

de facto dependant a person who is dependent on the family in which membership is claimed but who does not meet the regulatory definition of "family member" in the IRP Regulations; the person may or may not be a blood relative

de novo Latin for "starting afresh"; a *de novo* hearing is a new hearing

deemed rehabilitated an exemption from criminal inadmissibility; a person who was convicted outside Canada and who meets the criteria under s. 18(2) of the IRP Regulations may be deemed rehabilitated and permitted to enter Canada

delegation of authority the giving of decision-making power to someone else; for example, a minister may delegate authority to an immigration officer

departure order type of removal order that generally provides a person with 30 days in which to leave Canada

dependent child a person who is the biological or adopted child of a parent and is in a situation of dependency with respect to that parent, as described in s. 2 of the IRP Regulations

deportation order type of removal order that bars re-entry to Canada indefinitely

derogable rights refers to those human rights that can be temporarily suspended by a state in time of public emergency; for example, freedom of movement may be temporarily restricted or removed

designate choose someone for a position, duty, or responsibility

designated medical officer (DMO) a physician authorized by CIC to carry out a medical assessment

designated medical practitioner a local physician, authorized by the Canadian government

designated representative person chosen by the RPD to act and make decisions on behalf of a refugee claimant

detain keep a person in legal custody, such as in a prison or immigration holding centre, prior to a hearing on a matter

detention review hearing before the Immigration Division for the purpose of reviewing the reasons for detention under the IRPA

disclosure the release of documents to the opposing side in a proceeding

dual intent intention to become first a temporary resident and then a permanent resident

durable solution a lasting solution to a refugee's temporary status: local integration in the country of asylum, voluntary return to the refugee's home country (repatriation), or resettlement in another country

economic migrant a person who leaves her homeland to settle in another country, generally to work and improve her quality of life; the term may also refer to non-genuine refugees who use the refugee protection system without *bona fide* cause; *see also* migrant

espionage the practice of spying

ex parte a proceeding, or part of a proceeding, held in the absence of one of the parties

examination-in-chief the evidence given in an immigration proceeding by a witness; during the examination-in-chief, a witness is asked questions by the representative (counsel) who called her as a witness

exclusion order type of removal order that includes a one-year or two-year ban from re-entering Canada

Expedited Labour Market Opinion (E-LMO) an expedited Labour Market Opinion

Expedited Labour Market Opinion Pilot Project a program created by HRSDC to accelerate the application process for hiring temporary foreign workers in certain occupations

expert witness a person whom the Immigration and Refugee Board considers to have sufficient expertise in his field that he can provide information under oath; he can tell the tribunal what conclusions he reaches on the basis of certain facts and can give opinions about the facts

family member generally includes "(a) the spouse or common-law partner of the person; (b) a dependent child of the person or of the person's spouse or common-law partner; and (c) a dependent child of a dependent child referred to in paragraph (b)" (s. 1(3) of the IRP Regulations)

federal system of government division of law-making powers between the national (federal) and provincial governments according to subject matter

female genital mutilation (FGM) as defined by the World Health Organization, "all procedures that involve partial or total removal of the external female genitalia, or other injury to the female genital organs for non-medical reasons"

flight risk a person who is likely to fail to appear at an immigration proceeding in order to stay in Canada illegally

foreign national a person who is neither a Canadian citizen nor a permanent resident in Canada

fraudulent document a travel or identity document that (a) has been falsely made or illegally altered by a non-authorized person or agency; (b) has been improperly issued or obtained through misrepresentation, corruption, or in any unlawful manner; or (c) is being used by a person other than the rightful holder

GATS professional a person who seeks to engage in an activity at a professional level in a designated profession, and meets the GATS criteria

genocide an act or omission committed with intent to destroy, in whole or in part, an identifiable group of persons

ghost consulting a practice wherein a person who is not authorized to practise as an immigration consultant completes the application forms on behalf of a client but then has the forms submitted as if they were personally completed by the applicant

GIC member or appointee member appointed to the IRB by the GIC: the chairperson, deputy chairpersons, assistant deputy chairpersons, and members of the Immigration Appeal Division and the Refugee Protection Division

governor in council (GIC) the governor general acting with the advice and consent of Cabinet; formal executive authority is conferred by the statutes on the governor in council

Group of Five (G5) a group of five or more people who join together to sponsor one or more refugees

habeas corpus a writ requiring someone to be brought before a court to test the legality of detention or imprisonment

HRSDC confirmation *see* Labour Market Opinion (LMO)

human rights rights that belong to every individual simply because he or she is a human being; they set out the basic standards that allow people to live in dignity

humanitarian and compassionate (H & C) considerations factors that may be taken into account in deciding an immigration application or appeal and that may warrant an exemption from a requirement or obligation under the IRPA

hybrid or dual procedure offences offences for which the Crown prosecutor chooses to proceed either by summary conviction or by indictment

identity document a lawfully obtained document designed to prove the identity of the person carrying it (for example, a passport or birth certificate)

immigrant a person who wishes to settle (or has settled) permanently in another country (as opposed to a refugee, who is forced to flee)

immigration settling permanently in a new country

Immigration and Refugee Board (IRB) an independent quasi-judicial tribunal whose mission is "to make well-reasoned decisions on immigration and refugee matters efficiently, fairly and in accordance with the law"

Immigration Appeal Division (IAD) division of the Immigration and Refugee Board; under s. 63 of the IRPA, IAD members hear and decide sponsorship appeals, appeals against removal orders, residency obligation appeals, and minister's appeals

Immigration Division (ID) division of the Immigration and Refugee Board; ID members decide immigration matters related to admissibility hearings and hearings into the reasons for detention

Immigration Loans Program (ILP) special federal fund available to indigent refugees and immigrants who qualify

immigration resettlement plan plan tabled by the CIC minister each year that includes the number and types of foreign nationals who can come to Canada as permanent residents

immigration status the legal status that a foreign national may be accorded under Canadian immigration law (for example, permanent residence or temporary residence as a student, business worker, or visitor)

immigration visa officer a public servant working in a Canadian consulate or visa office abroad

inadmissibility (grounds of) statutory criteria under which a foreign national or permanent resident may be prohibited from being issued an authorization to enter or remain in Canada

inadmissibility hearing adversarial hearing to determine whether or not an applicant is inadmissible

inadmissibility report document that sets out the grounds of inadmissibility alleged by the officer

indictable offences serious offences such as murder, with longer periods of imprisonment and more complex prosecution procedures than those for summary conviction offences

individual rehabilitation a method of removing a ground of inadmissibility (criminality) that requires the applicant to apply to a visa officer, who will then consider whether certain criteria have been met

interdiction control activity that prevents illegal travellers and criminals from reaching Canada

Interim Federal Health Program essential and emergency health care coverage for refugees in need of assistance before provincial health care is available

internally displaced person a person who has been forcibly displaced but is still within the borders of her home country

International Covenant on Civil and Political Rights (ICCPR) an international agreement that obliges state parties to respect and ensure the civil and political rights of all individuals within their borders and subject to their jurisdiction

International Organization for Migration (IOM) an intergovernmental organization that works with partners in the international community to assist in meeting the operational challenges of migration, advance understanding of migration issues, encourage social and economic development through migration, and uphold the human dignity and well-being of migrants

intra-company transfer a category of work permit that assists multinational businesses to move executives temporarily to Canada, when required for business

intra-company transferee a US or Mexican citizen who is admitted to Canada under NAFTA for the purpose of assisting in the operations of a foreign company's Canadian parent, subsidiary, branch, or affiliate company

IRP Regulations Immigration and Refugee Protection Regulations

Joint Assistance Sponsorship (JAS) program a sponsorship program that involves both CIC and a private sponsor

jointly and severally liable refers to the legal doctrine that either partner in a relationship may be required to pay the full amount of a financial obligation—for example, where a sponsor takes on a co-signer, both may be liable for the full amount in the event of a default

judicial notice a rule of evidence that allows a decision maker to accept certain commonly known, indisputable, and uncontentious facts without requiring that they be proven with evidence

judicial review a court's power to invalidate legislative and executive actions as being unconstitutional or being contrary to law; a court's review of an administrative body's factual or legal findings (for example, a judicial review of a decision by a member of the Refugee Protection Division to reject a refugee claim)

jus sanguinis citizenship based on blood ties

jus soli citizenship based on the land of birth

Labour Market Opinion (LMO) an HRSDC document obtained by a Canadian employer in order to employ a foreign worker; also known as an HRSDC confirmation

landed immigrant *see* permanent resident

leave to appeal permission granted from a court to have a matter decided

letter of acceptance document that indicates that a foreign student has been accepted into a Canadian educational institution

local integration the process by which refugees become accepted into society, both as individuals and as groups, by their host country

low income cut-off (LICO) minimum income requirement for sponsors of permanent residents

Low Skill Pilot Project an HRSDC program designed to meet the labour market demand for temporary foreign workers in low-skill jobs

marriage as defined in s. 2 of the IRP Regulations, "a marriage that is valid both under the laws of the jurisdiction where it took place and under Canadian law"

medical surveillance a designation by the designated medical officer that provides for monitoring of an applicant's medical condition

member the title given to a decision maker in the Refugee Protection Division, Immigration Division, or Immigration Appeal Division of the Immigration and Refugee Board

migrants persons who are outside their country of origin; generally describes people on the move or people with temporary status or no status in the country where they live

misrepresentation a ground of inadmissibility under the IRPA that involves misstating facts or withholding information

multiple-entry visa document that allows a foreign national to enter Canada from another country multiple times during the validity of the visa

named cases sponsor-referred refugee cases

naturalization the process by which a foreign national, after being admitted to Canada as a permanent resident, applies for and obtains Canadian citizenship

non-derogable rights a person's core human rights, which must be respected and cannot be taken away or suspended for any reason (for example, the right to life, and freedom from torture)

non-political crime an act committed for personal gain with no political end or motive involved

non-refoulement *see refouler*

non-state agents persecutors of the refugee claimant who are not members of the state—for example, rebels or warlords

Notice of Arrival notice of a refugee's arrival into Canada that is sent to the sponsor

Notice of Decision a written decision by the decision maker, issued to those involved in the case, such as by the RPD to the refugee claimant and the minister

Notice to Appear notification sent to a person requiring attendance at a proceeding, and providing the date, time, and location

occupations under pressure a regional list of job shortages developed by HRSDC; if an occupation is designated an occupation under pressure, employers can more easily hire foreign workers for that occupation

officer under s. 6(1) of the IRPA, a person or class of person designated by the minister as an officer to carry out any purpose of any provision of the IRPA and who is given specific powers and duties

open work permit document possessed by a foreign student enabling her to work for any employer for a specific time period

oral representations arguments made orally, such as at the end of a refugee hearing

order in council an administrative order that serves notice of a decision taken by the executive arm of government

parallel processing processing the permanent residence application of the main applicant and those of sponsored family members at the same time, such as is allowed under the Live-In Caregiver Program

paramountcy a principle providing that if a law falls within the jurisdiction of both the federal and provincial governments, the federal government takes jurisdiction

pardon a grant under the *Criminal Code* resulting in an offence being deemed not to have occurred

peace officer a law enforcement officer having the power to examine people and perform search and seizure

permanent resident a person who has been granted permanent resident status in Canada and who has not subsequently lost that status under s. 46 of the IRPA; also known as a "landed immigrant" under older legislation

Permanent Resident Card (PR card) card issued to permanent residents after their arrival in Canada showing proof of immigration status

permanent resident status the enjoyment of most of the same rights and responsibilities guaranteed to Canadians under the *Canadian Charter of Rights and Freedoms*

permanent resident visa a document allowing a foreign national to travel to Canada and, after a successful examination at a port of entry, to enter Canada as a permanent resident

persecution sustained and systematic violation of basic human rights

person in need of protection a person who has been granted refugee protection under the IRPA because of a danger of torture or because of risk to life or cruel and unusual treatment or punishment; used when the refugee claim does not fall within the scope of the Refugee Convention

person without status a person who is not authorized to remain in the country; the person is not a permanent or temporary resident or may not have been granted permission to stay, such as a refugee claimant who is refused refugee status but is not yet removed from Canada

policy non-binding guidelines created by agencies to support the administration of statutes and regulations, and reflecting the government and agency's agenda

policy note a memorandum issued by an IRB business office to communicate to those affected about a particular operational matter in that local office

pre-approval blanket LMO program an HRSDC program that allows employers who wish to ultimately hire several foreign workers for the same type of position to obtain a blanket LMO

precedent a court ruling on a point of law that is binding on lower courts

prescribed senior official as referenced under s. 35(1)(b) of the IRPA, a senior official in the service of a government that has been designated by the minister as a perpetrator of terrorism, human rights violations, genocide, war crimes, or crimes against humanity

principal applicant the person who makes an application for permanent or temporary residence, for refugee protection, or for other immigration status; dependants (for example, a spouse or common-law partner, or any minor children) are considered derivative applicants and generally receive the same status afforded to the principal applicant

principle of paramountcy when both the federal and provincial governments have legislative power over a particular subject, federal legislation overrides any provincial legislation in conflict with it

probable grounds a standard of proof used by a decision maker; specifically, proof that something is probably true—more likely true than untrue

professional under NAFTA, a citizen of the United States or Mexico who has pre-arranged employment with a Canadian employer and whose occupation is listed in NAFTA

professional misconduct any improper action of an immigration consultant during the course of conducting business

prosecution a legal proceeding, such as a trial, against a person charged with a crime

protected person under ss. 96 and 97 of the IRPA, a person who is either a Convention refugee or who is in a refugee-like situation (for example, because she is in danger of being tortured)

Public Safety and Emergency Preparedness Canada (PSEPC) the former name of Public Safety Canada

Public Safety Canada the federal government department responsible for keeping Canadians safe from natural disasters, crime, and terrorism

quasi-judicial relating to or involving an executive or administrative official's adjudicative acts; quasi-judicial acts are subject to review by courts

ratification a confirmation to abide by an international agreement

reasonable grounds a set of facts and circumstances that would satisfy an ordinarily cautious and prudent person, and that are more than mere suspicion; a lower standard of proof than a balance of probabilities

referral organization under s. 138 of the IRP Regulations, "(a) the United Nations High Commissioner for Refugees; or (b) any organization with which the Minister has entered into a memorandum of understanding under section 143"

refouler French for "to return"; the principle of *non-refoulement* prohibits a country from returning a refugee claimant to another country or territory where there is a risk to life or a serious threat on account of race, religion, nationality, membership in a particular social group, or political opinion

refugee a person who is forced to flee from persecution (as opposed to an immigrant who chooses to move)

Refugee Appeal Division (RAD) a division of the Immigration and Refugee Board that is not functional because the section of the IRPA to allow appeals is inoperative

refugee claimant a person who has made a refugee protection claim where the decision is yet to be made; this term is used in Canada and is equivalent to "asylum seeker"

Refugee Convention *see* Convention Relating to the Status of Refugees

Refugee Protection Division (RPD) a division of the Immigration and Refugee Board; RPD members hear claims from foreign nationals in Canada who seek protection as Convention refugees under s. 96 of the IRPA or as persons in need of protection under s. 97 of the IRPA

refugee *sur place* a person who did not initially flee the home country, but while in another country became a refugee in need of protection because of changed country conditions or circumstances in the home country

refusal letter document sent to a permanent residence applicant outlining the reasons for application's refusal

regulations additional rules created pursuant to a statute by the governor in council, which fill in practical details for the administration and enforcement of the statute

relative as defined in s. 2 of the IRP Regulations, "a person who is related to another person by blood or adoption"

removal order order issued either after an examination or at an admissibility hearing instructing the person to leave Canada

removal ready refers to people who are subject to a removal order that is in force or to a security certificate that has been issued against them

resettlement in the context of refugee law, the relocation and integration of a refugee or person in a refugee-like situation from a camp or other temporary situation to another country where he can reside on a permanent basis; this option may be used when the refugee cannot return to his country of origin because of a risk to life or other serious problems

Resettlement Assistance Program (RAP) program that provides financial and immediate essential services to government-assisted refugees

residence in Canada a requirement for citizenship

residency calculator CIC website tool for timing citizenship applications

residual power power that is not otherwise delegated elsewhere; the federal government has a residual power to legislate in all subject areas that are not specifically assigned to the provinces

risk of cruel and unusual treatment or punishment and **risk to life** ill-treatment causing suffering that is less severe than torture

rules a category of regulation that has the purpose of establishing practices and procedures for the presentation of cases

s. 44(1) report *see* inadmissibility report

safe third country a receiving country that is any country, other than the country of origin, in which a refugee enjoys protection

Seasonal Agricultural Worker Program (SAWP) program that allows the entry of foreign nationals to work in the agricultural sector in Canada

security certificate a document providing for a removal hearing in the absence of the person named, where information must be protected for reasons of public safety

security deposit a bond that may be imposed by an officer where the officer has concerns about a temporary resident's intention to live up to the terms and conditions of admission

settlement plan details of a refugee sponsor's commitment to provide basic financial support and care for a sponsored refugee

significant benefit a ground of exemption from the usual requirement of foreign workers to obtain an HRSDC confirmation; the exemption applies to foreign workers whose presence in Canada will likely result in a significant benefit to the country and permits them to apply for a work permit without first obtaining the HRSDC confirmation

single-entry visa document that allows a foreign national to enter Canada only once, usually only for six months

solicitor–client privilege the protection of client information and communication shared in the context of a lawyer–client relationship

sponsorship a legal contract with the Canadian federal government to provide financial and other support to a foreign national for a specified period of time so that the foreign national may enter Canada as a permanent resident

sponsorship agreement holders established, incorporated organizations that have signed an agreement with the minister of CIC to facilitate refugee sponsorship

standard of proof the degree or level of persuasiveness of the evidence required in a specific case; for example, in the refugee context, "well-founded" is a standard of proof used when assessing the claimant's fear of persecution

state agents authorities of the refugee claimant's country of origin—for example, police and members of the military

stateless person a person who is not recognized as a citizen by any state

statutes written codes of law passed by legislatures, which typically deal with a particular subject matter; for example, the IRPA is a statute dealing with immigration and refugee matters

stay (of removal order) usually refers to a decision by a member of the Immigration Appeal Division where the member decides not to continue with an appeal against a removal order; the appellant is allowed to remain in Canada but must abide by certain conditions imposed by the member; if there is no breach of the conditions within the ordered period of time, the appeal is allowed, the removal order quashed, and the person permitted to remain in Canada; however, proceedings could be resumed at some future time if conditions are breached

subversion the practice of overturning or overthrowing

summary conviction offences less serious offences with a maximum sentence of six months in jail and prosecuted using streamlined procedures

summons a notice issued by the IRB requiring a person to appear for an immigration matter to serve as a witness

target number in the refugee context, the number of government-assisted and privately sponsored refugees that the minister commits to resettling in Canada each year

temporary resident a person who has permission to remain in Canada on a temporary basis (the main categories are students, temporary workers, and visitors)

temporary resident permit (TRP) a permit for temporary residence issued at the discretion of an officer to a foreign national who is inadmissible or does not meet the requirements of the IRPA; for example, a TRP may be issued to a foreign national for medical treatment in Canada in certain circumstances

temporary resident visa (TRV) document authorizing a person to board an airplane or ship to travel to Canada

terrorism activities directed toward or in support of the threat or use of acts of violence against persons or property for the purposes of achieving a political objective

terrorist group as defined under s. 83.01 of the *Criminal Code*, "an entity that has as one of its purposes or activities facilitating or carrying out any terrorist activity … and includes an association of such entities"

tickler system a reminder system for deadlines

torture infliction of severe bodily pain, especially as a punishment or a means of interrogation or intimidation

transit visa document that allows travel through Canada to another country by anyone who would need a temporary resident visa to enter Canada and whose flight will stop here for less than 48 hours

unaccompanied minors persons under the age of majority who are not accompanied by a parent, guardian, or other adult who by law or custom is responsible for them

undertaking a promise or agreement to do something

undocumented claimant generally, a refugee claimant who is not in possession of identity documents from his country of origin

United Nations High Commissioner for Refugees (UNHCR) international agency created in 1950 to protect refugees and provide assistance to them

Universal Declaration of Human Rights (UDHR) international declaration adopted by the UN General Assembly in 1948 setting out the fundamental human rights of all persons

unnamed cases refugee sponsorship requests referred to the CIC Matching Centre, which attempts to find a suitable match for a would-be sponsor

urgent need of protection term that describes, in respect of a member of the Convention refugees abroad class, the country of asylum class, or the source country class, a person whose life, liberty, or physical safety is under immediate threat and who, if not protected, is likely to be (a) killed; (b) subjected to violence, torture, sexual assault, or arbitrary imprisonment; or (c) returned to her country of nationality or former habitual residence (s. 138 of the IRP Regulations)

vacate nullify, such as may occur to a refugee determination that was obtained fraudulently

vicarious liability the principle by which an employer may be legally responsible for any actions or omissions of an employee, such as fraud or negligence

violence against women any act of gender-based violence that results in, or is likely to result in, physical, sexual, or psychological harm or suffering to women, including threats of such acts, coercion, or arbitrary deprivation of liberty, whether occurring in public or in private life (article 1 of the Declaration on the Elimination of Violence Against Women)

visa officer officer who works abroad processing immigration applications

visitor visa a temporary resident visa issued under the visitor class

visitor's record a record of information documented by a port of entry officer, stapled to the holder's passport; additional information may be kept on computer and referenced in the visitor's record

voluntary repatriation in the context of refugee law, the return of a refugee to her country of origin, of her own free will, once conditions have become safe

vulnerable term describing Convention refugees or persons in similar circumstances who have a greater need of protection than other applicants for protection abroad because their particular circumstances give rise to a heightened risk to their physical safety (s. 138 of the IRP Regulations)

war crime an act or omission committed during an armed conflict

warrant in the context of immigration, an order from any division of the Immigration and Refugee Board that gives the CBSA or the police the authority to arrest someone; a warrant is usually issued because someone has failed to appear for a hearing or other immigration proceeding

well-founded fear one of the four inclusion elements of the definition of a Convention refugee, assessed by the Refugee Protection Division in a refugee claim; the RPD member assesses whether a well-founded fear of persecution exists

withholding to hold back from doing or taking an action

witness someone who has some knowledge of an event and may have seen or heard what has happened; a witness provides testimony and may be cross-examined; any division of the Immigration and Refugee Board can issue a summons for a witness to appear before it

Women at Risk program program to resettle women who are members of the Convention refugees abroad class or humanitarian-protected persons abroad class

Index